MW01147291

EUGENE 1945-2000

EUGENE 1945-2000

*Decisions That Made a
Community*

Edited by Kathleen Holt & Cheri Brooks

The City Club of Eugene

To the people of Eugene, Oregon.
May the dialogue continue always.

TABLE OF CONTENTS

INTRODUCTION

ANYONE WHO HAS lived in Eugene, Oregon—or for that matter, anyone who has heard anything at all about it—knows this city is an active, involved community with citizens who readily voice their diverse opinions on most any given issue. When the City Club of Eugene formed in 1990, its members considered this particular community attribute a healthy application of democracy. The club took as its mission to "build community vision through open inquiry." That mission is the cornerstone of how this book was written. And that makes this book as much about Eugene's future as it is about its past.

This book includes milestones our community can be proud of. It acknowledges leaders who made a difference and helped shape Eugene into the progressive, innovative, and tolerant community it is today. The book also candidly reveals mistakes, missteps, and misguided decisions—things that we would probably do differently today if we could. We hope readers will enjoy these essays not only for their historical value, but also as a guide to future decision-making. Although this book is about Eugene's history, many of the issues and themes are common to other cities. Readers who don't live in Eugene likely will find it to be a useful reference for their community's future as well.

The City Club of Eugene is a civic organization whose members explore community and regional issues by preparing research papers, recommending positions on public-policy decisions and ballot measures, and hosting speakers at regular programs. The goal is to fully understand an issue by learning about different points of view. Club members believe that only by doing so can the community make the best decisions.

A book about Eugene's past half-century presented the club with the opportunity to identify key community decision points with the advantage of hindsight. To remain true to the club's mission, the book had to include a range of perspectives on our past, something that would not have been possible with a single author, or even a handful of authors.

To determine what topics to cover in the book, the club appointed an editorial board, which included both club members and nonmembers. All were long-time residents who had personally been involved in shaping the community. They identified twenty-two different topics to include in the book. The board hired two coeditors who, with the board, identified twenty-four different authors to write essays on each topic. (Typical of Eugene, the essays on government and the visual and literary arts required two authors apiece.)

The board directed each author to write about the people, decisions, successes, and failures of our community from 1945 to 2000 that made us the community we are today. To put City Club's mark on the book, the board went one step further. They asked each author to include their opinions as to whether or not Eugene is better off today as a result of those past influences and decisions.

The authors, editors, and club members have taken great pains to ensure the accuracy of the facts. Community members with firsthand knowledge of each issue were enlisted to review the essays. References are included to validate key information. Like any moment in history, much is subject to interpretation.

The point of this book is neither to glorify our history nor to condemn it. It is not even to try to persuade you to agree with the author's conclusions. The idea is that by adding the authors' interpretations of historical facts, the book will spawn a public conversation about our past decisions and whether they were for better or worse. Through this open inquiry about our past, the City Club of Eugene hopes to build community vision for our future.

Kathy Madison, Past-president
City Club of Eugene

PREFACE

HOW DID EUGENE come to be the way it is today? This is the question twenty-four writers considered when looking at their city's natural environment, demographics, planning, politics, community, and civic life: twenty-four writers from diverse backgrounds, all of whom live and work in Eugene.

However, this book is the result of efforts by an even larger community than those twenty-four writers. Included among them are dozens of board members, interviewed sources, reviewers, and other community members who provided assistance and support.

It has been a goal of all involved in this project to present varied, even contradictory, views of Eugene's past. Because—as is evident in many of these essays—Eugene wouldn't be Eugene without dissension. As laid-back as we seem, we don't just go with the flow when faced with issues that affect the quality of our lives. And we are not people who stay on the beaten path. We seek out forks and bumps in the road and strange off-channels. Thus, this is not a straightforward, chronological history. It is one that weaves and bobs and turns back on itself. A ride back into Eugene's past is a rocky, meandering one, not for the overly linear or faint of heart.

Yet in many ways, Eugene's history is similar to that of other cities its size: We boomed during the 1950s and 1960s. We reconsidered our values in the 1970s. We hit a recession in the 1980s. Our downtown struggled against our suburban malls. We built roads and schools. We elected leaders. We raised families. We rooted for our home team. We encouraged businesses to flourish. We celebrated our successes and grieved about our failures and losses.

But Eugene's story is also very different from other cities of its size. We fought for forty years about a lone cross on a butte. We developed a cutting-edge mass transit system. We were led, for a time, by a faculty member's wife, who changed the way we planned for the city's growth. We paved the way in providing alternatives in K–12 education. We finagled the best visual and performing arts community we could afford and now boast one of the best in the country for a city our size. We decided that, as a rule, kids having fun in sports was more important than winning. We served as a mecca for social services, a mecca for planning, a mecca for activism, a mecca for eccentrics and odd ducks.

Perhaps, Eugene does not shine as brightly as Portland or Seattle or San Francisco. And perhaps it long ago lost the blush of small-town charm. Eugeneans speak of their home sometimes with a kind of modest embarrassment; we are quick to point out our own shortcomings. And perhaps we are too quick to forget our heroic struggles, our hard-won compromises, our innovative solutions. But there are a lot of these, as this book shows.

It's been our pleasure—albeit at times our agony—to be a part of this project for the past year. We, along with the twenty-four authors and numerous reviewers, sources, and contributors, gladly take our place among all the other Eugeneans who've come before and who will come after us in asking, "How did we get to where we are today?" And we gladly offer you our answers to that question here within the pages of this book.

Cheri Brooks and Kathleen Holt, editors

CROSSWINDS ON THE BUTTE

By Ken Metzler

THE BREEZIEST LOCALE in Eugene is Skinner Butte. Winds of change—hot crosscurrents of emotion and civic philosophy—sweep frequently across the summit. They represent Eugene, metaphorically speaking. Real winds also blow there. They combine with heavy winter rains to fell an occasional tree and to batter down human-made artifacts.

Skinner Butte stands in the center of the city between the Willamette River to the north and downtown to the south. It represents the founding of Eugene by Eugene F. Skinner. In 1846 he built his cabin on the western side of the butte, the community's first structure. When Skinner first rode his horse to the butte's summit, he discovered rings of rocks, remnants of ancient ceremonial and signal fires. For the next 150 years the butte would continue to serve as a bearer of signals. Those with the will and the means would seek to place icons to signal an identity or a point of view for all to see.

Skinner founded a community that loves to disagree. Of Eugene and Mary Skinner's five children, two daughters became noteworthy for their historical disagreement. Citizens asked them, years later, the precise location of that long-vanished cabin. Amelia placed it on West 2nd Avenue, west of the butte. The older, Phoebe, who had lived in the cabin as a child, placed it higher on the slope, by Lincoln Street, a block away. Citizens placed stone markers at both locations, even while some local historians insisted neither was correct.

Emotions run high in Eugene. In 1929, upon viewing the

butte for the first time in twenty-five years, Phoebe Skinner Kinsey, then seventy-nine, burst into tears. "The ruthless hands of men," she wrote later, "have cruelly disfigured and ruined the natural appearance of the dear old butte that I loved so well." Had she the finances, she said, she'd "quickly bring it all back as God intended it to be."

Humankind had intruded. The butte's very birth was an "intrusion"—a geological term. Forty to fifty million years ago molten basalt lava squirted upward to form a hill 270 feet above the surrounding flatlands. Exposed basalt on the west side became a quarry, later a rock climbers' mecca.

There would be other human intrusions:

In 1890 the typical Eugene family owned a milk cow. How did they graze them? By intruding on the butte's grassy south side.

Years later fashion dictated that schools erect hillside letters as symbols of institutional chauvinism. Thus arrived the fifty-foot University of Oregon O in 1908, and the large E in 1915 for Eugene High School. The history of the O reads like a novel of intrigue and violence. Collegiate pranks resulted in the letter frequently changing color, mostly between Oregon yellow and Oregon State orange. But in 1929 it was blown up by a mysterious nighttime explosion that sent a twenty-five-pound chunk of concrete crashing through the roof of a downslope building. Similar late-night explosions occurred in 1952 and 1953. The rain of debris on nearby residences prompted angry citizens to petition the city to remove that dangerous nuisance. Students then built a wooden O (mysteriously carried away, eventually returned). In 1958 they built a heavy-gauge steel O (mysteriously dismembered by acetylene torches, missing for two years). When the steel sections reappeared, students reassembled them, and the O survived to the next millennium.

Consistent with Eugene's support of education, the butte once served as a scholarly retreat. The university built a telescopic observatory there in 1888. Unfortunately, clear nights were rare in

Eugene during the academic year, and the building fell into disuse. In 1905 it was intentionally dynamited to rubble one night. Fire promptly broke out, and the eerie nighttime glow alarmed many citizens. Much of the rubble remained until the 1950s.

There would be other explosions on the butte. Part of a massive beautification project undertaken in the 1970s was the destruction of a water reservoir built on the summit in 1906. So thick were the cement walls (eight feet at the bottom) that wrecking balls failed to do the job. Crews resorted to dynamite. The site was filled, covered with topsoil, and planted with ground cover in 1976.

The butte did not escape Eugene's obsession with trees. The south slope was treeless in 1914 when the butte became a city park. Volunteers cleared brush and poison oak and began planting shrubs and trees. A tree-planting marathon followed on Armistice Day 1934 when the city dedicated the butte as a war memorial. Once planted, trees become sacred cows in Eugene; public protests have greeted projects that involve tree removal. When a former Eugene mayor, Ruth Bascom, suggested cutting some Douglas fir trees on the north side of the butte—to prevent their encroaching on vulnerable oak trees—the idea fell flat. "Soon it's going to be all Douglas fir, which I think is a shame," she said. "It's still a valid concept, but I'm too chicken to get involved in that. You figure what battles are worth fighting for, and that one I decided was a no-win situation."

In the early 1920s, the Ku Klux Klan ranged through western Oregon, largely unchecked. When they reached Eugene, they burned crosses atop the butte and paraded on Willamette Street. They also encountered vigorous editorial opposition from the *Eugene Daily Guard*. Klan members retorted that they were interested only in "maintaining white supremacy and the Christian religion."

Other crosses claimed spots on the summit, starting with a war memorial after World War I. Another cross, glowing scarlet with neon tubing, appeared in 1936 as part of a Christmas celebration, courtesy of the Chamber of Commerce. A succession of wooden crosses followed until 1964.

Until 1964, the butte remained more a symbol of love than war. Who knows how many romantic encounters occurred there? In 1936 Don Hunter invited Dolores Van Cleave, a coworker at a downtown building, to join him for a picnic luncheon. They climbed the butte on foot. They began dating and had many lunches there. Eventually, they married.

In 1997 Don and Karri Karker stood on the butte with their three children. They recalled their frequent romantic visits to the summit as high school sweethearts fifteen years earlier. "It was so crowded sometimes with people partying and necking that you could barely find room to squeeze in," said Don.

In 1961 a twenty-eight-year-old architectural engineer and his wife, Ray and Lee Wiley, visiting from Iowa, drove to the summit. They fell in love—with the view. For five years they'd spent vacations searching nationwide for the perfect place to make a home and raise children. They found it. They thus added another chapter to the Oregon Trail legend, suggesting why immigrants from other states have consistently represented 60 percent of Eugene's post–World War II population.

The Wileys arrived in Eugene unaware that changing perceptions would embroil their newly adopted community in thirty-three years of often emotional dispute over the place of religion on that windswept summit of Skinner Butte.

Within a year after their arrival, the U.S. Supreme Court issued a landmark ruling that would have real if indirect impact on the butte. At issue was a simple phrase in the First Amendment of the U.S. Constitution: "Congress shall make no law respecting an establishment of religion, or prohibiting the free exercise thereof."

On that basis the Supreme Court in 1962 declared unconstitutional a New York state-mandated but voluntary nondenominational prayer to be read each school day: "Almighty God, we acknowledge our dependence upon Thee, and beg Thy blessing upon us, our teachers, and our country." Similar church-state decisions would follow.

What does prayer in the public schools have to do with symbols of Christianity overlooking the city? Occasionally newcomers posed just such a question—Ray Lowe, for instance.

When he moved from Massachusetts to Eugene in 1955 to take a job teaching clinical psychology at the University of Oregon, Lowe began asking about the cross on the butte, the wooden one with lights screwed in. Why does a Christian symbol stand in a public park? "And the people I talked to told me, 'Oh, Ray, it's rotting and it's going to fall over and nobody's going to do anything about it.'"

In short, Oregon's blustery weather would eventually rule on the constitutional question.

Sure enough, strong winds toppled the cross in January 1961— offering the perfect opportunity to settle a legal issue by doing nothing. But the *Eugene Register-Guard*, echoing public sentiment of the era, urged construction of a replacement. The light of the old cross, the editorial said, had "shone on men and women of all faiths—warming the hearts of the great majority as might any beacon focused on the common longing for peace and good will."

Changing winds would prompt a turnaround in the newspaper's editorial stance. The first breezes could be felt in 1963 when several college men sought a community project. They were members of a service fraternity called Alpha Phi Omega, composed of former Boy Scouts who had attained Eagle rank. The prospect of replacing the now reestablished wooden cross appealed to them—something concrete, windproof, vandal proof, with fluorescent lighting. They began raising funds and seeking a contractor. They found John Alltucker, head of the Eugene Sand & Gravel Company. He took a personal interest, even helped design the new cross.

But the young men's idealism struck hard reality. When they applied for the required building permit, the City Council first approved, then wavered in the light of public opposition. Some city officials and clergy privately urged them to look elsewhere for a project. This one could be touchy.

The ex-Scouts—standing "between the devil and the deep blue sea," as one of them put it—quietly dropped the project.

That left John Alltucker's completed cross gathering dust. The next step toward civic discord began at a weekly meeting of Eugene-area contractors late in 1964.

Alltucker recalled: "I was sitting next to Jay Oldham, who rents these big heavy cranes around town. He said, 'Hey, you still got that cross up there?' And I said yeah. He says, 'Why don't we go up there tomorrow and replace that old wooden cross? I'll furnish the crane at no cost if you'll send a crew up there to pour some concrete. So instead of turning on the old 50-watt bulbs on the old cross, we'll have that beautiful structure up there.'"

Alltucker agreed.

"So we hauled that cross up there and we went to erect it just about sundown. It started to rain like you cannot believe—the rain was going across sideways."

They had an equipment breakdown and decided to quit for the day. The cross remained on its trailer. A police officer drove up.

"He says, 'What are you guys doing?' We said we're putting up this concrete cross to replace the wooden one, and he said, 'Oh, that's beautiful.'"

The next day a newspaper reporter showed up. Alltucker was out of town and, according to the news account, his crew was evasive about who bore responsibility for the cross's sudden appearance. So the reporter, as Alltucker recalled, "writes this story about the 'mystery' of the new cross."

When Alltucker returned, his wife asked, "What have you been up to? We've been getting obscene phone calls."

The story twisted its way through the public consciousness, leading to such epithets as "Midnight Christians" and "Night Riders." That infuriated Alltucker. He said the crew had worked during daylight hours of two consecutive days, not at midnight. The new fifty-one-foot cross emerged without the blessing of the City

Council, however, and without the required building and electrical permits. Later the council voted 6-1 to grant the permits retroactively.

Catherine Lauris, the first woman elected to the Eugene Council, became the lone dissenter. She said, "I cannot defy the Constitution just to be popular." Citizens jammed the council meeting that night. Passions ran high. Lauris later called it one of the most frightening moments of her life. "The emotions of hate and fear—because we might take something away—were so heavy that you could practically rub it between your fingers." Lauris would pay a price for her outspokenness via hostile phone calls and letters.

Mayor Ed Cone spoke for the majority: "The new cross is certainly very attractive. Now that it is up, we should keep it there." Councilman Dick Crakes added, "I don't care about being pushed around by an agnostic minority. Many, many people love that cross and so do I." Councilman John Chatt said, "My first reaction was to chuckle about the cloak-and-dagger atmosphere of the thing. I feel like a teacher who knows a student has put something over on him. He smiles at it but knows the student's hand must be slapped."

The upheaval continued with stormy public meetings and an overflowing stream of letters to the newspaper.

"Those responsible for the flouting of both the City Council and the Constitution of the United States have succeeded in reducing a symbol of salvation to the level of a Halloween prank," said one writer.

Said another: "I get the feeling that the minority fringe has used this issue to open the doors to bigger and better ways to step on the toes of the majority who still believe that 'separation of church and state' guarantees us freedom of religion, not freedom from religion." The same anti-cross group, he continued, would not hesitate "to have all books removed from the Eugene Public Library that in any way show preference for one religion over another."

"Perhaps," said another, "they would like to remove the rainbow from the sky, which is God's promise that the earth would not be again overflowed in a deluge as at Noah's time."

And another: "We Christians have no right to force others to live under this sign of our faith."

The Eugene Ministerial Association held a meeting so divisive that several of the nineteen ministers present walked out of the room when a member proposed a resolution condemning the "clandestine" manner of the cross's erection. Rabbi Louis Neimand called it "an affront to civil authority." But passing such a measure, other clergy argued, would suggest that the ministers were taking a stand against the meaning of the cross. Baptist minister Vance Webster expressed dismay at groups seeking removal: "These groups have fairly well succeeded in making it illegal to read the Bible in our public schools, though vile and almost pornographic literature can be assigned to the students for reading. They have further made it almost impossible to teach anything about God in the schools, though atheism can be propagated without restraint."

The chairman of the association threatened to resign if the resolution passed, according to the weekly *Saturday Evening Post*, whose article raised the issue to national prominence. It was defeated. The association did pass a resolution asking the city to explore the constitutional issue.

Within days Eugene officials had received more than 200 communications—letters, phone calls, two petitions—about 85 percent of them supporting the new cross as it stood. John Alltucker began getting similar messages, eventually hundreds of them. He found some deeply touching. A woman said she was severely depressed and was enroute to commit suicide one evening. But she chanced to see the lighted cross on the butte. Her Christian faith rekindled, she drove to the cross where she vowed to return to her family.

Two Eugene ministers, Unitarian Reverend Carl Nelson and Presbyterian Reverend David White, formed an organization, Citizens in Support of Religious Liberty and Civil Authority, to campaign for removal of the cross. Carl Nelson recalled years later that "somehow the point never got across that we weren't against the cross; we were simply for religious freedom for everyone."

Some participants gained a certain notoriety. Reverend Nelson's mother sent him a letter, but had forgotten to include the house number. It was returned stamped "insufficient address." But a subsequent letter addressed simply to "The Minister Who Hates the Cross, Eugene, Oregon" arrived unerringly at his mailbox.

The outpouring of support for the cross puzzled some observers. Like most of the western United States, Eugene (population 70,000 then) did not possess solid religious connections. A 1971 study by the Glenmary Research Center would reveal that only 26.1 percent of Lane County's residents were church "adherents" (members and interested followers), as compared to 33.0 percent in Oregon and 49.6 percent in the U.S. population.

Whatever the public response, the courts would decide the fate of the cross because the issue was constitutional, not subject to popular vote. During the next three decades the courts conducted three trials and issued eight judicial rulings, five to remove the cross, three to preserve it on the butte.

In 1966 the first lawsuit, *Lowe et al v. City of Eugene & Alltucker, et al*, ran six days in state circuit court in Eugene. Ten plaintiffs, led by Ray Lowe, represented a variety of faiths—Unitarian, Episcopalian, Congregationalist, Jewish, Baha'i. Two were professors of religious studies. Two called themselves humanists. They all told why they felt the cross was inappropriate in a city park: It showed government was not religiously neutral, it displayed a governmental preference for one religion over others, and it made many uncomfortable. ("I feel more and more in a minority," said a Jewish businessman, Abe Brooks.) They said they would not object to a cross on private property.

One day a defense attorney was grilling witness Alfred Bloom, a university professor of religion, about which religious artifacts he'd want removed from public property. One was a "cross" that formed naturally in the Colorado mountains whenever snow fell.

Would the witness expunge that cross? Bloom recalled being "non-plussed" by such a question, "but the judge said I had to answer."

After a moment's thought the professor replied, "I think I'd wait for spring."

Defense attorneys argued that the plaintiffs had suffered no specific harm from the cross's presence. They said crosses had adorned the butte for many years and should enjoy heritage status like that of other religious artifacts on public property, such as religious symbols in the U.S. Capitol, seventy-one churches located on Forest Service land, three crosses on the shoulder patches of police uniforms in Las Cruces, New Mexico. They quoted a theologian: "It is in our national interest to keep and maintain our religious heritage; otherwise the government becomes the last word in totalitarianism."

Judge William Fort, however, called for the cross's removal. The city, he said, had no authority to place in a city park a structure "having as its primary purpose or effect a religious expression or function." His ruling sidestepped the constitutional question; he called the cross a violation of the city's own charter.

The Oregon Supreme Court overruled the decision in 1969. Six months later a shift in court personnel brought a reversal. The court ruled 5-2 that the cross must come down.

The U.S. Supreme Court declined to hear an appeal.

A new question intruded: Was the cross really a cross? Or was it "just a couple of sticks" whose meaning remained in the eye of the beholder, as one minister suggested? The American Legion post, in 1970, led a petition drive to refer the issue to voters. It sought to amend the city charter to call the cross a "war memorial." Voters approved the amendment by a three-to-one majority. The cross suddenly lost its religious significance. Or did it?

Back to circuit court for the answer. The cross supporters felt they had a stronger case this time, based on the 1934 dedication of the park as a war memorial. But in 1975, Judge Edwin Allen ruled that the cross must go. Its status as a "war memorial" was a non-issue, he said; on the basis of Oregon law, the cross was indeed a symbol of Christianity. "The only inference the court can draw from the evidence and from history is that the use of the cross as a symbol of death and sacrifice of the fallen soldier is derived from the crucifixion of Christ who sacrificed his life for mankind."

The decision precipitated another round of letters to the editor:

"How can people be so narrow minded? What if it is a religious symbol? Maybe if we had more crosses it would help this crazy mixed-up world."

"To me that cross in Skinner Butte means about the same thing as that wooden [crucifixion] device meant 2,000 years ago—political and racist terror, repression, and death."

The Oregon Court of Appeals upheld the decision in 1976, but the Oregon Supreme Court promptly overruled it, affirming the war memorial status.

The U.S. Supreme Court again declined to hear an appeal.

In 1991 a third lawsuit was filed in federal district court by Eugene attorney Charles O. Porter, a former U.S. Congressman. Catherine Lauris was among the plaintiffs, along with Jeff Lewis, a Republican activist, and Jimi Mathers. Judge Michael Hogan affirmed the cross's legality. "I find that a reasonable observer would not view the long-standing existence of the cross atop Skinner Butte as approval or disapproval by the city of their religious choices particularly in light of the fact that it serves a secular purpose described in the city charter."

But the U.S. Ninth Circuit Court of Appeals unanimously overruled that decision. The cross "clearly represents endorsement of Christianity by violating the wall of separation" between church and state, the court said. "There is no question that the Latin cross is a symbol of Christianity, and its placement on public land by the City of Eugene violates the establishment clause." Calling the cross a war memorial, said one judge, "might lead to the belief that only Christian soldiers are honored."

In a separate but concurring opinion, Judge Diarmuid

O'Scannlain pointed out a curious irony. In 1995 the U.S. Supreme Court decided that a Ku Klux Klan proposal to place a cross
on state property in Ohio during the Christmas season was protected by the First Amendment's free speech clause "as secular private expression." In other words, as Justice Clarence Thomas declared at the time, the Klan, by erecting a cross on public property, "appropriated one of the most sacred religious symbols as a
symbol of hate."

And there the issue ended. The city council, having spent
$23,000 defending the federal suit, had little stomach for further
legal machinations. Attorney William Wheatley, who had defended
Alltucker and other involved businessmen, prepared an appeal to
the U.S. Supreme Court on behalf of the American Legion. But an
East Coast delivery service somehow fumbled, and the papers arrived twelve minutes past the court's deadline.

So in 1997 the cross left its lofty perch, though not without a
final protest. A man confronted the removal crew with a shotgun
taped to his body, the muzzle beneath his chin. Touch that cross,
he told them, and he'd pull the trigger. After a three-hour stand-
off, police hustled him away. The gun was not loaded.

The crew delivered the cross to the hillside home of a loving
caretaker, the Eugene Bible College in southwest Eugene. The
thirty-three-year war was over.

But memories remained, and many participants said they'd learned
useful lessons from the experience. "This was one time in my life
that I put my security on the line, and it was a very good feeling,"
said Abe Brooks. Reverend Carl Nelson and plaintiff Jeff Lewis
learned that "in-your-face" confrontational tactics seldom help to
attain civic goals. Plaintiff Dirk Ten Brinke learned that "religious
questions are always explosive." Ray Lowe said, "I've learned to be
patient, but I'm not sure it's because of the cross—it might be old
age."

Broader civic lessons also emerged. "It exposed lots of people
to the basic constitutional issues of freedom of religion and free-

dom of speech," said journalist Don Robinson, whose *Register-Guard* editorials supported removing the cross.

"It reflected the changing character of Eugene where old customs were now subjected to scrutiny as never before," said professor Bloom. "Not everyone could be assumed to be Christian and accepting such situations."

John Alltucker faulted Eugene for "listening to its heart instead of its head."

Attorney William Wheatley faulted the city for a less-than-zealous legal defense in the 1996 federal appeals court hearing. He continued to insist that the cross was legal. "I would not have taken the case had it not been for the city resolution of October 8, 1934, specifically dedicating that park as a war memorial," he said. "They planted a tree up there for each fallen soldier during that ceremony. In the earlier history of this country a cross was deemed an appropriate and profound symbol of sacrifice—as opposed to a symbol of Christianity—for our fallen soldiers. You take that symbol and put it into a war memorial park—as opposed to putting it in Alton Baker Park—then the cross takes on a secular connotation."

Jeff Lewis found the controversy refreshing and healthy: "It had to open some eyes, and the more eyes you open, the better. Getting dissed is a small price to pay."

"Getting dissed" meant receiving spirited correspondence, such as this note sent anonymously to attorney Charles O. Porter: "We would like to meet you and your current 'client' on the butte Fri. night at 7 p.m. We will use piano wire to attach your worthless ass to the cross and shut your worthless mouth once and for all."

Folks began to miss the cross, however. Loren L. "Stub" Stewart, a World War II veteran and prominent lumberman, recalled looking out a window from his ninth-floor luncheon table at the Town Club and thinking to himself that the butte looked bare.

"I was real upset when they took the cross down," he said. "I looked up there and said, 'We've got to have something up there representative of a war memorial.'" He offered to finance a 100-

foot pole to support a giant American flag, together with a
$100,000 endowment to pay for its maintenance.

Amid dissension from opponents, flag supporters launched a
petition drive to refer the issue to voters. They passed it, 53 percent to 47 percent. The post-election controversy was short-lived,
especially after Stewart agreed to a smaller flag and shorter pole.

Past decades have seen many proposals for "improving" the
butte—including removing all human-made monuments and letting it revert to nature. Or leveling part of it to enhance the view of
the river from downtown. Or developing it for high-density housing. In 1928 a Portland landscape architect proposed building a
100-foot lighthouse-type beacon on top, installing steps from
Willamette Street to the summit, and adding formal gardens, a
museum, pools, and tennis courts. Others proposals have included
a tramway, a three-story restaurant, a large secular sculpture, an
ice rink, television stations, and an observation platform built of
logs to represent the lumber industry.

None of these occurred. But in the 1990s, the butte gained a
sinister reputation for crime and mischief. Police statistics cover-
ing a ten-year period through the 1990s show that officers went to
the butte area fifty-four times to cope with disorderly persons or
groups, forty-four for drug problems, forty-four for illegal camping, thirty-five for criminal mischief, thirty-three for loudness
(people, music, vehicles), fifteen for fights, fourteen for harassment, ten for indecent exposure, six for rape. A family retreated
from the top one day after spotting a teenager brandishing a rifle.
The butte suffered from off-road vehicles attempting to grind up
the slopes through fragile soil.

Based on such evidence—and pleading budget shortfalls—
the city's Public Works Administration announced in 1997 that
the road to the top of the butte would be closed permanently.
Only foot traffic could reach the summit.

The darkest hour of the butte's history, some said, among them
Ray Wiley, the engineer from Iowa whose 1961 visit prompted his
family's move to Eugene. The now-retired Wiley was incensed. He

fired off a letter to the editor of *The Register-Guard*: "The 'Top of Skinner Butte' is one of the few features of this community that is unique . . . only one city in the world has a 'Skinner Butte.'"

The tenacious Wiley continued to fight City Hall. The butte could be the city's "Crown Jewel," he said. *The Register-Guard* editorially supported his views: "There's no place like it and the city needs to find ways to preserve its easy accessibility." The city relented and agreed to keep the road open.

Wiley soon enlisted fellow members of the Eugene Rotary Club. He organized platoons of volunteers to clean up the mess—a "junkyard" Wiley called it—that years of neglect and vandalism had wrought. In less than three years they completed sixty-seven projects. They utilized 3,610 hours of hands-on work and expended about $52,310 worth of donated material, equipment time, and cash. With the help of others, Rotarians removed graffiti, painted structures, built trails, cleared brush (exposing the Eugene High "E" to view for the first time in decades). They placed big rocks to block the routes of off-road vehicle drivers. A maple tree planted, an osprey nest platform built, new picnic tables, drinking fountain, trash receptacles, a newly paved terrace, and many other enhancements—these led to what Wiley called a new attitude by citizens: "These changes have led to a significant improvement in the attitude and behavior of persons visiting the butte," he said. "As a result hundreds, maybe thousands, of local citizens have visited the butte for the first time."

Such evidence suggests that with good leadership and the right cause, Eugene can accomplish worthy ends. Eugene remains a feisty community, however, not averse to fighting over symbols. Issues are aired openly, aggressively, sometimes violently. John Milton, the seventeenth century English poet who wrote of Truth and Falsehood grappling on the open forum, would have loved Eugene.*

For those who possess patience and humor, Eugene is an interesting if bewildering city. Perhaps that's why immigrants fall in love, first with the region's good looks, then with the city's inner strength in displaying breezy debates that try to make democracy work, no matter how awkwardly, slowly, or painfully. And in the domain of windy entanglements, there's no place like Skinner Butte, with its glamorous views and its capricious political crosswinds.

* "Though all the winds of doctrine were let loose to play upon the earth, so Truth be in the field, we do injuriously, by licensing and prohibiting, to misdoubt her strength. Let her and Falsehood grapple; who ever knew Truth put to the worse in a free and open encounter?" John Milton, *Areopagitica*, 1644

Bibliography

Armbrister, Trevor. "The Cross that Inflames a City." *Saturday Evening Post*, July 3, 1965.

Bradley, Martin B., et al. *Churches and Church Membership in the United States, an enumeration by region, state, and county. 1990.* Atlanta: Glenmary Research Center, 1991.

Burton, Helen F. *The Cross: A Complete History of the Skinner Butte Cross.* Elmira: Self-published, 1997.

"Calls for service to all Skinners Butte locations." Computer print-out of crime statistics, Criminal Justice Data System, Eugene Police Department, 1990 to YTD, December 3, 1999.

Custer, Chuck. "History of the 'O.' " *Old Oregon*, October-November 1960.

"Development of Skinner Butte: A research report." The Metropolitan Civic Club. Archive: Department of Planning and Development, Historic Preservation Section, City of Eugene. June 14, 1964.

Eugene Daily Guard, 30 Jul. 1924.

Eugene Weekly, 10 Nov. 1994.

"Gimme an 'O' Gimme an 'E.' " *Lane County Historian*, Winter 1996.

Howe, Colby, and Robert Bohle. "The Skinner Butte cross issue: A study of the legality, bargainability, and future influence." Unpublished student paper. Manuscript collection, University of Oregon Library, Eugene, 1969.

Johnson, Douglas W., Paul R. Picard, and Bernard Quinn. *Churches and Church Membership in the United States, an enumeration by region, state, and county*. Atlanta: Glenmary Research Center, 1971.

"Just where was that Skinner cabin?" *Lane County Historian*, Fall 1996.

Kinsey, Phoebe Skinner. Letter to Eugene Daughters of the American Revolution.

Kosmin, Barry A. and Seymour Latchman. *One Nation Under God: Religion in Contemporary America*. New York: Harmony Books, 1993.

Lawrence, Henry W. "A natural landscape history of Eugene." *Lane County Historian*, Spring 1981, 1.

Maddox, Robert F. *Separation of Church and State: Guarantor of Religious Freedom*. New York: Crossroads Publishing Co., 1987.

Nelson, Lee, and Martin Schmitt. "Sic Transit Observatorium." *Old Oregon*, April-May 1955.

Nelson, Roy Paul. "The Case of the Midnight Christians." *Christian Century*, January 6, 1965, 22.

The Oregonian, 28 Jun. 1999.

"Park History Information: Skinner Butte." Archive: Department of Planning and Development, Historic Preservation Section, City of Eugene, undated, ca. 1985.

The Register-Guard, 3 Dec. 1936–16 Jan. 2000.

Seibert, Scott, compiler. *The Skinner Butte Cross*. News clipping and document collection. Eugene: Self-published, 1996.

Separation of Church and State Committee, Jeff Lewis, Jimi Mathers v. City of Eugene, Case 93-35094. Opinion, U.S. Court of Appeals for the Ninth Circuit, August 20, 1996.

"Shelton-McMurphey-Johnson House," descriptive flyer, Shelton-McMurphey-Johnson Association, undated.

Stark, Rodney. "Why Oregon? What Makes the State Attractive to New Religious Movements?" *Oregon Humanities*, Summer 1994, 22.

Toy, Eckard V. "Robe and Gown: The Ku Klux Klan in Eugene, Oregon." In Lay, Shawn, ed. *Invisible Empire in the West: Toward a new appraisal of the Ku Klux Klan in the 1920s*. Champaign: University of Illinois Press, 1992.

THE CHANGING NATURAL ENVIRONMENT

By Ed Alverson

IN 1945 EUGENE was a small, rural town of 36,000. Within fifty-five years, the city and its relationship to the surrounding landscape changed dramatically in response to population increases, economic changes, and broader-scale human alterations to ecological systems.

Though it seemed idyllic, Eugene's environmental setting in 1945 was, in fact, an outcome of dramatic changes that occurred during the previous century as a result of Euro-American settlement and the decline of American Indian cultures. Throughout its entire history, the character of Eugene's landscape has been closely linked to the values and aspirations of its human occupants, both in the past and in modern times.

Environmental Conditions, Circa 1850–1945

The Kalapuya people were hunters and gatherers who occupied the Willamette Valley for thousands of years before the arrival of Euro-American settlers. They were active participants in the interplay between humans and natural forces, helping to create a diverse landscape of prairies, savannas, and woodlands—all of which provided important resources for their subsistence. Prairies especially were the source of important edible plants, such as the bulbs of the camas lily, a food staple used similarly to the potato, and seeds of tarweed, a relative of the sunflower. Prairies that were especially wet in the winter attracted large flocks of ducks, geese, and other waterfowl. Savannas, composed of scattered trees with a grassy understory, were the primary habitat for oak trees, and their acorn crops served as an important food resource for the Kalapuya. The dense forested flood-plains of major rivers provided habitat for wildlife, such as deer and elk, along with much of the nutrient input that made the rivers productive habitats for fish.

Thus, the pre–Euro-American settlement landscape of the southern Willamette Valley was a rich mosaic of distinct habitats that supported a thriving human culture and a rich array of native plants and wildlife. Paradoxically, it was intentional burning of the prairies and savannas by the Kalapuya that kept forest trees from encroaching, thereby maintaining habitat diversity across the landscape.

Euro-American settlers who arrived in the southern Willamette Valley in the 1840s and 1850s and founded the city of Eugene appreciated the aesthetic attributes of the "natural" landscape, but they viewed it mostly as a source of agricultural land and raw materials for commerce. Bringing a can-do attitude toward developing the region, they paid little attention to the effects they were having on the native biota. As a result, the mid-1800s to the mid-1900s saw dramatic changes to the natural environment as prairies were turned into farmlands, timber was cut, and the emerging city of Eugene was built.

By the mid-1900s an emerging middle class had begun to appreciate Oregon's natural landscapes as sites for outdoor recreation activities. The Cascade Mountains and Oregon Coast were popular weekend and holiday destinations for sightseeing, camping, and fishing. However, because of the utilitarian perspective toward the Willamette Valley, the values of Eugene's natural environment were not widely appreciated. Although the unique landscapes and native species of the Willamette Valley were present, they were not recognized as characteristics that identified Eugene's "sense of place."

Since 1945, the attitudes that followed Euro-American settlement have persisted, and the natural environment has continued to change in response to human actions. However, some elements of the pre–Euro-American landscape have managed to survive, albeit in a fragmentary or altered state.

Meanwhile, as the philosophies of environmental thinkers such as Henry David Thoreau, John Muir, and Aldo Leopold took hold, views of the land and what it should provide expanded. Most citizens now recognize that natural areas play an important role in improving the value of the urban environment, and Eugene has a rich legacy of working as a community to preserve parks and open spaces as functioning natural habitats. The story of Eugene's natural environment is a work in progress that has its roots in the actions of our human predecessors many thousands of years ago. But the natural environment also has been greatly influenced by wider societal changes over the past half-century

General Impacts of Development and Urbanization, 1945–2000

In 1945 the urban portion of Eugene occupied only about six square miles, scarcely extending south of West 29th Avenue, west of Garfield, and ending at the south bank of the Willamette River. Small- to medium-sized farms dotted surrounding lands, with intensive agriculture occurring along the floodplain. Aerial photographs taken during the 1940s reveal a rather idyllic landscape of small orchards and fields intermixed with riparian strips and woodland patches, areas that now are filled by subdivisions, shopping centers, and freeways.

The diverse soils of the southern Willamette Valley brought agriculture to the floodplains and ranching to the hills. Areas south and west of Eugene—characterized by poorly drained clay soils in the valley bottoms and thin, infertile soils on the hillsides—served as pasture lands. In 1945 the extent of upland forests was limited, due largely to the lingering effects of Kalapuya burning—which was halted after the arrival of settlers in the mid-1800s—not because of intensive logging. The landscape character of many areas on the southern and western outskirts of Eugene resembled the prairies and savannas that had greeted the first white settlers.

George Watson, who grew up in the Bailey Hill Road area just west of Eugene in the 1930s and 1940s, remembers that animals typical of grasslands, such as the western meadowlark and quail, were once common, though they now are rare in the vicinity. Many now-common species, such as raccoons and black-tailed deer, then were seldom seen. Such species thrive in the brushy woodlands that are more abundant today than fifty years ago. Other wildlife species that are now common around Eugene, such as nutria, opossums, fox squirrels, and starlings, are recently introduced species that were rare or absent in 1945. Although these changes have occurred within the span of a human lifetime, the rapid growth of Eugene's population means that few residents have actually observed or experienced these changes.

A prevailing philosophy during much of the history of the United States has been that nature is an element separate from culture that exists to be manipulated and molded for the benefit of humans. Since 1945, the engineering of water resources has had a particularly significant impact on Eugene. During the first century of the city's existence, the frequent winter flooding of rivers and streams influenced land use within floodplains. Periodic flooding discouraged investments in structures that could be damaged by floodwaters. Although most homes in that era were typically built with basements, basements were poorly suited to areas prone to flooding or with a high water table.

During the 1940s, '50s, and '60s, the U.S. Army Corps of Engineers and the Bonneville Power Administration constructed a system of dams and reservoirs in the headwaters of the Willamette River to provide capacity for floodwater storage, as well as to generate hydroelectric power. This flood-control system largely—though not completely—eliminated flooding as a hazard to property within the former floodplain. The perception of flood control greatly facilitated urbanization in much of the Ferry Street Bridge, River Road, and Santa Clara areas during the '50s and '60s, although floods in 1964 and 1996 suggest that these areas might still be vulnerable to rare, extreme flood events.

Smaller streams flowing in Eugene's level valley floor also have been predisposed to regular flooding during the rainy season. Amazon Creek begins as a series of small streams that drain the north side of Spencer Butte and the ridgeline south of Eugene. In the 1940s, when these streams converged onto the flat prairie land, they tended to spread out in the winter and form a broad area of wet prairie in the vicinities of present-day Amazon Park and the Lane County Fairgrounds. Charlene Simpson, who as a child in the early 1940s lived south of the university near East 22nd Avenue and Kincaid Street, recalls that at that time the valley bottom along Amazon Creek upstream from 19th Avenue consisted only of vacant land that was covered with water at times because of winter floods.

Local efforts to improve the conveyance capacity of Amazon Creek began as early as 1925, but they were not very effective. After citizens appealed to the federal government for assistance, the U.S. Army Corps of Engineers, in 1951 and 1952, greatly enlarged the channel capacity and built levees adjacent to the creek from Chambers Street downstream to an artificial diversion channel at Royal Avenue that redirected most of the creek's flow westward out of the Amazon Creek watershed to Fern Ridge Reservoir. From 1956 to 1958, the Corps constructed the concrete-lined channel of Amazon Creek upstream from Jefferson Street to 24th Avenue and Pearl Street. These projects, as well as similar projects in other parts of the city and the installation of underground storm-drainage pipes, transformed a network of shallow, meandering streams into ditches fed by a network of hidden pipes. Such efforts served their intended purpose of drastically eliminating property damage due to flooding. But the process of remaking Eugene's natural creeks into an engineered drainage system sacrificed much of the streams' ecological function.

This re-engineering of nature paved the way for large-scale expansion of Eugene's urban area. Fed by dramatic economic and population growth during the post-war years, urban expansion led to a dramatic loss of agricultural lands, as well as natural or semi-natural habitats in Eugene. Between 1945 and 1995, the land area occupied by the city expanded from seven-and-a-half square miles to forty-two square miles, a five-fold increase in the urban footprint.

As Eugene grew and sprawled outward, the surrounding open spaces were filled by new streets, subdivisions, shopping centers, and schools. Although every landscape has a story to tell, a selection of sites representative of Eugene's native habitat diversity illustrates how Eugene's environment has changed.

Willamette River Floodplain: Goodpasture Island

Bounded on the west by the main channel of the Willamette River and on the east by Debrick Slough, Goodpasture Island in the 1940s was within the floodplain of the pre–flood-controlled Willamette River. In fact, the entire island was flooded in January of 1943, and such floods probably occurred at least once a decade. Because of the flood hazard, there were only a few homes or other buildings on the entire island. Most of the island consisted either of farmland or relatively natural riparian vegetation. Debrick Slough occupied a portion of an old channel of the Willamette, but the remainder of the quarter-mile-wide former river channel was primarily riparian forest. Another triangle of remnant riparian forest was found on the northwest part of the island.

During the 1950s much of the old river channel on the east side of the island was transformed by clearing the forest for gravel extraction, leaving behind a series of shallow ponds, now known as the Delta Ponds. Further gravel extraction occurred in the 1960s for the construction of the Delta Highway. Also in the 1960s, Valley River Center opened, and with a degree of protection from flooding provided by upstream dams, the island became an extension of urban Eugene, a transformation that has nearly come to completion. During the same era, Beltline Highway was con-

structed across the north end of Goodpasture Island, with a clo-
verleaf intersection placed in the middle of the old river channel.

Despite the history of alteration and urbanization, nature has
persisted in Delta Ponds, where the shallow former gravel pits provide habitat for a range of birds and aquatic animals. However, a
dike prevents most flows of water from the main Willamette into
the ponds, and consequently the water becomes stagnant at times.
The disturbed ground adjacent to the ponds has mostly been colo-
nized by Himalayan blackberry and Scotch broom, with patches
of native riparian vegetation persisting here and there. Only in the
ash-maple woods on the northwest side of Goodpasture Island
along the Willamette River does a small patch of riparian forest
persist in relatively intact condition, surrounded by new residential development. This small oasis of original riparian forest teems
with spring wildflowers and songbirds, a reminder of the character
of the Willamette River bottomlands in an earlier time.

Upland Prairie and Urban Forest: Skinner Butte

In the early days following Euro-American settlement, Skinner
Butte was a "bald hill," with open prairie on the east, south, and
west sides, and coniferous forest limited to the north slope. Early
photographs taken of downtown Eugene looking northward clearly
show the open character of Skinner Butte's dry south side. The
butte served as one of Eugene's first public parks, obtained from
Eugene Water and Electric Board in 1914. Its prominent location
and its links to Eugene's history have made it the site of a great
deal of civic attention. Converting the south slope from prairie to
forest was once seen, apparently, as an act of civic duty. Early tree-
planting efforts along the road to the summit involved blasting
depressions in the bedrock to create areas with sufficient soil depth
to support trees. And a mass tree planting in 1934, to commemorate Armistice Day, contributed especially to the establishment of
forest on the erstwhile prairie.

Among the most successful tree species established on Skinner
Butte are incense cedar and bigleaf maple, both native to western

Oregon. Many of these trees grew from the seeds of older trees that initially were planted around the Shelton-McMurphy House on the southeast side of the butte. The driest sides of the butte, particularly the southwest and west slopes, have resisted the transformation to forest and have largely become blackberry thickets, since the parks department stopped mowing the steep grassy slopes. However, scattered Douglas-fir saplings have taken root even here, and a future forest is developing.

Only on the steep western slopes of Skinner Butte, above the old basalt quarry, does a small fragment of prairie and oak savanna persist. Amazingly, this small remnant area supports populations of prairie wildflowers that have become quite rare in the Willamette Valley, including deltoid balsamroot, grass widows, and tapertip onion, along with Idaho fescue and Lemmon's needlegrass, two native bunchgrasses. Perched atop this steep slope, one can witness the contrast between the native prairie fragment, an archaic landscape in today's Willamette Valley, and the traffic and urban panorama that unfolds below.

The north slope of Skinner Butte tells a different story. It appears to have always supported some type of forest ecosystem, though it was probably in an early seral stage in the 1850s due to frequent fires. The historic presence of a forest ecosystem is reflected in the present diversity of forest trees, shrubs, and wildflowers. Although not sufficiently mature to be called "old growth," this could be called a "virgin" forest (since it appears to have never been logged), and the grove contains some Douglas firs and grand firs more than four feet in diameter. Numerous spring wildflowers, such as western trillium, Pacific waterleaf, and inside-out flower, carpet the ground under a multilayered canopy that includes Indian plum, vine maple, and bigleaf maple in the understory. However, over the past fifty years this forest community has been transformed by nonnative plant species that have escaped from nearby gardens, particularly English ivy, which is smothering the growth of native wildflowers on the ground and climbing tree trunks to reach the canopy.

Consciously or not, the vegetative changes to Skinner Butte reflect our cultural values: We value forest more than prairie. We have traditionally valued "useful" garden plants over native wildflowers. Despite efforts to "protect" the butte as a public park, we have set in motion a course of ecological change that is still in process.

Oak/Pine Savanna:
South Eugene, between Willamette and Hilyard Streets

When the first settlers arrived, much of the upland terrain south and southwest of Eugene was an open savanna. Fires set at frequent intervals by the Kalapuya prevented trees from establishing in thick stands and promoted the growth of native grasses and spring wildflowers. Oregon white oak was a prominent indicator of this habitat in the Eugene area, often accompanied by California black oak, ponderosa pine, and occasionally Douglas fir.

As a result of fire suppression, the higher and moister slopes gradually evolved into forests. But early agricultural use of some areas was limited to ranching, because of relatively dry, infertile soils, which maintained the savanna character of these landscapes.

In the 1940s the rolling hills in the Amazon Creek drainage, south of downtown, were entirely rural. The city dump, located in present-day Tugman Park, was the only intrusion of urban life to these rural outskirts. One low ridge, located east of Willamette Street and north of 39th Avenue, resembled a classic oak knoll with scattered, tall ponderosa pines. This ridge is apparent in the background of many older photographs of downtown Eugene taken from Skinner Butte.

Such places became prime building sites for residential neighborhoods, and with the post-war building boom, the ranching era faded into an era of curvy streets. Most of the streets running through South Eugene in 2000 were constructed by 1957; by 1968 the transformation to suburbia was complete. Only at the site of the landfill, which became Tugman Park, and in a few odd-shaped, privately owned lots, did remnants of the original oak savanna survive the transformation. Although many of the oaks were left standing where they were not in the way of construction, new homes were landscaped with the typical palate of exotic, ornamental plants. Some property owners, recognizing the special value of the oak savanna understory, have encouraged native wildflowers, such as the Oregon fawn lily, by waiting to mow their yards until flowering is complete and spreading the seeds of native species. Sometimes the transformation from a wild to an urban area is not as complete as it may seem.

Wet Prairie: Westmoreland area, between Friendly and Chambers Streets

A distance away from the Willamette River floodplain, soils on the valley floor become sticky clays—hard and dry in the summer but wet and gooey after the onset of winter rains. Poorly suited for agriculture, these seasonal wet prairies generally were used as pastures and for hay production. Because of drainage problems, early urbanization spread first along hillsides and avoided this wet valley bottom. In 1945 a large swath of wet prairie still existed in the Westmoreland area, south of West 18th Avenue between Friendly and Chambers Streets. Part of this area served as Eugene's first municipal airstrip from 1919 to 1954, after the Mahlon Sweet field was constructed northwest of Eugene. The old airstrip became a city park.

The 1950s and 1960s saw the construction of Jefferson Middle School on the site and the development of the field to look like an urban community park, with a community center, lawns, ornamental trees, sports fields, and tennis courts. Around the same time the surrounding lands became residential neighborhoods. By 1968 the Westmoreland neighborhood looked pretty much like it looks in 2000.

Despite the alteration of this landscape within a span of twenty years, several small areas within Westmoreland Park have managed to retain the native prairie flora. For example, between the community center and Polk Street (south of the tennis courts) lies a one-block-sized area of the native wet prairie that has persisted in spite of its use for pasturing animals, landing airplanes, and recreating citizens. Another patch of native prairie is found on the west side of the community center along Fillmore Street. As in presettlement days, the purple blooms of camas lilies are a major springtime feature of the prairie, and more than twenty-five species of native wildflowers and grasses also are present. The camas and some of these other prairie plants once served as important food plants for the Kalapuya Indians. It is ironic that one of the few landscapes within Eugene's city limits that still supports native flora and is linked to Native American cultures has survived only because of coincidence and benign neglect.

Toward the outskirts of west Eugene, where new development has begun to transform the landscape from rural to urban, larger areas of wet prairie habitats persist. Some of these sites, such as the Willow Creek Natural Area and the Lower Amazon Restoration Project, are protected by the City of Eugene, Bureau of Land Management, and The Nature Conservancy, partners in the West Eugene Wetlands Program. These larger areas of wet prairie are better able to support a range of native plants and animals than the Westmoreland Park and other small remnant prairies within Eugene's urban area. However, these urban remnants are important as reminders of how we have changed the surrounding landscape.

Remnants of the Past

Over the past fifty-five years, changes to Eugene's natural environment have closely followed demographic and economic trends. Conscious decisions to develop the landscape have determined the fate of ecological systems; so has management of natural forces, such as stream flows, and introduction of ornamental plants. Recognizing the degradation of certain environmental values, citizens and public officials increasingly have broadened the scope of civic objectives to incorporate ecological goals. Encouraged by the emphasis in Oregon on comprehensive land-use planning since the mid-1970s, the latest phase of urban resource management has worked to protect existing resources and, in some cases, to modify or restore areas damaged by past activities. Some examples are the Willamette River Greenway, West Eugene Wetlands, and protection of open space along the Ridgeline Trail.

While much of the environmental degradation that resulted from urbanization in the 1960s and 1970s was the direct or indirect result of federal transportation and public works projects, the current trend is for increased federal assistance to protect existing resources through land acquisition and modification of the built environment. For instance, in the late 1990s the U.S. Army Corps of Engineers and Oregon Department of Transportation lent their support to restoration projects along Amazon Creek. With the listings of salmon and steelhead in the Willamette River system under the Endangered Species Act, federal assistance is likely to increase.

Whether enough of these natural systems are left to maintain their ecological function is still an open question. Nature will always exist, of course, but whether Eugene's natural environment will be dominated by dandelions and starlings or camas and meadowlarks will depend upon the decisions and actions of current and future citizens.

Bibliography

Boyd, Robert. "Strategies of Indian Burning in the Willamette Valley." *Canadian Journal of Anthropology* 5 (1986): 65–86.

Johannessen, Carl J., William A Davenport, Artimus Millet, and Steven McWilliams. "The Vegetation of the Willamette Valley." *Annals of the Association of American Geographers* 61 (1971): 286–302.

Lawrence, Henry W., and Ann P. Bettman. *The Green Guide: Eugene's Natural Landscape*. Eugene, Oregon: Ann P. Bettman, 1982.

Williams, Jerrold. "The World According to Skinner Butte." *Lane County Historian* 43 (1998): 34–41.

COPING WITH GROWTH

By Karen Seidel

How Eugene Grew

EUGENE ENTERED THE twenty-first century with a population of almost 140,000 and a land area of forty-two square miles. It was not a Chicago or a Los Angeles; nor, contrary to some predictions, did it become a Portland or a Seattle. But Eugene was a vastly larger city than it was in 1950 when it claimed 36,000 people and 7.5 square miles of Lane County. By 1960 Eugene hit 50,000, became a "metropolitan area," and beat out Salem as Oregon's "second city." Within only seventeen more years, its 1960 population doubled. By 2000 Eugene's population was four times as large—with a land area almost six times as large—as it was at the midpoint of the twentieth century.

Three independent forces caused Eugene's 100,000-plus population growth between 1950 and 2000. The first was natural increase—the excess of resident births over resident deaths. This factor contributed to population growth most strongly during the 1950s and early 1960s, the Baby Boom years, when Eugene families produced upwards of three children each. The "Baby Boom Echo" was responsible for Eugene's small growth during the 1980s as it offset the large number of people moving away because of the economic recession.

The second force contributing to growth was annexation of populated areas. Following World War II, unincorporated regions surrounding Eugene grew rapidly. These areas needed urban services—some represented potential health hazards—and Eugene developed an aggressive annexation program. During the 1950s the city expanded westward and southward and, in 1960, for the first time, annexed large areas north of the Willamette River. In 1964 Bethel and Eugene voters approved the annexation of Bethel-Danebo, a seven-square-mile area containing more than 7,000 people. It represented the largest single annexation in Eugene's history.

Later in the 1960s and continuing into the 1970s, the rest of the Willakenzie area became part of Eugene, along with ridgeline lands to the south and east. After that, Eugene's only major annexation was the west-side industrial and wetlands area. Small, scattered annexations in the River Road-Santa Clara area occurred in the 1990s.

The third cause of growth was net migration—more people moved into Eugene than moved away. Responsible for more than half the city's 1950–2000 population growth, net migration was the most important of the three forces, and the most controversial. Most new Eugeneans wanted to close and lock the door after they arrived. However, economic, recreational, educational, and quality-of-life opportunities continued to attract people to this part of Oregon, especially during the 1970s and 1990s.

How Eugene Responded to Growth

Eugeneans never have been of one mind regarding the benefits and costs of population growth. Between 1950 and 2000, citizens, planners, and public officials thought long and hard about its challenges and implications. Growth management—of which population growth policy is one facet—is an enormously complex topic. The issues surrounding it include preservation of environmental quality, development of cost-effective infrastructure, protection of farm lands and open spaces, creation of family-wage jobs, provision of low-income housing, collaboration with neighboring and overlapping units of local government, and compliance with relevant state and federal laws. During each decade between 1950 and 2000, Eugeneans demonstrated different con-

cerns and pursued different strategies in their efforts to deal with
population growth.

1950s: Accommodating Growth

In 1945 Eugene, Springfield, and Lane County, along with other
units of local government, created the Central Lane County Planning Council (CLCPC) and gave it the task of conducting broad-
scale studies to promote sound physical and economic development in central Lane County. (CLCPC became the Central Lane
Planning Council [CLPC] in 1961 and Lane Council of Governments [LCOG] in 1970.) The founding of CLCPC was a historic
event because it established a basis for collaborative planning that
continues to this day. This unified approach meant Eugene's
growth-management policies were never conceived or implemented
in a vacuum, nor could they have been. The policies of adjacent
and overlapping local governments and districts all have had im-
pacts on one another.

Under the guidance of director Howard Buford, CLCPC prepared a long-range comprehensive plan for the Eugene-Springfield area (*Development Plan: Eugene-Springfield Metropolitan Region*, 1959). Based on population forecasts for the "full development" of planning units within central Lane County, the plan's
chief purpose was to identify suitable sites for public facilities (i.e.,
schools, parks, roads, etc.), so that those sites could be obtained
before rising land values made them too costly or development
made them unavailable. Although the population in and around
Eugene had been growing rapidly for twenty years, and the UO's
Bureau of Municipal Research had issued a series of studies for
Oregon's larger cities on the problems of the urban fringe, the
1959 Development Plan did not consider the need to limit the
area's population or geographic growth.

1960s: Restricting Geographic Growth

The balance of planning power changed in the 1960s as Eugene,
Springfield, and Lane County each established their own plan-

ning departments and sought more input into CLPC's decision
making. Eugene's first planning director, John Porter, and his staff
referred to the 1959 Development Plan and the eruption of federal, state, and county road building as "all the way to San Jose,"
an allusion to California cities torn apart by freeways.

Eugene planners wanted planning decisions to follow the city
council's goals and policies. The Eugene Planning Commission
stated its objectives to the council in 1965: "[We] believe that
Eugene needs a new general development plan . . . [that] would
be the Council's plan, a statement of official council policies on
the general development of our city. . . . We believe that the Council
will want to adopt such a plan as its own only if they have some
assurance of community support."

With the blessing of the council and under the guidance of
Planning Commissioner Betty Niven, Eugene convened its first
Community Goals Conference in 1966. Mayor Ed Cone invited
250 citizens to take "a square look at Eugene's future." While the
conference proceedings ranged over many issues, two metropolitan problems—air pollution and urban sprawl—took precedence.
Both problems were the result of unrestricted economic and population growth. Wigwam burners, field burning, motor vehicles,
and back-yard burning were worsening Lane County's air quality,
and leap-frog development was scattering homes onto prime farm
lands, where adequate urban services were unavailable.

The first community goal selected by conference participants
was "to protect and enhance the quality of our environment so
that Eugene will retain its appeal as a good place in which to live."
To accomplish this, they proposed that the city council look at
strategies that would increase housing density, preserve prime agricultural lands, and provide green belts and open space—all part
of what came to be called "compact urban growth." They were
realistic about the difficulties of solving problems related to sprawl,
given that Lane County had a very tolerant approach to development and that the Eugene Water and Electric Board's policy was
to extend utility services wherever it was economically feasible.

The conference assumed that Eugene's rapid rate of growth would continue but that "with some effort we shall be able to maintain in a larger city the quality of civic concern that is characteristic of Eugene today."

In the late 1960s CLPC prepared a new metropolitan plan for the Eugene-Springfield area. Known as the "1990 Plan," it was directed by the goals adopted by CLPC's Plan Advisory Committee in 1968, which in turn were guided by the results of Eugene's Community Goals Conference. The 1990 Plan rejected the growth accommodation objectives of the 1959 Development Plan and directly confronted the problem of urban sprawl. It sought to establish compact growth through an "urban service area" strategy. Urban services would only be provided within the boundary of the urban service area, which included Eugene, Springfield, River Road-Santa Clara, Glenwood, and other developed areas on the cities' edges. Its size and shape were based on the efficient service area of Eugene-Springfield's gravity sewer system, as well as on physical features, existing public facilities, projected population and employment, and vacant urban land.

Eugene City Manager Hugh McKinley and the CLPC Planning Advisory Committee, chaired by Ed Harms, provided strong support for this new planning strategy. The elected bodies of Eugene, Springfield, and Lane County adopted the 1990 Plan and the urban service area in 1972, transforming the way Oregon planners and residents thought about growth and development. A few years later, Oregon's newly created Land Conservation and Development Commission (LCDC) used the urban service area as the prototype for the "urban growth boundary," which became a required part of every Oregon city's comprehensive plan.

1970s: Attempting to Restrict Population Growth, Part I
The explosive migration to Oregon and Eugene during the late 1960s set off an equivalent explosion of anti-growth sentiment during the early 1970s. Slogans, such as "Visit us, but for heaven's

sake, don't stay" and "the famous radioactive vapors of the Columbia River will get you" and "Oregonians don't tan; they rust,"
attempted to discourage out-of-staters from moving to Oregon.
Along with Governor Tom McCall, vocal opponents of in-migra-
tion included Eugene's Jim Cloutier, creator of "Oregon Ungreeting
Cards," and the Joaquin Miller Society, named for a nineteenth-
century Eugene poet (for no discernible reason). The Miller Society was similar to the James G. Blaine Society, founded by Portland writer Stewart Holbrook during the 1940s to "save Oregon
for Oregonians," and resurrected by former *Register-Guard* reporter
Ron Abell. (James G. Blaine was a nineteenth-century senator and
presidential candidate from Maine who had nothing to do with
Oregon.) The Millerites proposed a $5,000 immigration fee and a
sixteen-foot fence along the shoulders of I-5 between Oregon's
borders with Washington and California. Along with members of
SNOB (Society of Native Oregon Born), they also suggested that
all nonnative Oregonians be expelled. If implemented, this proposal would have cut Eugene's population in half.

Such half-serious, tongue-in-cheek proposals were offset by
various city and state "livability" rankings that began to appear in
the national press. In 1971 *The Washington Post* listed the
Willamette Valley among seven areas in the country "where America
the Beautiful can still be found." Three years later *Newsweek* published an article, "Where the Future Works," that described Oregon as a paradise on earth. The Midwest Research Institute ranked
Lane County first among medium-sized metropolitan areas in 1975,
and in 1977 *Family Circle* judged Eugene to be second among the
ten best U.S. cities "in which to live a good life."

Between 1971 and 1974, Eugene's population grew faster than
any other Oregon city, and no-growth sentiments found their way
into official public discourse. A second Community Goals Conference in 1974 focused on the growth issue. Conference coordinator
Betty Niven told participants:

Eugene has itself experienced many of the benefits of growth. We are also suffering some of the detriments of growth. It is the assessment of the Community Goals Committee that a vote among the citizens to stop growth would be successful. [She was right—in 1977, 55 percent of survey respondents answered "yes" to the question, "Do you believe the City of Eugene should attempt to limit the growth of population in Eugene?"] It appears that more people came to this area to escape areas of excessive growth than the number who came here for the excitement of a larger place. Notwithstanding this appraisal of the public attitude, we do not see any legal means of stopping growth. At the same time, we recognize that the really critical factor in continued growth at the rate it has been occurring—nearly three times the national rate and twice the state rate—will lead to depletion of a resource we cannot renew: AIR.

Although Eugene's air quality gradually improved following local and state legislation that banned backyard burning, eliminated wigwam burners, and reduced field burning, the growth issue was harder to tackle. Conference participants and the city council agreed that "a city has a right and an obligation to adopt policies to direct and control the city's growth in order to protect the health of the inhabitants, to phase public improvements to match the city's financial resources, and to maintain its governability."

The two most important growth policies approved were 1) to strengthen the urban service area concept and 2) to implement a slower rate of growth, while maintaining economic viability. To accomplish the second policy conferees proposed inviting other taxing bodies in the metro area to appoint a joint citizens' committee to conduct a study of the costs and benefits of population growth and to develop growth policies and implementing tools.

When Springfield and Lane County declined to participate in a growth-management study, Eugene's city council directed the city planning department to carry it out. The study examined what other cities in the United States were doing to control or limit growth, reactions by state and federal courts to growth moratorium strategies, and new LCDC guidelines related to growth management. The study, along with subsequent public hearings and a 1978 Growth Management Conference, concluded that 1) a population growth moratorium would not be in compliance with court decisions or LCDC goals; 2) geographic management of growth should be continued; 3) greater efficiency and density should be pursued in Eugene's residential land use; and 4) widespread support existed for the city to adopt a growth-management program. The city "should pursue means of achieving this reduction in growth rate if it can do so without seriously impacting the cost of housing or . . . economic stability or simply shifting the fact and the problems of population increase from inside the city limits to the balance of the metropolitan area."

1980s: Encouraging Economic Growth

The issue of reducing Eugene's population growth rate became irrelevant in the early 1980s due to an absolute decline in the number of residents. Oregon's faltering timber economy and a national recession produced high unemployment rates, business closures, and major out-migration. Not surprisingly, improving and diversifying the local economy became the key concern of Mayor Gus Keller and Eugene's 1984 Community Goals Conference, led by Planning Commissioner Dorothy Anderson. Conference participants nevertheless reaffirmed their commitment to geographic growth management, a compact urban form, and environmental quality. They recognized the danger of overreacting to an economic downturn that would likely be short-lived.

In 1982 a new Eugene-Springfield Metropolitan Area General Plan (Metro Plan) replaced the 1990 Plan. The Metro Plan firmly stated, "To effectively control the potential for urban sprawl and scattered urbanization, compact growth and the urban service area concepts are, and will remain, the primary growth manage-

ment techniques." It established cities as the logical service providers and managers of urban growth. The plan also recognized
that decreases in average household size would increase the demand for housing, even without population growth.

"Quality of life" ranking centers continued to chronicle Eugene's
special character. Two organizations used ranking scales that pur-
ported to measure tranquility versus stress. Zero Population Growth
ranked Eugene eighth out of 192 American cities for "mellow-
ness." *Psychology Today* ranked Eugene 159th out of 286 metropolitan areas according to serenity-versus-stress measures. *The Register-
Guard* wondered, "What to make of all this silliness? Not much.
The causes of stress are many. Place of residence may or may not
be one. Some would find the Eugene-Springfield area too soggy,
too cantankerous or too smug. Others would find this area an
enlightened paradise."

1990s: Attempting to Restrict Population Growth, Part II

In the 1980s Eugene's city, business, and university leaders—led
by Mayor Brian Obie and City Manager Mike Gleason—developed a variety of strategies to improve and diversify Eugene's
economy. For instance, they formed the Business Assistance Team,
provided city services to large industrial sites in West Eugene and
the Chad Drive area, created the Riverfront Research Park, and
established the West Eugene Enterprise Zone. These proactive
development efforts bore fruit, culminating in the siting of Hyundai
Semi-conductor America in Willow Creek Basin in 1995.

Expanding local employment opportunities, coupled with
Oregon's economic recovery and California's recession, brought a
flood of new residents to the Eugene area. Oregon replaced Washington as the favorite destination of people leaving California.
During the early '90s Eugene's population grew by about 2,000
people per year. Eugene voters reacted negatively to this growth
surge by defeating a measure to widen Ferry Street Bridge to six
lanes in November 1994. In the same year a city survey found that
citizens ranked rapid growth as the city's third most pressing prob-

lem, behind crime and school funding. By 1996 growth had become residents' number-one concern.

In response, the Eugene Planning Commission recommended that the city undertake a comprehensive growth-management study to review the city's historic growth practices, establish priorities regarding future growth, and recommend changes to existing policies. In 1995 Mayor Ruth Bascom and the city council initiated the study, which included opportunities for community involvement. Mayor Bascom stated in *The Register-Guard*, "There's a basic conflict in people's minds: Is growth desirable, or is it something we should try to prevent? It can become a nasty debate. We need community dialogue that addresses that polarization in a constructive way."

Thousands of citizens responded to the city's "Shaping Eugene's Future" study. They participated in workshops, attended open houses and meetings, and completed surveys. When asked to choose among alternative growth scenarios, their answer was loud and clear: "When faced with four road maps for guiding Eugene's future, residents most strongly favored a slow-growth scenario that would promote denser development, prevent expansion of the urban growth boundary and direct public handouts to small companies and environmentally sensitive businesses," *The Register-Guard* summarized in February 1997.

The "Recycle Eugene" road map committed the city to stronger environmental protection, acquisition and protection of open space, and provision of various incentives for redevelopment and mixed-use and high-density development. Although many Eugeneans encouraged the city to do even more to discourage growth, constraints existed over the city's power to take such action. Eugene was obligated to follow the policies set forth in the Metro Plan, as well as state laws requiring local governments to accommodate and plan for growth.

After the council adopted the growth-management policies, the city planning staff worked to implement them. System development charges for new development were increased. The urban growth boundary was not expanded. Enterprise zone subsidies were revoked for new industrial development in West Eugene. Eugeneans passed a parks and open-space bond measure in 1998. In the late 1990s, staff worked on a land-use code update to implement the city's new growth management policies.

Postscript

Despite Eugene's changing demographics, its tremendous expansion, and changing ideas about growth and development among its citizens, it has managed to maintain its attractiveness and special character. In November 1999 the Arts and Entertainment Channel ranked Eugene seventh among the ten best places to live in the United States. This tribute, in a perverse sort of way, testified to the success of Eugene's 1950–2000 growth policies and planning practices.

Bibliography

Central Lane County Planning Commission. *Development Plan, Eugene-Springfield Metropolitan Region.* 1959.

Central Lane Planning Council. *Eugene-Springfield Metropolitan Area Preliminary 1990 General Plan.* 1969.

―――. *Three Valleys: An Examination of Growth Problems, Goals and Planning in Relation to the Eugene-Springfield Metropolitan Area.* 1968.

City of Eugene. *1974 Community Goals and Policies. Eugene, Oregon: Growth Chapter 3, Revised October 1979.* 1979.

―――. *1974 Eugene Community Goals and Policies.* 1974.

―――. *1984 Community Goals Conference Background Paper: Revisions to 1974 Goals.* 1984.

―――. *1984 Eugene Community Goals and Policies.* September 1984.

―――. *Community Goals and Policies.* April 1967.

―――. *Eugene Growth Management Study, Shaping Eugene's Future, Adopted Policies.* 1998.

―――. *Growth.* Background Paper for Community Goals Conference. May 1974.

―――. *Growth Management Study, Phase 1.* 1977.

―――. *A Growth Policy for Eugene.* Letter from Betty Niven to Community Goals Conference participants. May 8, 1974.

―――. *Shaping Eugene's Future, Phase 1: Setting the Agenda—Growth Management Report Card.* April 1996.

―――. *Shaping Eugene's Future, Phase 1: Setting the Agenda—Growth Trends Analysis.* April 1996.

Eugene Planning Commission. *Statement of Objectives from Planning Commission to City Council.* November 1965.

Institute of Policy Analysis. *City of Eugene Public Opinion Survey, November-December 1977.* Eugene, Oregon. 1978.

Lane Council of Governments. *Eugene-Springfield Metropolitan Area 1990 General Plan.* 1972.

————. *Eugene-Springfield Metropolitan Area General Plan, 1987 Update*. 1987.

————. Metropolitan Area Planning Advisory Committee. *Second Annual Review of 1990 General Plan*. August 1975.

BETTY NIVEN:

THE MOTHER OF MODERN

PLANNING IN EUGENE

By John Van Landingham

IN APRIL 1968, after almost five years of citizen committee meetings, surveys, drafts, hearings, letters to the editor, editorials, and planning commission and city council meetings, Eugene planning commission chair, Betty Niven, was conducting a hearing on a final draft of an ordinance to regulate signs and billboards in Eugene. In the late 1960s, pursuant to a ballot measure initiative, Oregon was phasing out highway billboards. Lady Bird Johnson led a national campaign to beautify highways, in part by removing billboards. Billboard owners were feeling the economic pressure. Brian Obie, then a member of Eugene's planning commission, was the owner of an outdoor advertising firm that owned or operated more than 100 billboards in Eugene. Fearing economic harm from the new sign code, Obie testified that his firm had "given generously" to charitable causes by allowing them free use of his billboards, and "the thanks we get is the taking of 70 percent of our business." Niven's response was typically quick, polite, and utterly effective at demolishing Obie's point. "I'm sorry to hear that by making contributions to public causes you thought you had purchased the right to put signs in public places and without regulations," she said. "I thought you made contributions because you were public spirited."

Who is Betty Niven? And what did she have to do with plan-

ning in Eugene? Rather than catalogue and describe the history
and contents of the hundreds of planning documents the city produced between 1945 and 2000, this essay will give a few examples
of what planning was like in Eugene at the beginning of the last
half century to illustrate how it has changed. Through her intelligence, political skill, and willingness to work hard for the good of
the community, Betty Niven is responsible for much of that change.

The Fringe Element

During the post-war 1940s and 1950s, Eugene experienced one
of its cyclical growth spurts. The national economy was booming,
with new construction surging for returning World War II veterans and their young families. More homebuilding, nationally, meant
more wood, more timber cut from Oregon's forests, and plenty of
timber jobs in Lane County. Eugene, in particular, experienced a
post-war population boom, because many veterans, often with
spouses and children, were taking advantage of the GI Bill to attend the University of Oregon.

There was a severe shortage of housing in the city right after
the war ended. Vets and their families were sleeping in cars and on
park benches. A veterans group bought 100 tiny "trailer houses,"
and the city allowed them to be placed in a small cow pasture on
the western edge of Eugene, in what is now Sladden Park in the
heart of the Whiteaker neighborhood. Others found housing just
outside the city in an area known to planners as the rural-urban
fringe, where housing and land were cheaper and no one paid any
attention to building code issues. Between 1930 and 1960, and
especially between 1945 and 1955, the population in this fringe
area grew much faster than the population inside the city. By 1956
the population of the fringe exceeded the population of Eugene
and Springfield. Eugene was being plagued by unrestricted urban
sprawl.

The fringe areas of those days—the Friendly, Glenwood, Bethel,
Bailey Hill, and River Road neighborhoods and, after the Corps of
Engineers built dams on the Willamette and McKenzie Rivers,

the Willakenzie and Norkenzie neighborhoods—raised concerns. City residents paid higher taxes for roads that fringe dwellers used to drive to their jobs in town. Fringe residents rarely had sewer service, and hepatitis and typhoid were realistic fears. Eugene used to respond to fringe-area fires and bill for the response, until it realized that the charge didn't cover the cost of maintaining the fire department. Shortly after the council decided to stop responding, half of Glenwood burned down, and the city took a lot of criticism for standing aside.

EWEB was cheering on the fringe, with Lane County's apparent support. By the 1950s water districts ringed Eugene, in large part because EWEB sold them water eagerly and cheaply. By the mid-1950s EWEB's water sales in the fringe area constituted 25 percent of all its water sales, almost equal to residential water sales inside the city. The fringe dwellers actually paid less for water than city residents, because city dwellers had to pay a sewer fee. And using federal timber receipts, Lane County built the roads that serviced fringe developments: Coburg, Willakenzie, Oakway, Irving, Royal, Barger, and Echo Hollow roads, and later Beltline, East 30th, and Northwest Expressway. In those years most local government viewed the promotion of development to be one of its responsibilities. After all, the federal government had just pulled the country out of the Great Depression, in part through huge public works projects such as the Bonneville Dam. That's what government did: build roads, courthouses, schools, bridges, dams, channels, and harbors.

In those days, planning consisted of figuring out what government would or should build and where. It was infrastructure planning. Advanced planning meant figuring out where roads and schools and parks should be to service and encourage growth, and then buying the land before it got too expensive. Planning also included a little bit of zoning to prohibit unwanted uses. "Unwanted uses" didn't mean huge polluting industrial plants. Rather, the most common unwanted use was the lowly trailer park. In a 1963 survey of Oregon local governments, one of the measures of

planning sophistication was whether a city regulated trailer parks.
When Lane County became the first Oregon county to create a
planning commission, in 1949, under a brand new state law, the
first thing it did was to get county voters to adopt a limited zoning
ordinance, applicable only in the urban fringe and along highways. It was prompted by public outcry over the placement of a
trailer park next to a school. The new zoning ordinance prohibited
businesses within 800 feet of a school.

Planning was done by the businessmen who made up the city
council and planning commission, occasionally with the help of a
blue-ribbon committee or outside consultant. Portland was the
first Oregon city to form a planning commission, in 1918. Eugene followed in 1925, along with Coos Bay, Corvallis, Medford,
Salem, and Pendleton, all by 1930. But most cities did not have
professionally trained planners on staff. Any staff work for a planning commission was done by a regular city administrator, who
added that task to existing duties.

After World War II ended, local leaders, like others throughout the country, worried that the economy would slide back into
the depression. Local businessmen and representatives of a "civic
group" (read: Chamber of Commerce) chipped in $10,000—a lot
of money in those days—to create a private advocacy group: the
Central Lane County Planning Council. The council agreed that a
"coordinated approach to development" was necessary. Development was considered a positive way to benefit the community by
creating jobs and avoiding economic hard times. Planning was
needed to encourage that development.

In 1945 Eugene, Springfield, School Districts 4 and 19, and
EWEB formed the Central Lane Planning Commission, the first
intergovernmental public planning agency in Oregon to provide
that coordinated approach. Initially named the Central Lane Planning Survey Committee, perhaps to indicate its intended temporary tenure, the CLPC evolved into our current Lane Council of
Governments (the name was changed in 1971). The first task for
the CLPC was to hire someone to actually do the planning. The

practice at the time was to hire a temporary consultant to prepare a development plan, but Herman Kehrli—the director of the Bureau of Municipal Research and Service at the UO—believed that planning should be institutionalized and ongoing. He persuaded the local governments to pay for a full-time planner, who would staff the CLPC as well as Eugene's, Springfield's, and later Lane County's planning commissions. Kehrli promptly hired Howard Buford from San Diego.

Howard Buford and the 1959 Development Plan

At first alone and later with a few assistants, Howard Buford staffed the planning commissions for Eugene, Springfield, and Lane County from 1945 to 1973. Much of the work was issuing permits and processing zone change requests and subdivision proposals. Buford is described as a man with vision, able to think about how Eugene should look in twenty or thirty years. He was modest and easygoing, but also so outspoken in his support of planning that he rubbed some people the wrong way, especially private-property-rights advocates.

Befitting his previous experience as a planner for the National Park Service, Buford's real love was parks—planning for their location, acquiring the land, and designing them. In the 1960s Buford wanted the state to buy the land around Mt. Pisgah, but state officials instead proposed to buy a site on the McKenzie River, now the Ben and Kay Dorris Wayside. Buford arranged a meeting with Tom McCall and showed the governor a photo of the Dorris site, taken on a dark and rainy day, and a photo taken of Mt. Pisgah, on a glorious, sunny day. McCall arranged for the state to buy both sites.

In 1957 the CLPC and Buford began gathering information for what would be this area's first comprehensive metropolitan plan. The result was a document rich in factual detail—the topography of each neighborhood, and the enrollment of every school—and with beautiful maps, showing both existing uses and future or proposed uses. "The present study," Buford wrote in the introduction to the 1959 Development Plan, "is a part of a continuing, long-range planning program designed to relate population growth trends in . . . the metropolitan region with the public facilities that will be needed once those areas are eventually built up." The plan assumed that full build-out of the region would be at a population of 232,000 people, with 3.5 in each dwelling unit.

Buford broke the city up into neighborhoods, using physical barriers such as roads or topography as boundaries. Each neighborhood would get a school and a park. And he named each neighborhood, such as the area south of 30th Avenue and east of Amazon Canal, which he called "Sunny Hollow." The plan recognized that there was significantly more land zoned for commercial use than was needed, but it still proposed extending the downtown commercial area west from Lawrence to Jefferson Street, apparently to provide enough land to build a new shopping mall, with customers driving to the site over the proposed new Washington-Jefferson Street Bridge.

There are big, limited-access freeways everywhere in the plan, several that have been built (I-5, the Washington-Jefferson Street Bridge, Highway 105, Delta Highway, Beltline Road, and the Northwest Expressway), but many more that have not. Those that did not get built, or were not built as freeways, include: a completed Beltline connecting West 11th Avenue to Bailey Hill Road; Spencer Butte Expressway, running from the Ferry Street overpass to Amazon Parkway, and then splitting; the First Avenue to Fourth Avenue Connector, running from the south end of Ferry Street Bridge to the Washington-Jefferson Bridge; and the Roosevelt Freeway, continuing the First to Fourth Connector west.

Buford also persuaded the federal and state highway folks to change their preferred route for I-5. After passing through Glenwood and reaching Franklin Boulevard at Judkins Point, I-5 would have followed Franklin Boulevard and then 6th Avenue running west to Highway 99 North and on to Junction City, effectively and artificially splitting Eugene in two. Instead, I-5 was built to divide Eugene and Springfield, an already existing and natural separation. This route also served another Eugene interest, avoiding freeway interchanges near the city, which might result in a new commercial district that could rival downtown. In hindsight, we see the downside of this choice. Interstate 5 runs through some incredibly good soil between the Willamette and McKenzie Rivers, and the interchange ended up being at Beltline, opening the way for Springfield's Gateway Mall, which competes with the downtowns of both cities.

Why didn't those freeways get built? And, perhaps more importantly, why were Eugeneans so keen on building them? The answers, of course, are never simple, especially in Eugene. But part of the answer is that planning began to change in Eugene in the early 1960s. And a big part of that change came about because of one person—Betty Niven.

Betty Niven Gets Involved

Betty Niven moved here when her math-professor husband, Ivan, took a position at the University of Oregon in 1947. She immediately felt that Eugene was different, more open politically (possibly because the *Eugene Register-Guard* did such a thorough job of reporting on local issues). In the post-war years, most women did not work outside the home; nor did they serve on city councils or planning commissions. The League of Women Voters was about to change that. But it was not the League that got Niven involved; the League required more process and patience than Betty had. It was instead a typical Eugene neighborhood issue: traffic on her neighborhood street.

Niven and her family had moved to a new house at 39th and Hilyard in 1956. A recently annexed area, Hilyard then was an oiled gravel road with no sidewalks from 24th Avenue south. Typical of fringe development, the street had not been built to city standards. Residents had to walk in the street. Niven went to a city council meeting and asked that the city install sidewalks. The council told her she would need to gather the signatures of her neighbors to show majority support. The councilors probably figured they would never see Niven again. But she did it. And she didn't stop there. She continued to go to council meetings to nag the city into following through.

Shortly after that, the mayor appointed Niven to the city's first urban renewal district advisory committee. And in 1959, when a vacancy came up on the Eugene Planning Commission, Niven called the mayor—commissioners then were appointed by the mayor, not the council—and told him that Eugene needed a woman on the planning commission. He agreed, and she served on the commission for fourteen years.

Niven's first planning commission assignment was an easy one, she thought, chairing the parks and recreation committee, which was responsible for a ten-year parks property-tax levy on the May 1960 ballot, expected to pass easily. When it lost, Niven went to work. She got the council to appoint a parks study group, which she chaired. The group included local heavy hitters, such as the president of the university, the manager of EWEB, the mayor, and a county commissioner, but it also included—for the first time in such an advisory group—ordinary citizens. Niven wanted the group to be visionary, which she felt required different viewpoints. And she wanted to have an understanding of what voters would support. She did something else different, something unheard of, even now: She had the CLPC staff members participate as full voting members of the study group.

The study group conducted what would now be called "focus groups," meeting with civic and service groups, giving informational presentations, and then reviewing surveys of what people thought about the levy and parks. They also held hearings. They found out what the people wanted and then acted on that information. The group revised the parks levy, reducing its dollar amount and time span, and changing the focus from large, regional parks to neighborhood parks, with an emphasis on activities for families and the elderly. And they worked out a compromise on a related controversial proposal, the Amazon Freeway, which had siphoned off some of the usual park supporters. The road was reduced from the proposed four lanes to its current two and was moved to the edge of the park. Niven emphasized these compromises when confronting the usual true believers, those folks who always seem to think that there is only one right way. In one hearing she is quoted as offering a guiding principle: "The planner must strive to place himself at a comprehensive standpoint, the hardest of all to reach—that of the city as a whole." The council referred the revised funding measure to the voters in May 1961.

Having crafted the best compromise she could, Niven then led a very savvy election campaign, utilizing the wisdom gained from a recent successful campaign to elect the first woman to city council, Catherine Lauris. The Better Eugene Committee, led by attorney Joe Richards, formed to raise money and buy radio spots, on one of which Richards played guitar and Niven and others sang, urging support for the levy. "Parks are for people, people are for parks" was plastered on 200 colorful signs in stores and buses around town. At twenty-four proposed park sites, they put up large plywood signs saying, "To develop this park, vote yes May 11." They organized more than forty in-home coffees, featuring the mayor or a councilor. They gathered endorsements from a broad cross-section, including the Chamber, the labor council, and elderly associations. The levy passed, with 60 percent of the vote. And in another trademark action, Niven did a postmortem, analyzing what worked and sharing that information with others.

All of these strategies—broad citizen involvement, working the details, surveying the public, seeking compromises, focusing on the needs of the city as a whole, and analyzing the results—would be used again by Niven and the Eugeneans who worked and learned at her side.

"The Hopes of the People"

The same ballots that began Betty Niven's planning career also changed the way Eugene planned for limited access roads, or freeways. That first election, when the parks levy failed in May 1960, included three other significant issues: authority to acquire a new city hall site, a downtown urban renewal district called the "Mulligan-Skinner Project," and a ten-year property tax levy for street improvements. The latter two failed as well.

The street levy was intended to fund the ten-year Arterial and Crosstown Street Program, which included three freeways called for by the 1959 Development Plan (the Spencer Butte Expressway, the First Avenue to Fourth Avenue Connector, and the southern portion of the never-completed Beltline). These freeways were not proposed because Eugeneans in those days loved cars more than they do today. Though the promotional materials mention driver convenience and safety, those arguments were secondary to the main goal: preserving residential neighborhoods and the downtown shopping core. Even before Valley River Center mall was built, downtown struggled. There were frequent discussions about the need for more free parking and the need to steer auto traffic—traffic of people passing through, not coming to shop—away from downtown to make it more accessible and friendlier for pedestrian shoppers. Traffic on the downtown portion of Willamette Street was viewed as "severing" the downtown. And teenagers drove their cars back and forth continuously at night in a ritual known as "dragging the gut." The freeways in the 1959 Development Plan, it was thought, would route through-traffic around downtown and get cars off residential neighborhood streets.

But the 1960 levy for the Arterial Street Plan was rejected by the voters. A front page *Register-Guard* editorial attributed the defeat to concern about running the Spencer Butte Expressway through Amazon Park. But that can't explain what happened next. Even though Niven's park study group (working to pass the park levy in the May 1961 election) modified the Spencer Butte Expressway plan to make the resulting Amazon Parkway smaller, opposition to the other freeways persisted. The owner of the Eugene Business College, whose business lay in the path of the proposed Spencer Butte Expressway, led an initiative drive for a ballot measure. In May 1961 the same voters who approved Niven's revised parks levy also approved this initiative, which amended the Eugene charter to prohibit the city from constructing a "freeway or throughway" unless the route was first approved by the voters, essentially requiring the city to get voter approval before the construction of any freeway. This law is still in the books, in Section 41 of the city charter.

In September 1964 Ivan Niven left Eugene for a nine-month visiting professorship at the University of California at Berkeley. He talked Betty into coming along and taking a leave of absence from the planning commission by noting that she could take classes at UC Berkeley's renowned planning school. Once there, Niven learned that the city of Berkeley had recently adopted a master plan with assistance from the planning school. Unlike Eugene's 1959 Development Plan, essentially a glorified zoning map, the Berkeley plan had community goals and policies setting out what the community's guiding principles were, what it wanted to preserve, and what it wanted to change.

When Niven returned to Eugene in the summer of 1965, she brought back the notion that Eugene needed a plan with goals and policies. Without some guiding principles, planners couldn't be consistent in reviewing development questions not answered by a zoning map. What, for example, should be the criteria for reviewing a zone change request? If the city approved a zone change at 29th and Willamette from single family residential to commercial use, shouldn't it agree to a similar request at 19th and Agate?

As Niven later defined them, goals are "broad statements of philosophy . . . describ[ing] the hopes of the people . . . for the future." Working with such concepts requires a certain level of intelligence and planning sophistication. Niven had always had the intelligence, now she had the planning sophistication.

Niven also wanted to emphasize the "community" in community goals. This would be grassroots planning, not planning by a Chamber committee. Planning with people, not for them. She wanted a meeting not of the elite, but of a cross-section of the town, representing everyone, and she wanted it to be a working meeting.

In the 1960s and 1970s the planning commission was perceived by many as being more influential than the city council.
The city manager and city attorney attended commission meetings. And the *Eugene Register-Guard* thought the meetings were
important enough to cover regularly. If the council tried to do
something other than what the commission had recommended,
the commission would demand a meeting to explain to the council—some would say browbeat it—why it was wrong. The
commission's strength reflected the quality of individual members, such as Niven, but also people like Jim Pearson, a calm, experienced lawyer whose primary client was a big homebuilding firm.
It also reflected the fact that those strong commissioners served for
a long time, longer than any councilor; there were no term limits
for commissioners then.

Niven sold the idea of community goal-setting to the commission, and the commission sold it to the council. An official
community goals committee, consisting of several councilors and
commissioners, including Niven, planned the conference, but much
of the work was done by Niven, who also conferred with a small
group of friends and like-minded people, such as Dorothy Anderson. That group also happened to be forming the Metropolitan
Civic Club, the precursor to the Eugene City Club.

There would be a lot of people—250 were invited. The committee made up a long list of possible invitees, including members
of previous city committees, acquaintances—the hairdresser of city
councilor Catherine Lauris, because she talked about civic affairs
while doing the councilor's hair—and all the (reasonable) people
Niven heard testify before the planning commission. The committee looked for "geographical, occupational, social, and political
balance." No group would be allowed to designate a representative; everyone was to represent himself or herself only. Niven figured that would make people more likely to think for themselves
and to act on behalf of the whole city, rather than their special
interest group. The conference was to meet as a committee of the
whole. Niven knew that subcommittees or break-out groups could

work through the issues more quickly, and that meeting as a large committee would require multiple meetings and risked lower attendance and involvement, but she wanted the conferees to consider all the issues, including how the issues interacted.

The mayor's letter of invitation went out to the 250 invitees in the spring of 1966, for three weekly sessions. Niven wrote ten background papers for the conferees on topics such as transportation, zoning, the environment, growth, and parks, with goals' committee review and revision. All but eighteen of the invitees attended, eighty people spoke during the conference, and forty-three later submitted written comments. Afterwards, Niven took the transcript of the conference sessions and the written comments to Hawaii, as she accompanied Ivan on a lecture tour. She edited and organized the material into nine substantive sections, with goals, assumptions, policies, and proposals for action. The conferees met again twice in the spring of 1967, after she returned, to finalize the conference report. Their decisions were reviewed by the planning commission and adopted by the council in April 1967.

Niven brought back another idea from Berkeley, too. Eugene needed its own planning staff; Buford could not do it for all four planning commissions anymore. Eugene was growing and needed more attention. Buford had baggage, having made enemies over the years. His efforts to make all three jurisdictions consistent resulted in compromises that limited what Eugene could do alone, and his history was in infrastructure planning and zoning, not goal-setting, long-range planning, and public involvement. Other people shared those concerns, and in early 1966 city manager Hugh McKinley hired John Porter, previously a planner with the city's public works department, as the city's new planning department director. Eugene joined Portland and Medford as the only Oregon cities having full time planners. Porter was a strong supporter of setting community goals, of citizen involvement—and of Betty Niven. Reversing twenty years of coordinated planning, Eugene was about to go off on its own, without Lane County and Spring-

field, but now with its own planner and its own citizen process
and goals.

A Blueprint for the Future

Only eight years after the adoption of the 1959 Development
Plan, the Eugene council adopted Niven's community goals and
policies document. Only eight years, but the difference is mind
boggling, in substance as well as process. Buford's introduction to
the 1959 plan stated explicitly that its purpose was to relate growth
trends with public facilities that would be needed. The closing of
Niven's preface to the Community Goals and Policies document
states, "We shall never reach our goals for Eugene if we do not
formulate and adopt policies to guide future private and public
physical development." It offered policies, not a zoning map. It
sought to guide, not to follow, growth trends. It set policies for
private, as well as public, development. The council declared the
goals and policies to be the "basis for guiding the Planning Commission, administrative staff and the Common Council of the City
of Eugene in making decisions relative to the comprehensive land
use plan of the City of Eugene and the development of the City of
Eugene and the general goals to be achieved by the government of
the City of Eugene."

The community-goals document is a simple one, compared to
the other, book-length plans Eugene has produced. Only twenty-
seven pages long, it includes five simple goals, twenty-nine assumptions, and nine chapters on substantive issues such as air and
water pollution. Each chapter includes several policies, followed
by a page or two of specific proposals for action. The five city goals
were, briefly: to protect and enhance the environment; to restore
clean air and rivers; to provide choice in education, employment,
housing, transportation, recreation, and culture; to establish land
uses consistent with the needs and well-being of all segments of
the community; to play a proper role in the development of the
metro area, recognizing problems that the city can address acting
alone and those that require intergovernmental cooperation.

Many of its assumptions are still relevant today. An increasing percentage of our population will be composed of persons who are members of minority groups. The shrinkage of the supply of housing within the means of low- to middle-income families will force public concern. The area surrounding Eugene will become an unbroken sprawl unless steps are taken to provide greenbelt breaks and to protect agricultural lands. The familiar ring of fir trees that fringe the hills around the city will disappear unless action is taken to preserve them. There will be an inevitable growth in the number of motor vehicles, probably at a greater rate than that of the population.

At the time, environmental concerns were growing nationally and in Oregon. Even so, the commitment to the environment in Eugene's community goals document is striking. Niven says now that the business community did not realize at first how influential the community goals document would be. The air and water policies included calling for "strict controls on all sources of air and water pollution: public, business and private," encouraging "only those industries to come to Eugene that are capable of a high degree of control over the emission of air and water pollutants," and giving first consideration to air and water "in the application of all other policy."

The plan's policies and proposals required developers "to direct their efforts toward our goal of achieving a beautiful city." It sought transportation plans that reflected the "reasonable needs of motorists" without subverting "all other aspects of city living to the demands of the automobile." It encouraged research to increase diversification within the timber and agriculture industries. It explored the feasibility of a farmers' market and encouraged high-density housing downtown. Of course, some of the ideas seem peculiar or quaint now, such as creating an intergovernmental "office of noise control" (and this was before the invention of leaf blowers). But it appears noise was then a big concern to the community, for the subject got a whole chapter in the plan.

One of the unique aspects of the document is the inclusion of social goals, particularly housing, in addition to the usual physical planning goals. Niven says that as they planned for the conference, she came to realize that housing was a planning issue. All the other goals and policies would impact housing, in particular by increasing the cost of housing. The policies and proposals regarding housing remain cutting-edge today: zoning that allows for maximum flexibility in design; a variety of housing types, including row houses, cluster housing, and manufactured homes; mixed income housing, downtown housing; and "because high densities can help reduce urban sprawl," provisions that encourage high density "under conditions of design control."

The community goals document did not sit on a shelf. The year after it was adopted, the planning commission overhauled the city's zoning code, implementing many of the new ideas. Niven and other representatives of the city took many of the document's proposals to Salem and succeeded with more than a dozen pieces of state legislation. Niven and a new ally, homebuilder and councilor George Wingard, got the council to create the City of Eugene Joint Housing Committee—Niven was a member—which began Eugene's long history of innovative work on affordable housing issues. John Porter applied the goals to the work on the planning staff, calling it "goal tending."

There were failures, or at least delays, concerning issues such as addressing EWEB's continued sale of water to the fringe area. The community goals document raised that issue as an example of a metropolitan problem that needed further work. Later, Niven and the planning commission arranged a meeting with the EWEB board to push for a resolution. But EWEB manager Byron Price staged the meeting at EWEB's Leaburg park, up the McKenzie River, and after a tour of the facilities and a long picnic lunch in the sun, Price declared that there wasn't enough time to get to that issue. It was not until 1978 that the city succeeded in getting EWEB to stop extending new water service outside the city.

The 1990 Plan and the Urban Services Area

The Eugene-Springfield Metropolitan Area 1990 General Plan (the "1990 Plan"), which was instituted in 1972, was "not a zoning ordinance or a blueprint for the specific development of particular buildings, highways, and so on" but rather a "long-range, comprehensive, [and] flexible guide for specific developmental decision making." Even though the 1990 Plan was a metro-wide plan, not just a plan for Eugene, its substance and organization flowed directly out of the Community Goals Conference. Small wonder—six of the seventeen voting members on the plan advisory committee had been members of the community goals committee, including Niven. And Niven and the planning commission invited Community Goals conferees to review a draft of the 1990 Plan to see how it related to the community goals and policies.

The 1990 Plan continued many of the community goals, such as protecting natural resources. But what makes it groundbreaking is the way it addressed a group of community goals—preserving the greenbelt, protecting the South Hills' tree lines, stopping fringe development—that Eugene could not address without the assistance of Springfield and Lane County. We may not be able to stop growth, the plan said in effect, but we can regulate and direct it.

The plan first addressed the preferred form of growth. After noting that the default form of growth at the time was scatteration, a leapfrogging urban sprawl, the plan committed to a compact urban growth form. The objectives were to preserve prime agricultural lands and open space, limit urban development in the flood plain, use urban services and tax dollars efficiently, preserve neighborhoods, reduce sprawl, minimize the need for beltline roads, preserve the area's character, and make mass transit more economically viable.

How does an area achieve compact growth? By an urban growth boundary (UGB), although the plan used the term "urban service area." Everyone was aware of the problems of fringe residential development. The cost to the fringe residents for improved roads, sewers, and stormwater control after annexation, and the resulting resentment by those residents, were still familiar following the 1964 annexation of the Bethel-Danebo area. An urban services boundary, beyond which urban services would not be extended, would limit fringe development and stop the creation of new water districts and EWEB water sales to those districts.

Setting the urban boundary involved some controversy. The Gonyea family owned much of the land in what is now known as the LCC basin. They donated land for the construction of the Lane Community College campus and wanted their surrounding lands to be included in the UGB so they could be developed. The City of Eugene opposed including the LCC basin, in part due to the extreme cost of running sewer lines over the 30th Avenue hill or through the riverbed rock along the Willamette, and in part because the city felt that there was plenty of vacant residential land already serviced inside the city. The LCC basin was designated in the plan for rural use—agricultural and residential development with minimum five-acre lots.

The resulting boundary was based on the amount of land already in the cities, as well as the topography of the area, which in some cases limited the use of gravity-based sewer lines. The plan also sought to protect farmland and wetlands. In thirty years, the boundary was extended by only 221 acres, with most of that coming in the addition of the Awbrey-Meadowview site in the late 1980s, as Eugene struggled to pull itself out of the early 1980s recession. Perhaps the initial boundary was too big, and we are just now growing out to it. Or maybe the 1980s recession, with its population loss and zero development, bought us some time. To my eye, though, the UGB has worked. Eugene doesn't have abandoned neighborhoods; redevelopment and infill are occurring; density is increasing; and we're surrounded by farmlands, not by fringe development and new water districts.

There was another significant controversy in the development of the plan. Late in the process, the draft plan map suddenly showed five sites in the metro area as designated for nuclear power plants to be developed by EWEB. The peripatetic Byron Price had gotten them inserted. One site was on McKenzie View Drive, and another was at the junction of the Willamette and McKenzie Rivers. Price tried to justify these locations by saying that the plants would use river water to cool the nuclear reactions, and that warmed water would be available to benefit local farmers. The plan advisory committee included Wayne Endicott, a taciturn farmer who was not too keen on land-use planning but who was quick to ridicule that idea—warm water does not make for better farming. The nuclear plant sites were deleted from the plan.

The 1990 Plan designated the Valley River Center area for commercial development. The area was part of Lane County—not the City of Eugene—farmland that only recently had been freed from the risk of flooding. After the 1990 Plan was adopted, a developer asked the county commissioners to grant a zone change that would allow for the development of a shopping mall. Niven recalls that the planning commission asked them to deny the request. County commissioners asked why the planning commissioners wanted to protect downtown businessmen. Niven explained, they didn't want to protect the businessmen, they wanted to protect the downtown. But Valley River Center was built with the help of county road funds, and later annexed into the city. To this day, the city is blamed, wrongly, for VRC.

One remarkable aspect of the 1990 Plan is that it institutionalized citizen involvement by establishing citizen-involvement goals. Early in the process, plan advisory committee members had difficulty understanding that it was their plan to design. By the end, Niven later recounted, the members had "a fierce commitment to the concept that planning should be based on goals and policies arrived at by citizens, and not planners." After the plan was adopted, the three jurisdictions each appointed seven people to the new metropolitan area planning advisory committee, with the task of monitoring compliance with the plan.

The State Gets into the Act

Eugene was not alone in worrying about land-use planning. Governor McCall did not trust Oregon's city councils, county commissions, and planning commissions to protect natural resources from the incredible growth the state was experiencing. He feared that Oregon's local governments were unable to stand up to the development interests that served this growth. McCall shared the common view that California had squandered its natural resources by allowing unregulated growth. He, along with many others, wanted to make sure that Oregon did not repeat California's mistakes.

The governor had tried during the 1969 session to get land-use legislation adopted, but succeeded only in passing a watered-down Senate Bill 10. Intended to relieve the property-tax pressures that were driving some Willamette Valley farmers to convert farm land to subdivisions, the bill required counties to zone for the first time and also adopt comprehensive plans. Lane County, for example, was largely unplanned and unregulated. But SB 10's shortcomings soon became apparent. There was no mechanism or funding for oversight or money to help the counties write the plans. Neither were there standards to evaluate the plans. The required plan goals related only to local concerns, not the interests of the state or other local governments. And no coordination was required.

Adopted in the 1973 legislative session, SB 100 was intended to address these growth concerns and fix SB 10's more glaring weaknesses. It created the Department of Land Conservation and Development (DLCD) and the Land Conservation and Development Commission (LCDC), a new statewide agency and citizen commission with enforcement powers. Now there would be a strong central planning body, requiring local governments to plan, coordinate with other public entities, and consider state-defined goals. LCDC had until January 1, 1975, to adopt those goals.

As the first chair of LCDC, McCall appointed L.B. Day, a labor organizer and former Republican state representative, and let Day hand-pick the other six LCDC members. Niven's friend

Dorothy Anderson was one of those Day selected. Like Niven, Anderson had followed her math-professor husband to the University of Oregon. She had helped with the 1960 parks study group and, later, served on the 1990 Plan advisory committee. Anderson was active in the League of Women Voters and lobbied in favor of SB 100. Day chose Anderson because he knew her from her lobbying—he mistakenly thought she was the state League president—and because he thought it would be politically wise to have one female member.

LCDC toured the state, holding dozens of forums to get public input on what the statewide goals should be. Some Oregonians viewed land-use planning as a form of communism, and LCDC members were hung in effigy. But hundreds of people all over the state also came out to express their support for the effort to preserve the Oregon they loved. LCDC adopted fourteen goals on December 27, 1974, beating the deadline by four days. Every local government in Oregon was now required to adopt a comprehensive plan complying with those goals, and to submit that plan to LCDC for approval.

Perhaps, the most unique and significant aspect of Oregon's current statewide land-use planning system came about because of Eugene. Nothing in SB 100's eleven "areas and activities" mentioned an urban growth boundary. That idea came from Anderson, from her experience with the 1990 Plan and her knowledge of Salem's adoption of the same concept. LCDC adopted the UGB idea as a way to address a number of the SB 100 goals, and the UGB is now integral to the statewide goals.

Despite concerns over compliance deadlines, the City of Eugene had been a strong supporter of SB 100 during the 1973 legislative session. Now other cities would have to do what it had done, and now Lane County would have to plan for its rural lands. But the city was not to be so happy with the application of the new law to the 1990 Plan.

Eugene was rather proud of its planning program and its plans. The city felt that the 1990 Plan met the requirements of SB 100 and asked LCDC to "acknowledge" that it did. Eugene also wanted its plan to be the first acknowledged. LCDC, however, had concerns. LCDC reasoned that SB 100 required each community to consider certain goals, and that consideration had to be through a broad citizen involvement effort that included coordination with the all the local public entities. LCDC questioned whether a plan adopted before the statewide goals were approved, as was the 1990 Plan, could have "considered" the statewide goals.

Eugene responded by having the planning commission declare that the 1990 Plan complied with all of the LCDC goals. LCDC disagreed, concluding that the 1990 Plan did not adequately address LCDC's economic development or the Willamette Greenway goals, that there had been a lack of coordination with EWEB and the school districts on future needs, and that the UGB needed to be more site specific. While appreciating Eugene's leadership in land-use planning, LCDC was seeing a lot of canned or boilerplate ideas, and it was determined to ensure that the first plan acknowledged set a solid standard of compliance with the goals.

Eugene resisted. John Porter was not happy about having the state muck about with our plan. The city wanted to go on to other planning matters, such as refinement plans. The dispute dragged on, and in that time gap Medford became the first local government to have its plan be acknowledged, in 1976. Finally, Eugene accepted LCDC's direction and agreed to revise the 1990 Plan.

The resulting 1982 Metro Plan was not much different from its predecessor. The introduction says that it "evolved from" the 1990 Plan, and was "not an entirely new product." It had the same UGB concept and the same UGB line. Outward growth of the two cities would occur through annexations with an "orderly and efficient" extension of services within the UGB. The only exception to the annexation requirement was a provision for sewer service in the River Road and Santa Clara areas to address the problem of failing septic tanks. The plan gives the two cities control over development—planning, zoning, permitting—within the urban transition area between the cities' boundaries and the UGB, thereby setting the stage for final resolution of the urban fringe problem.

Eugene, Springfield, and Lane County completed work on the Metro Plan in 1980, but not on the same product. The county insisted that the plan designate more land for industrial development; the two cities refused. Two versions of the plan were submitted. LCDC rejected both, and the three later compromised on the amount of industrial land, winning acknowledgment in 1982. In hindsight, the acknowledged Metro Plan still had too much industrial land, but that excess was needed when large parts of the industrial land inventory in West Eugene were later put off-limits as protected wetlands.

In 1986 the three jurisdictions undertook what was supposed to be a major update of the Metro Plan. Most of the work on the plan had been done before 1980, and it was based on the 1990 Plan with its data from the late 1960s. But lack of money and concern about inability to reach consensus led to a lesser "periodic review." The result was the 1987 version of the Metro Plan, with few significant changes (for example, which city "gets" Glenwood). The 1987 version of the Metro Plan was still in effect in 2000. While there have been talks about doing an update, the effort has been stymied by cost (Ballot Measures 5 and 47 limited local government funds) and consensus concerns. And the early 1980s recession delayed growth pressures for almost a decade. Instead, the local governments have revised the plan with several studies, addressing natural resources, as well as residential, commercial (Eugene only), and industrial lands.

The 1987 Metro Plan seems pretty remote to most Eugeneans, many of whom moved here or came to adulthood after its adoption; the 1982 version was the last one to go through a real citizen-involvement effort. Perhaps, as John Porter says, the Metro Plan suffers in comparison to the 1990 Plan, which was more supported by the community, probably because it came out of Niven's

1967 Community Goals Conference and its broad citizen participation.

Looking Back, Looking Forward

The planning commission is less influential now than it was in
Niven's day. Becoming a good commissioner takes time and experience. It is a complicated field. It is no coincidence that some of
our best planning commissioners served for long periods, such as
Niven (fourteen years) and Jim Pearson (sixteen years). With that
experience, they gained greater credibility and influence in the
community and with the council. Unfortunately, in the late 1980s
the council imposed term limits on planning commissions, a maximum of eight years. At the time Niven was appointed, the mayor,
not the council, made the appointment. Because the mayor serves
the whole city, the mayor's choices tend to reflect an effort to achieve
citywide balance. In the late 1970s the council took that power
from the mayor, and its appointments today sometimes reflect
narrower interests.

I met Niven in 1979, when I was a new lawyer representing a
group of low-income and elderly residents of two high-rise apartment buildings in Eugene. We were asking the city council to
impose a moratorium on a developer's proposal to convert the apartments to condominiums, forcing those tenants either to buy their
apartments or to move. We had already lost before a city advisory
committee, and our arguments had been ridiculed in the local
alternative newspaper by a prominent local economist. Desperate,
we packed the council chamber with white-haired citizens and
pleaded for help. When the developer got his turn, he was represented by a high-powered Portland attorney who threatened the
council with a big lawsuit if it dared adopt this crazy and "clearly
illegal" moratorium. Our spirits plunged. Council procedure allowed the proponents (us) to go first, followed by the developer,
and then speakers who "are neither for nor against." Usually no
one speaks then. This time, a small woman stood and introduced

herself as Betty Niven. While not endorsing our request, she thoroughly and efficiently demolished the Portland lawyer's arguments, making it clear to the council that a moratorium was clearly within its powers, and noting that she had just that day talked to an official in Chicago, where such a moratorium had recently been adopted to address the serious problems caused by condo conversions. Needless to say, we got our moratorium, and Niven thereafter worked closely with a council subcommittee to craft an ordinance that allowed condo conversions but required developers to pay to relocate low-income, elderly, and disabled tenants.

In 1995, when the planning commission was about to embark upon the second growth management study (there have been four), it invited former commissioners Niven, Pearson, and Jim Bernhard to tell us about their 1966 effort. Typically, Niven thoroughly and efficiently reviewed what they had done and why, and what they had learned, in about twenty minutes. She has kept files on all the issues she has worked on. When Niven finished speaking, we asked the other two if they wanted to add anything. Pearson smiled and said no, because as usual, "Betty said it all." He couldn't improve on it.

Betty turned eighty-two in 2000, and she lives alone in an apartment in a large retirement complex in South Eugene. St. Vincent de Paul and the city have named a street for her in a nearby city-funded subsidized townhouse development for low-income families. Niven is still busy. The retirement complex residents often watch videos together on Saturday nights. They'd been having trouble picking which video to watch. Since she's been there, she has instituted a resident survey to guide the choices. She's still a planner.

HEART MURMURS:

RESUSCITATING DOWNTOWN

By Jonathan Stafford

A Classic Downtown

MY MEMORIES OF downtown Eugene during the 1950s reveal a picture that could have been painted by Norman Rockwell. In those days downtown was the regional center of activity, not only for retail businesses but also for civic and cultural events. All the essential services and features associated with a center existed in downtown Eugene during that era.

If you needed to buy something, downtown Eugene was the best place to find it. National chain stores—the Bon Marché, JC Penney, Newberry's, Montgomery Ward, Sears, and Woolworth's—were located within a few blocks of each other, along with local department stores, such as Russell's and the Broadway. You could also buy groceries—at Safeway at 13th and Willamette, Newman's fish store on East Broadway, a number of bakeries, a doughnut shop. Hardware stores, wholesale and retail, were represented, too, with Quackenbush's, Eugene Hardware, and John Warren's (which also sold sporting goods), as well as the Surplus Store, an enticing repository of random items from shovels to shaving cream. Industrial facilities, remnants from earlier days when Eugene was much smaller, were found on the periphery of downtown. Establishments such as Scharpf's Twin Oaks Building Supply and Willis Small Feed, as well as wholesale warehouses such as Vitus Electric and Eoff Electric, were close to the railroad and the industrial area along the millrace.

People lived downtown—in apartments above ground-floor

retail shops, as well as in single-room-occupancy hotels. The Eugene Hotel and the Osborne Hotel provided dining and meeting rooms for residents. A variety of services, from attorneys to bankers, from tailors to doctors, dentists, and pharmacists, were available downtown, along with general offices. The *Eugene Register-Guard*, which promoted itself as "a citizen of the community," housed its offices and presses downtown. You could also get your car gassed and serviced.

The Christmas Parade, Pet Parade, and Rodeo Parade all routed through downtown, which also was the venue of the quaint custom of window-shopping. Warm summer evenings brought people to promenade in the streets and look at window displays in the stores, generally closed at that hour, and to experience chance encounters with others involved in the same activity.

Exhaust Clouds on the Horizon

In spite of the evident prosperity, signs began to appear that, in Eugene as well as the rest of the nation, downtown areas were not well. A fundamental shift was occurring in how people viewed where they lived, where they shopped, and what they expected from their transportation system. During such a shift, it's often difficult to understand what is occurring and what the consequences will be.

The population of Eugene burgeoned between 1950 and 1960. Post–Word War II prosperity enabled more people to own automobiles and to use them more often. This trend eventually led to cars outnumbering people. Left over from the days of fewer cars was the expectation that there should always be roads to drive on and a parking space in front of where you wanted to be, and that anywhere you wanted to go would be within easy walking distance from where you had parked.

The breakdown of historic patterns—the close conjunction between housing and employment, such as the railroad workers living near the railroad yard in the Whiteaker area and professors living near the university in South Eugene—accelerated during

the '50s. Greater mobility made it possible for housing to lie far-
ther away from places of employment and for retail and service
outlets to locate on arterials in strip developments. Cheaper land
at the edges of town became the site of drive-in restaurants and
supermarkets, such as the Big Y, located where Highway 99 split
into 6th and 7th Avenues. Such factors increased the use of the
automobile, leading to traffic congestion and parking problems,
along with concerns among merchants that people would stop
shopping downtown.

Although automobiles allowed for rapid movement, cars took
up a lot of space when not in use. Downtown's density of activity
arose during an era of fewer cars, when many trips were made on
foot. While a typical office allows 150 square feet per occupant, an
automobile takes at least twice as many square feet for parking.
Thus, a three-story office building requires six times as much
ground area to park cars for its tenants. Though Eugeneans proposed ingenious solutions to this car storage problem, such as using alleys for parking, most were not accepted. The contradiction
of maintaining the same density of activity in downtown Eugene
while accommodating the cars to support it did not admit a simple
solution.

Attempts were made to address the traffic problems, but funding
was limited. Highway 99's route through town expanded from
just 6th Avenue to 6th and 7th Avenues. The railroad relocated closer
to the river to allow for the expansion of Franklin Boulevard. Streets
such as 18th and 24th were widened to provide better travel routes.
Many downtown streets became one-way. In 1955 signals at the
intersection of Broadway and Willamette were adjusted to an
"amble-scramble" configuration, allowing pedestrians to cross the
intersection in all directions, including diagonally. When traffic
moved again, all pedestrians remained on the curb.

The construction of Interstate 5 alleviated congestion by allowing traffic that had been funneled through downtown on Highway 99 to bypass Eugene entirely. It also required a connection to
Eugene from the freeway, which became I-105 and the Washing-

ton-Jefferson Street bridge. Beltline and Delta Highways were not far behind. With access provided by the new road infrastructure, the enclosed shopping mall became the preferred solution to the problem of accommodating both cars and shopping across the nation. The standard practice was to find a location near a limited access highway, build a large, air-conditioned building with major department stores at the ends of a connecting mall lined with smaller stores, and surround it with acres of free parking. The relatively remote location and the parking-lot barrier around the stores made access by means other than automobiles difficult, if not impossible.

The Long Walk to the Pedestrian Mall

But in 1945, long before the idea of a suburban mall gained currency, was the notion that creating a pedestrian-only precinct free of the noise and fumes produced by automobiles would enhance the downtown experience. Fred Cuthbert, a professor in the department of landscape architecture at the University of Oregon, proposed closing Willamette Street to cars and providing parking areas at the perimeter. The idea did not go anywhere at the time, but the seed was planted.

The idea of a pedestrian mall reemerged in 1956 when a group of downtown business owners suggested that part of Willamette Street be closed to automobiles on a trial basis. A subsequent poll, however, found that 80 percent of the merchants on Willamette Street actually opposed the idea. In 1958 Frank Shearer, president of the city council and eventual chairman of the Eugene Renewal Agency, expressed conditional support for building parking areas on the downtown perimeter in conjunction with a traffic-free shopping area. In August 1959 Eugeneans celebrated the Oregon Centennial by constructing blockhouses on Broadway at Oak and Charnelton, closing the street to automobile traffic. The experiment provided citizens with a preview of what a pedestrian mall might be like. The experience of crossing the street without having to watch for cars was enthusiastically embraced. Downtown was still the regional center for shopping and services at the time.

Meanwhile, other parts of downtown were changing. In 1954 the Architect's Collaborative, a group of architects and other volunteers, were asked to find the best place for a new county courthouse. They quickly realized that the Eugene-Springfield area was the most logical place. After a yearlong study, a plan emerged for a county-city government and cultural center between Willamette and Pearl Streets and Broadway and 5th Avenue. The plan also proposed an auditorium and cultural precinct for the area east of Skinner Butte to the Willamette River, even though this area was separated from downtown by the railroad and a proposed First Avenue to Fourth Avenue Connector along the south face of the butte.

The plan envisioned an area for county uses north of the Park Blocks in the general location of the existing county courthouse and public-service building. It visualized a new city library on the site of the present Park Blocks, with a new city hall north of the county area between 6th and 7th Avenues. The area between 6th and 5th Avenues would be reserved for state and federal offices. The area between Pearl Street and the Ferry Street Bridge viaduct, north of the railroad tracks, would be devoted to a cultural center, with an auditorium described as "large enough to hold a state grange convention . . . or a concert attracting thousands of persons," along with a museum, zoo, and other buildings for the community's benefit.

The plan called for large areas of surface parking, along with extensive changes to the road system to get cars to the parking lots. Some of these ideas, such as I-105, the Washington-Jefferson Bridge, and the Beltline, came to pass. Others, such as the First Avenue to Fourth Avenue Connector, never were built.

Though the collaborative's plan was not followed in its entirety, it did lead to construction of the downtown civic center of government buildings. The county courthouse relocated across the street from the old courthouse; a new city hall was built adjacent to the courthouse; and, in 1958, the plan helped convince the state government to locate an office building in Eugene's downtown civic area.

The Park Blocks, adjacent to the courthouse, underwent change as well. During the mid-1950s Eugeneans began to consider the arena, which formerly contained a bandstand, horseshoe pits, and lawn areas, a detriment to the genteel character desired downtown. In 1957 the park was rebuilt under the new concept of a contemporary urban park—emphasizing space, form, texture, and indestructibility, rather than romantic informality and social interaction. Lawns became hard surfaces. Trees remained, but flowers were banished. Shortly after this improvement, the alley connecting Willamette and West Park, between 8th Avenue and Broadway, became a pedestrian walkway. The walls of the adjoining buildings were painted in light colors with abstract shapes.

In terms of the commercial buildings downtown, not much occurred in the two decades prior to the 1950s. The depression and materials shortages following World War I kept development from occurring. Surveys in the early 1960s showed that more than two-thirds of downtown's buildings had been constructed prior to 1930. Half the buildings were rated "substandard" and another fifth as "borderline." The public infrastructure was crumbling. Streets were severely crowned from repeated overlays and needed reconstruction. And some of the oldest water, sewer, and steam mains in Eugene lay buried underneath downtown streets. Overhead, the electrical and telephone lines were unsightly and unreliable.

Despite fireproof exteriors, many downtown buildings posed serious fire risks, as a series of major fires demonstrated through the late 1950s and early 1960s. John Warren's Hardware and Sporting Goods store on Willamette caught fire in July 1956. The Elks Club on 7th Avenue burned to the ground in December 1958. The clothing store topped by a hotel at Broadway and Willamette burned in the late 1950s. Other fires during the 1960s destroyed buildings on Broadway, including Thompson's Records and the Home Bakery.

At first, large-scale plans to improve downtown foundered for lack of money. Urban renewal changed that. The passage of the Housing Act in 1949, expanded in 1954, provided federal dollars to renew deteriorating infrastructure and commercial buildings in urban areas. After the passage of ORS 457.130, federally funded urban renewal became a reality in Oregon. Planning began, in 1958, for two urban renewal projects in Eugene, with the mayor and city council acting as the formal urban renewal agency.

The first, the East Campus Urban Renewal Project in the university area, cleared land for campus expansion in 1961. The second, the Mulligan-Skinner project, was to redevelop three-and-a-half blocks around 7th Avenue and Pearl Street into a civic center. The cost of $1.5 million was to be shared by the federal government and the city, with $87,000 paid for by the city. But at a special election in 1960, citizens rejected the plan by a margin of three to two. Opposition centered on the specter of "socialism" and federal "intervention" into local affairs, as well as federal fiscal waste. In 1961 voters were in a more expansive mood and passed a $2.4 million bond issue for a new city hall.

In 1964 and 1965, as a proposed enclosed shopping mall to be built across the river from downtown became more real, downtown business owners began to fear its potential effects. They began to promote the idea of urban renewal, not centering on a civic center, but rather on the decaying retail core. In December 1965 the city named six citizens to the Eugene Development Commission. In 1966 the city applied for federal funds for planning and implementation of the Central Eugene Project. In 1967 an additional member was added to the commission, and the city council designated its urban renewal authority to this commission, which became the Eugene Renewal Agency (ERA).

The Eugene Renewal Agency carried its work forward, culminating with the *Urban Renewal Plan for Central Eugene Project*, published in December 1968. The plan's objectives were to "improve the Project Area through redevelopment and rehabilitation of substandard buildings, to eliminate blighting influences, to modify the street system and to provide pedestrian amenities." More specifically, it sought to reorganize and consolidate the commercial area, providing expansion possibilities for retail outlets and a new site for a major retail development on the block between Willamette and Olive Streets from Broadway to 8th Avenue.

The plan also called for more adequate parking, better traffic circulation, a pedestrian mall, and an auditorium-convention center "adjacent to the Civic Center and the retail core to provide additional nighttime activity and variety in the area." Such public improvements, the plan noted, "will stimulate private investment in new developments to protect the existing economic base and bring about an increase in tax income to the City and County."

Federal approval of funding for the urban renewal plan came in March 1969, and during the construction season of 1970, downtown street, sewer, water, and fire systems were replaced and improved. Following the underground work, construction commenced on the pedestrian mall, with its decorative fountains, rain-protection covers, paving, lighting, restrooms, and playgrounds. Dedication of the pedestrian mall occurred in February 1972.

Chasing the Retail Rainbow

The motivating force behind urban renewal was to preserve downtown Eugene as a primary shopping area for the region. The competition was stiff, not only from the soon-to-open Valley River Center, but also from commercial developments along major arterials. The plan was formulated, and the dollars came to implement it. Yet thirty years later, downtown Eugene was no longer a major player in the retail market. In spite of correctly doing all that it could, Eugene was unable to retain the major retail outlets downtown had in 1960 or attract other major retailers.

However, some things had been done correctly. Sufficient land to accommodate the retail square footage in place by 1970 had been zoned for downtown uses west of Lincoln Street. While no serious consideration was given to developing this area as an enclosed shopping mall, by the 1960s it did have the primary characteristic necessary for development of an enclosed mall—easy access to a freeway. But land ownership downtown was fragmented, and assembling and clearing enough property, dealing with infrastructure issues (such as easements for underground utilities), vacating streets, and the like presented too many problems for a developer to consider building an indoor mall next to downtown. From a developer's standpoint, the shorter the time from buying the land to collecting rents from retailers, the better. Thus, developing a green-field site is more attractive than trying to assemble properties under separate ownerships, especially since many properties west of downtown had been bought by speculators who believed downtown would grow in that direction, and property would gain in value. In theory, the city could have assembled land for a Valley River–type development, but it is unlikely that the political climate of the day would have allowed this to happen, and certainly not quickly enough to provide an attractive alternative to the green-field site across the river.

In 1969 Valley River Center was slated to add more than 800,000 square feet of retail space to the Eugene-Springfield area. There would be more retail square footage than could be supported for a few years, but population growth would remedy that situation. In order for downtown to retain a significant share of retail sales, outmoded buildings had to be remodeled or replaced by well designed, appealing retail spaces. A June 8, 1967, report by the Real Estate Research Corporation suggested that the West Broadway mall, between Willamette and Charnelton, was an appropriate area to concentrate retail activity. Two major stores were already there, Sears and the Bon Marché, and the addition of one or two additional department stores, along with smaller retail outlets, would create a viable shopping district—if adequate parking could be provided.

The solution to the parking problem—then as now—was to build garages. Prior to urban renewal, downtown merchants formed an improvement district to construct the 10th Avenue Overpark. Other parking garages were slated for the half-blocks on either

side of West Broadway and Charnelton. In the interim, urban renewal removed housing to provide surface parking for the Bon
Marché and Sears.

The parking was there, the land was bare, there was a pedestrian mall with anchor tenants—in short, all the pieces of a shopping mall were in place, except the enclosure. Yet no Nordstroms
showed up in Eugene to build a store downtown. Reasons for this
failure remain speculative. By the time the pedestrian mall downtown was dedicated on February 13, 1971, signs of a national
economic downturn were beginning to appear, and given the sen-
sitivity of the local economy to national trends, potential retailers
may have judged the risk too high, especially in light of the excess
retail floor space in the area.

Probably the greatest impediment was the mindset of corporate decision makers, who were dedicated to enclosed, air-conditioned shopping malls. Perceptions with little or no basis in reality
may also have played a part. Eugene has the reputation as a wet
place, even though most of the time when it is raining, it's a gentle
rain. Parking lots downtown were seen as too remote from store
entries, even though the travel path from car to door may have
been greater in shopping malls. And the parking garage alternative
was seen as unsafe. There may also have been the perception that
major retailers would eventually flee to the mall, even though the
addition of another large department store would have been a powerful incentive to keep them downtown.

By 1977, when no major retailer arrived, ERA tried again by
contracting with a Berkeley, California, firm, ELS, to provide an
architectural concept to entice a developer to bring another major
department store downtown. One of the unstated aims of this
effort was to demonstrate to Sears how it could enlarge its downtown store, so it would not have to move to the mall. Barry Elbasani
of ELS proposed establishing a galleria on a diagonal from Broadway and Charnelton to 11th and Willamette, creating space at 11th
and Willamette for a new department store, as well as space for
Sears to expand east. Additionally, the galleria would create space

for parking structures at Broadway and Charnelton, and another site for a department store on the southwest corner of Broadway and Charnelton. The aim was to convince a potential developer that an "enclosed mall" could occur in downtown Eugene. But the plans and diagrams produced by ELS proved insufficient to lure a major developer with a national retailer in his pocket. The retail paradigm of that time was that money could be made in regional malls, not in downtowns. Another demerit for this plan was that it required structured parking, while surface parking was the rule for regional malls.

National trends conspired to create difficulties for the downtown mall, too. Tax laws allowing accelerated depreciation favored the construction of enclosed malls over freestanding department stores. Downtowns, with their grid street patterns and fragmented land- and building-ownership patterns, were not easily adapted to the enclosed shopping mall. To create a "suburban mall" downtown, a number of activities—financial, civic, office, residential and cultural—would have to be abandoned in favor of exclusive retailing. But would such a "downtown" still be truly a downtown?

Despite pledges by managers of local department stores to stay, one by one their boards of directors decided to move them out of downtown into shopping malls. As the majors moved out, locally owned stores followed. Offices that did not need to be close to the government center continued the exodus to suburban areas, where parking was provided with the rent. The services that depended on these offices, such as office supply stores and restaurants, no longer had the demand downtown to survive and likewise moved away.

The Pedestrian Mall as Whipping Boy

As the most visible part of the urban renewal project, the pedestrian mall became the lightning rod for criticism of the program in general. Downtown merchants fought features on the publicly owned portions of the mall that, ultimately, resulted in benefits for downtown. When the Masonic Building at 10th and Olive was demolished in the early 1970s, just after the pedestrian mall was completed, wheelchair-bound Brownie, who ran Brownie's Popcorn Stand, was evicted. A public outcry arose at the loss of this downtown institution, and the city searched for a suitable place for him to relocate. When it was proposed that he relocate in the middle of what had been Broadway, some downtown merchants complained. How could public land be used for individual profit-making activities when they were paying hefty taxes on their land? Was this not socialism of the worst kind? Wouldn't it clog up the mall? But Brownie persisted, and his popcorn stand was built in the middle of Broadway.

In the late 1980s, when the mall seemed particularly desolate, consultants associated with William H. White, a pioneer in the study of how people act in public spaces, came to Eugene to make recommendations about enlivening the downtown mall. They noted that its physical geometry—sixty feet between building faces—created a formidable distance between one side of the street and the other. They recommended that carts and kiosks and movable street furniture be allowed on the mall to help reduce its width.

Yet another controversy occurred around the establishment of the Saturday Market, which originally set up shop on the broad sidewalks at the 10th and Oak Overpark. Again, the use of public land by "non-taxpaying" transient merchants irritated established merchants, who failed to recognize that the Saturday Market generated pedestrian traffic downtown.

Meanwhile, enterprising "alternative" merchants took advantage of the abundance of temporary rental spaces in buildings about to be demolished. Record stores, delicatessens, craft stores, and "head shops" catered to the younger population. The appearance on the mall of longhaired, scantily clad, dirty, sometimes-stoned youth rankled merchants, who felt they kept traditional shoppers away. Downtown business owners felt doubly put upon because

Valley River Center, being "private property," could keep these "undesirable" youth off their premises.

One area in which legitimate criticism might be leveled is the original urban renewal plan's failure to address the housing issue. Apartments that existed within the urban renewal area were systematically demolished, the tenants given relocation assistance. However, even though early planning documents and studies indicated that dense housing on the edge of downtown would be of great benefit—providing opportunities for workers to live close to their work, thus reducing the need for parking—no mention of housing remained in the final plan. When all the efforts to find a major retailer for downtown failed, attempts were made to place housing at 11th and Willamette, and Broadway and Charnelton. In both cases, developers were unable to obtain financing. Had the urban renewal plan included areas beyond the limits of the area drawn, reserved those sites for high density housing, and offered incentives to make the housing more affordable, downtown would have benefited. It is interesting to note that downtown housing in the Tiffany Building occurred in a building slated for acquisition and demolition in the original urban renewal plan.

Even though covered walkways were included as part of the mall, during this period there were still concerns that the rain and weather kept people from shopping downtown. Somehow there existed in the public's mind that it did not rain at Valley River Center like it did downtown, even though one's exposure to rain from car to door at Valley River might exceed that from car to door downtown. As part of a study to provide more complete weather protection for downtown, Otto Poticha proposed that free umbrellas imprinted with advertisements for downtown businesses be provided for shoppers, who could pick up an umbrella as they left a store and leave it by the door as they entered another. Even though the program cost would have been modest compared to any other solution, and exposure of downtown businesses increased if, as expected, these umbrellas were to find their way out of downtown, the renewal authority did not adopt this program. Perhaps because they were still wedded to the notion of attracting another large retail store, which would prefer a more permanent rain cover.

At the turn of the millennium, the character of downtown has changed dramatically from that of 1960. Although it is no longer the area's regional retail center, it remains the cultural and civic center. The 1954 guide for development still has relevance, resulting in major offices from all levels of government collected compactly together. The return of the library to downtown promises to increase activity there, as does the addition of high-density housing to the periphery, on West Broadway between Charnelton and Lincoln Streets.

What else changed? In the early 1980s citizens of Eugene finally were able to pass a bond measure to build a performing arts center. Located across the street from a large hotel and city-funded convention center, the Hult Center and Eugene Conference Center provided an attractive draw to downtown Eugene.

Though improvements to infrastructure—water, sewer, steam, and underground electricity, as well as street improvements—still functioned, most of the mall had disappeared by 2000. Willamette Street from 10th to 11th Avenues was reopened to vehicular traffic in 1985, with a singularly unattractive design. Touted as a panacea to problems on this stretch of Willamette, fifteen years later the effects were not yet evident. In 1987 reconstruction of the mall occurred on West Broadway, between Willamette and Charnelton; public restrooms and rain covers were removed. Thirteen years later, descendants (figurative if not literal) of the hippies of 1972 were creating the perception of danger and unpleasantness on this portion of the remaining pedestrian mall, and initiatives were underway to reopen this portion to automobile traffic as well.

In 1992 Olive Street, between 8th and 10th Avenues, opened to cars. Fortunately, lessons learned from the 1985 Willamette Street opening were applied, and a better design resulted. Gauging the success of this effort is not easy. One successful restaurant occupies a portion of the west side of Olive, between 8th Avenue and Broadway, but other frontage has not shown the same signs of prosperity. In 1993 US Bank of Oregon bought the site at 8th Avenue and Willamette Street. In 1996 the rest of the Willamette Street mall reopened to vehicular traffic. But in 2000 many vacant storefronts remained in the two blocks that face the newly reopened street.

Becoming What It Could Be

The centripetal effect the automobile had on Eugene's urban form could be only dimly perceived in the 1950s. Access to downtown was seen as crucial, and completion of the Washington-Jefferson Bridge was, in 1958, the highest priority road project for the city council, who were unaware that this would facilitate the creation of Valley River Center within the decade.

In the thirty-some years since the urban renewal project formally began, downtown lost all its major retail outlets: the Bon Marché, JC Penney, Newberry's, Montgomery Ward, Sears, Woolworth's, and the Broadway. National corporations with head offices outside of Oregon own all except the last of these retail outlets. With national trends dictating that suburban malls are the place to be, coupled with the corporate belief that money cannot be made in downtown areas, it is not surprising that efforts in Eugene to influence decisions made so far away were unsuccessful. And it is not surprising that with major stores gone from downtown, small local stores would have a difficult time surviving.

Though urban renewal did not achieve its primary goals of retaining a significant portion of the region's retail sales downtown, it did meet other goals. Unsafe buildings were demolished, others were rehabilitated, failing infrastructure was replaced, additional parking was provided in parking structures, and an auditorium-convention center was built.

Identifying trends that will shape society and urban geography over the next thirty years is not simple. Will fuel cell technology enable personal transportation to continue as it is in the face of global petroleum shortages? Will Internet shopping spell the demise of big box retailers and shopping malls? Will the Internet, used as a source of locating goods, allow smaller specialty stores to prosper? Will something that no one has thought of come along to change the way goods are sold? What effect will the demographic shift to an older population be? Answers to some of these questions may be significant, others irrelevant.

Where urban renewal had a large part in directing the activities that led to specific goals, it was generally successful. Where other agents were required to act to achieve a goal, and urban renewal sought to influence those actions, it was less successful.

Authors Note: Perhaps a weakness of my essay is that it derives mostly from personal recollections and did not rely on the memories of others. Bob Hibschman of the City of Eugene development department provided use of his "short file" on urban renewal in Eugene, which contains articles from the *Eugene Register-Guard*, copies of other articles, memoranda, notes, press releases, and excerpts from official urban renewal documents. Microfilm copies of the *Eugene Register-Guard* were examined to confirm dates and sequences of events relating to Eugene in the 1950s.

GETTING TO KLATAWA:

NOTES ON FIFTY YEARS OF

TRANSPORTATION IN EUGENE

By Ross West

A Pivotal Year

TAKE A WALK along Columbia Street between 22nd and 23rd Avenues, and in the middle of the roadway you'll find trolley-car tracks. These are relics, reminders of a time gone by, like the toppled columns of a Roman temple or a dinosaur bone jutting out from an eroded creek bank. This wasn't Eugene's only trolley line; another ran along Willamette Street. Over the years there were many others, some electric, some mule-drawn. The last of the trolleys rumbled and clanked to a stop in October of 1927, replaced by motor-driven buses. Having outlived their usefulness, the last few of the once-fine street cars were set afire not far from Franklin Boulevard. The flames, sparks, and smoke spiraled skyward, signaling the end of an era.

This same year marked another turning point. A train passenger in Eugene could choose from any of eleven trains departing each day for Portland and any of eleven departures for the return trip. Train service has been in decline ever since, down to the current level of two passenger trains per day to Portland. As was the case with the streetcars, the death knell for train travel sounded in the sputter and roar of the internal combustion engine—buses to a small extent, but primarily the personal automobile.

American flier Charles Lindbergh twice dazzled the world in May of 1927. First he set the record for the fastest flight across

North America. He then topped even this impressive achievement when, after thirty-three-and-a-half hours and 3,600 miles in the air, he landed at Le Bourget Field outside Paris, becoming the first flyer to complete a nonstop crossing of the Atlantic and forever changing our perception of how close and easily reached are even the farthest shores.

Much nearer to home, a 1927 editorial in Eugene's *Guard* newspaper characterized traffic congestion as "one of the city's principal problems at this time." Oh really? The entire 1927 population of Eugene would fill fewer than half the seats in Autzen Stadium. And yet the perception of too much traffic was as commonplace then as it has been ever since.

As early as 1927 many of the issues, trends, advances, and perceptions that would shape the evolution of transportation in Eugene between 1949 and 2000 were already in place.

Treating the Symptoms in a City No Longer

In the western part of the United States, the slope of progress rises at a precipitous incline. Just four fifty-year jumps backward from 2000 land one at 1800, before the Lewis and Clark expedition. Three jumps—1850—and settlers were pouring westward over the Oregon Trail, bringing the total population of the lands that make up present-day Oregon to about 25,000 with natives still outnumbering newcomers. Two jumps back—1900—and Oregon, now a state, was growing fast in the midst of an economic boom based on exports from forests, fisheries, farms and ranches.

By 1950 we'd come a very long way. Oregon's 1.5 million citizens were learning of the Soviets exploding their first atomic bombs, of Mao forming the People's Republic of China, of scientists at Harvard developing the "world's most powerful computer"— a ten-ton machine measuring fifteen by thirty feet. A young crooner named Sinatra was getting a promising career going, and Clark Gable charmed audiences from the big screen at the McDonald Theater in downtown Eugene. Long ago, Aristotle observed that a city of more than one hundred thousand is "a city no longer," having grown into something larger and of a different quality. According to this definition Eugene made this important transformation between 1950 and 2000. In this period, the Eugene-Springfield metropolitan population surged from 77,000 to nearly 230,000. Eugene's physical size expanded as well, more than quadrupling from seven-and-a-half square miles in 1950 to thirty-eight square miles in 1990. Population projections estimate that ten or fifteen years into the new millennium, Eugene will be close to 300,000 inhabitants; by 2050 the Willamette Valley will be crammed with nearly 4,000,000 human sardines—an amount of growth equal to sprinkling the valley with an additional thirteen cities the size of Eugene or three the size of Portland.

As the population continues to bulge, our greater numbers are going to squeeze the urban growth boundary, putting added strain on everything from the water supply and street maintenance to the availability of a restaurant table on a Saturday night. Population pressures will increasingly be the motive force behind the political decisions we make, the taxes we pay, and the quality of life we experience. And all these folks—ever more, ever more—will need to get around.

How is that going to happen? What will getting them around do to the look and feel of the town? What are the options, the trade-offs, and how much is this whole thing going to cost anyway?

These are the kinds of questions that have occupied citizens, business leaders, politicians, and transportation and land-use planners since 1945. As time passes and the pressures increase and the answers become ever more difficult and more costly, it is important to recognize and acknowledge the fundamental cause of the discomfort: plain and simple, more and more people. Unfortunately, the will to reduce these population pressures is far beyond the scope of the American social and political psyche. Since we are unwilling to address the underlying disease, we will therefore be forced to expend enormous energies treating the symptoms.

The Four-Wheeled Partial Evil

In his 1798 "Essay on the Principle of Population," Thomas Robert Malthus sounded the alarm that the ever-increasing number of humans was hurling civilization toward some sizable problems. When he wrote his essay, the world had less than one billion people; in 2000, we number more than six billion. Malthus predicted that we could not continue growing "without occasioning partial evil."

He wasn't thinking of the automobile, but as things have turned out the car, along with the vast structures required for its support, may be an excellent candidate for the role of "partial evil"—a blessing and a curse. The automobile must be at the center of any consideration of where we've come from and where we are today.

Our dependence on the car is growing, with no end in sight. Consider these facts: There are more of us every year, we own ever more cars per capita, and we are driving those cars more and more miles. Imagine a graph showing all three of these lines trending upward. Now for a bit of wicked fun, superimpose onto this graph a fourth line, bright red for emphasis, increasing even more sharply than the other three. This line represents the effort transportation planners have put into plans aimed at getting people to decrease automobile use.

The problem is not that local transportation and land-use planners have done a crummy job—far from it; but rather, tremendous forces ranging across society, history, economics, technology, and politics have worked to make the privately owned automobile the transportation option of choice for most Americans. Factors contributing to this trend include: the colossal federal investment in the interstate highway system beginning in the 1950s (which put an exclamation point on shifts in public support away from mass transit and toward improving roads for personal transit—cars—that began in the 1920s); the baby boom and the increased postwar prosperity this generation has enjoyed; comparatively inexpensive gasoline prices and the associated (and sometimes quite messy) geopolitical efforts exerted to keep them low; the earning of a driver's license as one of the central rites of passage for American youth.

As the car took its place as the primary mode of transportation, it became an ever more potent force shaping the way Eugene and other American towns and cities developed. The post–World War II era saw a sharp rise in the number of people living in suburbs and commuting, usually by single-occupant automobile, to a job in a city center or other place of employment. The five-day-a-week tidal influx of suburban cars, coupled with the increasing numbers of cars owned by city dwellers, called out for more and broader roads and more and more parking. Zoning laws changed, segregating commercial, industrial and residential areas. Public policy extended sewer, water, and power to new developments, and new regulations supported vehicle access by providing for parking, adequate road widths, paving, etc. Along with a motorized public came the notion of shopping centers and eventually malls— mercantile islands in an asphalt sea—and the withering effect they had on many downtown shopping districts, including Eugene's.

Automobile dependence has it share of critics who assail the habit with arguments ranging from the polluting effects of auto emissions to global warming to "unsustainability" to the evils of consumerism. As time moves forward, these opinions may hold increasing sway over public policy. But the fact is, 80 to 85 percent of the populace now depend on cars to get around. For better or for worse, it is a system that has coevolved with the way most of us live our lives here in America at the beginning of the new millennium.

Level of Service F

In transportation planner lingo, "level of service F" is what the rest of us call gridlock. In 1994 planners for the Lane Council of Governments were thinking about how to avoid level of service F on West 11th Avenue. They had looked at the trends, crunched the numbers, and concluded that by the year 2014, without a fix, West 11th would be a parking lot.

The commuter's nightmare is the planner's challenge. Local transportation planners have long been aware of the central fact of transportation in the Eugene-Springfield metropolitan area: an east-west configuration with no limited-access transportation corridor along its axis. Such a thoroughfare would shift large numbers of motorists off the block-to-block street grids.

Creating such a corridor has been on transportation planners' minds since the early 1950s. Their responses have taken a number of forms, beginning with the idea of hooking up Franklin Boulevard to Highway 126 at Greenhill Road. Next, in the late 1950s, planners favored an extension of I-105 across the Willamette River to connect with Roosevelt and on through West Eugene. Concrete plans, but no concrete poured.

Still desirous of that elusive east-west connector, planners once again sharpened their pencils, readied their slide rules, went back to the drawing board and came up with a number of expressway proposals. One was called the "Skinner Butte Freeway," a ribbon of highway that would extend west from I-5 along the south bank of the Willamette through downtown to the Washington-Jefferson Bridge area. Another, the Roosevelt Freeway, would take off from this area to West 11th.

This round of plans did not sit well with a large and vocal contingent within the community concerned about the effect of such building on the riverside area, as well as life in the Whiteaker and Roosevelt neighborhoods. The force of this opposition killed the proposals. One enduring result of this fight was a 1976 amendment to the city charter requiring that for any new freeway or throughway project to proceed, a majority of Eugene voters must give the green light.

Increasing Complexity and the Crystal Ball
Still unsolved, the east-west traffic problem was creeping inexorably toward level of service F, and something had to be done. In the 1980s voters approved an alternate—or stop-gap—plan to improve 6th and 7th Avenues and extend the West Eugene Parkway.

Longtime residents will remember the enormous amounts of vit-
riol and *Register-Guard* ink spilled over this plan. For readers not
around at the time, it was in many ways a replay (or rather, pre-
play) of the same kinds of growth versus no growth conflicts that
have remained a source of tension in the city ever since. Anti-tree-
cutting activists voiced their concerns alongside citizens who felt
that bigger roads would not only divide neighborhoods, but also
invite more car use in an ever-escalating spiral.

These events illustrate the idea of "unintended consequences,"
as described in Edward Tenner's 1996 book, *Why Things Bite Back:
Technology and the Revenge of Unintended Consequences.* Part of
Tenner's notion—which Malthus, not to mention *Frankenstein*
author Mary Shelley, would doubtlessly second—is that as we
bound toward what we hope is a better, easier, technologically
enhanced future, we create whole new sets of problems.

Did the designers of the Roosevelt Freeway intend to compromise neighborhoods? Did those who protested the proposed route
of the freeway intend to kill trees on the avenues? Did the builders
of Valley River Center intend to devastate downtown shopping?
Probably not. More likely they envisioned better transportation,
neighborhoods, and shopping options.

Looking backwards through time it's easy to be brilliant—and
if we had tomorrow's newspapers today we could make a killing in
the stock market or betting on sports. Looking forward, however,
is a different matter. We are, as Tenner's book makes both tragi-
cally and comically evident, remarkably ill-equipped to look forward through time. But the job of a planner is, in one sense, to do
just that.

A case in point: The interstate highway system was making its
wide, smooth presence known locally in the form of I-5 in the
early 1960s. Eugene's planners refrained from commercializing
the areas near the interstate highway. With the guidance of Eugene Planning Director John Porter, planners focused on the downtown area. A missed bet in terms of economic development or a
visionary move to protect Eugene's livability? In contrast, Spring-

field was more open to commercial development of these areas, a bias that helped pave the way, decades later, for the Gateway development. An economic windfall or a mall and some sprawl? The answers to these questions remain unclear today. We don't have a functioning crystal ball any more than did the planners who responded to the new interstate highway forty years ago. This inability to predict the future with certainty holds true not only for planners, but also for politicians who guide the process, citizens who bring forth their own ideas and opinions, editorial writers who stake out a position, and anyone else attempting to envision tomorrow today.

Compounding the problem further is the number of chefs deciding what seasonings should go into Eugene's transportation soup. The nature of our transportation-planning system gives everyone from the Federal Highway Administration to the Oregon Department of Transportation, Lane County, and Springfield access to the spice rack.

Road building at our suburban fringe is a critical example. Many of the major roads that have fostered suburban development in Bethel, River Road, and Santa Clara were not built by the city. Instead, they are county roads, funded by timber receipts that flowed to county road-building coffers. Specifically, this arrangement accounts for most of our high-volume, fringe-connecting roadways: Belt Line, 30th Avenue, Delta Highway, Northwest Expressway, and the extensive improvements to River Road.

While forces outside the city exert control over many transportation decisions that affect those within its boundaries, city planners control other decisions through their efforts. And during the second half of the twentieth century, a telling sea change occurred in planning for Eugene's future transportation needs. The change is summarized in a draft version of TransPlan, the area's hotly debated—this is, after all, Eugene—master transportation planning document of the 1990s.

This summary, for all its inelegant and highly abstract language, succinctly describes decades of sweeping changes in values, methods, and intentions. It provides a cipher for understanding the sometimes mystifying actions of those charged with putting our transportation future into blueprint form:

> [T]here has been an evolution in what is expected from a region's transportation system and commensurately with the decision making for and content of the region's transportation plan. The evolution has included the following shifts:
> From: Emphasis on methods and data in support of programming transportation system improvements
> To: Improved information on a wide-ranging set of impacts for a wide variety of capital, operational, pricing, lifestyle, and land-use strategies.
> From: A focus on the efficiency of highway networks and corresponding levels of service (speed and travel time)
> To: Multimodal systems operation and broad performance measurement.
> From: A focus on how to get from point A to point B
> To: A broader context of transportation's role in a community and in the global, national, state, and local economic market.
> From: Acceptance of land use patterns as a given and not part of the solution set
> To: Use of land use strategies in connection with corresponding transportation policies as a major strategy.
> From: A focus on transportation system user benefits and costs
> To: Broader concerns for the equitable distribution of benefits and costs within the community.

In short, the trend in city transportation planning is toward a greater appreciation for interconnections, equity, and a broader view of how plans affect community.

So What Works?

In comparison to the complicated and at times contentious challenges associated with transporting people within the city, efforts to develop a functioning air transport system have been a much smoother ride.

Mahlon Sweet was the most effective and persistent early advocate for air travel in Eugene, according to Christopher R. Mellott's *The Eugene Airport*. Sweet, who along with partner Rollo Drain owned the Sweet-Drain Automobile Company (too bad these guys weren't plumbers), was the driving force behind Eugene's first airport. Opened for operation in 1919, the Eugene Air Park was way out in the boondocks near West 19th Avenue and Chambers Street. The first municipally owned airport on the west coast, the Air Park serviced the community until it was devastated by a fire in 1950 and finally closed in 1954.

Luckily, Sweet, the tireless evangelist of air transport, had begun lobbying for a second air field as early as the 1930s. The new field was first used in 1943 and named to honor its energetic promoter. During the period when Eugene was a two-airfield town, the Air Park serviced the needs of private aircraft and the new airport handled commercial traffic from United Airlines, West Coast Lines, and others. A number of expansion and improvement projects followed, most notably a large-scale renovation in the late 1980s, which included rechristening the facility as "the Eugene Airport" but retaining an honor for Sweet by naming the terminal building for him. By century's end, the Eugene Airport was serving more than 60,000 passengers per month.

While Sweet was a force in creating, supporting, and developing air transportation for Eugene, he was in one sense merely the local manifestation of a trend taking place all across the country in cities with the demographics to support air facilities. A much more unusual, and unusually successful, effort toward better local transportation options led to the city's renowned bicycle system. Anyone who has ever spent a sunny afternoon near the bike paths along the banks of the Willamette River knows that Eugene's bicycle system is one of the best parts of its transportation mix. You'll find young and old, cruisers and racers, roller-bladers, walkers, joggers, and three-year-olds riding like tiny rajahs in their Burley bike trailers, Styrofoam helmets for turbans—all savoring their own slice of the good-life pie.

Eugene's bikeways are an in-progress success story. The system includes twenty-eight miles of off-street paths, seventy-eight miles of on-street bicycle lanes, five bicycle/pedestrian bridges across the Willamette River, and connections to Springfield's bicycle system and county bikeways.

The first baby step in Eugene's long march to becoming a bicycle-friendly city took place in 1970, when mayor Les Anderson, himself a bike enthusiast, suggested forming a five-member bicycle committee with representatives of various city departments. By early 1971, City Manager Hugh McKinley, another cyclist, added five lay members to the committee—among them future mayor of Eugene Ruth Bascom. This core group formed the mechanism by which the force of citizen desire for and enthusiasm about improving conditions for cycling got transferred into the levers and pulleys of city government. Further institutionalizing its commitment to pedal power, the city added a bicycle coordinator to the payroll in 1973.

The Bicycle Committee's booth at the 1972 and 1973 Lane County Fairs featured a suggestion box for ideas to improve local cycling. Citizens' most frequent suggestion was for a bike and pedestrian bridge to the new Valley River Center. The same suggestion came up again and again at public hearings on the Eugene Bikeway Master Plan in 1974. Not long after, Oregon's Senator Bob Packwood was able to bring home the pork for what became the Greenway Bridge.

Oregonians spoke in favor of biking with the passage in 1971 of the state's "Bicycle Bill," which earmarked one percent of state-gas-tax funds for bicycle and pedestrian paths. A state law encouraged a "Willamette River Greenway," setting the stage for devel-

oping the riverside paths, and a series of further state actions helped
with acquisitions, easements, and condemnation.

Local agencies, too, were spawning good ideas. Three of the
other bike bridges that span the Willamette came about as the
result of a willingness on the part of various local agencies to cooperate for the civic good. In 1970 the Eugene Water & Electric
Board was planning a conduit to carry steam across the river. EWEB
offered to design the structure with bicycle and foot traffic in mind,
if the University of Oregon and the county would assume the additional costs. The three found a way to cooperate, and the splen-
did Autzen footbridge has been a reality ever since.

The Willie Knickerbocker Bridge near I-5 had a similar genesis, as did the Owosso Bike Bridge, a mile downstream from the
Greenway Bridge. Knickerbocker, by the way, was an eccentric
bike enthusiast remembered for leading mid-century parades
through downtown Eugene atop his stripped-down one speed.
His specialty was trick riding, standing on the bike seat or defying
disaster with handlebar handstands. He was a local fixture, a rain-
or-shine rider, and a favorite with kids for decades before his death
in 1960 at age ninety-two.

Eugene's newest bridge, the Peter DeFazio Bicycle Bridge between EWEB and Alton Baker Park, carries on the tradition of
citizen input shaping the bike system. Fourteen citizens and six
city staffers participated in the Ferry Street Corridor Citizen's Advisory Committee that delivered a report in December of 1995,
calling for the bridge as part of the $30 million Ferry Street Bridge
redevelopment project.

At the end of the century, the bikeway system was in the midst
of significant expansion. The riverside bike loop was nearing comple-
tion with a new path along the east bank of the Willamette River.
On the west side of town, the long-in-the-works connector along
Amazon Creek to the Fern Ridge Reservoir extended as far as Terry
Street.

A Measure of Who We Are

Like all aspects of transportation in Eugene, the bus system has evolved over time. Beginning in the 1920s, when motor buses replaced the city's trolley cars, the system passed from one owner to another. Oregon Motor Stages had the unfortunate timing of taking ownership in 1929 as the nation's economy collapsed. OMS hobbled through the Great Depression and was looking for a buyer when it was saved by the economics of the Second World War. Full buses kept the company in the chips until after the war when, with the resurgent availability of gasoline and personal automobiles, passenger numbers plummeted. In 1947 City Transit Line took over operations for a decade before handing over the keys to another operator who, in the period of just two years, drove the entire operation over the cliff of bankruptcy.

Taking matters into their own hands, the drivers kept the system limping along—going so far as to use their own personal cars for a time—until a new company, the Emerald Transportation System, could be formed. A driver-owned co-op, Emerald Transportation gradually expanded its service area. In late 1958 Emerald began to amass a distinctive fleet of twenty Volkswagen microbuses that plied the streets of Eugene for much of the next decade. But financial stability remained elusive for Emerald Transportation and other providers of mass transit, even as unimaginable amounts of state and federal transportation dollars subsidized car travel.

Bus companies up in Portland, for example, were headed for financial disaster by 1969. In an effort to prevent a loss of service in the Rose City, the state legislature passed ORS 267, which defined how transit districts could be formed, thus allowing for the formation of Portland Transit District (now Tri-Met). The cities of Eugene and Springfield, along with Lane County, petitioned Governor Tom McCall to establish a similar district for them, resulting in the formation of the Lane Transit District in 1970.

Since its inception LTD has racked up an impressive record of service—fifty million riders by 1987, 100 million by 1996. In

2000, a fleet of 112 well-maintained buses rolled from a new down-town terminal as far as Thurston, Lowell, Veneta, Santa Clara, Junction City, and McKenzie Bridge. All LTD buses are wheel-chair accessible (since 1985, seven years before federally mandated), and all are fitted with bike carriers.

Although LTD is another obvious candidate for what has worked well in the local transportation scene, the success here is, at least on the surface, less clear cut than the city's bicycle pro-gram. The primary difference is that the bike program costs little and supports a popular form of transportation (bikers account for about 3.6 percent of all trips taken in the Eugene-Springfield area), while LTD is enormously costly (roughly $30 million in 1999) and accounts for only about 1.8 percent of local trips taken. Half the bang for vastly more bucks.

Is it worth it? Some people say no. There is something about a huge bus rolling along nearly empty that seems to hit a nerve for some in the community, prompting the occasional peevish letter to the editor in *The Register-Guard*, decrying what is perceived as an inefficient use of precious resources. Indeed, since the forma-tion of LTD the bus system has been, year after year, a costly service.

But cost is quite different from value. Value is: getting large crowds of fans (some of whom we'd all just as soon not have be-hind the wheel) in and out of Duck football games and the County and Country Fairs; shuttling students and employees by the thou-sands in and out of the UO, LCC, and K–12 schools; serving as transportation for people without the resources to own a car or without the ability to operate one; being a mass-transit option for people who do own cars but find it more convenient, economical, or environmentally responsible to take the bus. In times of trouble the bus system has been an especially valuable civic asset, most notably during the two oil shortages of the gas-rationing 1970s, when bus use spiked. For the past thirty years Eugene has chosen thoughtfully, generously, compassionately, and wisely to keep this transportation option open.

While Eugene has been, and continues to be, swept along in national trends over which we have little control, the bus system is an exception. Oregon's urban-growth-boundary guidelines and strong land-use-planning system provide the tools with which to affect the future of how Eugene develops. Currently accepted local transportation theory has it that in combination with these tools, strong and steady support for the bus system—including the planned "Bus Rapid Transit" system—will shape that future in a way that fosters livability as the city grows larger and more closely packed.

Knitting History Together

In the history of transportation in Eugene, one event stands out from all the rest—singular, spectacular, illuminating. The event puts all the other details and ruminations about transportation in perspective the way that a near-death experience can provide a sobering glimpse of The Big Picture, the stuff that really matters.

It happened at just the same time as the pivotal transportation changes described in the first paragraphs of this essay. Eugene was, in mid-August 1926, abuzz with excitement. The weeks and months of planning, organizing, and practice were about to blossom forth into, perhaps, the most hallucinatory moment in the city's history—Ken Kesey and the Pranksters notwithstanding.

Months of work by "several thousand" actors, dancers, singers and choir masters, musicians, stage hands, set designers, lighting specialists, costume makers, choreographers, composers, directors, and many more were about to come together at Hayward Field in the world premier performance of "Klatawa: A Pageant of Transportation." The occasion of Klatawa—from the Chinook word for "to travel" or "to go"—was the joining of eastern and western Oregon with a Southern Pacific rail line between Klamath Falls and Eugene. Not only did this help join the halves of the state previously separated by the Cascades, it also would eventually provide a link to the Central Pacific Line in Nevada, thus giving Oregon a new transcontinental railroad and all the associated benefits.

Klatawa was only part of the three-day "Trail to Rail" celebration, an all-out, city-wide transportation-focused theme party. Other festivities included street dances, displays of locomotives, open air-boxing matches (refereed by Bill "Hayward Field" Hayward himself), and a daily "Air Circus" featuring parachuting, "unbelievable stunts," and flocks of planes flying in bomber formation. The Trail to Rail Queen and other members of the Royal Party won their titles in a two-month-long contest, during which, according to the celebration program, "seven million votes were cast."

But the jewel in the celebration's crown was, without doubt, Klatawa, presented in part because "there is no more dramatic episode in the history of the world than that of the development of transportation in the Oregon Country in the past seventy-five years." *Katie bar the door!*

The ebullient write-up about Klatawa in *The Guard* explains a bit further, detailing the pageant's "central theme of transportation, which seems so prosaic at first glance. But set against the background of the history of human civilization, expressed in a series of dramatic episodes which glow with color and are alive with romantic suggestion, with music adding its haunting thrill and a great chorus melodiously giving utterance to the emotions roused by the scenes beheld by the eye, transportation becomes 'Klatawa,' the symbol of human progress, the thread with which history is knit together."

These folks—our predecessors—took their transportation seriously and celebrated it with gusto. The "dramatic episodes" worked out in Klatawa go back as far as the Mayan civilization and work forward to the advent of air travel.

One especially atmospheric episode described in *The Guard* epitomizes the superabundance of Klatawa and the spirit of those participating. "No dance could be more brilliant and full of kaleidoscopic mingling of color and movement than 'The Forest Fantasy' in which more than a hundred girls and young women participated. The dance reached its climax when, among the maples, the birches, and the firs, all suggested beautifully in the costumes of the dancers, the forest fire represented by swift rushing scarlet-clad maidens, flashed in and out. Then came the pattering rain, represented by maids in snowy garb, who drove the flames away as the music softened." And that music, in keeping with Klatawa's titanic proportions and cyclonic intensity, was nothing less than Wagner's celestial fusillade "Die Walküre."

"The Forest Fantasy" was just one segment of Klatawa, accompanied by ten other major production numbers, plus sundry overtures, musical interludes, invocations, processions and other lavish grandiosities.

Perhaps only those few remaining seniors who may remember seeing or participating in Klatawa have a sense of the true scope of the spectacle. But even viewed through the distance of time and the words of others, it is certain that the lights above Hayward Field burned with a magical brightness that night, the choruses reverberated magnificently, the dancers danced with a breathtaking lightness of step.

All the folks at Klatawa, on stage as well as in the bleachers, got to Hayward Field somehow. Maybe they walked, maybe they took a streetcar or bus, maybe they drove. Maybe they took one of these eleven handy trains a day down from Portland to be part of the extravaganza. To them, Klatawa was a symbol of transportation, progress, and the spirit of the age.

Three quarters of a century later, the spectacle takes on an added meaning. Those trains, those buses, those cars that brought folks to Klatawa are pretty much gone today, rusted, crashed, burned. What remains is memory. For train buffs and old car hobbyists the sweetest of memories might be of the vehicles themselves. For the rest of us, it is Klatawa that we remember, or our own Klatawas in the form of that concert at the Hult Center, the Ducks whooping the Beavers, where we were on New Year's Eve, 1999—who we were with during those precious charged moments, who we dreamed ourselves to be, the lights, the music, the look in that pair of eyes across the room. How they got to Klatawa, how we get to our Klatawas, well, sure, that's important and practical, a necessity worthy of our best and most thoughtful planning efforts. But getting to Klatawa is preamble, transit not target, significant mostly in that it allows us to find our place before the house lights dim and the stage lights begin to shine.

Bibliography

Bikeways Oregon Inc. "Bicycles in Cities: The Eugene Experience," Vol 1-12, Eugene, Ore., 1981.

Boorstin, Daniel. *The Seekers*. New York: Vintage Books, 1998.

A Citizen's Guide to TransPlan (Friends of Eugene) Sept 14, 1999.

Eugene City Charter (adopted 1976)

The Eugene Guard, Aug. 20, 1926.

Eugene Weekly, Sept. 23, 1999.

Headley, Paul, Lane Transit District Historical Notebooks (unpublished)

Henry, Charles T. "On Building the Bicycle Habit (A Commuting Alternative)." June 14, 1978.

Hulce, David et al. *Willamette River Basin—A Planning Atlas*. Pacific Northwest Ecosystem Research Consortium. Version 1.0. 1998.

Inman, Leroy. *Beautiful McKenzie: A History of Central Lane County*. Roseburg: South Fork Press, 1996.

Loy, William G., Allan, Stuart, Patton, Clyde P., and Plank, Robert D. *Atlas of Oregon*. Eugene: University of Oregon Books, 1976

Malthus, T.R. *An Essay on the Principle of Population: Or a View of Its Past and Present Effects on Human Happiness*. Cambridge: Cambridge University Press, 1987.

Mellott, Christopher R., *"The Eugene Airport."* Springfield High School Junior/Senior Writing Project, 1999.

Moore, Lucia, McCornack, Nina, and McCready, Gladys. *The Story of Eugene*. Eugene: Lane County Historical Society, 1995.

The Other Paper, Sept. 1999.

The Register-Guard, 18 Sept.–14 Nov. 1999.

Rider's Digest, Lane Transit District, September 1999.

Tenner, Edward. *Why Things Bite Back: Technology and the Revenge of Unintended Consequences*. New York: Alfred A. Knopf Publisher, 1996.

Trail to Rail Celebration Guide (including a Complete Program for Klatawa a Pageant of Transportation), Eugene Ore. (Oregon Collection, Knight Library, University of Oregon)

TransPlan Summary: Improving our Transportation Choices, Lane Council of Governments, August 1999.

TransPlan, Revised Draft, May 1999.

The Runoff—Newsmonthly of the Many Rivers Group of the Sierra Club, Fall 1999.

West Eugene Parkway Supplemental Needs Analysis. Lane Council of Governments, Sept. 1994.

ENTERPRISE IN THE WILD WEST

By Nancy Webber

"We go westward as into the future, with a spirit of
enterprise and adventure . . . . Eastward I go only by
force, but westward I go free."
— Henry David Thoreau

IT WAS THE director of the Census, not the historian Frederick
Jackson Turner, who proclaimed the western frontier officially closed
in 1890. Three years later, at a meeting of the American Historical
Association, Turner said that the frontier was the foundation upon
which American political and economic freedom was built. Without a frontier, democracy and free enterprise would not endure. In
other words, America could survive only on the resources of its
domestic colonies and overseas territories.

It was an admission, fully realized by historians only at the
end of this century, that the West we claim as symbol of independence and self-reliance exists mostly in our imagination. It is true
that long past the Census Bureau's proclamation, there are still
five counties in Oregon with fewer than two persons per square
mile, the traditional census measure of "frontier." It is also true
that Eugene was built by a remarkable and colorful collection of
fortune-seekers, gandy dancers, and gyppo loggers who experienced
the boom and bust cycles of a raucous beginning.

Yet the West of imagination was hardly a place of solitary entrepreneurs, whose labor alone built the farms and mills, the towns
and cities. From its territorial beginnings westerners were dependent on outsiders to develop the seemingly limitless supply of

natural resources. Rather than the independence and self-reliance of the individual envisioned in Thomas Jefferson's agrarian society, the organizing principals of the frontier economy were those of government subsidies, outside venture capital, and organized labor.

Eugene was, in Turner's terms, a colony of the American empire, and so it remains. It is a town dependent on the federal government to determine allowable timber harvests and on Korean and Japanese investment to create new jobs. The last great story of the century involved Eugene's labor organizations, united and energized after nearly twenty years of declining membership, marching through the streets of Seattle at the World Trade Organization meeting to protest the stampede toward globalization, and its presumed loss of domestic jobs.

As the extractive industries of a natural resource-based economy continue to decline, we look east for government support to retool the timber economy. We look beyond Wall Street to the venture capitalists of the Far East to develop new industries. Whether Eugene is poised to take advantage of the emerging global economy is not so much a question as it is a hot debate in a town that is determined to buck trends and find its own way.

Located near Sitkum on the Coquille River, there is a tree that reaches 329 feet toward the horizon. It takes nine to ten adults with arms outstretched to encircle its thirty-six foot, six-inch circumference. In this one tree there are more than 52,000 board feet of lumber, enough to build five houses for the average American household. The world's largest coastal Douglas fir, it is a reminder of the giants that have propelled Eugene's lumber and plywood mills nonstop for nearly 150 years.

From 1937 to 1987, Oregon was the leading timber-producing state in the nation and Eugene the industry's hub. The city was known as the "timber capital of the world," a title challenged only by Springfield and Coos Bay. For a brief period during World War II, shipbuilding topped timber as Oregon's leading industry, employing 120,000 workers. Even so, production of lumber and plywood reached record levels as the industry stretched to meet the needs of national defense.

More than 160,000 workers came to Oregon for jobs during the war. It was a population shift larger in numbers and more profound in its social impact than the first migration across the old Oregon Trail. For the first time among the immigrants there were significant numbers of African Americans and Latinos. Although Oregon was still 90 percent white, people of color could now be counted.

The war economy peaked in January 1945, and the war's end meant massive layoffs in the defense industries coupled with the return of more than 1,516 soldiers to Lane County, according to the Selective Service Records of the State Archives Division. However, the closing of the munitions factories and the shipyards and the need to employ returning soldiers would not signal a return of a 1930s-style depression. Housing was at a premium. The orders for lumber and plywood could not be filled fast enough. The nationwide housing shortage kept more than two hundred sawmills operating in Lane County. It was common to see wigwam burners along Highway 99 smoking twenty-four hours a day to incinerate the sawdust shavings and bark. (What was considered "waste" in the 1940s was valued in the 1990s as a by-product used in pulp, paper, particle board, and other engineered wood products.) By 1946, said Carlos Schwantes in his book, *The Pacific Northwest*, timber regained its place as Oregon's number one industry.

The biggest management concern in the postwar timber economy was that a glut in the lumber market would drive prices unacceptably low. In 1948 William B. Greeley of the West Coast Lumberman's Association (WCLA) spoke in favor of an industrial price fix, telling the Eugene Chamber of Commerce that communities should not "sacrifice too much to the god of competition." Greeley called for "sustained yield" in the industry, by which he meant something very different than the term came to mean in later years. Greeley advocated for consolidation within the industry. By closing down the smaller operators, the remaining larger companies could control both the timber harvest and the profits.

Nils Hult, whose family operations began in Lowell and included operations in Junction City and Horton, defined the situation of the mid-sized family firm in a speech before the Willamette Valley Logging conference in 1958. As quoted in Michael Thoele's, *Bohemia*, Hult said: ". . . without exception I would say our ownership is insufficient to sustain our operations on a perpetual yield basis. We are dependent primarily on public stumpage. The question has always been how much of our limited capital can we put into timber and land, and how much into plant investment. We don't have enough for both and somewhere along the line we have that decision to make. If we make the wrong decision, it can be fatal."

Hult's remarks proved to be prophetic by the end of the century. The companies who chose to put their money into land survived the volatile years to come, while the companies who invested in mills and machinery were forced to sell. At the time of Hult's speech, however, many owners chose a third route: They would rely on contracts with the national Forest Service to harvest federal lands.

As the demand for lumber grew, the owners of many companies kept cutting at higher and higher levels. The year of peak production on Oregon's private lands was 1952; the last privately owned virgin stand was cut in 1955. The mills, built to handle the old-growth giants, needed a new source of supply. Only in the national forests were there sufficient old-growth trees available to supplement private stands. Pressure grew to open greater tracts of public lands to harvest.

Since the time of Gifford Pinchot, the first chief of the National Forest Service in President Theodore Roosevelt's administration, the national forests were managed "for the homebuilder first of all," according to Charles Wilkinson in *Crossing the Next Meridian*. At the time Pinchot outlined his vision for the newly formed agency, the cut on federal lands was only one billion board feet per year. Time and time again Pinchot defined the purpose of the national forests as the "greatest good for the greatest number" and, although he acknowledged other commercial uses, to him that meant timber production now and for future generations. By 1944, the average annual timber harvest jumped to 3.3 billion board feet from all national forest lands. The Forest Service's "sustained yield" policy suggested that federal lands could provide a perpetual supply, if the service allowed eleven billion board feet, and no more, to be cut each year. Of that total, the Pacific Northwest's region six would supply 4.5 billion board feet.

Other forces were at work in the gradual decline of the industry after 1955 besides supply. Competition for public contracts was fierce. Some mill owners faced a second front in the fast-growing southern pines, which were ready for harvest in about half the time as the second growth of the Pacific Northwest. The postwar Japanese demand opened a new market, but the Japanese wanted raw logs and bypassed American mills to process timber to their own specifications.

The results of these forces were frequently a consolidation of companies and a loss of jobs. Throughout the sixties, Lane County employment in lumber and wood products had its ups and downs. A report by Brian Rooney for the Oregon Department of Employment showed the decade began with 13,500 jobs in its primary industry and ended with 13,600, a net gain of only one hundred jobs but a loss in the share of the labor market from 23 percent to 17 percent.

Beginning in the 1960s the U.S. Congress passed several laws that reoriented the work of the U.S. Forest Service. The Multiple Use–Sustained Yield Act went beyond Gifford Pinchot's statement on the management of the national forests to include outdoor recreation, range, timber, and watershed management, and the protection of wildlife and fish. It broadened the responsibilities of the Forest Service, and as management plans began to change, the battle between environmentalists and the timber industry over the use of the national forests exploded, too.

The Wilderness Act of 1964 set 9.1 million acres beyond the reach of the saw blade, and by the 1979 passage of the Endangered American Wilderness Act, 2 percent of all the land in the lower forty-eight states were set aside as wilderness.

The timber industry claimed that the forests were capable of providing an annual harvest of 4.5 billion board feet per year from this region and that locking up land as wilderness was a threat to their timber supply. Environmentalists viewed the newly preserved wild lands as just the beginning of an effort to protect biodiversity and wilderness for recreation. The debate reached a fever pitch that often masked other issues within the industry.

At Oregon State University, a team of foresters led by John Beuter published their research on the future of the state's timber industry. The 1976 report, *Timber for Oregon's Tomorrow*, projected a significant decline in the harvest between 1976 and 2000 because of the maturity of private stands and public timber policy. Beuter concluded that private stands could not produce enough timber to meet demand and that the allowable cut on federal lands would have to increase to maintain the status quo.

Beuter found that private owners were harvesting at a higher rate than the inventory could support, a level that could not be maintained beyond 1985. He projected a decrease in the harvest of almost 60 percent in Lane County between 1985 and 1995, because of a severe depletion of mature trees. Even with a policy change to increase the allowable cut on public lands, the harvest would probably decrease by 12 percent.

During the 1970s the evidence of Beuter's projections was readily apparent. The stronger companies were buying weaker ones in a race to shore up supply. The consolidation sought by William B. Greeley of the WCLA to keep prices up by limiting the supply was now becoming a reality. The export of raw logs to Asia was eroding the job base in mills. Those plants that remodeled could process lumber with fewer employees. Workers watched their jobs leave on boats bound for Asia, in the computer technology that replaced the sawyers, and with every company that moved south or closed its doors altogether.

The backdrop of Eugene as a timber town was Eugene as a union town. The International Woodworkers of America (IWA), with membership as high as eighty percent, helped rank Oregon sixth in the nation in union membership in the late 1940s. The wood-products unions negotiated the first strong settlements in 1946 and set national trends for labor agreements after World War II. With the pent-up demand of a working class raised in the depression and restrained by a world war, consumer spending and the wages to support it were a high priority. The unions' leaders worked hard to transfer the postwar prosperity to their membership.

In June 1954, unions negotiated for a 12.5-cents-per-hour raise. Management did not respond. More than 6,000 workers in Lane County joined in the regional walkout. After three months, the governors of Oregon and Washington appointed a nonbinding negotiations team. Workers returned to their jobs with the promise of a settlement, and in December an agreement was finally reached to provide a 7.5-cents-per-hour raise.

The strike brought the industry's weaknesses into focus. Both labor and management had concentrated so much on the postwar boom and its economic fortune that danger signs in the industry were ignored. Even though the timber harvest on private lands reached its peak the very next year in 1955, it was decades before the problems precipitated by a diminishing supply were addressed. When the industry finally recognized the problems, rather than restructure, companies habitually turned to the federal government for relief and an increase in timber sales.

By 1980, the IWA took a contract first negotiated with Bohemia Lumber and in a uniform-pattern bargaining agreement, much like is done in the auto industry, it negotiated set wages and benefits for 65,000 workers at ten companies in the region. The three-year contract was the strongest the Sawmill and Timber Workers Union and the International Woodworkers of America ever had. It

called for wage increases in each of the three years and contributions to health insurance and pension funds.

But it was an agreement that could not hold. The early 1980s
brought a national recession, and by 1986, 60 percent of Oregon's
loggers lost their jobs. Marcus Widenor of the UO's Labor and
Education Research Center (LERC) reported that those who remained in the industry were asked by their employers to give back
$3.87 to $4.62 per hour. In the first five years of the decade, there
was an out-migration of 1.7 percent from Lane County. Lane
County's wood products workforce fell from a high of 16,000
workers in 1973 to 10,100 by 1986. The Western Council of
Industrial Workers lost 50 percent of its membership.

At the same time Georgia Pacific, Weyerhauser, Willamette
Industries, and Pope and Talbot, all with operations in Lane
County, reported record earnings. Georgia Pacific, whose Eugene
operations included hardboard and veneer plants, plus a resin plant
and distribution center, reported a net income of $458 million, an
all-time earnings record that was a 55 percent increase over 1986.
The company's CEO credited the increased profits to improved
operating efficiency and the export market.

The jobs concentrated in the natural-resource industries, once
10 percent of the state's job base, never returned. In 1991, the
lumber and wood products industry employed only 8,000 Lane
County residents, the lowest level of employment recorded by the
Oregon Employment Department in more than thirty years of
annual reports. Employment shifted to services, the public sector,
recreational vehicle manufacturing, restaurants, and retail. "If the
kind of drop that occurred here had occurred in the country as a
whole it would have been called a depression and not a recession,"
said Margaret Hallock, economist and director of LERC.

Yet the community, like many others throughout the Northwest, was embroiled in a controversy over the northern spotted
owl that threatened to close large tracts of federal and private forest lands. Many people blamed the industry's decline not on tech-
nological changes or the export market, but on the owl.

The story began in the early 1970s with a government inter-agency task force concerned with the biology and sustainability of forest ecosystems. Rather than recommend uncounted species for inclusion on the threatened and endangered species lists, they looked for an "indicator species" that could provide information about its habitat and the animals in its food chain, predicting the health of the old-growth ecosystem. The task force recommendation, that three hundred acres around each owl-nesting site be protected from logging, was intended to protect the forest itself from the fate of midwestern and European deforested areas that are no longer capable of producing commercial trees.

As is true of many government reports, this report was debated among the scientists and economists involved in its creation, but languished within the federal bureaucracy. It wasn't until environmentalists perceived that the federal agencies would not or could not act that the Seattle Audubon Society petitioned for protection of entire ecosystems on behalf of the spotted owl under the National Forest Management Act.

The Scientific Panel on Late-Successional Forest Ecosystems, a successor to the first task force, delivered a report that said: "There is no 'free lunch'—that is, no alternative provides abundant timber harvest and high levels of habitat protection for species associated with late-successional forests. In order to give fish and wildlife species even a moderate chance of survival, timber production would have to drop by well more than half of historical and planned levels." The report concluded that the allowable cut in the Northwest should be reduced from 4.5 billion board feet to no more than 1.7 billion board feet to achieve a medium-to-high probability of sustaining the ancient forests and their dependent species.

Industry and labor advocates argued that the resulting job loss was unacceptable. In one of many decisions Judge William Dwyer delivered during the spotted owl controversy, he found that "job losses in the wood products industry will continue regardless of whether the northern spotted owl is protected. A credible estimate is that over the next twenty years more than 30,000 jobs will be lost to worker-productivity increases alone."

Estimates of job loss from protection of the spotted owl ranged from 13,000 to 32,000. While the estimates of the environmental organizations were probably low and the industry and government figures were probably high, coupled with the preexisting nationwide recession and resulting decline in housing starts, and the increase in the export of raw logs, the impact was devastating.

Men who had worked all their lives in the forests and the mills had three choices: move, collect unemployment, or return to school in hopes of training for jobs in other industries. As a result of President Clinton's Forest Summit in September 1993, a lucky few were accepted into the Jobs-In-The-Woods program. The Oregon Department of Economic Development created a program to provide jobs that kept fishers and loggers working in their own communities on technical jobs in streambed and wildlife habitat restoration. The jobs were dependent on Forest Service and BLM contracts with very few private industry jobs immediately available.

An economic transition is difficult, particularly when the community is unprepared to make it. Beyond the experimental Jobs-In-The-Woods program, retraining efforts focused on the high-technology industry. The rationale was if other university towns prospered from the connection between academic research and technology companies, perhaps Eugene could too.

The strong relationship that existed between higher education and the high-tech industry in Silicon Valley or Seattle was not as well developed in Eugene. Since World War II, California and Washington leaders in education, industry, and government had focused their efforts on building strong research facilities within their states' university systems and strong ties to the industries that needed their services.

According to Richard White in his book, *It's Your Misfortune and None of My Own*, between 1940 and 1945, California received 45 percent and Washington 15 percent of the federal industrial facilities contracts that flowed to the eleven western states. By contrast, Oregon received just 5 percent. These defense-related industries influenced research at the universities, which in turn helped to bring about new industries unknown before the war. Among the nation's fastest growing industries between 1950 and 1966 were cathode-ray picture tubes used in television sets, semiconductors, computers and peripherals, and nonferrous metals.

These companies often were located in research parks on or near university property. According to a study done by the Battelle Memorial Institute, while more than 180 university towns established research parks and witnessed growth in one or more of these new high-technology industries, Eugene and the University of Oregon did not follow the pattern.

Gerald Kissler, senior vice provost for planning and resources at the UO, studied the relationship between university-level research and economic development. In his 1993 study, he found that California and Washington received more money, placed more emphasis on research, and paid better salaries to research faculty. The State of Washington concentrated its resources and students on two campuses, while Oregon, in the same time period, spread its resources and students among the four campuses of Oregon Health Sciences University, Oregon State University, Portland State University, and the University of Oregon. Although the two state systems enrolled nearly the same number of students, Washington received 60 percent more state funding. Washington schools also received $303 million in federal grants and contracts to Oregon's $124 million. Kissler concluded, "it's no accident that Washington and California have many more high-technology companies than Oregon does."

When Data General, an electronics firm headquartered in Boston, approached the UO in 1977 regarding a research partnership to support a manufacturing plant the company was thinking of locating in Eugene, the reception was not warm. In a report by Jack Condliffe and Alean Kirnak called "Cone-Breeden Controversy," UO Vice President N. Ray Hawk said, "I couldn't see our getting involved with any kind of manufacturing firm on a university site."

Data General briefly looked at the Cone-Breeden property north of Beltline Road and adjacent to I-5. The owners wanted to develop residential housing, which required extension of storm sewer lines from the city's system. It was one of several properties that the Boston electronics firm had expressed interest to city planners, but not to the owners, in using for a new plant. Either use required annexation to the City of Eugene in order to provide necessary services. For the last six months of 1976, city planning officials worked to acquire federal funds for the $750,000 storm sewer system without drawing public attention.

When the story broke in January 1977 citizens quickly organized against annexation. At a public hearing on February 28, the establishment of Eugene—a group that included University of Oregon President William Boyd, Lane Community College President Eldon Schafer, Chamber of Commerce President Emerson Hamilton, and Lane County Labor Council Executive Secretary-Treasurer Irvin Fletcher—testified in favor of the proposal. Aligned against them were those who objected to the conversion of agricultural land to industrial use, cost, and traffic congestion. Some opponents favored urban infill over annexation for residential housing. Others believed that an electronics plant would attract skilled workers from elsewhere rather than provide jobs for Eugene-area workers who would need to be trained.

By April the City of Eugene and the Boundary Commission approved the annexation request despite continued objections from a growing number of citizens. Data General, however, decided to locate elsewhere. Eugene was a perfect site for the company, with a university nearby, a skilled labor pool, an airport that was just minutes away, and a beautiful place to live. The reason the company gave for its decision was the lack of available land. Perhaps the nearly four hundred acres was not enough, but many believed that the company was deterred by a negative attitude toward business.

"That was a very important moment," said Margaret Hallock. "Cone-Breeden crystallized the debate. We need more jobs, but we have to preserve the land, livability, the way of life as we've known it."

Hallock believes that the city did not respond quickly enough in the land-use dispute. Given a choice, where Costco now stands, she would have preferred to see a manufacturing plant, such as Data General, because of the skilled jobs it could have provided. The controversy was an illustration of Eugene's continued ambivalence toward new industries. In 1974 Hewlett-Packard backed away from Lane County and selected Corvallis for its first Oregon facility. When the next phase of the timber crisis hit, Eugene could not support its population with a diversified economy that included new jobs in light-industrial manufacturing.

In 1987, Batelle Memorial Institute was contracted to conduct a feasibility study on the development of a research park at the University of Oregon. The study found that the UO had many programs that could contribute to the growth of Eugene's industrial sector. In its recommendation to move forward with plans for the research park, the study concluded that the city and school would benefit by attracting new light industry, especially the computer industry, to the region to help to diversify the economy.

The study site was a tract of 147 acres that stretched from Eugene Water and Electric Board to the I-5 Bridge between Franklin Boulevard and the Willamette River and included the UO soccer fields and a section of the Willamette River Greenway. The site sparked a new approach from those opposed to development, the creation of a "recreation/natural resources zone." The proposal called for an amendment to the city's land-use zoning ordinance that mandated the creation of a "zone" whenever a petition with seven thousand signatures requesting the designation for a particular area was presented to the City Council. Organizers mounted a petition drive to place the proposed zone on the ballot.

The first effort failed, but on a second attempt, backers succeeded in placing it on the November 1988 ballot. A *Register-Guard* editorial called it "one more in what seems an endless parade of obstacles to any effort by Eugene city government to facilitate economic development." Ultimately the measure failed by a 2–1 margin with 47,000 votes counted. Off to a rocky start, the original developer, Carley Capital Group, then filed for bankruptcy. A report by a review committee to UO President Dave Frohnmayer in 1998 says the zoning controversy and change of developers delayed the project by an estimated three years.

At the time, the park was projected to create one thousand to four thousand new jobs by 2003–2008. In 2000 park tenants employ more than three hundred people with an annual payroll of $15 million. Fifteen tenants include UO-affiliated projects and software and Web design companies. In their 1998 report, the Riverfront Research Park Review Committee found that the campus community significantly opposed the project and supported the preservation of open spaces. The committee also noted that the park was doing a better job of fulfilling its mission than is generally known. Their recommendations included the creation of both a community relations plan and a business plan, further study before additional development is undertaken, and the hiring of a developer.

Abe Farkas, former director of planning and development for the City of Eugene in the late 1980s, said, "There was some thought that the university would be a pivotal player in turning around the Eugene economy, but the leadership changed and the focus dispersed. When President Paul Olum left the university and Brian Obie decided not to seek a second term as mayor, attention was basically drawn elsewhere—to the west-end industrial expansion and development potential surrounding the new *Register-Guard* building, on former Cone-Breeden lands."

The venture capital for high-technology development eventually came, but the biggest investors were Asian rather than American firms. In the 1990s Sony Disc Manufacturing from Japan and

Hyundai Electronics from Korea settled in Lane County. Once again the community expressed its ambivalence toward economic development and did not welcome Hyundai, a computer disc manufacturer, with open arms in 1997.

The firm located in the West Eugene Enterprise Zone, which qualified the company for a projected $34 million in property tax abatements. (An *Oregonian* report said the actual figure for the five-year exemption will be closer to $65.8 million.) When the firm applied for permits to expand the initial plant, it faced a formidable challenge to receive an exemption from state and federal land-use laws to build on 10.5 acres of wetlands. It took the considerable skills and influence of many civic leaders, including former governor Neil Goldschmidt, to resolve the issue in favor of the company with the Corps of Engineers, the county commission, and city council. Four years after the initial permit was granted, the company requested an exemption from the West Eugene Wetlands Plan on an additional 7.7 acres, over the objection of citizen advocates. Undaunted by wetlands permits, civil suits, or the potential loss of tax abatements, Hyundai expected to increase its current workforce of 800 to 920 employees in 2000.

Although Hyundai has struggled, the increase of low-wage production jobs has been steady and dramatic. In the nearby Greenhill Technology Park, Rosen Products Inc., producer of flat panel display screens for cars and boats, employs 250 workers. *The Register-Guard* reported that another west-end company, HMT Technology Corporation, which makes thin-film disks for computer hard disk drives, added 725 jobs to Eugene's technology sector. Brian Rooney reported that between 1990 and 1998, new technology companies created 4,200 new jobs in Lane County, a 75 percent increase. During the same period the lumber and wood products industry lost 3,100 jobs, a 30 percent decrease.

While the addition of these jobs has helped to diversify the economy, Eugene appears to have skipped the development of high technology industries with strong ties to the research and development capabilities of the university. Gerald Kissler believed that unless and until there is a significant increase in faculty salaries from the state legislature and institutional support for research, the UO would not see the $250 to $300 million that it is capable of attracting on an annual basis. In addition to the benefits to the university, it is in the industries spawned from the research-and-development relationship that many economists see the future of the middle-income wage earner.

Instead Eugene seems to have exchanged the middle-class jobs in the timber industry for a set of higher-wage professional jobs and another set of low-wage retail, service, and manufacturing jobs. As 1999 ended, Monaco Coach Corporation, the luxury recreational coach manufacturer, was the county's largest private, local employer. Since 1988 more than 67 percent of the new jobs created in Lane County have been in the services and retail trade industries. The newest national firms to locate in the city exemplify this trend: Levi-Strauss Financial Services, providing "back office" accounting and data processing services, and Accutel (GMAC Finance), a call service center.

The impact can be seen in what is traditionally considered downtown as well. In 1971 the city limited vehicle traffic in the center of town and created a pedestrian mall. Major retail anchors Sears, McKenzie Outfitters, J.C. Penneys, and others began to abandon what were once prime locations downtown for the suburban malls. Despite many efforts, the retail sector has never recovered.

Abe Farkas cited many vision documents and attempts to revitalize the retail sector, but he described in particular detail an effort that fits a familiar pattern. At the corner of Oak and 8th Avenue, city planners envisioned a multi-use building that included a Nordstrom store, plus a new downtown library. Citizens were concerned about housing the library in a retail building and voted against municipal funding for the project, and Nordstrom wasn't interested. Still smarting from a decision to locate Portland-based retailer Lipman-Wolf at Valley River Center rather than Seattle-based Nordstrom, company officials told the city that when Nordstrom needed Eugene, Eugene didn't want them. Now that Eugene was asking, Nordstrom had bigger markets for expansion plans.

Development on the former Cone-Breeden lands provided further proof of an economy in transition. In 1999 it was one of the largest growth areas in Eugene, with new residential development and retail outlets. KEZI/Chambers Communications, with its new sound stages, attracted feature film productions from Los Angeles and the new Levi-Strauss Financial Services brought 170 new finance-related jobs to the area.

As 1999 came to a close, not one of the top fifty Oregon businesses reported by the *Oregonian* was a Eugene-based timber products company. Since 1990 the annual volume of timber harvested on Lane County's public lands fell by 670.5 million board feet, a 94 percent drop, and 122 wood products firms closed their doors permanently. Neither could the city boast of a locally owned high technology firm among the top fifty publicly owned firms. Eugene's Centennial Bancorp and Obie Media Corporation were the only firms to make the list.

The $20-per-hour jobs of the timber industry have been replaced by the $10- to $13-per-hour jobs in the retail, service, and manufacturing industries. The new labor force, unlike the timber industry, is not unionized. Between 1979 and 1993, inflation-adjusted wages for college graduates increased by 10 percent and fell for high school graduates by 12 percent. This gap, once tempered by union demands for increased middle-income wages, is expected to grow.

The Oregon Employment Department projects 84,000 new Lane County residents by 2015. The sectors with the most growth are expected to be the high-income professional and technical group, largely in computer-related work, and the low-wage production jobs in the manufacturing sector, other than lumber and wood products.

In this time of extended growth, the question facing Eugene is not if the city will recover from the most devastating downturn in its economic history, second only to the Great Depression, but how. The frontier of government subsidies, strong organized labor, and foreign venture capital may be finally coming to a close. The organizing principles of Eugene's next fifty years have yet to be defined.

Bibliography

Battelle Memorial Institute. *A Feasibility Study of the Riverfront Research Park*. Columbus, Ohio, Battelle Columbia Division, 1987.

Beuter, John, et. al. *Timber for Oregon's Tomorrow: An Analysis of Reasonably Possible Occurrences*. Corvallis, Oregon: Oregon State University, 1976.

Condliffe, Jack, and Alean Kirnak. *Cone/Breeden Controvservy: A Case Study in Land Use and Economic Development*. Survival Center/Associated Students, University of Oregon, 1977. Coursework in the Departments of Political Science, Sociology and Urban and Regional Planning.

Conlin, Joseph R. *The American Past: A Survey of American History*. New York: Harcourt Brace Jovanovich, 1990.

Final Report of the Riverfront Research Park Review Committee to President David Frohnmayer, October 15, 1998.

Hallock, Margaret, and Steven Hecker (ed). *Labor in a Global Economy: Perspectives from the U.S. and Canada*. Eugene, OR : Labor Education and Research Center, University of Oregon, 1991

Kissler, Gerald R. *Economic Growth and Competitiveness: Higher Education and the Development of Oregon's New Economy*. Eugene, Oregon: Office of the Vice President for Academic Affairs and Provost, University of Oregon, 1993.

Multiple Use and Sustained Yield Act of 1960.16 U.S.C.

Nash, Gerald D. *World War II and the West: Reshaping the Economy*. Lincoln, Nebraska: University of Nebraska Press, 1990.

O'Donnell, Terrence. *That Balance So Rare: The Story of Oregon*. Portland, Oregon: Oregon Historical Society Press, 1988.

"Oregon Live: Special Reports: Top 50 Businesses," *The Oregonian* (Portland, Oregon), February 14, 2000.

Oregon State Department of Veteran's Affairs: Selective Service Records 1943–1945.

Oregon Daily Emerald, 26 July, 1988.

The Register-Guard, 29 Apr. 1988–20 Feb. 2000.

Robbins, William G. "Lumber Production and Community Stability: A View from the Pacific Northwest." *Journal of Forest History* 31 (October 1987).

Rooney, Brian. *"Eugene/Springfield MSA (Lane County) Economic Data Sheet 1978-1998,"* Salem, Oregon: State of Oregon: Department of Employment, 1998.

Rooney, Brian. "Labor Force in the Eugene Metropolitan Area. 1958-1999," Salem, Oregon: State of Oregon: Department of Employment, 1999.

Schwantes, Carlos Arnaldo. *The Pacific Northwest: An Interpretive History.* Lincoln, Nebraska: University of Nebraska Press, 1996.

Selective Service Records 1943–1945. Salem, Oregon: Oregon State Archives Division, 1945.

Thoele, Michael. *Bohemia: The Lives and Times of an Oregon Timber Venture.* Portland, Oregon: Oregon Historical Society Press, 1998.

Wilkinson, Charles F. *Crossing the Next Meridian.* Washington, D.C: Island Press, 1992.

White, Richard. *"It's Your Misfortune and None of My Own": A New History of the American West.* Norman, Oklahoma: University of Oklahoma Press, 1991.

Widenor, Marcus R. *"Pattern Bargaining in the Pacific Northwest Lumber and Sawmill Industry: 1980–1989.* Eugene, Oregon: Labor, Education and Research Center, University of Oregon, 1991.

OF COUNCILS, MAYORS, AND MANAGERS:

EUGENE'S GOVERNMENT

By Rosemary Howe Camozzi and David Thompson

IN MAY 1944, the month before D-day, Eugene voters fundamentally altered the city's charter, approving an amendment to
adopt the council-manager form of government. Where previously
the mayor and city council ran the day-to-day affairs of city hall,
now a paid professional, a city manager, was in charge. Eugene
thus joined hundreds of other U.S. cities with a council-manager
plan, a Progressive Era reform intended to remove political parti-
sanship and corruption from city hall, and to improve efficiency in
city government.

"Eugene represents a big business deserving full-time supervision," said A.L. Hawn, one of the councilors who helped put the
charter amendment on the ballot.

Proponents of the council-manager plan in Eugene envisioned
the backlog of civic projects the city could start after the war ended.
Under the old system there was a sense that city hall couldn't get
things done. The part-time, unpaid mayor and council had their
own businesses or jobs to deal with, and nobody was truly in charge
of the day-to-day business of the city. When the Army Corps of
Engineers, for instance, asked the city for data on Amazon Creek
to help with its Willamette Basin flood control plan, city hall
couldn't provide it, and the Chamber of Commerce had to step in.

But not everyone agreed the city needed a professional administrator. The most prominent opponent of the city manager plan

was Mayor Elisha Large, who argued that it was dictatorial, that it would raise taxes, and that it was actually a covert attack on the Eugene Water Board (later known as EWEB), an independent municipal corporation run by its own manager. (As the argument went, once the council got its city manager in place, it would claim one manager was enough and attempt to seize control of the utility.) Large succeeded in keeping the council from putting an argument for the plan in the voter's pamphlet. However, an opposing argument appeared with this warning: "THE PLAN IS TYRANNICAL, OPPRESSIVE AND UNAMERICAN."

But plan's proponents had a powerful ally in the editor of the *Eugene Register-Guard*, William Tugman, who ran a series of editorials in favor of the amendment. Rebutting the claim that the plan was undemocratic, Tugman wrote: "How much real democracy do we have now? How about the secret meetings of council or committees of council cliques which have long been subject of complaint? How about the many years during which relatives and friends have been wangled onto the payroll with little regard for merit? How about the repeated violations of sound practice requiring open bids on purchases? There has been nothing very bad, but the practice has often been far from good."

In the end, the charter amendment squeaked by with a vote of 2,781 to 2,532. The history of Eugene city government from then through the end of the century is largely the story of the interplay between eight city managers and the councils and mayors they served. Henceforth, the mayor and eight-member council, as the city's legislative body, would appoint a city manager to implement the policies they set. The manager, as head of administration, would prepare the budget, make purchases, organize departments, hire and fire staff, enforce ordinances, and provide information requested by the council. Furthermore, the manager could participate in all council discussions. If the council lost confidence in its manager, it could—with five votes—choose to find a new one.

Deane Seeger, the First Manager

Deane Seeger was a business manager at a Boeing aircraft plant when the council hired him as its first city manager. When he started in February of 1945 the city had a new mayor, construction magnate Earl McNutt, and an ambitious list of projects. By spending thriftily through the depression and the war, the city had practically eliminated its debts and even managed to build up some cash reserves. A new swimming pool topped the list of projects the council was anxious to start, and as the city's business agent, Seeger flew to San Francisco to get a deal on surplus pool equipment. The council also put him to work on planning the city's first sewage treatment plant, applying for federal funding to help build the city's segment of the Amazon Canal, implementing downtown's system of alternating one-way streets (Eugene was the first city in Oregon to try such a thing), overseeing park and airport improvements, and undertaking a slew of road, alley, and sewer jobs.

The city manager's first test as head of city personnel came when the police chief, Otto Pittenger, slapped a fourteen-year-old who had marched into the chief's office with a group of friends to complain about being barred from the community recreation center, where the boys went when cutting school. The boy's battered but defiant face appeared on the front page of the next day's *Register-Guard*, along with the announcement of the chief's resignation. Pittenger supporters, unhappy the chief had been forced out, kept Seeger up until 2 *a.m.* with angry phone calls. They presented a petition to both the manager and Mayor McNutt calling for the chief's reinstatement—not that there was anything McNutt could do about it, for under the new system neither he nor the council was permitted to influence the manager on personnel matters. And if the city were to be run professionally, the chief of police could not smack kids around in his office. Seeger remained firm. Pittenger had to go.

One of the larger physical changes to the city in the postwar years was the widening of Franklin Boulevard as part of the state's transformation of Highway 99 between Eugene and Goshen into a "modern four-lane superhighway." In related projects, Seeger oversaw work on realigning the dangerous right-angle turns where Highway 99 passed through downtown and where too many log trucks had spilled their loads on too many cars. Nearby, the city was building a viaduct to tie the new superhighway in with the new Ferry Street Bridge that the county would build. In 1946 Eugene voters had approved a half-million dollars for the city's share of this work, known as the "Millrace Junction Project." The old millrace was involved because the council opted to fill the end of it, from Broadway to the river, in order to reduce costs and simplify right-of-ways. The tail end of the race would flow through a pipe beneath the highway. But first the city had to buy the millrace from the Eugene Power Company, and with the voter-approved bond in hand, the council directed Seeger to do just that.

Dug by pioneers to tap energy from the Willamette River, the millrace had lost its industrial value once the city was able to provide electricity. But the two-mile-long waterway remained a popular recreational site for townspeople and students. When the city acquired the race, however, it was in sad shape. A flood had knocked out the concrete intake by Glenwood, and the race had gone dry. Many in the community wanted to see it restored. Millrace enthusiasts used the initiative process to pass bond measures in 1946 and 1948 to finance restoration work. They raised matching funds, they obtained right-of-ways, and they formed an association to pressure the council to take their cause seriously. When businessmen along Broadway took it upon themselves to begin filling the race where the city had left off, students and townspeople rallied to the site and formed an automobile barricade to block the dump trucks. Seeger frequently met with the Millrace Association to discuss restoration plans and to explain financial and engineering obstacles. And there were always obstacles—the single largest probably being that the city council wasn't as enthusiastic about putting water back into the ditch as were others in the community.

The millrace was still dry when, after four years on the job, Seeger stepped down as city manager to work for the League of Oregon Cities. The council liked Seeger and tried to induce him to stay with a raise. The Eugene Chamber of Commerce liked him, too, and made him president for a few years.

Oren King

In 1949 Eugene elected a new mayor, Edwin Johnson, and hired a new city manager, Oren King, who had been the city manager of Pendleton. The council continued cooking up infrastructure projects on which to turn their city manager loose. During King's four years on the job he supervised construction of the city's first sewage treatment plant, launched a ten-year program to create a network of cross-town arterial streets, and oversaw the laying of a lot of blacktop and sewer lines. By 1953 the city had seventy-seven miles of paved roads—nearly twice what it had at the end of the war. But through annexation the city had gained nearly eighty more miles of dirt and gravel roads, and the number kept growing.

First on King's list was a project the public demanded: restoring the millrace. With money from the voter-approved bonds and the Millrace Association's matching funds, the council directed King to start work on a pumping station to put water back into the dry canal. But victory soon turned to disillusionment, as the town learned that the outtake pipe laid beneath the highway in the Millrace Junction Project wasn't wide enough to return the water flow to its original rate. The grand old millrace—once known as "Eugene's Crater Lake"—had been reduced to little more than a murky, slow-moving storm sewer.

Robert Finlayson

When King left in 1953 for another city manager job, the council replaced him with Robert Finlayson, who had been city manager of Oregon City. Roads and sewers occupied much of Finlayson's attention, and he added more streets, curbs, and sewer pipe than ever. Continuing work on the airport, the park system, and the Amazon Canal also kept him busy.

Through the 1950s the old lumber town experienced sharp growing pains, and the city council got embroiled in a string of notable controversies, particularly during 1954. It started in January with a $700,000 bond measure for off-street parking downtown, a joint product of the council and the Chamber of Commerce. But voters objected to spending public money to create parking for the benefit of merchants, and they rejected the measure by a six-to-one margin. The council and chamber regrouped and continued to work on the issue. But the first modest municipal parking lot wouldn't open until the early '60s. In the Bethel area, west of town, the council twice in 1954 held contentious annexation votes. After the first failed, and Bethel attempted to incorporate into its own city, the council redrew the line to leave out parts where anti-annexation sentiment was strongest while still capturing industrial development. The second vote succeeded. Also in 1954, a referendum overruled the council's decision on where to locate the new public library. Voters disliked the council's downtown site, opting instead to build at 13th Avenue and Olive Street.

But 1954's ugliest controversy came when the city council held an unpublicized meeting at the home of Mayor Johnson. At the meeting the council informally agreed to overturn a planning commission recommendation for zoning the newly annexed strip of land between the millrace and the river. An editorial by William Tugman blasted the council for conducting public business in "secret sessions." After voters rejected the council's zoning decision in a referendum, the council spent an hour at its next meeting castigating Tugman, kicking off a heated exchange of letters and editorials. In a telling glimpse into the mindset of the council at the time, one councilman wrote: "…it is essential we have private conversations where we let our hair down and talk freely, argue by ourselves perhaps and by the interchange of opinions reach a sound decision, if possible. We shall never freely discuss many things before the public." In the end the council agreed not to have any more meetings in private homes.

Throughout the turmoil, Mayor Johnson, owner of a downtown furniture store, managed to provide a sense of leadership to the council, if not to the wider community. But things started to fall apart after Johnson stepped aside at the end of 1956. The city attorney was convicted of tax evasion, the president of the council died in a plane crash, and the new mayor, John McGinty, who was working in Colorado on a logging operation, was out of the city longer than the sixty days then allowed by the charter. When he failed to get back to Eugene for the meeting in which the council might have granted him an extension, the council declared his seat vacant and found a new mayor.

Former city councilor and Republican state legislator Ed Cone replaced McGinty. Although Cone was far more attentive to the duties of mayor than McGinty had been, his own lumber operation, the family mill in Goshen, took the better part of his attention. Finlayson continued doing his job, but a leadership gap had formed at city hall, and he did not fill it. He was perceived as too cautious, too slow to act, and unwilling to take initiative. The council grew frustrated, feeling its policies weren't being implemented. Dissatisfaction with what was—or wasn't—going on at city hall spread through the community. It all boiled over at the beginning of 1959 when a newly elected city councilor, Hobie Wilson, made a motion to fire Finlayson on the spot. Wilson's audacious move drew one supporter and a sharp rebuke from the council president, who objected that such a thing "by a new councilman who doesn't have the most rudimentary knowledge of city government as yet [is] highly objectionable to the older council members." Still, Finlayson got the message. And though the five votes needed to oust him weren't there, the sentiment was. He stuck around long enough to help a new city manager get oriented, but he didn't announce his future plans after he resigned.

Hugh McKinley

Into the gap stepped Hugh McKinley, and he filled it well. During his fourteen-and-a-half years as city manager of Eugene, McKinley gained national recognition within the profession, becoming known as "the city manager's city manager." As the son of a Reed College political science professor, McKinley was attuned to public administration from an early age. He was city manager of Grants Pass when Cone contacted him about the imminent job opening in Eugene. McKinley brought a new professionalism to city administration. One of his first memos informed the public works department that employees could no longer accept Christmas turkeys from contractors. He was affable and accessible: His open-door policy made it possible for anyone in the community to see him. When a woman who had been selling velvet paintings on a busy corner was told she could not conduct business on the street without a license, she stormed into McKinley's office saying she was "so angry she could just spit!" McKinley heard her out, asked her to please not spit in his direction, and somehow, the two parted friends.

During McKinley's tenure, Eugene underwent tremendous physical change, growing from a city of about 50,000 people in ten square miles to one of about 95,000 people in twenty-eight square miles. The 1960s were filled with capital improvement projects. Under McKinley, the city continued its cross-town street program, laid more sewers, made more airport improvements, built new fire stations, bought land for parks, and opened a new city hall. The city's rapid growth meant no shortage of problems. Every major street project turned into a neighborhood battle. The extension of Pearl Street into Amazon Park to create an expressway linking downtown to 30th Avenue sparked a 1961 initiative petition leading to a charter amendment that prohibited the city from building "limited access roadways" without a public vote. The city overturned this amendment a few years later, only to have voters put it back into the charter in 1972, following an outcry over a planned freeway that would have torn through the Whiteaker neighborhood.

As the decade marched on, the business of city government grew increasingly complex, and McKinley created the position of assistant city manager to free himself from the day-to-day minutiae of administration, allowing him to better focus on problem solving.

As the societal changes of the '60s took hold, the lock that businessmen and professionals had on the city council for so long was broken. The composition of the council broadened, and clearly defined liberal and conservative blocs emerged. City government's role evolved beyond public safety and infrastructure to include social concerns, such as low-income housing, environmental protection, and equal rights. With federal money from the Community Development Block Grant Program, the city began financing social service agencies. Opportunities for public involvement in government grew. The city put together a human rights commission in 1964. In 1967 some 250 people attended the landmark Community Goals Conference to hammer out a set of broad policy objectives to guide the city council in decision making (one of the direct results was the preservation of the city's South Hills). The goals document gave elected officials and staff alike consistent policy guidelines to work from. It also gave city councilman Les Anderson the platform for his successful 1968 mayoral campaign.

Anderson, publisher of a lumber-market newsletter, embraced the mayor's role as spokesperson for the city. This permitted McKinley—whom Cone had left to handle much of the city's public relations chores—to fall more into the background. Anderson's cool head was just what the city needed as social upheaval spilled into city hall. Issues such as the Vietnam War and rules for the new downtown pedestrian mall drew so many young protestors to council chambers that the fire marshal had fits. The young activists disregarded time limits for public speaking; they harangued elected officials, called them fascists, and waved North Vietnamese flags in their faces. Anderson managed not to inflame the situation, and he helped restore order by leading the council in setting conduct rules for meetings. Meanwhile, McKinley worked closely with police during times of civil unrest, sometimes standing beside the police chief just behind the front lines. During one antiwar demonstration at the University of Oregon, McKinley and

the police chief took position in the ROTC building, which police
believed the demonstrators intended to burn. From there they
watched as a cordon of riot cops held off the name-calling, bottle-
throwing crowd. Years later, McKinley still found it amusing that
the tennis players on the nearby Alder Street courts seemed
undistracted by the wild scene, even when the tear gassing began.

McKinley was not shy about using the authority he had under the charter to participate in policy discussions right up to the
vote. The council welcomed his input. If he were absent from a
council discussion, inevitably someone would ask, "What does
Hugh think?" McKinley provided leadership, which can be dangerous territory for a city manager, who risks the perception of
stepping over the line into policy making. But McKinley negotiated this terrain with such agility that it was rare for anyone to
complain. Still, there was occasional grumbling, such as the time
City Councilor Fred Mohr said: "He's gone beyond the role of city
manager. He's a policy maker, and he's very effective at it." Anderson framed it differently: "He presents a problem in a way that
makes you feel like you've made the decision."

When McKinley left Eugene in 1975, it was for San Diego,
the second-largest city in the nation with a council-manager form
of government. Four hundred people turned out for a farewell dinner. Governor Bob Straub, who planned to attend but couldn't
make it, said in written remarks that McKinley had as much influence on city politics in Oregon as "anyone in history."

Charles Henry

To replace McKinley, the council selected Charles Henry, city
manager of University City, the largest suburb of St. Louis, Mis-
souri. Henry's work developing neighborhood associations there
was a strong factor in the council's decision.

Henry provided a low-key contrast to McKinley, who left his
successor a box filled with pages from the city's 1905 charter,
scrawled with notes for revisions. The old 1905 charter was due
for an update. It was almost 300 pages, poorly organized, ambigu-

ous in places, and full of anachronisms, such as the grant of power
for the city to regulate town criers, prohibit opium houses, and
punish "lewd women of ill repute." Henry inherited the job of
overhauling the charter, and under his supervision, city attorneys
whacked it down to thirty-eight pages. In the process they clari-
fied the 1972 freeway amendment so it couldn't be construed to
mean every new city street had to be approved by voters. They also
stripped most of the language from city employees' hard-won collective bargaining amendment—over strong objections of the employees' union—and they transferred authority over library staff
from the library board to the city manager. Voters approved the
revised charter in 1976, the same year that Anderson, after two
terms as mayor, called it quits.

So Eugene entered 1977 with a new charter as well as a new
mayor, Gus Keller, the manager of a downtown sporting goods
store. Keller was soon reminding everyone that the charter granted
the mayor veto power. It was a power no one could recall the mayor
having ever used. But Keller used it three times, aggravating the
council's liberal majority, which complained that Keller wasn't the
consensus builder that Anderson had been.

Anderson, for his part, wasn't out of the limelight just yet.
Keller appointed him to head a commission working to create a
civic auditorium. Eugene's arts set had long bemoaned the lack of
a fitting venue for performing arts. It was one thing to squeeze into
the stands at Mac Court for Duck basketball, but quite another to
do for an evening with Jascha Heifetz. In 1972 and again in 1973,
the Lane County Auditorium Association, a private group, put
forth auditorium bond measures. Both lost by close votes. Neither
the downtown business establishment (reeling over the mess urban renewal had made of downtown) nor the city council had
gotten fully behind the auditorium idea on the first two go-arounds.
But in 1978—with the council's backing, business community
support, and a slick ad campaign—an $18.5 million bond for the
project passed. Arts supporters cheered. Charles Henry got to work.
He launched the project, appointing staff and the architectural

firm, and supervising the construction contracts. Henry also helped with negotiations to lure a major hotel to build next door to the Hult Center, as the auditorium would later be named. As an enticement, the city pledged to build a conference center and parking garage at the site. The Hult Center vote squeaked through just in time, for the following year the nation began to slip into a recession that would hit Lane County particularly hard.

But city finances were in bad shape before the recession even started. Revenues through the latter half of the '70s weren't keeping pace with inflation or growth. Meanwhile, Henry was beginning to have trouble keeping pace with the increasing demands of his job. Neither he nor the council realized it at the time, but diabetes was draining his strength. In 1980, with the local economy in a tailspin and a budget shortfall forcing the city to cut payroll and services, the council wanted someone new. Henry helped recruit Mike Gleason, who took over in January 1981, just as the Hult Center's roof was going up.

Mike Gleason

The thirty-six-year-old Gleason, who previously had been city manager of Walla Walla, Washington, stayed on the job for fifteen years, breaking Hugh McKinley's record by a half-year. Like McKinley, Gleason grew up around local government; his father was head of the Multnomah County Commissioners. Where Henry had lacked energy, Gleason bristled with new ideas and enthusiasm. Although this drove some of the older city staff crazy, it was just what the council was looking for. "We're awful lucky to have the guy," said Mayor Keller.

Gleason came on the scene as the city struggled with the most troubled economy it had seen since the depression. Mill closures, layoffs, and bankruptcies were widespread, and unemployment rates climbed into the double digits. Wood-products workers who still had jobs accepted wage and benefit cuts. Many people fled the area, and Lane County's population actually began to decline. "For Sale" signs sprouted everywhere, but no one was buying. The only bright spots were the opening of the Hult Center and its next-door neighbors, the Eugene Hilton hotel and conference center complex, in 1982.

Economic development became the city council's top priority. Issues that had previously divided the council died down. The growth debate that had emerged in the '70s fell dormant. The council wanted to bring back jobs, and it wanted jobs that wouldn't dry up every time the wood-products industry faltered. When Brian Obie moved from the council to the mayor's seat in 1984, he brought to the job the same intense drive that helped him turn his outdoor advertising company into one of Eugene's most successful businesses. The dominant theme of Mayor Obie's tenure was the "public/private partnership." One result was the creation of the Eugene-Springfield Metropolitan Partnership, an agency jointly funded by private contributions and public tax dollars to recruit new companies to the area. Another result, which didn't come to fruition until the mid-'90s, was downtown's Broadway Place development, which combined a publicly built and owned parking garage with a privately built apartment, office, and retail complex.

Gleason zealously implemented the council's economic development policies, helping to set up an enterprise zone in West Eugene and overseeing the installation of new sewer, water, and power lines for industry; launching the Riverfront Research Park; upgrading the city's transportation system with airport improvements; and widening 6th and 7th Avenues. Although Gleason's style didn't always mesh with Obie's, he got the results the city wanted, and the council was pleased with his job performance.

By the time insurance agent and former minister Jeff Miller was elected mayor in 1988, the economy had turned around, and the council's agenda was broadening to once again include issues such as homelessness and human rights. Both on the council and off, murmurings began to crop up that the city manager had acquired too much power and did too much work behind the scenes. The first serious crack in Gleason's council support appeared when two members, arguing that elected officials should have some con-

trol over administration, launched a failed attempt to limit the
city manager's authority to hire employees, contract with the city
attorney, and merge departments. A sore spot had been Gleason's
merging of police and fire into a single department without consulting the council. Still, Gleason continued to get overall positive
performance reviews into the '90s—despite his sometimes abrasive manner and the growing belief that he attempted to manipu-
late the council through the information he presented to it.

The economic development policies of the '80s appeared to
pay off in the '90s. High-tech companies such as Spectra-Physics,
Symantec, and Molecular Probes set up shop in the city. In 1995
Hyundai announced plans to open a semiconductor chip manufacturing plant in West Eugene. But by then, the council's temperament had changed. A four-member anti-Gleason bloc had
formed on the council in 1993, and it disliked both the city
manager's continued pro-growth agenda and his way of working
behind the scenes to advance it. Although the fifth vote needed to
oust Gleason never materialized, clashes between the city manager
and the council frequently occurred. In one case the council attempted to reinstate a staff position that Gleason had eliminated,
raising the question of whether the council was exceeding its authority by meddling in administrative affairs.

Gleason wasn't the only problem the council had—in-fight-
ing, insults, and general strife unrelated to the manager marred
council meetings. Mayor Ruth Bascom, the city's first woman
mayor, found it impossible to build consensus with the group on
much of anything. The atmosphere grew so hostile—at one meeting a councilor flung a sandwich at a city employee—that some
staff refused to attend council meetings.

In 1996 council turnover undid the anti-Gleason faction, and
Gleason, having outlasted his enemies, resigned to take a less stress-
ful job as manager of the Lane County Fairgrounds. Not long before leaving city hall he received the top award of the International
City/County Manager's Association, which noted his contribu-
tion to the city's nationally recognized wetlands program, its air-

port expansion, its community policing effort, and its use of a community survey to involve the public in budget cuts.

Vicki Elmer

The council picked Vicki Elmer, who had been head of public works in Berkeley, California, as Eugene's next city manager. Elmer was an administrator with a liberal bent who came recommended as smart and innovative. She talked a lot about "transparency" and "community-based government," which seemed to be just the antidote to the Mike Gleason years. But as it turned out, she was the wrong person for the job in just about every respect. She didn't have the experience or skills needed to oversee the city, nor did she have the temperament to successfully manage its 1,300 employees. In her one short year, city hall was thrown into disarray, and an atmosphere of fear and confusion prevailed.

Elmer rarely asked for the advice of her staff before making decisions. She consistently used the buzzwords "cost-effective," "transparent," and "community-based," but her actual mode of operation seemed just the opposite. At her annual review, both council and staff accused her of spin-doctoring and out-and-out lying. One executive staff member wrote, "If transparency is a value, then why does she ask staff to bury information, cook the numbers, or explain away information? I question her commitment to the community."

She was hired just as major budget cuts were needed in the wake of Measures 47 and 50, which limited property tax revenues. She began the difficult process of trimming both services and staff only weeks after she got here, but made a political gaffe when she spent thousands of dollars to redecorate her own office. Three months after she was hired, a protest over the removal of more than two dozen trees from the construction site of Broadway Place erupted into violence. Police teargassed and pepper-sprayed protesters. As the city's chief administrator she came under fire for the way the city handled the incident.

The first major public indication that something was amiss

was the firing of Leonard Cooke in January of 1998. Cooke, the city's first black police chief, was extremely popular with the minority community. Elmer flatly denied that she had pressured him to leave, but a letter made public from his attorney told a different story.

The staff lost further confidence in her integrity after Elmer proposed in a meeting to move the city's long-time human rights analyst to another position. When a flood of calls to her office made it obvious that she had made a big mistake, she denied ever considering the change in an e-mail that went out to her entire staff. Her quick retraction set off waves of criticism.

Her annual review was scathing. Several councilors wrote that Elmer didn't take the time to make policy recommendations to the council, or to discuss them. Her interest in community involvement did not show itself in the way she operated. One councilor wrote, "I have no sense of the direction of organizational change. Change without clear expectations or outcomes tends to be chaotic and works against the public good."

The staff was much harder on her, turning in written recommendations that read like an indictment. One staff member summed it up by saying, "I never in my wildest dreams thought that one person, in conjunction with lack of leadership on Council, could cause so much chaos and destruction."

The council apparently concurred, because on March 18, 1998, it fired her by a vote of six to two. With Elmer's departure, Eugene was left with no manager, no assistant manager, no planning and development director, and no police chief. City government was in a shambles.

Jim Johnson

Once again, it was time to hire a new manager. This time, the city council stuck with the tried and true. Jim Johnson was already doing a fine job as interim manager while the post was vacant. Johnson had spent the previous twenty-three years in local city and county government, including seven as the county's chief administrator. He was known for his even-handed and low-key management style, thoughtfulness, and honesty. The council saw no reason to look any further and voted seven to one to give him the job.

Johnson was a natural fit with Jim Torrey, a hands-on, businessman mayor who was at city hall just about full time. The city began to see progress once again. Voters had approved bonds for a new library (rejected on several previous occasions) and more land for city parks. The city had a new police chief, a new planning director, and a new library and recreation director. Johnson's one-year review was glowing, with the council and mayor giving him their highest rankings in sixty-nine out of seventy-one categories. His staff gave him high marks as well. The city's engine went back to humming right along.

Gleason, curious about how Johnson got along with so many different people, once asked him the secret of his success. Johnson replied: "My job is to help people reach their goals. I cheerfully and skillfully implement even what I think are bad decisions."

As the twentieth century neared its end, a proposal was building steam to amend the city charter to permit pay for the mayor and city council. Several times over the years, this idea had made its way onto the ballot, but never beyond. However, in May 2000 a majority of voters finally agreed that the mayor and councilors should be paid ($1,500 a month for the mayor, and $1,000 for the council members, with annual adjustments for inflation). The reasoning was the same as it had been back in 1974—the last time the idea had been on the ballot. Proponents argued that the council's workload had grown so time-consuming that it was not fair to expect people to volunteer for the positions. Another argument was that pay would expand the pool of candidates to include working people who couldn't otherwise afford to serve on the council.

One argument against paying city council members was that—intentionally or not—paychecks would increase the inclination of elected officials to try to influence city administration, which the charter puts exclusively in the hands of the city manager. The tensions resulting from what councilors would feel they ought to do—no longer as volunteers but as paid city officials—and what the charter allows them to do might create pressure to change Eugene's form of government to one in which elected officials could legitimately have a hand in the day-to-day running of city business.

Three months after the compensation measure passed, the council announced that it would fulfill another one of its goals for 1999–2000 by appointing a committee to review the city charter. Among other things, the council wanted the committee to take a look at changing the city manager's role, including giving the council a say in the hiring and firing of department heads and in reorganizing city departments.

Bibliography

City of Eugene. Charter. Revised version. 1976

Frederickson, George H., editor. *Ideal & Practice in Council-Manager Government.* International City/County Management Association, 1995.

Kane, Paul. "You Say You Want an Evolution (Evolving Relationships Between City Councils and City Managers." *American City and County* (September 1999).

Mehnert, Paul Jefferey. *The Urban Development of West Eugene.* Ph.D. thesis. Eugene: Dept of Geography, University of Oregon, 1981.

Mushkatel, Alvin Howard. *Citizen Response to Annexation.* Ph.D. thesis. Eugene: Dept. of Political Science, University of Oregon, 1975.

Nalbandian, John. "The Contemporary Role of City Managers." *American Review of Public Administrators* (December 1989).

The Oregonian, selected articles, 1945–2000.

The Register-Guard, selected articles, 1944–2000.

THE RAGING TORRENT:

A HALF CENTURY OF EUGENE ACTIVISM

By Alan Siporin

"Rebellion liberates stagnant waters and turns them into a
raging torrent."
— Albert Camus

IT'S TEMPTING TO cut to the chase and plunge directly into
the raging '60s. But the springs that fed this great torrent bubbled
under the surface in the preceding decades, and it's from those
years the trickles of Eugene's activism began to emerge. Even with
the benefit of hindsight, however, many of the earliest droplets
don't appear to herald what was to come: A "starvation dinner" as
World War II wound to an end, put together by Leslie Brocklebank
and conscientious objector Charles Gray to feed starving people in
Europe; Ken Kesey and his fraternity brothers, in the mid-1950s,
turning on to the beat poetry of Ferlinghetti and Ginsberg; and a
larger, more visible stream—University of Oregon students protesting against the military draft in 1950.

Something was happening in the '50s, saturating the entire
country. Television exposed millions of middle-class white kids to
the Civil Rights movement. From the comfort of their own homes,
the baby boomers, mostly grade-schoolers at the time, witnessed
scowling white cops with billy clubs and dogs attack black women
and children. The understanding of these young white kids was
limited. They perceived black subjugation as a product of, and
exclusive to, southern white bigotry. But a stream of consciousness
had been set in motion.

The Time

Racism was everywhere, including Eugene. And it wasn't confined to the Skinner Butte cross burnings of the '20s. In 1963 the city uprooted the black community concentrated near the Ferry Street Bridge. Dan Goldrich, then a member of the Congress of Racial Equality (CORE) and the University of Oregon faculty, says CORE stepped in to assist families in relocating.

Inexorably, like a stream carving its way through clay and rock, the Civil Rights struggle moved north and west. Inner cities erupted. Many of America's middle-class, white baby boomers, then in their teens and twenties—ages of natural personal rebellion—identified with their black counterparts. But they still didn't have an inkling of the depth of black oppression.

The Vietnam War changed that. At first, opposition to the war, like white opposition to racism, was mostly altruistic. The concern was for the Vietnamese who were victims of U.S. policy. But the war escalated, and the demand for fresh troops increased. U.S. involvement in Vietnam went from a few thousand military advisors in 1963 to more than half a million troops by early 1968. The floodgates sprang open in 1964, when Congress overwhelmingly passed the Tonkin Gulf resolution. The House and Senate combined had only two dissenters. One of them was Oregon's Wayne Morse.

More and more middle-class white kids headed off to war, joining the disproportionally high numbers of African Americans, Latinos, Native Americans, and poor whites. Some returned in body bags; many came home damaged—in body or mind or both. After a while everyone knew someone who had been there, was there, or was likely to go. Draft-age men were like rats in a cage, waiting for a giant hand to reach in, pull another victim out, and hurl him against the wall. The depth of the black struggle was no longer so far removed.

Demonstrations erupted on college campuses throughout the country, including the University of Oregon. And like the Civil Rights struggle, television beamed the devastation and death of the Vietnam War—and the rebellion against it—into America's living rooms. Some activists were dedicated to nonviolent tactics. Others felt the killing of Vietnamese civilians demanded that the war be stopped by any means necessary. Fires were set inside the University of Oregon ROTC building. The physical education building burned to the ground. A powerful bomb devastated three floors of Prince Lucien Campbell Hall. Police with clubs and tear gas confronted thousands of demonstrators. As many as two hundred National Guardsmen were deployed in the streets of Eugene. The Black Panthers maintained a separate presence, skirmishing with local police and organizing breakfasts for kids.

Meanwhile, peaceful antiwar marches drew as many as four thousand participants. At one rally speakers included Wicks Beal, a city councilor who had been an observer at the Paris peace talks, businessman-mayor Les Anderson, and UO student body president Ron Eachus, who had visited Hanoi.

Community-based activists organized study groups. Campus protesters held teach-ins. Charles Gray created a display at an antiwar meeting at the South Eugene High School auditorium. A bar graph demonstrated spending on various needs such as health care and education. Gray says the bar for arms control and disarmament "amounted to a few inches while the bar for military spending went around the auditorium three times." Gray and others later painted the bar graphs on 13th Avenue on the University of Oregon campus.

As the war dragged on, the antiwar movement was infused with fresh activists—returning Vietnam vets and more kids coming of draft age. Tax-resistance work picked up, too. Individuals refused to pay the portions of their taxes that went to war. Later, in 1971, resisters produced a rubber stamp and stamped IRS leaflets with red ink that told people half their tax dollars funded war.

Eugene sent disproportionately large numbers of people to rallies in other cities, a practice that continued in the '70s, '80s, and '90s. In April 1968 a huge contingent of Eugene activists joined a gigantic antiwar march in San Francisco. Black Panthers from Eugene and Black Student Union members from the University of Oregon hoisted a banner that read: "No Viet Cong ever called me nigger." But alliances between white and black activists were often difficult. When Goldrich first opposed the war, black allies he worked with on Civil Rights issues accused him of deserting them. He was in good company. Dr. Martin Luther King Jr. caught flak for that, too.

Black and white differences weren't the only divisions. As the movement grew factionalism increased. Marion Malcolm says Eugene was still better than most places. "We lacked the sectarianism common to other communities, like Berkeley." There were divisions in Eugene, too, Malcolm says, "but you could always count on people to come together as a coalition for a march."

In 1972 more than one hundred Chicanos and Native Americans from Eugene and nearby banded together to occupy the gymnasium of the vacated Adair Air Force Base outside of Corvallis. The action coincided with the occupation of the Bureau of Indian affairs office in Washington, D.C., and was one of several demonstrations throughout the country demanding better treatment of Native Americans.

And neighborhoods organized, too. The *Whiteaker Neighborhood News* ran articles on democratic economic development. Activists lost the battle to stop the building o the Washington-Jefferson Bridge, which cut the neighborhood in half. But, Goldrich says, they "won the war by launching citizen-involved land use planning that continues today."

And beneath it all was a drum beat—literally—and a guitar lick, maybe a horn, and some vocals. Like the Civil Rights movement, the blues rolled north and west from the deep south, creating an undercurrent of rhythm-and-blues that exploded into rock 'n' roll. From Dylan to the Dead to local bands in cities and towns throughout the country, something was happening.

All these streams mixed together, sweeping over the national landscape: The oppression, the awakening awareness, battling the established powers, internal struggles, and growth within the movement, music, the birth control pill (make love not war!), the automobile—and drugs. Would the '60s have happened without LSD and marijuana? Probably. Too much was in motion. The awakening of awareness was more important than the turning on to pot and acid. But psychedelics were a short cut—another river for millions more to enter the current and add to the raging force. "Drugs aren't necessary to find grace," says Ken Kesey. But it's one of the ways he prefers "over hunger and grief."

A huge number of people had arrived at the prime age for rebellion at the same time. The baby boomers, the largest population bulge in history, had come of age. The '60s were such a rush in large part because so many individuals were experiencing similar stages of personal rebellion at the same time. A growing awareness of injustices and contradictions in the established ways and systems was fueled by national and worldwide movements for rights and justice. Under these conditions, the volatility of the time was unavoidable. Certainly, many people never went beyond getting high. They joined the party and missed the movement. But other '60s activists funneled their rebellion into an attempt to create something better—especially in Eugene.

The Place

In 1968 Bill and Cynthia Wooten opened the Odyssey Coffee House at 7th and Willamette. "Real change," Cynthia Wooten says, "necessitates a place where people could come together and talk about life and personal evolution." The Odyssey quickly became that, and more. People were drawn to the Odyssey as a music venue. Local musicians performed, including Ken Kesey and the Merry Pranksters. Paul Olswang broadcast live on KWAX and later, with the help of Tom Krumm, on a frequency that was a precursor to KZEL. A cramped closet space under the stairs was turned into Switchboard—a hot line and bulletin board where people connected for rides and housing. A Switchboard partnership with local churches allowed suburban families to offer their homes as overnight youth hostels. Eugene had become a primary destination "because it was developing an infrastructure," Wooten says.

Businesses with a distinct counterculture hue sprang up, ranging from the Crystal Ship music store to the Wildflower Garage to the People's Cafe. In the fall of 1968 the first Oregon Renaissance Fair was put together as a benefit for the Community School—an independent alternative school. Between five and six hundred people attended. From the beginning, Wooten says, the fair was seen as "more than fun in the woods and selling things." The fair was to be a demonstration for living outside the industrial world in a more natural way, "a rural marketplace where people could support themselves through the selling of hand-crafted goods." Rather than attempting to tear down the capitalist economy, fair founders hoped to create a parallel economy. "Another way," Cynthia Wooten says, "a counterculture."

Although the fair had a renaissance feel, it developed its own unique Oregon identity, reflecting counterculture and rural influences. To many, it seemed misnamed. But it was legal pressure from the California-based Renaissance Faire that forced the fair in 1977 to change its name to the Oregon Country Fair.

Gill Harrison, Lotte Streisinger, and M'lou Zahner, along with other potters, formed the Crafts Guild, primarily as a way to buy materials cooperatively. Out of that, in 1969, came the Saturday Market, an attempt to create a Latin American– or European-style urban marketplace in Eugene. In 1970 the Springfield Creamery, owned and operated by the Keseys, opened the Health Food and Pool Store in Springfield. The same year a group of young doctors and physicians started White Bird. The Willamette People's Food Cooperative opened in southeast Eugene. The Council of the Poor held meetings to organize a food co-op for Eugene's west side. Internal power struggles prevented it from getting off the ground, but some of the people who showed up wound up taking the idea and started a food-buying group that worked out of Bill and Vicky Nelson's garage.

Thirty households participated. The concept proved so popular they moved the operation to a rented warehouse at 3rd Avenue and Lincoln. In March 1972 Bill Nelson and Paul Bestler, looking to rent a different warehouse, seized upon an unexpected opportunity and bought the McDonald Candy Company building at 4th Avenue and Willamette. By then the Growers Market Food Co-op was handling more than 150 orders made up mostly of produce, grains, and cheese. They figured they could afford to buy the building with the revenue the market generated each week. With volunteer labor they could renovate the second floor of the two-story building and provide inexpensive office space for community groups. Within a year the orders were topping three hundred. The Wootens' Odyssey concept of place had evolved another step. The Growers Market Building was *owned* by the community.

And this loosely defined community even placed a voluntary tax on itself. Businesses, worker collectives, and cooperatives volunteered a small percentage of their income each month to form the Community Sustaining Fund. New businesses could apply to the fund's board to borrow seed money to get started, or existing businesses might request funds to get over a tough stretch. By 1974 the market was filling more than 550 orders a week. And volunteers put together several gigantic orders and delivered them to senior-citizen homes. As many as three thousand people in the Eugene area were getting their food through Growers Market. The downstairs remained an unimproved warehouse with drab, concrete walls and a low, barren ceiling. But every Thursday it became a bustling food market with the colors and smells of oranges, apples, bananas, and truckloads of fresh produce. People arriving in Eugene connected with others there. The building had become the gathering place for the counterculture—the community center.

The upstairs, now renovated into individual office spaces, housed a bigger, better Switchboard, Jackrabbit Printing Press, *The Augur*, Women's Press, and Hoedads. And two large separate central rooms provided free meeting space. Growers Market generated enough surplus income to help fund another group's plans to buy the Woodsman of the World Building. The WOW Hall became a community center for performing arts. Local groups, as well as touring musicians, played there. Wallflower Order, a local women's dance collective, got their start at the WOW Hall before going on tour internationally.

The People

Back in 1970 Jerry Rust, John Sundquist, and John Corbin formed the Triads, a tree-planting collective. Workers shared the profits equally. From the outset they conceived of an alternative to the tree-planting contractors, who ripped off workers for their own profits. When new workers joined the crew they became worker-owners. The three original partners had given way to many worker-partners, and the Triads renamed themselves the Hoedads (after the tree-planting tool). Within a few years they had grown to more than a hundred strong.

Similar growth spurts were happening with other worker collectives. Genesis Juice had gone from a privately owned business employing half a dozen people to a worker-owned collective of nearly two dozen. Zoo Zoos restaurant, a worker collective, took over the Fifth and Blair space once occupied by the ultra-hip, but privately owned, Lighter Brown Darker Brown Restaurant and Rescue Station.

Debbie and Charlie Glass started Starflower by selling cheese and herbs out of the trunk of their car in 1972. The couple's primary interest was in organic and natural foods, but they always conceived of Starflower as a feminist-based, non-hierarchical company. Within a few years Starflower was known up and down the west coast as a feminist outfit, run by women. When Shoshana Cohen first joined Starflower she was "in awe of the women driving these big rigs, and being so self-confident."

Historians and the media offered America's daughters few role models. Now, women were finding models among their peers. Twenty-three-year-old Jane Gibbons was "in awe" of eighteen-year-old Kate Thompson operating Jackrabbit's printing press. Crescent Construction was a women's builders' collective, Mother Kali's a feminist book store, Amazon Kung-fu, a self-defense collective. The Women's Prison League started the Women's Transitional Living Center, and the Women's Health Center collective held weekly educational sessions on women's health issues. Eugene's feminist community built a reputation as one of the strongest in the country.

Women were feeling empowered like never before. The *Roe v. Wade* decision signaled that equity in pay and the Equal Rights Amendment were worth more effort. Women's groups formed, some for political action, some for personal support.

Still, much of the same old sexism persisted in the alternative culture. Men often dominated the meetings and monopolized the reins of leadership. Some women undertook the task of educating men. Others felt the depth of sexism in society necessitated a complete separation from men.

In the midst of battling the establishment, people were turning inward, exploring their own contradictions. Marion Malcolm says, "The context of the work is a patriarchal, racist, sexist, homophobic society; therefore the issues must be dealt with internally, too." Learning about sexism was woven into the fabric of most worker collectives. Running a food co-op sometimes meant spending an entire meeting conducting self-education about sexism.

Weighing bananas, packaging granola, combating sexism— and all the while being watched by the FBI. The bureau believed members of the Weather Underground were among the many Growers Market users. Agents never spotted anyone. Right under their noses, however, *Prairie Fire*, the manifesto of the Weather Underground, was printed at night at Jackrabbit Press. And for years one of the primary coordinators of Growers Market was a guy whom everyone knew as Pogo. He turned out to be Silas Trim Bissell, wanted by the FBI for an antiwar bombing in Seattle. Agents probably came face to face with Pogo and never knew it. Maybe all hippies looked alike to G-men.

For several thousand people the Growers Market Building had

become the epicenter of a new ideal, with all the various collectives, cooperatives, workers' guilds, and alternative businesses radiating outward. Jane Gibbons remembers "really belonging, a sense of family and of cooperation." It was 1975. The Vietnam War was finally over, and Richard Nixon was on the run. The counterculture was winning. So what happened?

The Grassroots

What did *not* happen was activism's decline. Quite the opposite. That single raging current that was the Vietnam era split into dozens of major rivers. It had to. Too many different problems demanded attention. And enough leadership had developed for activists to tackle numerous separate causes. Protest had not given way to community-building. They coincided. And intertwined. But this fragmentation from a single issue (the war) had a downside, too. Without central leadership projecting a cohesive national strategy, global corporate power continued to expand. Perhaps it would have grown even more powerful, however, without numerous grassroots victories.

Activists say as many as ten nuclear power plants were scheduled for construction in Oregon. But thanks in large part to the statewide bicycle tour of the Eugene-based Dr. Atomic's Famous Medicine Show and Lending Library, Trojan became the only nuclear power facility in Oregon. Activists from Oregon also battled Washington State's nuclear power industry, the Trident missile base in Bangor, the Hanford nuclear reservation, and the B1 bomber. Eugene became the first community in the nation to vote on its nuclear future, approving a bond issue in 1968. But activists Jane Novick and Chris Attneave mobilized a broad coalition, including housewives, farmers, and fisher people, and in 1970, voters reversed the earlier decision.

Dozens of separate grassroots efforts combated the spraying of chemicals using 2,4-D and 2,4,5-T. Barbara Kelley led the early charge in Eugene with SOS, Save our Ecosystems. From the nearby Five Rivers area, Carol Von Strum battled sprays and published *A*

Bitter Fog, alerting people to the presence of dangerous chemicals all around them. In 1978 the Northwest Coalition for Alternatives to Pesticides was formed, from seventeen anti-spray groups. Led by Mary O'Brien, Norma Grier, and others, NCAP became a nationally renowned research arm and clearinghouse, freeing up local groups to concentrate their efforts on halting spraying in their own backyards.

Organically Grown, a co-op of Eugene-area farmers, formed. The Willamette Valley Immigration Project organized to educate and defend migrant farm workers and tree planters in Oregon. The Northwest Forestry Workers Organizing Committee researched the range of working conditions in the forests. Both groups were Eugene-based.

Perhaps the early trickles to save Oregon's old-growth forests began with Rachel Carson's publication of *Silent Spring* in 1962. Or on the first Earth Day in 1970. But it was the Reagan years that turned the war of the woods into another flood of activism. Dozens of groups sprang into action, fighting in the courts, in Congress, and in the forests. Eugene members of Earth First! and the Cathedral Forest Action Group blocked logging roads in an effort to halt logging and awaken the media. Meanwhile, Eugene-based groups like the Western Environmental Law Clinic, the Oregon Natural Resources Council, the Native Forest Council, and numerous national environmental organizations went to work lobbying Congress and filing suits in court.

Forest activists not only had to battle the powerful timber industry; they also had to deal with the federal agencies that administered the national forests. Like Vietnam vets whose war experiences awakened them to the contradictions of U.S. policy, Forest Service workers, too, rebelled against their agency's actions. When Jeff DeBonis, after more than a decade as a Forest Service timber-sale planner, founded the Association of Forest Service Employees for Environmental Ethics, he was flooded with members.

Environmental activists made at least one big mistake. They didn't seek out alliances with timber-industry workers. However, one group, Eugene's Labor Action Committee, understood the need to establish ties between leftist activists and traditional blue-collar workers. They published a paper, *Stand Up*, and distributed it to workplaces throughout Eugene. The organization faded in the early eighties, but Dennis Gilbert, along with other original members, established the Eugene Springfield Solidarity Network in 1989, in large part to support the Morgan-Nicolai door plant workers in their strike. ESSN has been supporting workers and building relationships between various groups ever since.

While some Eugene activists battled against local and regional problems, others fought evils globally, often because the causes originated in the United States. Eugene's South African–divestiture movement recognized the relationship between apartheid and the finances behind it and eventually succeeded in forcing the state of Oregon to withdraw its investments from South Africa. Activism against U.S. policies in Central America began with self-education. Soon, members of groups like the Eugene Committee for a Free Chile and the Committee in Solidarity with Central American People were enlisting popular support to counter the devastation and murder financed by the U.S. in Chile and El Salvador, and later in Nicaragua and Guatemala. Innovations like the sanctuary movement brought these Third World struggles home, and organizations like Witness for Peace placed U.S. activists in the lands and homes of the victims of U.S. policy.

McKenzie River Gathering, a social-change granting foundation, started in 1976 with money donated by Charles Gray and Leslie Brockelbank. Their inherited wealth troubled them because of stock connections to military contracts. Gray says they perceived "the U.S. economy as a system with inherent injustices." They felt compelled to live simply and to form community. Giving away their wealth was only part of it. They gave up the decision-making power, too, gathering a group of activists together to determine who would get the funds. Five years later, when the funds ran out, MRG recruited new inherited wealth and established itself for the long haul. During the next two decades MRG would fund hundreds of Oregon groups advocating for human rights, community building, and the environment.

MRG located in the Growers Market Building. NCAP rented an office there, too. Mike Gravino established Garbagios, a recycling operation, in an unused downstairs portion of the building. The significance of a central gathering place not only played out with the Growers Market Building and the Odyssey Coffee House, but also with the CALC office.

Clergy and Layman Concerned, established nationally in 1965 to oppose the Vietnam war, opened a Eugene chapter in 1966, and *Layman* in the group's name became *Laity*. Linda Reymers, longtime MRG staff person, says CALC became the "incubator" for numerous new organizations. Coalitions involved several groups, but CALC was often the key player, and Marion Malcolm, more often than not, the key staff person.

Several groups dedicated to Central America work trace their roots to CALC. When President Carter moved to bring back the draft in 1979, a number of groups and individuals, spurred by Vietnam veterans, mobilized. CALC's guiding hand played a crucial role in the formation of the Coalition Opposing Registration and the Draft. CALC staffer Cynthia Kokis worked directly on the Nestle boycott, started in response to Nestle's promotion of their baby formula in Third World countries. Local South Africa work originated in the CALC office, too. CALC efforts continued throughout the '80s and '90s. The Second Chance Renters Rehab Program got its start there. And CALC organized a multicultural kids' camp that was the genesis for a cadre of young activists called Youth for Justice.

By the early '80s the Growers Market food co-op had peaked, and orders were declining, but the upstairs remained a community center. Through the years the Chicano Affairs Center, Eugene Peaceworks, the Industrial Workers of the World, the Saturday Market office, National Abortion Rights Action League, the Lavender Network (a gay rights organization), the Oregon Natural Resources Council, the Western Fire Ecology Center, and the Big

Mountain Support Group (a Native American rights group) rented space. As the century came to a close, tenants included Support Coalition, a federation of eighty groups in eleven countries working on human rights in the mental health system, the Center for Rural Affairs, and MRG, still going strong.

The Augur, an alternative paper, had long since folded. It didn't take long for the *Willamette Valley Observer* to fill the breach, but several years later, it went under, and a void set in. *What's Happening* began as an events calendar. Eventually, it took on local reporting, too, filling Eugene's need for an alternative paper. Later, it changed its name to *Eugene Weekly*. However, the *Weekly* didn't satisfy everyone's alternative needs, and *The Other Paper* formed. *The Comic News* attempted to fill the humor void.

From the end of the Vietnam War to the turn of the century, new organizations continued to spring up throughout Eugene. Groups addressed a wide range of issues from animal rights to disability rights. The Lane County chapter of the American Civil Liberties Union began protecting a broad range of citizens' rights, beginning in the late '60s. A couple of decades later, Sponsors formed to assist former inmates making a transition from prison to society. Organizations ranged from the Rape Crisis Network to the Eugene-Springfield Tenants Union. Eugene-based groups included Mobility International, the Interfaith Sanctuary Network, the No-GWEN Alliance (a group that stopped an Air Force communications tower from being built in Eugene), and AIDS support groups. When incidents of racist, anti-Semitic, and anti-gay violence increased, Communities Against Hate formed. Eugene's Spencer Butte Middle School became the nation's first school to declare itself a racism-free zone.

Activism occurs throughout America, but Malcolm says Eugene "is a place where you can still believe what you do makes a difference." She says activists always had access to their congressional representatives. And unlike representatives in California and Washington, Oregon representatives weren't beholden to military contractors because Oregon didn't have a defense industry. And

Oregonians cared about integrity and independence, Malcolm says. "It's no accident that Oregon had Wayne Morse." Goldrich says House members Charles Porter and Jim Weaver deserve credit, too, "for taking stands that weren't always popular."

Although activism continued on many fronts, the notion of a counterculture did lose steam. The success of the Oregon Country Fair casts some doubt on that hypothesis. Back-to-the-landers disappeared from the Eugene scene, but showed up for this annual gathering of the tribes. Others, though, went back to the big city, as Seattle and San Francisco lured people with better jobs and more wealth. Urban renewal eliminated the Odyssey. Growers Market shrunk below one hundred orders from the peak days of more than 550. Starflower closed.

Growers Market's success spurred private health-food stores to open in various neighborhoods throughout Eugene. This coincided with more people working regular hours, making their co-op time commitment difficult to fulfill. Later, even mainstream supermarkets began to carry the bulk foods once found only in alternative stores. The co-ops had been co-opted.

Cynthia Wooten says, "We were victims of our own success." And issues like land use, growth, and natural resource laws made it clear that alternative folks had to play the game in the mainstream political arena. Bill Wooten ran for the state senate in 1970, and for a county commission seat in 1972, losing both attempts. By 1976, using the people power of Hoedads, Jerry Rust won election to the Lane County Commission. Cynthia Wooten won seats on the Eugene city council and, later, the state legislature. Ron Eachus, the former University of Oregon student body president and antiwar leader from the late '60s, became chair of the State Public Utility Commission in the '90s, where he battled corporate powers like US West.

In 1976, Ken Kesey gathered some of the most forward-thinking people in the state at the Bend in the River Conference. Wooten says, "It was akin to convening a new party." Perhaps the event was ahead of its time. People talked about direct democracy through electronic voting. But the Internet was still years away. Neverthe-less, networking would be the legacy of Bend in the River. Pro-gressive connections were made there that continued until the end of the century.

The Opposition

Activists were making inroads, but the counterculture decline ac-celerated during the '80s. Dan Goldrich thinks Ronald Reagan had an enormous impact, "reorienting the whole political culture to his competitive, individual thinking—knocking out democratic, cooperative-style thinking."

Reagan energized conservatives at the grassroots level, too. From anti-abortion activists to timber-industry workers, the Right mo-bilized. Progressives questioned the legitimacy of calling organiza-tions like the Yellow Ribbon Coalition "grassroots" when they were financed by corporate funds. But there was no doubt many blue-collar workers resented liberal gains and were countering with their own brand of activism.

Battling the military-industrial complex had been daunting enough. Now progressive activists faced a mass movement calling itself the Religious Right and claiming the moral authority from God. In Oregon, an anti-gay charge was led by Lon Mabon and the Oregon Citizens Alliance. They had some successes. Spring-field became the first city in America to pass a law to single out gays and lesbians for discrimination. But activists mobilized quickly. Huge numbers of heterosexuals as well as gays and lesbians stood up for human rights. Statewide measures similar to the Spring-field ordinance were defeated. Singling out one group of people for discrimination had undermined the conservative Christian claim to a moral high ground.

George Bush's war against Iraq demonstrated how much the government had learned about countering activism. A well-orches-trated public relations campaign convinced a large majority that Saddam Hussein was a new Hitler who murdered babies. But ac-tivists saw the same foreign policy contradictions that were present in Vietnam and Central America. They went to work, educating and demonstrating. And Eugene, once again, proved to be one of the leading centers of protest in the country.

The counterculture had failed to create an Ecotopia in Eugene, but the battle to hold the ecological line continued into the '90s. Citizens' groups lobbied for less growth, defeating several projects that would have brought more jobs to Eugene, but more congestion as well. And, in some cases, dangerous chemicals, more pollution, and destruction of wetlands.

Within days of the 1995 press conference announcing the decision by Hyundai, a multinational corporate giant, to build a huge computer chip factory in West Eugene, concerned citizens were calling each other. Neighborhood groups led the initial charge, but in no time at all Citizens for Public Accountability had formed. The concerns varied, ranging from doubts about the advisability of building on a wetland sight to the use of toxic chemicals to Hyundai's hiring practices.

In the final year of the century Eugene's media spotlight shined on a new group of activists calling themselves anarchists. The problems they sought to address were familiar—corporate destruction of resources and people. But the anarchists complained their ideas received no coverage until they destroyed property. This debate wasn't new, either. Seventies activists who occupied the Trident base in Bangor refused to cut barbed wire when they scaled the fence because they had decided against destroying property. They got plenty of attention. On the other hand, Charles Gray received comparatively little coverage in 1983, when he and others nearly died, fasting for forty days to protest the nuclear arms race.

Whether activists are right or wrong on any given issue or tactic, vigilance by the citizenry is essential. How much greater would the oppression of people of color have been without the Civil Rights movement? How many more would have died in Vietnam, and how many other Vietnams would there have been? How many nuclear power plants would dot Oregon's countryside today? Would the countryside even be inhabitable if not for antinuclear activists? For democracy to work, activism should be the norm. For many people in Eugene, for the last half century, it has been.

Oregonian Ben Linder, the first American killed in Nicaragua, wrote in his journal upon his arrival there, "So why am I here? Adventure is part of it. Proving myself is also part. Doing good is a very large part. The rest I guess will be known in time."

Perhaps all activists should ask themselves Linder's question. Are they here only for adventure? Or are they here to do good?

But nonactivists in a democratic society must ask themselves a question, too—Henry David Thoreau's query of his friend Ralph Waldo Emerson. In 1846 Thoreau was jailed when he refused to pay his taxes because of his opposition to the Mexican War. Emerson visited him in jail and asked, "What are you doing in there?" Thoreau reportedly replied, "What are you doing out there?"

Author's note: I considered writing this essay in first person because of my direct involvement in several of these groups. However, my leadership roles were limited to a relatively small number of these organizations. For the sake of full disclosure, I participated in the decision making in the Grower's Market, the Grower's Market Building, MRG, and the Coalition Opposing Registration and the Draft.

Bibliography

The Augur, selected articles, 1970–1973.

Camus, Albert. *The Rebel. An essay on Man in Revolt.* Vintage, 1951. First American edition, 1954.

Drukman, Mason. *Wayne Morse: A Political Biography.* Portland: Oregon Historical Society Press, 1997.

Eugene Register-Guard, 1970–1977; *The Register-Guard*, 1989–1999.

Hartzel, Jr., Hal. *Birth of a Cooperative: Hoedads.* Eugene: Hulogosi Communications, Inc., 1987.

Kruckewitt, Joan. *The Death of Ben Linder: The Story of a North American in Sandinista Nicaragua.* Seven Stories Press, 1999.

Masse, Mark H. "Healing House: The Colorful History of White Bird Clinic." *Lane County Historian* (Fall 1994): 61–67.

Thoele, Michael. *Bohemia: The Lives and Times of an Oregon Timber Venture.* Portland: Oregon Historical Society Press, 1998

Zinn, Howard. *A People's History of the United States.* New York: Harper Collins, 1980.

THE CITY IS THE PEOPLE:

THE HISTORY OF ADVOCACY FOR

GAY AND DISABLED RIGHTS

by Gretchen Miller

AT MID-CENTURY, Eugene, like most other cities, successfully ignored various types of residents who did not "fit in." Gay and lesbian people were accepted if they did not "flaunt" themselves; that is, they were acceptable if they kept quiet, made their sexual orientation and family structure invisible, and caused no trouble. Disabled people were in a somewhat similar situation. Parents were encouraged to institutionalize retarded or mentally disabled children. Physically disabled children were home-schooled or went to special, separate schools. Physically challenged people, people with limited mobility, were generally expected to stay home. This changed fairly quickly during the last half of the century, a time period when Eugene moved from hiding away to accepting, encouraging, even appreciating several different kinds of residents.

Gay Rights

In New York City, on June 28 and 29, 1969, outside a gay bar called The Stonewall, gay men, drag queens, transvestites, and others, tired of being rousted, arrested, and beaten by police, fought back. The Stonewall Riot is generally regarded as the dawn of the age of gay rights in America. The Civil Rights movement of the 1950s and 1960s, which brought the organization of class as well as racial justice to the fore, provided the groundwork for this and other gay rights protests. Stonewall brought a similar movement to gay men. A few years after Stonewall, the gay rights movement arrived in Eugene.

Although homosexuals certainly lived in Eugene before then, they had no obvious gathering place or public culture. Gay people often went to Portland to socialize. Prior to the 1950s, gay men gathered at the Osborne Hotel bar (called Room 13). Couples owned businesses together in Eugene and were invited out socially together, but no one mentioned it. Closeted decorum was the rule. In the 1960s, Seymour's restaurant was a gathering place for gay men, along with the Hunter Room at the Greyhound bus depot, a mixed gathering place where people of all sexual persuasions felt equally welcome. That space eventually became Perry's, which was known as the gay bar in town for years afterward. Later in the decade, the Riviera Room bar behind Seymour's became the lesbian bar, which was also accepting of others who felt unwelcome elsewhere, including interracial couples.

Social hot spots aside, the first organized gay rights group in Eugene was the Gay People's Alliance. The GPA began organically, as so many groups in Eugene seem to, in October 1970, when a speaker from the Gay Liberation Front in Portland spoke at the Erb Memorial Union on the University of Oregon campus. The room was packed that night with forty or fifty men and women of all cultures and backgrounds, most of them university age, but a fair sprinkling of older people, too. They were an enthusiastic crowd, and after the speech, many adjourned to Bill and Cynthia Wooten's Odyssey Café downtown. That night, they agreed on a regular meeting time for a continuing group, the GPA. In 1975, the GPA became a UO-affiliated organization called the Gay and Lesbian Alliance (GALA). The organization is known today as the Lesbian, Gay, Bisexual, and Transgendered Alliance (LGBTA).

Dick Crawford recalls that after the first GPA meeting he received telephone calls from gay men, faculty members, and adults employed in the community, all of whom were appalled at the openness of the participants. Although he was on the UO faculty himself, Crawford supported the younger GPA members. From then on, he says, he had no older friends and almost entirely socialized with younger men. He says the older men, who had previously been his friends, never came out, but spent the rest of their lives living in the closet, which had been the rule until the 1970s. Crawford became a spokesperson for gays and lesbians in classrooms and public forums.

The GPA quickly began to work toward a "gay rights ordinance," a city ordinance that would outlaw discrimination on the basis of what was then called sexual preference. The GPA proposed the ordinance to a skeptical Human Rights Commission in July 1972. GPA members painstakingly educated and ceaselessly lobbied the HRC for six months. At first the HRC's reaction was dubious. The chair of the commission, Bobby Edwards, an African-American man, indicated that he believed homosexuality to be unnatural and resented attempts by homosexuals to compare their plight to that of blacks.

Roy Poole, an African-American doctoral student at the UO, voted for the ordinance as a statement of opposition to discrimination. José Romero, the only Latino on the commission, said that at the beginning of the process he was inclined against the ordinance partly because of "cultural bias" against homosexuals and partly out of fear that the commission's anti-discrimination efforts would be diluted if more groups were added. After six months of study and work, Romero decided that the ultimate question was "whether discrimination against homosexuals was, in fact, occurring." Concluding after the hearings that it was, he cast the deciding vote to recommend the ordinance to the city council.

The recommendation went to the council in November 1973, on the same day that the gap in the Watergate tapes was announced. The *Eugene Register-Guard* reported that the Eugene City Council voted "along sex lines" against the ordinance: The five male councilors voted against the ordinance, the two female councilors for it. Mayor Les Anderson, who would only vote in case of a tie, commented, "I think the trend is in your favor, and I think someday your request will come because it involves fair treatment for all. But at the present time I see no particular benefit for the city of Eugene to stand alone, to experiment...."

Anderson was right on both predictions—the time for the ordinance did come eventually. And Eugene was never willing to "stand alone" in the forefront of the movement. These early efforts laid the foundation for the later ordinance, as each time the subject was raised, it was more acceptable to more people.

On Sunday, June 27, 1976, in honor of Stonewall Day, supporters of the gay community rallied at City Hall and marched to Washburne Park. In previous weeks, paint had been spattered on the walls of the Riviera Room, eggs thrown at patrons leaving the bar, and a dead possum left on the doorstep. Several gay men and lesbians reported telephone death threats. On the Tuesday night after the march, rocks were thrown through windows at Starflower, a lesbian, feminist, natural food collective, with a note saying, "Queers not welcome here." Starflower's delivery truck windshields were broken by chunks of cement, and the word "queer" was spray painted on a truck. Although the support rally had encouraged another outburst of homophobic vandalism, gay people continued to organize. The idea of a gay rights ordinance surfaced again.

Again, supporters painstakingly educated the city council, working with any member who was at all receptive, attempting to put a face on homosexuality. Terry Bean, the owner of Cassaday's, a gay tavern on 13th Avenue, was influential in the campaign from the beginning. Don Powell, who had chaired the successful election for kindergartens in District 4J the year before, was another. Powell had worked with councilor Betty Smith during the kindergarten campaign, as well as with most of the other progressive and education-minded politicians in town, and he called on those friendships and alliances in the gay rights campaign.

UO law professor Dom Vetri drafted the ordinance, and on October 24, 1977, after long hours of hearings, the council passed the ordinance 5–3. Because the vote was so close, another was required, and the ordinance was officially adopted a month later, on November 28, 1977. Opponents promptly filed referendum petitions, and the struggle continued.

A tremendous coalition developed to oppose the referendum, including straight as well as gay people. Many gay people, who had never dreamed they would ever do so, came out to strangers, going door to door or appearing at forums, explaining what the ordinance meant to them. Efforts were widespread across the community. A theatre group called Footlight Faggots and Lesbian Thespians formed, with Connie Newman, Jena Bisgyer, Chuck Spencer, Sho Cohen, Sally Sheklow, and others, putting on performances around the community. The group tried to combine visibility, education, a get-out-the-vote drive, and humor. When Sally sang, "I'm a D-Y-K-E dyke," it said something about presence in the community, in a most good-natured but inarguable way. Supporters raised more than $50,000, a record at the time.

The campaign was rocky at times as the "No on 51" campaigners had trouble agreeing on strategy and tactics. Relations between gay men and lesbians, as well as between gay and straight campaigners, were often strained. Despite resolutions to work together, separatist tendencies among the lesbians and gay men had the two groups meeting separately from time to time. The organized group, called Eugene Citizens for Human Rights (ECHR), decided to act by consensus and to end each meeting with a session criticizing how the meeting had run. Some strong gay rights supporters quit participating in the organized campaign and continued to work on their own. The campaign continued with great effort, and the number and quality of volunteers of all types was overwhelming at times. Vetri and Rosemary Batori, a long-time feminist activist in town, were co-chairs of the ECHR and spoke at many churches, to civic groups, on radio and TV programs, and anywhere voters might be found. Bean and Powell continued to organize, raising money and consciousness.

The issue was the talk of the town, which was seen as a victory for gay rights: If the subject was talked about at the dinner table and on the front page of the newspaper, it must be a respectable topic. The issue was argued in other campaigns that year. At one city council candidates' forum, as most of the opponents of the referendum pussy-footed around the issue, Eric Hawes, councilor from the Bethel area, simply responded, "I am not a bigot," and sat down. Gay people wore buttons reading, "What do gay people want? Ask me." For many people, the decision each day, or even several times a day, whether and where to wear the button, meant coming out in ways and to people that they never had. The trend was irreversible.

Despite best efforts, the referendum succeeded and the ordinance was repealed, 22,898 (61%) to 13,427 (37%), abolishing the gay rights law in May 1978. The loss was devastating to many people, who had somehow, despite knowing better, believed that if they did their utmost for a good cause, what was right would prevail. The organizational experience, however, was valuable as even bigger electoral struggles were still to come. The gay and lesbian community and its allies gained enormously in political sophistication and experience during the campaign, and the lessons were remembered.

In 1987, Governor Goldschmidt issued an executive order banning discrimination in employment by the state on the basis of sexual orientation. The Oregon Citizens Alliance immediately filed petitions for a referendum that would overturn the order. Lane County organized in opposition to the statewide measure, which was put before the voters in 1988. Harriet Merrick, an account collection officer for the UO who had also been active in the local campaign in 1978, chaired the Lane County effort. She points out that although Ballot Measure 8 overturning Goldschmidt's order passed statewide, it failed in Lane County. Ably aided by the ACLU and its director, Dave Fidanque, Merrick sued the State Board of Higher Education, seeking to have the new statute held unconstitutional. The Board adopted rules that instructed employees to continue to comply with the previous anti-discrimination policy, while not violating any other state law. Merrick argued that the rules were confusing and contradictory at best, giving her no guidance on how she was to act as a supervisor and making her uncertain about her own position at the university. *Merrick v. State Board* (1992) held the ballot measure unconstitutional, in effect restoring the executive order.

The OCA, feeling strong after their 1988 victory with the voters, filed another statewide ballot measure, which was eventually on the November 1992 ballot. This measure would have added to the Oregon constitution language prohibiting the state from "recogniz[ing] any categorical provision such as 'sexual orientation,' 'sexual preference,' and similar phrases that include homosexuality, pedophilia, sadism, or masochism." It then required that the state "assist in setting a standard for Oregon's youth that recognizes" those unrecognized categories "as abnormal, wrong, unnatural, and perverse." The Eugene-born, and by then Portland-based, political action group, Right to Privacy, called a statewide meeting in response to the OCA filing. Alan Brown, William Warren, Aleta DeJung, George Link, Ron Schlittler, and Kathleen Cooper from Eugene drove to Salem together. The lessons of the failed campaign in 1988 were emphasized: Start early and organize the grassroots.

The group held its first meeting at Central Presbyterian Church. Twenty people signed in that night. The second "No on 9" meeting was held at Koinonia Center, with some forty-five people attending. About half the attendees were gay, roughly half were women, and not everyone was white—a trend that continued throughout the campaign. The campaign caught the edge of a wave bigger than anyone expected. The outpouring of opposition to Ballot Measure 9 from allies all over the world, and from straight allies whose support was unanticipated, was overwhelming. Lynn Pinckney tells the story of her stepfather saying that he opposed the measure, not because he liked homosexuals, which he didn't, but because if "they" could "do it" to the gays, then "they could do it to [him] next." Characterization of the issue as bigotry and discrimination, rather than as a referendum on homosexuality, was critical to the success of the campaign.

Eugeneans were more active than ever, using some of the same tactics as before, as well as new ones. Gay people came out at work, to their families, at school, at the health club, at the grocery store, at the gas station, in PTA meetings and churches, everywhere. Drama, music, and sports were pressed into the service of the campaign to make the issues real and meaningful. Money was raised in unprecedented amounts, literature mailed, doors visited, and all the mechanics of a political campaign were worked. By this time the gay community had more computer and campaign expertise, better precinct and voter targeting, and the campaign was able to use resources more effectively. But the main thing the campaign had were volunteers. Sometimes there were so many volunteers it was hard to know what to do with them all. Volunteer massage therapists rubbed shoulders of phone bankers. Volunteer bakers brought rolls and bagels for canvassers. Musicians entertained at rallies to raise money and entertained volunteers on breaks. Counselors offered free services to volunteers for debriefing. Lawn signs were everywhere. The first words our youngest son read were at a political rally, when he said excitedly, "Mom, Mom, look! That sign says 'No on 9.' "

In the spring, Sally Sheklow, Vicki Silvers, Linda Phelps, Jill Sager, and others began organizing a Pride Day celebration that turned out to be an organizing tool for the campaign. The event was held in June (as is traditional to commemorate the anniversary of the Stonewall riots) outside the community center along the Amazon Slough. Along with many others, Greg Evans, former local NAACP president, gave an impassioned speech drawing parallels between racism and homophobia and urging all victims of discrimination to unite and prevail, rather than be divided and conquered. WYMPROV! presented a patriotic medley including the crowd pleaser, "He's a Grand Old Fag." The event included booths from most of the gay-and-lesbian-operated or supportive groups in town, and many allies. Those who had been active had the chance to network and cooperate to make their actions even more effective. And, of course, the media coverage was a chance to show gay and lesbian people having a good time on a sunny Saturday in June—ordinary people of all ages and sizes, shapes and colors, just having a good time in the park.

By September 1992, 300 people marched with PFLAG (Parents and Friends of Lesbians and Gays) in the Eugene Celebration parade, wearing all colors of the rainbow, waving placards and banners. *Register-Guard* columnist Don Bishoff reported it was the "largest and loudest" contingent in the parade. At a downtown intersection on 8th Avenue, parade viewers on the tiers of the parking garage took up the chant, "1, 2, 3, 4, Equal Rights and Nothing More," with such enthusiasm that the windows of the buildings shook. That the group took a first place ribbon seemed appropriate.

The campaign was hard on a lot of people in the community. Many gay people made sure that their passports were current and kept an emergency stash of money handy just in case. Some people were refugees from Hitler, or had parents who were, or lost family in the Holocaust. Many of these people were particularly traumatized, to the point of making specific plans to flee from this persecution, if it should come to that. Such fears may sound exaggerated now, but the people who made these plans were deadly serious; they felt their lives were at stake. Counselors offered special sessions for people stressed out by Measure 9.

The OCA ballot measure failed, 60,384 to 54,832 in Lane County, and 742,271 to 564,232 in Oregon, on a swell of opposition rising in the last days before the election. Gay people across the state breathed easier for a time. The campaign had to be rerun two years later, when Measure 13, the daughter of 9, was put on the ballot by the OCA. That ballot measure also proposed a constitutional amendment, of gentler language but identical intention.

For many people the wild enthusiasm was gone, replaced by tired determination. There were still plenty of volunteers, gay and straight alike. The mailing lists were fairly current, and many people picked up just about where they had left off before. It wasn't such a party the second time. However, most activists, both gay and straight, believed that they had no choice but to continue the political fight until the OCA stopped. Once they were out of the closet or committed to equal rights, they couldn't go back. The canvassing, phone banking, fundraising, and all the political chores continued, with some of the same players and some new ones. The educational efforts continued, with more people coming out to neighbors and coworkers, perhaps without quite the same enthusiasm as before, and without as much fear of the consequences this time, but with determination. In Lane County, the vote was 41,240 "no" to 29,478 "yes." Statewide, the measure was defeated 257,100 to 236,675.

As the gay and lesbian communities become more open, more diverse, and more mainstream, it is harder and harder to describe the social and cultural events. At this writing, the most recent political event was the passage of the Eugene gay rights ordinance in 1994. I was the only attorney on the Human Rights Commission for a period during the 1990s when it became obvious that the 1976 human rights ordinances were outdated. A small subcommittee agreed to take on the project of rewriting them. They worked with deliberate speed, but after about a year presented a proposal to the HRC for a restructured human rights ordinance, based more on mediation than on enforcement and which included protection on the basis of sexual orientation, as well as source of income. In fact, the proposed ordinance lacked serious enforcement powers, but the expansion of protection was nonetheless seen by some as a threat.

The HRC was overwhelmingly supportive, as was the city council. Well-attended hearings were held at both levels. Fifty people testified in front of the city council, quoting the Bible on both sides, telling stories of discrimination and mistreatment from both sides, and generally adding to the feeling of being in a play (and not a very well-written play at that) in which everyone had said their lines many times before. In July 1994, the city council passed the ordinance. It was clear before the start of the meeting that there would be six votes in favor. A few days before the vote, local ACLU director Dave Fidanque, remembering the last go-round, pointed out that with six votes, an emergency clause could be added. Thus, the ordinance could not be referred, but instead would be subject to an initiative petition to repeal it. This would allow the ordinance to go into effect, so that an election would be held based on what actually happened when the ordinance was in place, rather than on fears and speculation. The emergency clause was added and adopted, and although opponents took out peti-tions for an initiative to repeal the ordinance, they were never turned in and no election was held.

During the period between the referendum on gay rights in 1976 and the passage of the gay rights law in 1994, the UO made great progress, too. It was the first public university to include gay and lesbian rights protection in its non-discrimination policy. It also established a President's Task Force on gay and lesbian con-cerns that led to considerable reforms on campus.

Les Anderson's prediction came true. So many other local or-dinances had been passed around the country that Eugene was nowhere near the forefront of the movement. Because of changes in society and the social climate, the "love that dared not speak its name" had become one in a range of acceptable choices for many people. But, another OCA measure was on the November 2000 ballot, and the Springfield city charter still contains the discrimi-natory provisions passed in 1992. Optimists see progress, pessi-mists see the work still to be done, activists persevere, and gay, lesbian, bisexual, and transgendered people have children and sing and dance, just like everyone else, all over town.

Rights and Advocacy for the Disabled

When Lisl Waechter arrived in Eugene in the early 1950s, she was shocked. In Germany, where she lived until her family fled Hitler, she had trained at a neuropsychiatric institute and at a specialized nursery school and had worked with severely retarded children. Here she found that the only public money spent on the mentally disabled was spent on institutions, such as Fairview, and parents were commonly urged to institutionalize their children at an early age. Waechter had worked with disabled children wherever the family stopped on their trek—she worked in a nursery school in Holland and set up a specialized program in Boston—so when her husband found work in Eugene, she started a nursery school for retarded children. It began with a meeting of parents on October 26, 1952, and at first the school consisted of five children in her dining room. Eventually it became the Pearl Buck Center and changed life for thousands of developmentally disabled children and adults.

Some of the same parents formed the Lane County Association for Retarded Children. The Unitarian church, then located at 11th and Ferry, let the group use a small building on their property. In 1954, the group became a United Way agency, which assured a little more stable funding. In 1958, they moved to the old Skipworth juvenile facility on Marcola Road, a much larger and in many ways more suitable facility, while they raised money for their own building. Money crises were nearly continuous, in part because Waechter saw the need and started the program first, believing that the funding would follow. With the help of many dedicated volunteers and staff, her faith was justified time and again.

Waechter was not an outspoken person or a public-oriented figure. She was more comfortable working with children or at home with family and a few friends. Yet for years she cheerfully gave speeches to every civic group who would have her and actively sought donations for the school from local businesses. With a great deal of community support, Pearl Buck Center opened in its own building in 1959, and continued to grow. Eventually the center received funding from local school districts to help educate children from those districts. The center cobbled together funding from state mental health funds, CETA workers, and continued local grants and donations, for two decades increasing its programs. In the '70s public schools began enrolling the trainable mentally retarded, and by 1978, or even a year or two earlier, the center had no educational programs, as the children were in public schools. It was painful for Waechter and some of her coworkers to see this, as they struggled for many years to offer parents a choice. However, federal legislation and changing expectations made the change inevitable, and Pearl Buck Center today operates a day-care program for the children of retarded adults and vocational programs for developmentally disabled adults. The public schools have taken over education of disabled school-age children.

Another community institution had a somewhat similar trajectory. The Easter Seal School provided classes for children who were physically impaired, though cognitively able. Children who use wheelchairs, braces, or crutches, for example, today are mainstreamed into all public school classes. In the 1950s, '60s, and early '70s, they went to school at Easter Seal School. In 1968 ESS started a program for children with learning disabilities, children who would certainly be in regular public school today. Easter Seal School no longer has such classes, but it does have the largest warm-water therapeutic pool in Oregon, which is used by people with all kinds of disabilities.

The city of Eugene has always officially recognized disability issues as human rights issues. The human rights committee included a commission on the handicapped beginning in 1975, and those functions were incorporated into the larger commission when the structure was changed in 1990. This has been both the cause and effect of the high profile disability issues have in town. The city usually considers access issues, noting in publicity that meetings will be held in accessible rooms, that assistance-listening devices are available on request, and that interpreters will be provided with advance notice. Although often no one takes advantage of these services, disability advocates agree that seeing this announcement makes them feel much more included as part of the commu-

nity. Just like anyone else, they could attend meetings, understand the proceedings, and make themselves heard, if they chose
to do so.

The University of Oregon had a special-education program in
the 1970s and '80s that researched and developed educational
programs for disabled students and was, perhaps, the best in the
country at the time. By the early '70s the university was running
the Specialized Training Program, which taught severely people
useable vocation skills, such as assembly of electrical parts. This
research program had major spillover effects in the community.
UO faculty like Tom Bellamy, Rob Horner, Hill Walker, and Dan
Close did internationally recognized work. Their efforts fed the
community with educated, bright, compassionate, and dedicated
people who continue to work in these fields.

The university-trained people intersected with Dorothy
McNair, another of Eugene's strong women who wouldn't take no
for an answer. McNair's son was blind and used a wheelchair. She
was initially driven by her concern that he have a full and normal
life and that he be cared for after she was unable to care for him.
She started McNair House, a group home still located on Coburg
Road, and the Exceptional Family Advocacy Center to help others
in similar situations find the resources they needed. McNair pushed
the funding and building of McNair House through the federal
Department of Housing and Urban Development in nine months,
far less time than the two-and-a-half years HUD told her to expect. She was an unusually persistent advocate for the disabled,
and even federal bureaucrats found it easier to expedite her project
than to take her calls.

There are many other venerable institutions in Eugene serving
people with disabilities. The Eugene Hearing and Speech Center,
started in 1955, was for years the largest accredited hearing and
speech center west of the Mississippi. Eugene Emergency Housing for decades provided emergency housing and stabilization for
mentally ill adults at the Hawthorne Apartments and other locations. The Ulhorn Apartments on West 13th Avenue across from

the fairgrounds, named for Bill Ulhorn who created and advocated for EEH, have apartments for head-injured adults. Marshall Peter has been with Direction Services since 1977, advising parents and people with disabilities of what is available and how to access it. That was one of many federally funded programs when it started and is now one of only two in the country that successfully made the transition to local funding without completely changing its mission. Goodwill Industries, the Laurel Hill Center, and the Alvord-Taylor Homes are just a few of the numerous Eugene institutions created and sustained with the energy of many committed staff and volunteers.

For people with physical disabilities, Eugene is one of the most accessible cities in the world. The Rehabilitation Act of 1973, federal legislation requiring some accommodation of people with disabilities, landed on receptive ground here. At least in part because of the work of the leaders mentioned above and because of the continuing work at the university, the disabled community was ready to demand access.

Shortly after Anet Mconel arrived in Eugene in 1974, she attended a women's dance at Scarborough Faire, an arcade of tiny shops with a small performance area in the back. Women were dancing without their shirts and cheerfully made way for Mconel, who has impaired mobility. This seemed a lot friendlier than the community she had recently left, San Francisco, so she stayed. In 1975 she and some friends attended a conference at the UO and created Iron Duchess, a feminist disability rights advocacy group. Iron Duchess sponsored self-defense classes for women with disabilities, ran bake sales as fundraisers, sent women to a National Organization for Women conference in Los Angeles to advocate for disability issues, and worked for accessibility locally. Mconel, Susan Sygall, and others picketed the residence where the Federal Secretary of Health, Education, and Welfare was staying, just south of town. Although he did not meet with them, the protesters believed that the coverage of their actions—women in wheelchairs on a rural Oregon road, sitting by his mailbox—favorably influenced later meetings with federal officials.

Alicia Hays is another homegrown activist. Her consistent, matter-of-fact insistence on equal access resulted in a number of successes in Eugene, including the ramp to City Hall. She was a member of the Community Development Block Grants (CDBG) committee for years, and Marshall Peter remembers working with her each year to make sure that some money went to accessibility projects (such as curb cuts) and that projects that were funded were designed with access in mind. Hays was involved with the Private Industry Council, was repeatedly president of the Eugene Commission on the Rights of the Handicapped (as it was then known), and in both capacities worked with the city building and public works departments. Quietly and behind the scenes, she helped sensitize legions of building permit inspectors to access issues so those concerns could be brought up early, while changes could be made economically.

Bjo Ashwill remembers being one of a group picketing the 5th Street Public Market because it did not have an elevator. The issue went through the Eugene Committee on the Rights of the Handicapped where the market was given a five-year extension after pleading poverty. Five years later the managers were back asking for another extension, and the protest began. Activists wheeled up and down the sidewalk in front of the market carrying signs, "Equal Access for All." A hearing in the McNutt Room was packed; many waited outside in the courtyard because the room was overfull. The market spokesman said that most of the market was accessible without an elevator, all but the third floor. Susan Sygall asked, "What if it were you in a chair?" He responded that any publicity is good publicity.

The market did put in an elevator, and since then all floors have been accessible. Ashwill recalls warmly that, at about the same time, the Smith Family Bookstore on 13th Avenue put in an elevator without seeking exemptions and without picketing or public pressure, just because it was the right thing to do. The fact that there are quite a few businesses like Smith Family is what makes Eugene an accessible city.

Ashwill worked for some years at LCC in the disabled student services unit. Although the campus was relatively accessible, there were always problems. The doors to the administration building were large, heavy, and hard for disabled people to use. The administration's response was to install a bell, so that a person in a chair could ring to be let in. Then, the people inside wanted double doors installed, because of cold air sailing in during the winter. The double doors would have made access nearly impossible for people with impairments. Ashwill and some activist students finally convinced the administration that a bell was not equal access, so automatic door openers were installed.

Ashwill has been on the Eugene CDBG advisory board, continually reminding people of access issues. In one recent housing project, 5 percent of the units were handicapped accessible. The rest were designed with one small step up into the front door. Ashwill pointed out that this design would prevent people from visiting friends in the other units, and it would be very simple to make all the units more accessible to everyone. Eugene has been fortunate to have people willing, patiently and persistently, to point out these matters over and over again.

Susan Sygall returned to Eugene in 1979 after going to Australia on a Rotary scholarship. She realized that she had an incredible experience and decided that every disabled person should have the opportunity to participate in international exchange. She and Barbara Williams, both graduate students at the UO, started Mobility International USA (MIUSA), with world headquarters in Eugene. Many people said that an international organization aimed at providing international exchange could not be run from Eugene, and suggested she move to New York City or Washington, D.C. Sygall said of those years that they accomplished so much partly because we "didn't know exactly what we were doing, [so] we had no limitations." Sygall is quick to credit "a ton" of community support as essential to the success of MIUSA, suggesting that perhaps a place like Eugene is exactly the right place for such a program. Businesses donate meals, community service organizations help with logistics, hundreds of community members open their homes for home stays, bus passes are donated for exchange participants. Sygall said this wouldn't happen in a less-supportive community.

She had help from others, including, from the very beginning, Linda Phelps, Mary Boomer (now Mary Lee Turner), and Rod Hart. At first MIUSA was under the auspices of the Lane County Wheelchair Basketball team, which was a charitable organization with IRS approval. The first $500 was given by John Alvord, which was matched by the Downtown Rotary, for $1,000 seed money. In 1983 MIUSA hosted its first international exchange of people with and without disabilities, providing home stays and organized activities. Since then the organization has organized exchanges involving more than 1,500 people and seventy-six countries.

Eugene has completely accessible buses. LTD has wheelchair lifts on every bus and has consistently been a leader in providing transportation for the disabled. LTD got the idea that equal means equal—that equal access means every bus, not every other bus or a call-a-ride system—far earlier than most transit systems. The city has used CDBG money for curb cuts at corners for years, steadily expanding the areas in which wheelchairs can freely travel. Participants in MIUSA exchanges in Eugene travel on LTD, use the curb cuts, go to movies, use the bathrooms, attend meetings, and take these ideas home to countries where disabled people are less valued. MIUSA plans the exchanges not only to share information and offer new experiences, but also to give people new skills to take home, so they can become advocates in their own communities. The home-stay process also gives Eugeneans a chance to see their town through the eyes of an outsider, always finding things to appreciate and things to improve.

During the second half of the twentieth century, Eugene was a leader in providing opportunities and access for people of all sexual orientations and for people with all kinds of disabilities.

Some people appreciated and cultivated diversity, some tolerated it, and of course some did neither, but Eugene has been a more accepting community than many. Posted on the wall of the city council chambers is a quotation from Shakespeare's play *Coriolanus*, "The city is the people." Eugene has taken steps to ensure that the city reflects and empowers all the people, not just the wealthy, the light-skinned, the straight, or the able-bodied. Never forgetting how much remains to be done, and never forgetting that eternal vigilance is the price of inclusion, we should still take time occasionally to reflect that we have been given a heritage to live up to.

DEALING WITH RACE

By Peggy Nagae

THE HISTORY OF race relations in Eugene is one of discrimination and harassment, of relocation and displacement, of marginalization and invisibility. People of color received access only to inadequate housing, or were denied housing altogether. Property deeds with restrictive covenants allowed houses to be sold only to whites. Police made stoppages based on skin color. The government conducted labor raids. Racist individuals burned crosses in the yards of people of color. But Eugene's history also includes efforts to stem the tide of racism. Many of these efforts have resulted from action by communities of color, including the local NAACP, the Latino Coalition, and the University of Oregon ethnic students unions. Others resulted from action of the mainstream white community.

According to the 1990 U.S. Census, people of color made up approximately 7 percent of Eugene's population, a rate only slightly lower than that of the entire state of Oregon, measured in the same census at about 10 percent. As the city, along with the rest of the country, moves toward greater racial diversity, citizens must continue their efforts to stop racism in all its forms.

Housing Discrimination

In the late 1940s, almost a dozen African American families lived in the Ferry Street Bridge area, dubbed "Tent City" because most residents' homes were wooden floors with a tent pitched over the top. Among these families were the Johnsons, Reynolds, and Mims, who had moved to Eugene in the early 1940s and who lived in this vicinity for a period of time. When the county wanted to change the structure of the bridge in the late 1940s, these families and dozens of other African Americans were forced to find housing in other areas.

The Reynolds family bought a house on West 11th Avenue, an area that was virtually segregated. According to Lyllye Parker, the fourth daughter in the Reynolds family, the only white people who lived on their side of the street were white women who had relationships with black men. Lyllye remembers that there were no modern conveniences, no flush toilets, and not even a well for water. But, she said, there was community. "There was a lot of love on West 11th."

Although this area was beyond the Eugene City limits, the deplorable housing conditions caused a stir in the city. In 1952, a *Eugene Register-Guard* article addressed this housing area as "The Negro Problem in Eugene: What Should We Do?" and described the West 11th area as muddy swampland. *The Oregonian* also covered the story and asked the question: "Who's responsible for helping members of a racial minority find decent housing, when they're living in an area apparently barred from installation of water, sewers or septic tanks?"

In an attempt to answer this question, organizers set up a meeting at the First Presbyterian Church. More than 100 representatives from Eugene and Lane County groups gathered to hear a discussion by a panel of government officials and state experts. Panelist Edwin Berry, executive secretary of the Portland Urban League, stated that "records of racial discrimination in Salem and Eugene are among the worst in the state." A report by the league charged "the Eugene situation as disgraceful and horrible."

Although the meeting yielded no immediate solutions, a civil rights organization called Lane County Fellowship for Civic Unity was formed in March 1952, with H.V. Johnson, a prominent Eugene lawyer and former minister, as its president. In addition to Johnson, Civic Unity's founders included a group of concerned white citizens who were from the League of Women Voters, churches, and the *Eugene Register-Guard*, as well as other civic leaders who wanted to focus on better housing and employment for the black community. There was, however, no thought of integrating Eugene, and little was ultimately accomplished for the black community.

Eugene's middle-class communities did not readily accept African Americans as neighbors, and inadequate housing continued to be the number-one complaint for many African Americans during the 1950s and 1960s.

In the 1970s Eugene resident Bill Powell recalls an incident involving an apartment complex he had purchased. The apartment manager called Powell the week after the purchase. The two had not yet met. She asked if he was the new owner, and when he said yes, she told him that she had "these niggers at the door and wondered if it was still the policy to not rent to them." He replied, "I'll be right there." When she met him at the door and saw that he was black, she asked how long she had to move out.

In the Latino community, for those whose first language is Spanish, there have also been incidents of housing discrimination. According to Guadalupe Quinn, a long-time Eugene leader in racial justice, these incidents have often involved landlords taking advantage of the language barrier. Some tenants signed agreements with no real knowledge of their content and then had to pay for things they had not broken. Or during a walk-through of the premises, the landlords checked things checked off as working when they were not.

Bill Powell said that throughout the 1970s, 1980s, and 1990s, when his family bought property, exclusionary references had been grandfathered into the deeds. One such reference was recorded in Lane County Records on November 16, 1946, and stated: "No persons other than those of the Caucasian Race shall own, use, lease, occupy . . . portion of said premises, providing that this restriction shall not prevent occupancy by domestic servants of a different race employed by an owner. . . . " He said that the lan-

guage gave him a sense of what had occurred in Lane County and
Eugene, and that his experience seemed to be pervasive.

Racial Profiling

Selective harassment based on skin color has also been a part of the
history of race relations in Eugene. In 1963 UO professors and
students organized the Eugene chapter of the Congress for Racial
Equality (CORE). One of their early studies focused on police
harassment in Eugene, which they defined as the "systematic, patterned police bias in using their authority to follow, stop and in-
terrogate Negroes." What we call racial profiling today, they called
patterned harassment, stating:

> A number of individual minority group members have tes-
> tified before the Human Rights Commission of the City of
> Eugene as to their treatment by individual policemen. Al-
> though this testimony has resulted in an impressive picture
> of patterned harassment, police officials and others have
> denied the pattern. Instead, in each case the policeman's
> behavior was considered idiosyncratic, or the result of inex-
> perience, or at worst, misguided. The testimony of the Ne-
> gro was considered reliable, and the policeman in error only
> after every conceivable excuse for the policeman's behavior
> had been exhausted. Never was a general pattern of police
> misconduct acknowledged.

In its report, CORE asserted that until systemic, patterned
harassment is understood to cause such treatment—whether as
the result of an official policy or an unofficial practice—no effective change could occur. CORE charged that where whites were in
a superordinate position, blacks in a subordinate one, and institutions had made a "historical accommodation to a substantially
segregated society," patterned harassment occurred. This phenom-
enon was not specific to law enforcement, nor did it mean that the

police necessarily had racist motivations. It involved systemic forces and the conscious allowance of a racial hierarchy.

CORE's survey found a pattern of racial differentials in police stoppage. African Americans were more often stopped than whites: 52 percent of the African Americans surveyed were stopped at least once during this period, while only 3 percent of the whites surveyed were stopped. Other findings also indicated selected stoppage based on race.

Yet when this issue was brought before the Eugene Human Rights Commission's subcommittee on city government, CORE's report was given short shrift. The committee questioned its validity and, after interviewing African Americans who had been stopped by the police, concluded there had been no pattern of harassment of minority group members by the police. In most instances, the subcommittee instead found that either there had been a good law-enforcement reason for the stop or police officers had exercised what was termed "poor judgment," which was never deemed as overt discrimination. The committee did make several suggestions, such as asking the police department to develop a procedure that would reduce multiple stops of innocent blacks, emphasize civil rights training, and recruit qualified African Americans for police work. At the same time, Eugene Police Chief Art Ellsworth and City Manager Hugh McKinley questioned the validity of CORE's report, with the latter going as far as saying that he "didn't think it was statistically sound."

Some thirty-five years later, race profiling remains a concern. African Americans and Latinos, especially, are stopped based on their race, but now there is national awareness about race profiling and even a statewide mandate for police to keep local statistics on the races of those stopped. Eugene Police Chief Jim Hill signed an official pledge in 1999, along with police officials throughout Lane County, condemning race-based profiling by any law enforcement agency and stating that the only valid police practices are those free of discrimination or suspicions engendered by race.

La Migra

Like African Americans, Latinos have also experienced seemingly uncalled-for police stoppages based on race, but Latinos also have been the target of raids by the U.S. Immigration and Naturalization Service (INS), also called La Migra. Guadalupe Quinn, program coordinator for the Network for Immigrant Justice, says that the Latino population in Eugene has grown by more than 70 percent in the 1980s and 1990s. This increased population, as well as anti-immigration sentiment characterized by the passage of Proposition 187 in California, has affected Eugene, stirring up more animosity toward Latinos.

In 1998 La Migra conducted a raid at the Aramark Company in Eugene and two months later at Latino-owned businesses in Eugene and Springfield. They also raided homes with the aid of local police. The May raid started in the early evening and continued throughout the night. According to the *La Migra (INS) Raid [Task Force] Report*, compiled by the Migra Raid Task Force, a community-based group, "The workers were kept in constant movement, while shackled on a bus [going] from one location to another with the heater on high causing nausea to many of the workers."

The raid report adds that La Migra treated workers with legal documentation as if they were undocumented workers, often transporting them miles away from their homes and detaining them for hours, after which they were released with no transportation assistance. Out of fear, many Latino children were pulled out of schools, and workers did not return to their places of employment for days.

During the May raid, the workers were handcuffed and their feet were shackled in front of their coworkers. They were told to "shut up," that they had no rights, and were accused of selling drugs. At the interrogation site, they were not allowed to use the bathroom or the telephone and had to sit on the floor, many still in tight handcuffs, for up to five hours. During questioning, INS officials gave them papers to sign, which many could not understand. It was later discovered that the papers were voluntary deportation documents. According to interviewees, those who requested a hearing were intimidated and verbally abused or told they would need to pay a $5,000 bond to get a hearing. Many were handcuffed for twenty hours without interruption and had to go to the bathroom, eat, and move around in handcuffs. Men, women, and children were flown to Juarez, Mexico, even those who had requested a court hearing.

When people from the Migra Raid Task Force met with the INS, the agency denied all allegations. Instead, it claimed the workers were treated with respect, given the option of requesting a hearing or voluntary deportation, and allowed to use the telephones. It said that they had never requested money from the workers.

From housing discrimination to patterned harassment to La Migra raids, forms of targeting left many people of color feeling that they could not live safely in Eugene.

Displacement

Twila Souers, former coordinator of the Indian Education Program for School Districts 4J, Bethel, and Fern Ridge, said that historically Native American people have suffered—at the hands of non-natives—cultural destruction, loss of language, and the taking of their land. She said that the history of native people has been one of displacement, generally to places and situations with fewer and poorer resources than once had been available.

Examples include the theft of the land on which Eugene exists, broken treaties, and Indian boarding schools. In more recent times, they include changes in funding from CETA (Comprehensive Education and Training Act) to community block grants, which caused a shift in revenue sources from the federal to the local government and a change in priorities. Under CETA, American Indian social service programs, which allowed native people to provide services for native people, received direct funds from the federal government. According to Bob Tom, retired education director of the Confederated Tribes of Siletz Indians and one of the people who started the Urban Indians of Lane County in the early

1970s, most Indian social service programs in Eugene lost money through Reaganomics and the shift to community block grants, because the monies were put in the hands of local governments to be used as they felt necessary. Often, American Indian needs were ignored.

Another example of displacement occurred in the early 1970s at the University of Oregon. George Wasson and other native students formed Speelyi Ah Ahtum, predecessor to today's Native American Student Union, in 1968. A few years later, the Native American Program, an academic support group, was established. The two organizations created a community within the university for native students, who could get academic support and have their values, background, and practices understood.

The university decided that an academic program for each different racial group was not "cost effective," that a multicultural center for all groups would be better. Program supporters believed that within the different ethnic student programs, "one size does not fit all." They believed that more than simply providing academic support, these programs served the specific emotional, social, cultural, and advocacy needs of different ethnic students who often felt alienated, isolated, and ostracized from the majority of the campus.

For Indians, the familiar struggle to retain services and resources was on again. Students, faculty, and community allies waged a nine-month campaign, brainstorming ideas, rooting out funding sources, planning a campaign, and meeting with university administrators. Not just Indian students were involved. "It used to amaze me," Bob Tom said. "I'll always remember sitting in the Longhouse where there were Asian, blacks, Chicanos, and white students strategizing." But in the end, the program was collapsed into one for all groups and relocated to a multicultural center. For this community, the loss of the program was not about cost-efficiency, consolidation, or nonduplication of resources; it was about being displaced and losing a part of their community.

Invisibility

Displacement was also the experience of Asian Americans across the country during World War II, when many Japanese were sent to relocation camps. But invisibility has also been part of the Asian American experience in Eugene.

Many long-time Eugene residents, such as Art Johnson, Ada Lee, Ken Nagao, and Tony Lum, recall that very few Chinese and Japanese even lived in Eugene during the forties and fifties. Lee, who moved to Eugene in 1954 to attend Northwest Christian College and is now a local businesswoman, recalled that those who did live in town taught at the university or owned small businesses, such as restaurants. Angie Dean, founder of the Filipino American Association and one of the founders of the Eugene Asian Council, said that there were Filipino women in Eugene right after World War II. They had either married Anglo-American soldiers or Filipino men who had immigrated to the area. In the late fifties, Tony Lum became the first Asian American in a fraternity at the University of Oregon.

During the 1970s and 1980s Asian Americans became politically active and worked with other people of color to bring better understanding and acceptance of diversity issues to the Eugene 4J School district. Asian-American teachers and community activists like Misa Kawai Joo, longtime activist and teacher at Jefferson Middle School, and Ansellmo Villanueva, minority community liaison for District 4J School District, participated in a Multicultural Education Committee and a Racism Task Force for the district. They advocated for an equity specialist position to respond to racism. Asian Americans also joined city commissions and changed the complexion of those groups. Joo said that many had been the founders of the Asian American Student Union at the UO, where they started political, social, and cultural activities focused on Asian American issues.

Active and involved, many Asian Americans feel they have had good relations within the community and that they have gained a voice. But others feel differently. In 1995, Garrett Hongo, an author and professor in the University of Oregon's creative writing program, wrote an essay entitled "Lost in Place" for the *Los Angeles Weekly*. The essay described his experiences in Eugene as a father of two sons, having to grapple with issues of race and identity, as a person of color, and speaking openly about his feelings of isolation and alienation. He wrote, "People in the supermarkets assume I'm a foreign student on academic sojourn. I'm not supposed to be here—I'm not part of their community, but just passing through, using the post office or dry cleaner. I have become a stranger in their village. An exile."

The *Eugene Weekly* reran Hongo's article and an avalanche of response followed. The issue disappeared faster than any other, and for more than a year afterward, people asked for copies. People talked about it all over Eugene. Then-editor Debra Gwartney recalls walking into a pottery sale at Faye Nakamura's and hearing people talk about it. She joined the conversation and half of those present admonished the paper for running an article that was tearing the town in two. The other half thanked her for reprinting it because they said it was about time people talked about those issues.

For some Asian Americans, Eugene has been a haven of good business and good relations. For others, with their history untold and their presence unknown, the experience has been dehumanizing. Invisibility has meant marginalization and pressure to assimilate into the dominant culture, though assimilation is neither wanted nor possible.

Human Rights Commission

Through governmental bodies such as the city council, Human Rights Commission, and Eugene police department, and through many county-based organizations, attempts have been made to achieve racial justice and pluralism in the city.

Established in 1964 by vote of the Eugene City Council, the Human Rights Commission duties include serving as a watchdog on diversity issues and referring and investigating complaints. Since its inception the HRC has conducted numerous surveys and advised the mayor and city council regarding resolutions and ordinances concerning human rights and issues of race, gender, sexual orientation, national origin, disabilities, and age.

Since 1969 the city council has passed ordinances prohibiting discrimination in employment, housing, and public accommodation based on race, color, religion, sex, or national origin. The council declared that such discrimination deprives people of their rights and also "menaces the institutions and foundations of a free democratic society and threatens the peace, good order, health, safety and general welfare of the community."

Have these actions made a difference in race relations? Yes, said UO sociology professor Lawrence Carter, who was actively involved in the Eugene civil rights movement, and Guadalupe Quinn, director of the Network for Immigrant Justice. They said that open-housing laws provided something of a safety net for communities of color against blatant discrimination and a basis for forcing recalcitrant landlords and property owners to capitulate. Other state laws prohibiting local law enforcement agencies from using their resources for detecting or apprehending persons solely based on their foreign citizenship have also formed a kind of safety net, especially for Latinos. Quinn said that her group has used this law to remind the Eugene police that they are not to help the INS, and it has been effective.

New Initiatives

Race issues in Eugene have created conflicts but also have been catalysts for new ways to find new expression, maintain radical perspectives, and stop the erasure of people's histories. Many in the community have found ways to foster their culture and maintain their dignity. Here are a few examples.

• Racism Free Zones: Racism Free Zone schools were developed after an African-American sixth-grader in 1986 protested the presence of pictures depicting African Americans being lynched in his classroom. After complaining to his teacher to no avail, Zakee Ansari went home and told his mother, Bahati Ansari, who took her complaint to the teacher and principal at Jefferson Middle School and to the school superintendent, Margaret Nichols. When Ansari described the school debacle, Nichols was said to have responded, "I don't know anything about racism, but is it anything like sexism? I understand sexism."

"I believe it is," Ansari answered. From that conversation, a National Racism Free Zone was formed at Jefferson, and Cal Young and Spencer Butte Middle Schools and Adams Elementary have adopted similar creeds. Each year the schools hold annual Rededication Ceremonies, where every student and staff member signs the Racism Free Zone Declaration.

Students at these schools say they feel safe at school. They know they will not be harassed, and if one student is not respecting another, the school and the students will intervene. They also know that something can be done about disrespectful acts. For example, when a swastika was put up in the girls' bathroom at Jefferson Middle School, the students from the Celtic Club responded by announcing over the PA system that cultural pride is about sharing your culture, not hiding in some bathroom and scrawling hate messages on the wall. This is an example of how empowered students can combat racism around them.

• Asian Council: According to Tony Lum, the Asian Council was organized in 1982 as a vehicle to pass ideas back and forth among Asian groups. Additionally, the council's goal is to encourage the Asian ethnic communities to organize ethnic-specific groups. The council sponsors the Asian Celebration, one of the biggest Pan-Asian efforts in the west. When it first began, the Asian Celebration attracted 500 attendees; at the end of the century, more than 16,000 participated in the event.

• Catholic Spanish Mass Community: After years of periodic bilingual masses at various Catholic churches, or driving a priest down to Eugene from Salem to conduct the masses in Spanish, or simply doing without, St. Mary's Catholic Church began holding a weekly Spanish language mass in 1992. Dedicated parishioners helped make the masses happen. The majority of the parishioners who attend the Spanish masses are Mexicans and other Latinos. The sanctuary is filled to capacity, with just a few Anglos in attendance. When Rose Marie Villanueva inquired about one Anglo-American's consistent attendance at the Spanish language mass, he said that he attends because "this mass is alive!" Now, other Eugene churches also have services in Spanish.

• The Ganas Program: The Ganas (meaning desire) program originated in 1996 from a conversation between Jim Garcia, then-UO assistant director for the Office of Multicultural Affairs, and Roscoe Caron, an eighth-grade teacher at Kennedy Middle School. As they talked about Latino students at Kennedy, Caron described the dilemma: New Latino students did not feel welcomed and returning Latino students did not feel a part of the school. Garcia says that as a result, many were performing under their potential, had negative interactions with teachers, and fought with other students.

Together, Garcia and Caron created a program with goals that focus on self-confidence, learning diverse Latino cultural history, exercising bicultural student leadership, and enhancing academic performance. Under the program, university students meet biweekly with middle-school students to tutor them, discuss Chicano/Latino history, provide guest speakers, and develop other culturally relevant activities. The younger students are educated about their own cultures and empowered to be leaders, while the college students serve as role models.

• Clergy and Laity Concerned: In 1980 Clergy and Laity Concerned (CALC) moved to make racial justice a key issue. Marion Malcolm, who served on the staff of CACL for twenty-five years, recalled, "It was not necessarily easy to see where there might be

racism because often there were only white people in many meetings, so no one necessarily noticed that other racial groups were
missing." She added, "I learned enormous amounts when I worked
side by side with people of color at CALC, when I went places
with them. They had to have a wariness that I might have [known]
only if I was somewhere by myself at night, as a white woman.
Moving around the community by bus and waiting for a bus was
a different experience for Bahati Ansari, who also worked at CALC,
than for me; the Dairy Queen and supermarkets were different
experiences for her." Malcolm came to understand that the daily
cost of racism must be enormous. She said she began to realize
that everyday experiences could be like "hundreds of paper cuts all
over your body," as Carla Gary, director and advocate of the UO
Office of Multicultural Affairs, described it.

To foster their commitment, CALC, renamed Community
Alliance of Lane County, started conducting "Unlearning Racism"
workshops. They also initiated several programs. Communities
Against Hate conducted research and action projects to counter
the activities of the extreme right in Oregon. The Immigrant Rights
Program worked to increase community understanding, banish
stereotypes, and defend immigrant rights, and also helped form
the Network for Immigrant Justice, which fights anti-immigrant
legislation, La Migra raids, and INS abuses. Youth for Justice Program empowers young people to take a stand against injustices,
such as racism, sexism, and homophobia, and to learn grassroots
organizing and leadership skills.

Conclusion

When asked about how she viewed racism at the end of the century, Misa Kawai Joo said, "There's been an explosion of diversity
in this community. It is no longer centered around the university.
There are a growing number of Latino people from both Mexico
and Central America. There are enough Korean people to merit

three Korean churches, and African Americans and other people of color are taking their rightful place in this city as advocates."

By 1999 Eugene boasted several ethnic celebrations: Asian Celebration, Obon, Cinco de Mayo, Kwanzaa, Juneteenth Celebration, and others. The University of Oregon has several programs dedicated to students and faculty of color. According to Jane DeGidio, the UO director of student retention programs, the UO has a program called "Reach for Success," which brings middle school students of color from across the state to campus to learn about opportunities to further their education.

With celebrations, university programs, and increased racial diversity, many feel that Eugene is a nice place, an easy place for different kinds of people to live. However, this has often translated into surface appearances of racial harmony without true underlying racial integration. UO professor Lawrence Carter said, "Most white people in Eugene are well-behaved, but—as a rule—many do not make long-term commitments unless they are in the driver's seat. Most white people do not talk to black people until they establish dominance, no matter how bizarre it gets." Others have said that those who are prejudiced do not have to deal with racial issues openly; they have not been confronted with the issue much.

Others agree. Marion Malcolm said, "White people do not think Eugene is racist. It doesn't affect them. When white people think about racism, their minds move toward racial conflict, and it is not something they have to confront as part of their lives. They might have read that people of color get stopped more by the police, but lots of white people here can live their whole lives without significant interaction with people of color."

The real challenge that lies ahead is continuing to bring people together to work cooperatively on race relations in order to build Eugene's future. Jane DeGidio, who has lived in Eugene for more than thirty years, said, "Race relations in post–World War II Eugene is a work-in-progress, filled with every emotion imaginable: from anger to hate to despair to hope. Success will take more than hopes and dreams; it will take action as well."

Are citizens, institutions, and businesses of Eugene ready for the multiracial future? Ready for the challenges? Are they ready to change personal behavior? Ready to change institutional policies and practices that fail to foster diversity, inclusion, and community? Or are people too comfortable and institutions too arrogant to think about changing? Will change come only with crises or will change be born from vision? The answers are not obvious. The dialogue has begun.

Bibliography

City of Eugene. "Minutes for the Common Council Meeting."
July 8, 1963.

————.*Eugene Area Historic Context Statement.* Eugene: Planning
& Development Department.

————. "Report of Activities." Subcommittee on City Government, Human Rights Commission, August 24, 1965.

Congress of Racial Equality. "Report of Community Relations
Committee, Eugene Chapter, Congress of Racial Equality
(C.O.R.E.)."

Edson, Christopher Howard. *The Chinese in Eastern Oregon, 1980–
1890* . San Francisco: R and E Research Associates, 1974.

Gamboa, Erasmo. "Oregon's Hispanic Heritage." *Oregon Humanities*, Summer 1992.

Hongo, Garrett. "Lost in Place." *Half and Half.* New York: Pan-
theon Books, 1998.

Migra Raid Task Force. *La Migra (INS) Raid Report: A Socio-Economic Impact Study.* Lane County: 1998.

Oregon Daily Emerald, selected articles, 1997.

The Register-Guard, selected articles, 1952–1999.

Spicer, Florence LeVan. *Adapting to the times: My Life 1907 – 1975.*
Eugene: Vesta Publishing Services, 1991.

Toepel, Kathryn Anne. "The Western Interior." *The First Oregonians: An Illustrated Collection of Essays on Traditional Lifeways,
Federal-Indian Relations, and the State's Native people Today.* Portland: The Oregon Council for the Humanities, 1991.

Turpin, Cheri, and Mark Harris. "A Eugene Black History Perspective."

YouthBuild. "The Mims Family History." 1998.

University of Oregon students paint the O on Skinner Butte
Photo credit: Division of Special Collections & University Archives,
University of Oregon Library System.

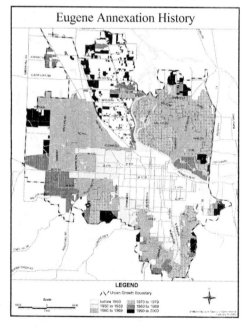

Photo credit: Lane Council of Governments

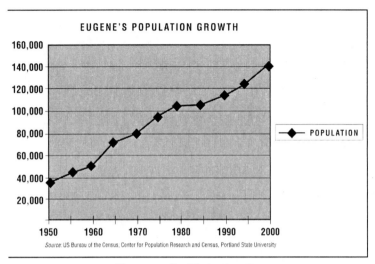

Photo credit: Katherine Getta

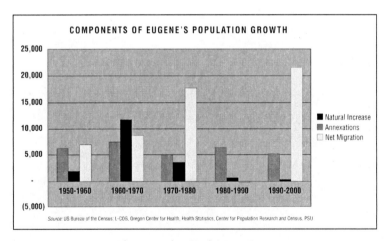

Photo credit: Katherine Getta

Photo credit: U.S. Army Corps of Engineers

Photo credit: Spencer Gross

Left: Goodpasture Island-Delta Highway area, 1940 and 1999. Farmland, orchards, pasture and woodland in 1940 have largely been replaced by highways, neighborhoods, and shopping centers in 1999. Debrick Slough flows from south to north through the center of the 1940 photograph, when it was an overflow channel for the Willamette River during times of flooding. Portions of Debrick Slough have been replaced in the 1999 photo by Delta Highway and the adjacent Delta Ponds, which were excavated for aggregate and fill. Other portions of Debrick Slough still occur in their original locations. Other than Delta Ponds, the few remaining natural areas include the maple woods along the Willamette River on the northwest corner of the photos, and an oak savanna located just north of Beltline Highway near the eastern edge of the photos.

Downtown Eugene, 8th and Willamette
Photo credit: Dot Dotson Photo Archives

Downtown Eugene, Willamette Street
Photo credit: Dot Dotson Photo Archives

Wigwam burner in West Eugene
Photo credit: Lane County Historical Museum

Saw logs
Photo credit: Dot Dotson Photo Archives

Mahlon Sweet Airport
Photo credit: Dot Dotson Photo Archives

Lane Transit District microbus fleet
Photo credit: Lane Transit District

Mayor Les Anderson at downtown event
Photo credit: Lane County Historical Museum

Students stage a sit-in on the steps of Johnson Hall at the University of Oregon. Photo credit: Division of Special Collections & University Archives, University of Oregon Library System.

Lisl Waechter (standing, with glasses), children, and staff try out new playground equipment at the Pearl Buck Center. Photo credit: Courtesy of Pearl Buck Center

Congregants at a Spanish mass at St. Mary's Catholic Church, 2000.
Photo credit: Alex Dupey

First Christian Church
Photo credit: Dot Dotson Photo Archive

Tom Payzant at a reception hosted by the
Eugene Branch Association for Childhood Education, 1973.
Photo credit: Courtesy of Eugene School District 4J

Johnson Hall on the UO campus, 1978
Photo credit: Division of Special Collections & University Archives,
University of Oregon Library System.

St. Vincent de Paul, West 11th Avenue store, 1959
Photo credit: Courtesy of St. Vincent de Paul

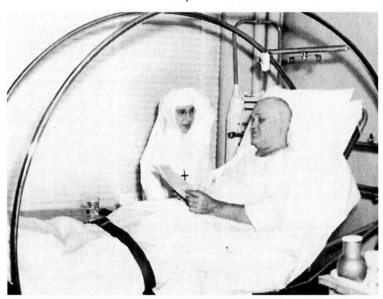

A nun and patient at Sacred Heart Hospital
Photo credit: Courtesy of PeaceHealth

Sculptor Hugh Townley talks to children about his sculpture in Alton Baker Park, 1974. Photo credit: University of Oregon

McArthur Court on the University of Oregon campus, the site of sporting and performing arts events. Photo credit: Dot Dotson Photo Archives

Kids play on a local park jungle gym, circa 1960s.
Photo credit: Courtesy of City of Eugene Parks and Recreation

Willie Knickerbocker, the bike guru, 1925
Photo credit: Lane County Historical Museum

COMMUNITIES WITHIN:

STORIES FROM EUGENE'S

COMMUNITIES OF COLOR

By Kimber Williams

Where do we find community?
MORE THAN GEOGRAPHY, the bonds are hard to predict, impossible to force. Rather, they evolve with imperceptible momentum—rising from shared experience, common struggle, the ongoing process of daily living. Every individual story its own chapter.

For Eugene's communities of color, the sense of community has been forged with time, reminding us that we live our history every day, that where we come from is never too far away from where we now stand.

The Ladies of the Club
From the beginning, it was the language she missed the most—a simple identification with voice and cadence and something familiar.

"Spanish? You almost never heard it spoken on the street," said Cristina Ciprés-Jácome, a Spanish-language immersion teacher at Buena Vista/Meadowlark Elementary School who arrived in Eugene in 1970 as a young bride from Mexico. "That part of you was still seeking," she said, "always seeking."

Of course, Ciprés-Jácome hadn't expected Eugene to offer the cultural conveniences of Mexico City, where she had grown up. In 1970 barely a few hundred Hispanic residents were settled here.

Most were from Mexico, drawn to the University of Oregon—a doorway opened wider by affirmative action—or jobs in the thriving industries of the day, including lumber mills and railroads. In fact, local Hispanics often joked that you used to be able to count every family member living here—on one hand.

For Mexican immigrants, Oregon in 1970 offered few cultural amenities. It was an unspoken rule: You came here to accept the culture, which was not expected to return the favor. Grocery stores then never dreamed of carrying the dried peppers and ground masa, jars of mole and fresh chilies that were kitchen staples back in Mexico—items plentiful in today's supermarkets. In Eugene's business community, it was decades before Mexican restaurants— among the first Hispanic enterprises to open here, and often funded by friends and family, not local banks—took root. To attend a Spanish-language Catholic mass, you might have to traipse over to Alfonso Cabrera's backyard to hear the priest from Salem or Portland, who ventured down I-5 perhaps once a month. No groceries, no music, no culture, no clout. No fiestas, no barrios, no places to meet people with a shared background.

At least there was "The Club." Created in 1965, Club LatinoAmericano soon came to represent many things to many local Hispanic women. It was founded as an informal social-civic group, but for new Latina immigrants, it quickly assumed the role of a second family, a support group like no other. Many of the women were stay-at-home mothers with small children. Language could be a built-in barrier to fitting into the new culture.

Consider Julieta Hughet, for example. A teacher in Mexico, she visited Eugene while on vacation in 1965 and met her husband on a blind date. They corresponded for a year. Neither knew the other's language, but they eagerly found translators to decipher their courtship. When they married, Hughet recalled, "I still couldn't speak English, and he couldn't speak Spanish. We had a dictionary next to us all the time."

But it wasn't just the language. It was the culture, the connections that she missed. "In Mexico, families would get together all the time," Hughet said. "Here, come Sunday, and nobody would drop by, just drop in and visit you. The first two or three years you just miss that powerful part of life."

Kathryn "Catalina" Hidalgo, one of the founders and the club's senior matriarch, initially viewed the club as a way to brush up on her own Spanish skills, which she found little opportunity to use in Eugene in the early 1960s. Raised in Nebraska, her own father was from Spain and insisted on keeping the language alive. "We were always required to speak Spanish to my dad in our home," recalled Hidalgo, who has lived in the same house on East 27th Avenue since 1942. "The main thing was that we wanted to talk," she said. "It was a powerful need. We just needed to hear the language."

What started as a conversation over coffee grew. For years the club was the closest thing Eugene had to a Spanish-speaking Junior League. Money from their community fundraising dinners routinely helped support orphans in Mexico and, occasionally, local families in need. Members rented a hall, fixed traditional foods, made costumes, and put on programs—events that also helped introduce the culture to the larger community at a time when there seemed to be little Hispanic presence in Eugene. "The appreciation we felt kept us going," Ciprés-Jácome said. "In some cases, the people who came had no idea where Mexico even was."

In the absence of mothers, sisters, and aunts, The Club became a surrogate family, a lifeline into a new world. Meeting in one another's homes, they shared recipes, home medical remedies, and parenting tips. Children came too, in diapers and portable playpens and toddling underfoot, the way it had been back home. When someone's parents would visit from Mexico, women in the group would giddily "share" them—a strategy to help stave homesickness.

"It was my home away from home—a way to continue the tradition, the culture, and to stay in touch with the language," recalled Guadalupe Jones, a Spanish teacher at Monroe Middle School who came to the club twenty-three years ago. "We would have potlucks, get-togethers to just talk about different things we had experienced. A lot of us shared the same backgrounds. In my case, I was the first of all my brothers and sisters to be away from home."

Initially, almost all of The Club members were from Mexico and were married to American men—not unusual in Eugene's early Hispanic community where marriage to an Anglo spouse sometimes helped open doors that had once been closed. Most were homemakers and had small children. Nearly all were Catholic. Spanish was their first language.

Rebeca Urhausen was lucky. She has been a club member for twenty-two years and is cofounder of Fiesta Latina, Eugene's most visible Hispanic celebration, held each May. Growing up in Mexico City, her mother had insisted that she study English. Without it, the experience it Eugene could have been isolating. "Without the language, without support, it was not that easy," said Urhausen, who helps place Hispanic workers through Barrett Business Services, a Eugene employment agency.

By 2000, the organization had evolved into more of a social than service club, and a majority of its twenty-five to thirty members are career women, with less spare time on their hands. Some in Eugene's larger Hispanic community credit Club LatinoAmericano as being the early keeper of the culture, the glue that helped hold together the first tenuous threads of the community—particularly among women.

The children, the church, and the club—for many Eugene Latinas this was a not just a powerful social trinity, but a point of civic identity. Sometimes, club membership dwindled to only a handful, but still, they met. "The moral support was Number One," recalled Ciprés-Jácome. "I never really thought about our group having something to do with cultivating our local culture, but I can see that. There are so many people I've known through it."

In thirty-five years, members of the club have witnessed profound change in Eugene, and in their own lives. Hispanics can actually find some sense of community within the larger Eugene community. Increasingly, they move here with families, rather than as single adults. Public schools welcome their children without questioning their immigration status.

Hispanics also represent the state's fastest growing minority group. In the 1990s, Oregon's Hispanic population exploded, jumping 77 percent. Census figures from 1998 show nearly 12,000 Hispanic residents in Lane County, about 3.8 percent of the population.

Hispanic names appear throughout the business community, university system, and political circles. Agencies such as Centro LatinoAmericano, which provides social services and support to area-Hispanic families, now exist to help provide social services to many of the city's new immigrants, backed by a budget of $700,000. Father Mark, the bilingual pastor of the parish at St. Mary's Catholic Church, attracts a standing-room only congregation at his weekly Spanish-language mass, which draws about 500 parishioners each Sunday afternoon.

Pick up a brochure from any state agency, and you'll probably find it printed in both Spanish and English. And Eugene school children have the chance to study in Spanish-immersion programs—a fact that makes Ciprés-Jácome feel as if she's truly come full circle. There was a time when she almost never heard Spanish spoken in Eugene. Her ears used to ache for it. Now, she's immersed in the language every day.

As an educator, Ciprés-Jácome is deftly fluent in both English and Spanish. But the power of language can take her by surprise. "I think the most difficult thing, still, is I can operate [in the community] on a professional level and a social level and feel comfortable, but when I'm with Hispanic people my personality changes," she said. "I feel a lot more outgoing, more comfortable in the language, explaining myself, communicating my view of life."

From the beginning, that's what made Club LatinoAmericano so natural—and so important. "With our group, we didn't have to establish anything. We viewed life in a different way—our own way. Not right or wrong, just different," Ciprés-Jácome said. "Sometimes, it's good to remind yourself that's OK."

Coming Home

It is said that if you're black, the debacle of the Ferry Street Village is one of the first stories you hear when you arrive in Eugene—unsettling but important information. At the end of World War II, town leaders quietly permitted black families in need of housing to piece together their own neighborhood on the north side of the Willamette River, in the shadow of where Ferry Street Bridge now stands. In 1949, plans for a new bridge changed everything. Issues of planning and place collided.

Despite the state's long-standing hostility toward black families—prejudicial laws and attitudes hardly welcomed them—an increasing number made their way West by the 1940s, looking for war-time jobs widely promoted in shipyards and munitions plants. A smattering came to Eugene and stayed.

They found a town that made it almost impossible to rent or own property. However, county officials allowed black families to build homes along the north bank of the Willamette River, effectively creating a rural ghetto. There, families grew their own vegetables in small plots, fished on riverbanks, raised their children, and worshipped in a crude church with a canvas roof.

By all accounts, Ferry Street Village was a humble neighborhood, consisting of homes fashioned with scrap lumber or whatever materials were available. Without city services, residents relied on outhouses and water that was hauled in from local service stations. Flooding from the nearby Willamette was a soggy seasonal problem. And yet, here was a community, at one time home to more than twenty families, many of them founders of today's black community.

Washington. Reynolds. Johnson. Mims. To many, the names from 1930s and 1940s are the bedrock, the foundation of the black community they now know. Their stories are local history.

Among Ferry Street dwellers who stayed to be Eugene's first black property owners were C.B. and Annie Mims, who borrowed $5,500 to buy two houses on the northernmost reaches of High Street. Their household would become a touchstone for many black families, who sometimes rented rooms there. The Mims's family also opened their doors to well-known entertainers such as Nat King Cole and Ella Fitzgerald when they were turned away from local hotels.

Or folks like Bertha Johnson, who moved from Atlanta, Georgia, to Oakridge, Oregon, then to Eugene in the early 1940s. Her husband, Charley, spotted a newspaper ad appealing for railroad workers to migrate to Oregon. When they first moved to town, the family wound up staying with Leo and Pearlie Mae Washington, another early black family famous for opening their doors to those banned from all-white hotels and boarding houses.

In 1949, the Lane County Commissioners announced plans to replace Ferry Street Bridge and raze the village—a decision that angered many blacks as well as some whites. When a handful of University of Oregon leaders jumped into the fray, openly protesting the treatment, DeNorval "Dee" Unthank couldn't stay away.

Unthank's interest was both professional and personal. As a student of architecture at the University of Oregon, he was interested in the village as a fascinating community planning dilemma. But as the son of one of Portland's first black physicians, Unthank also understood the physical need for community, the desire to claim a sense of place.

"I remember at the time, some of us from the school went to meetings and tried to be of help," said Unthank, a Eugene architect. "People were being taken advantage of pretty badly. It was a hostile situation in a lot of ways. Part of the university community and the larger community were very worried that the real-estate community and other interests were trying to sell them a pig in a poke.

"We tried to offer support, but many local blacks here were worried that we were just trying to get in their business," he added.

"We'd all gone through something like that wherever we lived, anyway." It was "part of being a black person in America, the name of the game," Unthank recalled. "From the time you were a little kid, you knew you had to take care of yourself. [Ferry Street Village] was handled pretty badly, but nothing any different from people trying to burn our house down in Portland."

When Unthank's parents had moved from Kansas City to Portland in the early 1930s, they found neighbors weren't anxious to have a black family in their midst. Regardless, his father served many patients that the medical community didn't care to, including blacks, Asian Americans, and Roma. "That was one reason my parents weren't too excited about me coming to school [in Eugene]," Unthank said. "They thought I'd have more opportunities elsewhere."

Despite the protests, Ferry Street Village was relocated out on West 11th Avenue, on a site that was once little more than a boggy slough. Those who didn't move in time saw their homes leveled, sometimes with belongings intact.

The controversy marked an important moment. Although the relocation spurred both anger and activism, some credit it for opening a new level of civic dialogue between Eugene's black and white communities. It marked the beginning of years of slow change. "A lot was happening on an individual level, along with state and national civil rights trends," Unthank recalled. "Up until 1950 and 1951, when the legislature began to turn laws around, it was an uphill battle, every step of the way. Then, things changed. But it took a long time. In Eugene, particularly."

In 1951, Unthank married while still at the UO. His first wife was white. When they began dating, she was kicked out of her sorority. When they married, news of it made *Time* magazine. "It wasn't as emotional as it could have been or should have been or maybe really was," Unthank said. "We were students, busy going to school. You just did what you had to do and never tried to worry about it. That's the way I was raised."

Following graduation, Unthank stayed in Eugene. He formed

a construction company with his friend, Dick Chambers, and started building houses. After a few years, Unthank joined Wilmsen-Endicott, among the city's largest architecture firms at the time, where he became a partner. He later formed his own partnership, leaving his architectural thumbprint on homes, schools, and government buildings throughout the state.

In 2000, there is no Ferry Street Village to create a built-in sense of community and unity for black families, no particular neighborhood to come home to. Talk to young black leaders, and some will admit that it can actually be difficult to find a place to connect, particularly for newcomers.

"Where do we find community? I'm still struggling with that one. If you find out, let me know," jokes Diamond Livingston, a codirector of the Eugene-Springfield chapter of the National Association for the Advancement of Colored People (NAACP), who works for the State Services to Children and Families Division. "Actually, for me it's probably within our black churches," she said. "But for those who don't go to church, I think it can be a struggle."

Angel Jones, who moved to Eugene in 1999 from Richmond, Virginia, to become executive manager of the city's library, recreation, and cultural services, agrees. "I attend Bethel Temple Christian Family Center, and it gives me comfort, encouragement, the feeling that there is someone else out there with the same issues. I'm not alone when I feel people stare at me wherever I go, or always ask, 'Where are you from?' because they just know I can't be from here," she said, chuckling.

Despite limited opportunities for physical connections, unity exists among the black community. But to outsiders, the connections may be invisible, unseen until they are required by circumstance, such as the protests provoked by the forced resignation of former Eugene police chief Leonard Cooke.

"When issues arise, you feel the cohesion, people pulling together and standing behind one another—there is support," said

Marilyn Mays, diversity manager for the City of Eugene and codirector of the local NAACP. "But can you get in your car on a Saturday afternoon and drive to the park and hang out with people of your race the way you can in larger cities? No. I think we lack having places to go and congregate as a community that way.

"I moved to this community about five years ago with no family here," Mays said. "The church really became my family. We use the words 'church home' and that is really what it becomes— the place you build friendships, bonds, and a sense of support."

For someone like Dee Unthank, who has seen decades of change in Eugene's black community, the perspective is different. Compared to the forced segregation of Ferry Street Village, he sees enormous gains. "Black community? I'm glad to say that we have some now," he said, chuckling. But Unthank doesn't quantify progress by the fact that he has witnessed local black leaders become county commissioners or city police chiefs. Not by the growth of a community-wide Martin Luther King Jr. celebration or the influence of local groups like the NAACP, who in the late 1990s challenged Eugene police to make good on their pledge to end racial profiling, the identification of suspects solely by race.

Rather, it's the fundamental diversity of the local black community that pleases him most. No longer are black neighborhoods segregated; no longer are local black families employed only in the service sector, nor are they among the community's poorest residents. He sees new faces, new talents. He sees progress.

"I think of the variety of people who've come and participated in various fields and have broadened the base, and I feel that we're fortunate to have their contributions," he said. "It isn't just a matter of a 'you-and-them' thing any more. It's taken a lot of growing. But I'm amazed at the people I see that I don't even know—people from various companies and professions.

"And it's absolutely wonderful. Amazing and wonderful."

Unity People

In high school, Lela Ross remembers the awkward tug of social segregation. Black classmates wondered why she didn't identify with them. White classmates didn't always know how to treat her. Being a child of mixed ethnicity, she decided, was "its own distinct culture."

"My mom is white, my dad is black, and they're both hippies," she said, laughing. "It was totally different from what either one of those groups knew. I had to make my own culture."

An eighteen-year-old student at Lane Community College, Lela Ross realizes that she had the confidence to create her own identity, in part, because of her home life. And also because of the organization that her parents helped found, which created a community for Lela that stands "like an extended family."

It was in 1983, while helping plan a community-wide celebration around Martin Luther King Jr., that Lela's parents, Sarah and Randy Ross, and others decided to build a multiracial organization. "The effort of all of us coming together, people we knew and associated with, felt really good. We wanted to build a multicultural organization," she said. Later that year, they launched HONEY (Honoring Our New Ethnic Youth, Inc.), a group with goals of supporting interracial families and building harmony in society.

Sarah and Randy met in 1974. She was white and from San Francisco. He was an African-American musician from Los Angeles. Their friendship stayed strong, grew into something deeper. Both had children from previous relationships. But even in laid-back Eugene, interracial couples could still cause heads to turn. "Hey, even black people were unusual in Eugene back then," Sarah Ross recalled. "We kind of knew who every family was."

It wasn't easy. Walking down the street together, the couple would endure taunts from passing vehicles. "A lot of our friends of color were really afraid to go out into the country, into rural Oregon," she said. "It never stopped us. We'd go to the coast or wherever, and people really did stare. But I became accepting, trying to

understand. I didn't take it as hateful, just people who were igno-
rant of anyone different than themselves."

In their twenty-three years together, Randy and Sarah have
had four children. Added to the children they each brought to the
relationship, that makes nine kids—nine wonderful kids representing a mixture of races. "Having a lot of kids kept us in a low-
income situation," Sarah admitted. "That was hard. And we had
to kind of find ourselves, as a community."

In time, the Rosses began connecting with other mixed-race
families who also shared less-than-conventional configurations. She
recalled it as a natural evolution, families who just found each
other. Recruiting was primarily word of mouth. "It wasn't just
black or white, but other combinations, too," she said. "There was
even a black and white lesbian couple. Most were people of some
black and white heritage."

Within this group, they discovered a natural kind of community building that was important, especially for their children—a
sense of recognition, of belonging. "When you see your kid as the
only kid of color in a classroom, it's still not unusual," Sarah said.

Seventeen years later, HONEY is on the cusp of going statewide, under the auspices of the Oregon Council of Multiracial
Affairs. HONEY offers something Sarah Ross sought for her own
children all along—a way to look around their community and see
other mixed-race kids and feel pride and identity. "It takes a lot of
self-esteem and courage to say, 'Yes, I'm a mixed-race person, it's
fine with me.' I guess it gives the kids permission to own that
heritage instead of letting society dictate that, 'You look like this,
so you must be that.' Instead of letting friends or the neighborhood you live in dictate identity."

She's seen it work. Her twenty-year-old son, Tumasi, is a junior at Southern Oregon College majoring in international studies,
Spanish, and creative writing. A football player and vice president
of the Black Student Union—that's who he is. While one of her
children will say that she's of mixed-race, another chooses to say

that he's black, which is fine, Sarah Ross said. "It's having permission to choose some of it or all of it," she explained.

Lela Ross considers herself lucky. "I've had a sense of HONEY being there for me ever since I was a baby," she recalled. "I always had the support I needed." Picnics and groups campouts, just being able to talk to someone else who knows how it feels to walk into a restaurant or department store and get "the look" that sometimes comes with darker skin color—Lela likens the organization to providing the security of a community embrace. Looking back, there have been times when that safety net was important to help with everyday struggles.

"Sometimes you feel really separate," she explained. "I've been called 'nigger' while walking down the street in Eugene. It's demeaning, but the hurt I feel is more because I feel sorry for them. I want to help them—that's what affects me more than the actual name calling. Just knowing that no one is born racist. It's what they've learned and grown up with."

Lela likes Eugene. She likes the fact that she doesn't have to choose a racial group to identify with. "I'm attracted to people who are open-minded, basically," she said. But she also knows that when she meets someone like her, who knows what it is to grow up in a mixed-race family, there is an automatic relationship, a shared experience.

Ross likes to believe that HONEY isn't an island unto itself but a group that builds bridges into other corners of Eugene's communities of color. It's there when it's needed. "Not every interracial family in town is connected," she admitted. "But many are. Others have said, 'I don't need a group like that,' almost in defiance. They want to try so hard to be color-blind that they don't want to fit in, not even identify with interracial folks."

Which is fine, Ross said. "We try not to be adversarial. We're unity people, in unity with whoever wants to be with us. I know I see myself as a multicultural person, and I love it. I'll be glad when the rest of the world moves in that direction."

Staple of Life

Her mother made frybread—small, flat rounds of sweet dough that crisped to a golden brown when cooked in hot oil. And even now, when Wilma Crowe helps schoolchildren measure out the ingredients—flour, baking powder, sugar, salt, yeast, and milk—it is a contemplative act, a communion of ritual and memory: *South Dakota. Standing Rock. Her father, a college-educated man, a Lakota Sioux. Her mother, a white woman. The warm smell of frybread.*

"Bread is symbolic for many cultures, a staple of life," Crowe said. "That's just part of our culture, like putting on a pair of moccasins." And so, Crowe makes frybread, kneading it and patting it out and generously dispensing it the way some dole out a good story. "Oh, I make it all the time," she said, laughing. "Someone will say, 'Grandma, I haven't had any frybread in awhile,' and the next thing you know I'm making it up."

Some call her the Frybread Queen. This makes Wilma Crowe laugh. "Word does get around," she demurred. "I do make frybread."

But she's also making lessons, working with schoolchildren, young adults, even University of Oregon students—because she loves children, she'll tell you, no matter how old. "Children have been my forte, I guess," she said. "I can't imagine my life without working with them. They teach you so much, if you just listen . . . and watch."

Many see eighty-one-year-old Crowe as a living treasure, part of a circle of elders who form the very foundation of the patchwork tapestry of tribes that constitute Eugene's Native American community. She's seen as a woman who came to this town at a time when few American Indians had found their way into urban centers. A woman who stayed.

Though Crowe was born on a reservation in South Dakota, the land had already been opened to white homesteaders. Her parents were among only three Indian families left in their farming community. Still, to leave the reservation, they had to have government consent. There were no pow-wows, because Indians weren't allowed to attend any kind of gathering and prohibited from practicing their own spirituality. Instead, they were encouraged to attend the Catholic Church.

Crowe can still remember the day that she was officially anointed a United States citizen. She was six years old when Congress deemed that native people could be recognized as citizens on June 2, 1924. "Then we could leave the reservation whenever we wanted to," she said. "The first thing we did was get in a buggy and go buy an ice cream cone."

When her family relocated to Southern Oregon, Wilma Crowe met the man who would become her husband. His last name was Crow—he had added an "e" to avoid bird jokes. And his family had come from old pioneering stock. "His great-grandfather settled Crow, Oregon," she said. "His people were among the first whites in Jacksonville."

They moved to Eugene in 1944, a town with virtually no minority community. "There were a few black families who lived out West 11th, a few students at the University of Oregon," she said. "That was it." The town was largely hospitable, though she can remember that her father ("he had black hair, looked every bit the Indian") was refused service in restaurants and movie theaters from time to time. It was a difficult time. Through the 1950s, a number of Oregon Indian tribes lost government recognition and were disbanded. Tribal lands were taken; members were expected to assimilate into the larger, white culture.

Over the years, Crowe occasionally met some of the Valley Indians, people who had come from the tribes that had long traversed the Coast Range and Willamette Valley, including the Siletz, Coquille, and Grande Ronde tribes—distinctively different groups with their own histories, languages, and cultures. It wasn't until the early 1970s that the roots of today's urban Indian community really took hold. Through the decade, tribes fought for re-recognition, which marked the beginning of a hard-won restoration of identity.

"I know when I was going to school, I was not supposed to be an Indian—it was like, 'Don't tell anybody.' You know, 'the only good Indian is a dead Indian.' All the old stereotypes," recalled Nick Sixkiller, an education specialist for the Siletz Indian tribe, who grew up in Oregon and has lived in Eugene for nearly thirty years. "Over time, that attitude began to change."

The UO served an important role, helping create a place to come together. "It was 1974 and a young man by the name of Bob Tom was at the University of Oregon," Crowe recalled. By then, Crowe knew of perhaps a half-dozen Native American students and their families in the area. Tom helped them create a Native American Student Association. "In the beginning, we had potlucks and then started in on the culture, beading and drumming and dancing and singing," she said. "It escalated from there." In time, when UO students would sponsor a pow-wow, "Indians from up and down the coast of Washington and Oregon would come, mostly to renew our culture, to talk about each other's culture," Crowe added.

To help preserve culture, they looked to children. "It's always been children—they've been the main issue, and education our biggest goal." That's how Wilma Crowe went back to school. This time, as a teacher. Through the NATIVES/Indian Education Program, she began working with the children of urban Indians.

"At Jefferson Middle School we meet twice a month for culture classes, singing, dancing, and beading," she said. "I try to get each child to look to their own background, research what their food and clothing must have been." And once a month, they make frybread. "At the end of the year, we put on a heritage day," Crowe said. "That's important, even if they're blond-haired and blue eyed, it doesn't matter. If they have a connection, they should know it."

Crowe looks about her community and sees many teachers who've made a difference. People like Dwight Souers, an award-winning science educator at Willamette High School who helped open doors at the school for weekly evening meetings for the Native American community. Or his wife, Twila Souers, who long coordinated the NATIVES program for the 4J school district. Today, Crowe knows that eighty-five to ninety tribes are represented among Eugene's urban Indians—probably four to five hundred students in K–12 classrooms, alone.

Different backgrounds, different cultures. "Here in Eugene, urban Indians tend to be intertribal," Sixkiller said. "We're all pretty generic in the way we do things. Being urban means we're losing a lot of our traditional ways. That's what I try to remind kids in school—you have to go back to tribal lands to see how people really are. Still, we celebrate who we are."

With the confluence of different tribes from across the country, it's not always a smooth journey. "There's a saying that we'll fight among ourselves, but if anyone turns on us, the whole tribe turns on them," Sixkiller said, laughing. "It's kind of like a mother and her kids. We fight among ourselves all the time, politics between tribes, whatever. But fundamentally, we're always united, trying not to forget our ancestors, yet live in a modern world. It's really tough to live in both worlds."

For many Native Americans, pow-wows remain the primary source of community in Eugene. "Years ago, you'd have to look for them," Sixkiller said. "Now, you can find them almost every weekend. We're a pow-wow rich place." To help form another connection for Native Americans, Sixkiller hosts a weekly radio show on KRVM, "Indian Time," which offers two hours of Indian music, traditional, contemporary, and pow-wow oriented fare. It's the first and only show of it's kind in Western Oregon and a way to feel connected.

"The feedback has been more than I ever dreamed," he said. "I never thought I'd have a listening audience like I do—Indian and non-Indian alike. Tons of phone calls." That marks a big change. The Cherokee Indian who once thought he was supposed to hide that fact now finds his cultural perspective in high demand.

During the school year, Sixkiller often takes time after work to instruct young people in drumming and traditional songs, pow-wow etiquette and protocol. The pow-wow is community—a magnet that has brought people together for generations, working still.

Wilma Crowe knows. To attend a pow-wow "makes me feel wonderful. To see all those brown faces—even if they're not brown—to see all those faces and know that we're all connected somewhere, to the land and to each other." And at the age of eighty-one, she can still dance, five, six hours without any problem. "I love every minute of it," Crowe said.

The Art of Building Bridges

As a Japanese-American woman in Eugene in the early 1970s, Misa Joo said it was easy to feel alone. She remembers that as she walked through crowds, she would subconsciously look for a piece of herself. "Every time I saw a head of black hair, my own head would snap around, an automatic response, to see who it was, to see if I knew them," explains Joo, a teacher at Jefferson Middle School.

It wasn't just the general absence of color in the local landscape of faces that she missed. It was something more—a sense of continuity and permanence to this place. More often than not, ethnic faces in Eugene at the time meant new faces. Faces that would come, stay briefly, and leave.

"I missed the multigenerational feeling," she said. "I missed seeing black hair in the landscape. Some of us [Asian-American residents] ended up at Indian community gatherings because that was the only place you would see grandmas and little kids in one room."

Not that she had grown up near an ethnically rich community herself. Joo came from Caldwell, Idaho—not San Francisco or Seattle. Joo chose to stay in the Northwest. She went to college in Idaho and taught school for three years in Washington before transferring to Eugene. In time, a class offered at the University of Oregon caught her eye. John Beckwith, a Chinese-American scholar, was offering a class in ethnic studies called "The Asian-American Experience."

"I went thinking I could meet people," Joo said, laughing. "In Eugene, there are no real ethnic neighborhoods. We're scattered.

If you see someone on the street, it's not always easy to walk up and say, 'Hi, I'm lonely.' "

When she walked into the UO classroom, Joo was surprised to find more Asian-American faces in one room than she had ever seen before in Eugene. "There were Asian-American students and older people, maybe in our late twenties and thirties," she said. "It was a good start, but it was a class. You read books, listened to the teacher. He was smart, put us on projects to develop something in the community, investigating our experience historically."

It wasn't a common history. Looking at the people around her, Joo saw Asian Americans rising from many different cultures and countries, including Japan, China, Taiwan, Korea, the Philippines, Indonesia, and Southeast Asia. At first, there was much to be learned from each other.

But Joo saw the class as making a fundamental difference in the lives of Asian Americans in Eugene. From the class, two important projects emerged with legacies that still live on. First, the development of the Asian American Student Union (now called the Asian Pacific American Student Union), which was launched directly from the class. Second, was the Asian-American Cultural Center, a now-defunct organization that became the seedbed for today's Eugene/Springfield Asian Council, a civic group credited for successfully drawing together diverse strands of the area's Asian-American community and founding an annual Asian Celebration, which draws thousands of people to the Lane County Fairgrounds each year.

At first, the Asian-American Cultural Center was little more than an excuse to come together, to see that you weren't invisible and to create community where none had seemed to exist. But then it grew into something more. "One focus was to bridge with the student union to do things with students, because it's lonely to come here," Joo said. "Another focus was political action. Then, there was the excuse to get together, to cook together. And finally, we tried to be some kind of community presence. We were definitely part of the ethnic pride movement, worked on restitution

and redress, links to other communities of color, international issues. There definitely was a political-action component."

And because some in the cultural group were teachers, they
targeted multicultural education as a goal for change. "I was older,
but a lot [of Asian Americans] were coming into college because of
the ethnic studies movement," Joo said. "The idea of the school
curriculum reflecting more, so that all students felt included and
that the information was correct, that became a burning issue for
us."

In drawing the Asian-American community together, Joo found
that there was also a "reaching out," particularly to other local
communities of color. "The kinds of relationships we made with
other communities, it was just important. It wasn't just these separate communities. I remember it as a fun, exciting time."

But even as the community stabilized, it constantly seemed to
shift. Asian Americans would come and go, arriving to attend or
teach at the UO or pursuing job opportunities until they hit the
"cultural" glass ceiling. "It was like you quickly reached the maximum of what you were able to do here. There were bigger opportunities for professional growth other places."

But even as they moved on, they left change in their wake. "As
people moved away, they had skills about caring for people across
cultural boundaries," Joo said. She recalled them with the same
fondness you regard alumni or close class members. "There are so
many," Joo said. "Eugene was a stop-off place in their lives. Most
moved to larger Asian centers, San Francisco, Hawaii, Seattle. But
some of us stayed. There is something here, that bridging to other
communities, that was so valuable to me. I would miss it. I like
that."

Years later, the embers of the Asian-American Cultural Center
were stirred again. Joo heard from Vern Ho, a friend from the
1970s who later became a consultant. Ho and other community
leaders, including Ken Nagao, Tony Lum, and David Toyama,
wanted to create a new organization. They sought a group that
would build more bridges, foster friendship, understanding, and

harmony. A group that would help, even encourage, the larger community to understand Asian-American cultures in return.

That group became the Asian-American Council, which is an important central hub to Eugene's many Asian-American ethnic groups. "They sent representatives to work together and it turned out to be really wonderful," Joo said. "The council kind of provided support for all these separate communities to grow and do their thing.

"In Eugene," she added, "the key thing is crossing lines to support one another. No one group can do anything without other people involved, because we're small. But I like that, by the way, the art of building bridges." In the early years, it seemed that Eugene's Asian-American community "couldn't do anything alone," Joo joked. "The support came from up and down I-5. We had to connect with Seattle, Portland, Ashland, San Francisco."

Sometimes, it felt like the hardest obstacle to living here wasn't abject racism, but a wall of misunderstanding, or worse, indifference. Equally frustrating was the feeling that institutions would sometimes treat them as "model minorities," hiring one Asian-American employee and then bragging to other communities of color that they had a diverse workplace. "It was a horrible position to be in," she said. "We had to make our position clear in those days that diversity is a good thing, but hiring a few Asian-Americans was not getting the job done."

Today, Misa Joo sees change. Not perfect change, not change without room for improvement, but change, nonetheless.

No longer does she feel that people look at her and assume she's a university student, here and gone, without roots to connect her to this town. "People in Eugene don't see us as people who flew in for the weekend," she said. "For instance, they now see Taiko (drumming) as a Eugene thing. The kind we play is Japanese-American in spirit, anyway. So you see, what we do has been influenced by this diverse society we're lucky enough to live in."

At Jefferson Middle School, a public school with a reputation for diversity and inclusion, Joo has found a happiness she couldn't have imagined. "For the first time in my life as a professional, everyone who works here and goes here believes that they have a right to be here and to feel safe," she said. "That means I don't leave anything at the door. Other places, I come in with my college degree, all my coursework, but I have to leave what I learn at home and part of my culture outside the door because its not 'relevant.'

"At Jefferson, the tone is set. It's incredible what happens when everything is relevant and included. I've never had the feeling before. What happens is all these huge ideas come up, and everyone wants to play, supporting each other."

From studying Taiko drumming to participating in an annual cultural fair, from planning a peace symposium to attending River School, where students study different perspectives and talk to people from the Warm Springs tribe, "people aren't afraid to put their ideas out there," Joo said.

"I'm not saying everything is fixed in Eugene," she said. "But I don't feel lonely any more. I can actually call this place home."

Bibliography

The Register-Guard, 31 Jan. 1993–9 Apr. 2000.

Richard, K. Keith. "Oregon denied first blacks rights, freedoms."
Oregon Historical Quarterly, Spring and Summer 1983.

OUR SHARE OF CHURCHES:

RELIGION AND VALUES IN EUGENE

1945–2000

By Alice Evans

A LOOK OVER time at the character of our town reveals qualities that never seem to change. Nature shapes character, and we are a town at the head of a verdant valley nestled between the mountains and the sea. Wildlife enters our dreams and becomes a part of our mythology. A river runs through us, and so does a major human thoroughfare. We love where we live, or we hate it. People are always coming and going, leaving traces of themselves behind. We enjoy our eccentricities, our recreation, and our spirituality. We are called to look for something more. We can be depended upon to be paradoxical. We are eclectic. As *Register-Guard* religion and values reporter Jeff Wright sees it, we are embedded in traditional Christian beliefs and styles of worship even as we're one of the weakest areas of Christian faith vis-à-vis the rest of the country.

Who Are We? What Do We Believe?

Entering the new millennium, it's very natural to wonder: Who are we? What do we believe? It's a way of reassessing, looking back as we move forward. While some Eugene evangelicals eagerly, perhaps anxiously, anticipate the Second Coming of Christ—one small evangelical church I drove by on New Year's Eve 1999 had a nearly packed parking lot at midnight—most Eugenecans shrug their shoulders in indifference. Many in Eugene may be on a spiritual search, but few search in church.

Those who opt for organized religion in Lane County, according to a 1990 study, attend in greatest numbers Roman Catholic churches, followed by Latter-Day Saints (Mormons), Christian Churches and Churches of Christ, and Foursquare Gospel (Pentecostal). But organized religion hardly reflects the dominant atmosphere of Eugene spirituality. Eclecticism would probably win out if a different sort of poll were taken.

What I've noticed and partaken of in the twenty-five years since I first came to Eugene on the back of a BMW motorcycle is this: We are politically correct, we are New Age, we are freethinkers, we are Christian. We are hippies and ex-hippies, tree-huggers, social-activist joggers, mountain climbers, fun loving, Mormon, Jewish, Sikhs. We are Catholic, Tibetan Buddhist, Quakers, and every combination thereof. We're metaphysical, mystical, hot-tubbing shamans. We are independent survivalists whose ancestors followed the Oregon Trail to a new land of independence; we came here seeking Nirvana or Ecotopia in the '60s and never left. We summoned our friends and relatives to join us. We consult the I Ching. We interpret Tarot. We practice Tai Chi. We eat tofu. We meditate, we pray, we chant, and we Sufi dance. We leave no stone unturned. And sometimes, we are stoned.

We have our dark side and we know it because we are Jungian. We prefer psychology to religion, though many of us juggle both. We have learned to reconcile. We know how to breathe. We are yogis.

What Does It Mean to Be a Eugenean?
What Are the Values We Share?

As 1999 drew to a close, I put these questions to a number of Eugene pastors and people whose lives have focused in one way or another on religion and values.

Lois Barton, one of the founders of the Eugene Friends Meeting (Religious Society of Quakers), said that when she and her husband moved here from Philadelphia in the late 1940s, they were really impressed to find businessmen in shirtsleeves. "This was the kind of laid-back atmosphere typical of Eugene," she said. "There's not a lot of protocol about appearance and behavior." In 1999, Barton found Eugene "still an open and accepting kind of atmosphere, where you can make a go of it without getting caught up in the eight-to-five rat race."

Minnesota native Steve Overman, senior pastor of the Eugene Faith Center since 1988, "got saved" when he was a University of Oregon student in the early 1970s. He described Eugeneans as "people who care about our way of life. We're known for that and it's part of our fabric." He sees us as countercultural for the most part, people who desire to maintain a simple, environmentally sound lifestyle.

Rabbi Yitzhak Husbands-Hankin of Temple Beth Israel said the word that floats through his mind regarding our shared values is *hopefulness*. "I've always felt that Eugene was somehow a symbol of hopefulness." Rabbi Yitz, as his congregants fondly call him, came here from Pittsburgh in the early 1970s, cello in hand. In the big cities in the eastern United States, so much was already created and in place, he said. When he arrived in Eugene, he felt that instead of seeing a chalkboard already filled with drawings and scribbles, he was seeing a community still fresh and vital and in the process of creating itself.

Benton Johnson, retired professor emeritus who taught the sociology of religion at the UO from 1957 to 1996, said that while he and his wife were a little put off by the lack of formal manners when they first arrived in Eugene from the South, he was "very much favorably impressed by open and candid goodwill toward one another in impersonal encounters." Johnson was also "struck by how literate people are here, just ordinary people." He noted also a "willingness to tolerate lifestyle diversity—gay and lesbian, for example." In Eugene, you "don't push your religion on other people," he said. But people "will tolerate so long as you don't try to convert someone else in a harsh way."

Oregon native Sherry Lady, associate pastor of the metaphysical Unity of the Valley Church, pointed out, "The westward movement is still happening, and coming to the West Coast are still those independent seekers who want a different lifestyle." She described her own spiritual journey from Christian fundamentalism to New Thought Christianity as "the good Eugene search." What she found in Eugene was opportunity and a sense of freedom from debilitating judgment. "You can live any way you want to live here," she said. "Somehow we set a real model as a community, a model of acceptance and celebration of all the different expressions of spirituality."

Greg Flint, senior pastor at First Congregational Church, sees a darker side to Eugene. Take a look at the downstairs bulletin board at 5th Street Public Market, he suggested. There, you'll find "at least one poster, if not more, for every sort of New Age healing and of all the different therapies packaged as holistic thinking." Flint, who came to Eugene from Minnesota in 1985, described what he perceives as a broad definition of spirituality here—"broad and eclectic from Pentecostal speaking in tongues to Reiki to massage therapy to crystals." What he saw on the bulletin board, he said, revealed "quite a fascinating story—the story of who we are."

The problem with Eugene's broad definition of spirituality as a value system, according to Flint, is Eugene is a very "narcissistic" place. "We talk a lot about community but don't understand it as covenant with our neighbors. Here, community means everybody does their own thing. Covenant means, we take seriously the responsibility we have with and for each other." In Eugene, said Flint, the common thinking is: "I want to be free to do what I want to do when I want to do it. I am focused on my own wellness, my own wholeness.

"We talk about Eugene as if it were a kind of Nirvana—we like trees, we recycle—but we're a drug culture and we're not talking about it. From the '60s, we inherited the Me-generation, narcissism, and a really narrow view of Eastern religions that pulls out of them self-nurturing things and plugs in a culture of drug tolerance."

Mainstream or Countercultural?

Kimball Hodge, senior pastor since 1990 at First Baptist, Eugene's oldest church and one of its largest, likened Eugene to other liberal college communities, specifically Berkeley and Santa Cruz, but described Eugene as nonetheless very unique. "It's never been an average community," he said, adding that Eugene has had an intellectual and liberal bent since the UO started but became a university community in ways others have not. He noted that countercultural movements come out of causes, and that despite our reputation as a countercultural community in a kind of laid-back way, "strong opinions—legalism—remain in everything you do in Eugene, even such a seemingly simple activity as planting trees in your backyard."

Hodge went on to describe a community that tends to turn everything on its head. What once was countercultural has now become mainstream, and vice versa. He noted two examples, Saturday Market and the Eugene Celebration. Both events take place in the same downtown area as First Baptist and were once considered countercultural, but now, according to Hodge, they represent the mainstream culture of Eugene. First Baptist Church, which was once representative of mainstream Eugene culture, has become, over time, "countercultural in this community," Hodge asserted. "The pre-1960 church," he said, "was not countercultural but part of the culture. Now, we're the odd ones out, not thinking with the same kind of mind as our community in general thinks with."

Greg Flint made a similar observation. "Churchgoers are in a minority now," he said. "Anyone who participates in a faith community is in a minority. What is now truly mainline is not going to any church—nothing," Flint said. "People in Eugene go to the DAC [Downtown Athletic Club] and to coffee houses, they put on Spandex and go run, they climb Mt. Pisgah, go to the Coast, or to the mountains. All churches that are healthy now, be it First Congregational, Faith Center or the synagogue, recognize it's a different world and you can't do things in the same way."

The 1930s and '40s were still a period of legalism in church life, said Kimball Hodge. "If you didn't come, you sinned against God." While God was still "probably at the core of everything through the '50s" in terms of what people believed in as truth, Hodge said, "now the only thing at the core are certain scientific principles and mathematical equations."

Especially in the 1960s, Hodge noted, "we experienced the move from absolute to relative truth. People's beliefs are now up for grabs—morally, spiritually, and ethically. American society in general has moved away from values of tradition and moved to values of change. People believe change is good, tradition bad." Most churches that have stayed in a traditional mode, he said, are not succeeding.

Because people have so many choices, churches now need to cater, said Greg Flint. Taking a broad view of religious practice, Flint mentioned these things: "Competition is much more part of a church's life. People have much more of a consumer mentality. There's no denominational loyalty anymore. It used to be if you were a Methodist then you were always a Methodist. Churches are competing for people's time. If they're going to come on Sunday morning, then what you do had better be very good."

According to sociologist Benton Johnson, old mainline churches in Eugene constitute a smaller proportion of total churches than they would in other parts of the country. The decline of mainline denominations, he said, "is disproportionately greater in the West than in Texas or parts of the South," a decline spearheaded by those born after World War II. "There's no sign of a real turn-around coming, although the decline has slowed," Johnson said, adding: "People don't feel institutional religion has much to offer, and they don't feel that good responsibility that people should go to church."

Unchurched Seekers

According to a 1990 study reported in *The Register-Guard*, Oregon is one of the three least churched states in the nation, tied with Alaska one-tenth of a percentage point behind last-place Nevada. In top-place Utah, eight out of ten adult residents regularly attended religious services, while Oregon, in contrast, showed only 32.2 percent of adults in attendance against a national average of 56.6 percent. Nationally, church attendance had increased by 5 percent over a similar study published in 1980. Going exactly the opposite direction, Oregon had fallen by 4 percent, and Lane County by 5 percent. Lane County, and particularly Eugene, represents the lowest of the low.

Many of the people I spoke to not only mentioned this study, they emphasized it. Pastor Gregory Flint said his hunch is that "Eugene may have the lowest percentage of people involved in a faith community of anywhere in the country."

Pastor Steve Overman called the study's findings "a reality check" for the community's religious leaders. Interpreting the findings, Overman mentioned the long-time western disregard for tradition and the fact that "a lot of people migrate here for the purpose of independence." The bright side of the picture for Overman is that people in our area who do attend services go because of personal conviction rather than peer pressure.

In an interview with *The Register-Guard*, UO sociologist Mimi Goldman said it's not that Oregonians are less religious than the rest of Americans but just less likely to go to church. She described us as "believers but not belongers."

Anyone with eyes to see and ears to hear knows that Eugene is a community of spiritual seekers. Few may join their faith to community, but many believe in a higher power and fluidly define their own ways to worship.

And Yet, We Do Have Our Share of Churches

A list of churches in *The Register-Guard* church calendar pages of January 1945 shows sermon topics of these denominations—First

Baptist, Unitarian, Christ Church Unity, Central Presbyterian, First Christian, First Congregational, and a few others. St. Mary's Episcopal Church was set to burn its mortgage. First Baptist was hosting "an evening of Negro spirituals." The Eugene Council of Churchwomen was making clothing for women and children of the Philippines with material furnished by the U.S. government. Many area churches were participating in a World Day of Prayer, and the Northwest Christian College was sponsoring a talk by a well-known rabbi. The front pages throughout January and February 1945 were dominated by war news—local men missing in action or reported killed. Theologian-editor Paul Hutchison, speaking at the UO, said no compromise is possible between the concepts of totalitarianism and Christianity.

Many of the same churches still exist and are still prominent Eugene institutions. A few became mother institutions to smaller churches planted in outlying areas of the city. New denominations and new faiths have found a place here in the ensuing fifty-five years.

In 1999, a look at the telephone directory's Yellow Pages under the heading "Churches" shows six pages listing literally hundreds of churches—denominations ranging from Pentecostal Assemblies of God to Zen Buddhist. While Christian denominations dominate the listings, also represented are Jewish synagogues, a Muslim mosque and cultural center, a Buddhist priory, and a rich array of other spiritual centers. Eugene has a thriving Tibetan Buddhist contingent led by refugee Tibetan lamas. Eugene also houses an active Sikh community composed mostly of white middle-class professionals. Eugene has a Hindu presence as well as an estimated five hundred plus community of practicing Moslems. The Unitarian Universalist Church, whose congregants take an intellectual approach to spirituality and find their inspiration in religious pluralism, grew in attendance by about 42 percent in the last three years of the millennium. Membership stands at 245 at the beginning of the year 2000.

The Eugene Friends Meeting functions as one of the most

tolerant of Eugene denominations, a crucible quintessentially eclectic—operating with a core group of bedrock Christians who are closely associated with Jesus, and an increasingly large group of newcomers, many of whom, said Lois Barton, are unhappy with past religious experiences and have a hard time dealing with Christian terminology. While this is "trying" for many long-time members, Barton described the Meeting as nonetheless having "a spirit of warm acceptance." She painted a picture of a congregation with a long history of social activism that continues to embrace the social underdog. Whether working nationally with such organizations as American Friends Service Committee or locally with Clergy and Laity Concerned (CALC—recently renamed Community Alliance of Lane County), members of the congregation are "not buying souls," Barton said, "we're meeting the human needs of people in desperate situations."

Some Eugene churches have been around in one form or another since the beginning of Eugene's history. Oldest among them, First Baptist was organized in 1852 and still resides in the same block where it's been since 1868. It rivals Faith Center as the largest congregation in Eugene. Pastor Kimball Hodge recalled the charismatic wars that went on between First Baptist church and Faith Center starting in the 1960s and running into the '70s, a time of what he described as "dueling pulpits." Both congregations were active church planters in that era.

First Christian Church, formally organized in 1865, used to be the largest church in town. Senior Pastor Dan Bryant, an Albany native, said that during the 1920s and 1930s, one thousand people used to attend Sunday services, with a record of 1,200 during "rally days." Even until the 1960s, he said, 400 or more people attended worship, but the numbers have been in the 200-250 range ever since.

Bryant noted that in the aftermath of World War II, churchgoers were faced with the need to "intellectually come to terms with the Holocaust. The whole 'death of God' philosophy developed after that," which had a huge impact on Eugeneans "with our high level of education." Bryant went on to explain, "People have been coming to a new and different understanding of God. People put together new models that adapt scientific understanding to religious understanding, or they have to abandon a religious system."

John Koekkoek, pastor of First Norkenzie Christian Church since 1973, cites the significant presence of the Northwest Christian College in the Eugene community. Students from NCC bought the property upon which his church stands, began meeting in a tent and held vacation Bible school. "They came to the wilderness of north Eugene about 1956," he recalled. "Quite a number of Christian churches were started or influenced by NCC and staffed by their students." His church was very small in the '60s but forty years later had about six hundred members.

The oldest Catholic parish in Eugene, St. Mary's, was established in 1887 following more than thirty years of in-home services held by traveling priests and was, by the time of its centennial celebration, serving more than 1,200 families. Monsignor Edmund J. Murnane, whose fifty-nine-year career included the pastorship of St. Mary's Catholic Church from 1950 to 1969, established five other Catholic churches in the Eugene-Springfield area, the UO Newman Center, the Carmelite convent west of Eugene, and two of the area's major social service agencies (Catholic Charities and St. Vincent de Paul). Murnane was influential in establishing Serenity Lane, an alcohol and drug treatment center. But what others described as his proudest accomplishment was the founding of Marist High School in the mid-1960s, a visionary effort that involved persuading members of the religious order of Marist Brothers to move from East Coast to West. In a *Register-Guard* article, one of his parishioners, Ellen Lyford, said Murnane loved people and "was at home with the highest of the high and lowest of the low, and was just as friendly with all of them."

In 1997, St. Mary's offered in addition to English mass the largest Spanish service in Eugene, drawing more than three hundred people on Sunday afternoons—a contrast to early years when services were held in both English and German. In a town with a growing Hispanic community estimated by some at roughly 10 percent of our overall population, many denominations in addition to Catholics—including Baptists, Episcopalians, Mormons, and Jehovah's Witnesses—now offer a separate service in Español. Centro de Fe, affiliated with the Pentecostal Assemblies of God, is entirely a Spanish-language church.

In contrast, Eugene has a black population of less than 2 percent. Church of God in Christ Bethel Temple is a Pentecostal denomination and one of three churches in Eugene whose congregation consists largely of African Americans. Reverend Arthur Shankle has been pastor for more than thirty-eight years; he is presently the longest standing pastor in Eugene. Steve Overman said Shankle "built [the church] with his own hands."

St. Mark Christian Methodist Episcopal Church, the oldest predominantly black church in Lane County, was founded in the late 1940s in what a *Register-Guard* article described as "a black shantytown located on the north side of the Willamette River near the Ferry Street Bridge." After disappearing under the blades of bulldozers during bridge construction in 1949, St. Mark's was built and rebuilt off West 11th. One early pastor, Reverend Herman Riley, recalled for *The Register-Guard* that the church was both a spiritual center and the social hub for the black community. In the early 1990s, under the charismatic leadership of a female pastor, Allidees Beckham, the church was known for its outreach ministries. In 1996, Beckham estimated that nearly one-third of the church's regular Sunday congregation was non-black.

Founded after World War II, Temple Beth Israel (TBI) was aligned with Judaism's mainstream Conservative movement for most of its history. After a period of growth and change that culminated in a painful split, a small, orthodox group founded a new synagogue in 1994. With the main body of the congregation still intact, TBI became in 1996 the ninety-first synagogue in the country and the second in Oregon to formally affiliate with the

Reconstructionist movement, a liberal branch of Judaism that embraces contemporary interpretations of Jewish traditions.

Scholar Phil Zuckerman described TBI as progressing from a small, humble congregation in the 1950s and 1960s, through growth in the 1970s, then truly booming in the 1980s. Rabbi Myron Kinberg arrived in the mid-1970s when the temple had 118 families. By the early 1990s, it had 350 and in 1999 not only enjoys record numbers, but has embarked on an ambitious fundraising campaign to build a new temple.

Rabbi Yitzhak Husbands-Hankin, who worked with Kinberg the full eighteen years of his stay in Eugene, described him as a "great community builder who had an extraordinary influence on the city." Husbands-Hankin noted Kinberg's commitment to causes of justice and the wide range of friendships he developed.

Kinberg was spiritually grounded, but a new model, said Husbands-Hankin. "He was a wrestler, an athlete, with a unique blend of abilities and great personal warmth. He taught Jews not to closet their Judaism, but to wear it proudly as a gift and to offer the goodness of it out into the world. He showed Jewish people how to live in two cultures simultaneously in a comfortable and whole way. Here was a rabbi that could hit a homerun."

Second largest denominational presence in Eugene after the Catholic churches, Mormons, who attend the Church of Jesus Christ of Latter-Day Saints, are known for strict morals and emphasis on family values. A highly structured organization with many leaders, Mormons are close knit, believe they will be judged for their works, believe that marriage is eternal, and put an emphasis on genealogy. Taught to abstain from tobacco, tea, coffee, and alcohol, Mormons are commonly stereotyped by those outside the faith. As one young Mormon put it to a *Register-Guard* reporter in a 1990 article about the opening of a new Mormon missionary center in Eugene: "People think that maybe we're robots, and we have no personality and we're going to convert the whole neighborhood. They think we're brainwashed, suit-wearing, bike-riding clones. I haven't met any missionaries like that." In 1990, the

Mormon church had at least 7,500 members in central Lane County, up from 6,000 in 1976. The membership has continued to show strong growth.

At century's turn, the largest single church in Eugene is one that didn't even exist in 1945—the 2,500 member Faith Center, one of three Eugene Foursquare churches. Founded in 1952, Faith Center rose to prominence in the community under the leadership of the late Roy Hicks Jr., whose untimely death in an airplane crash in 1994 caught *The Register-Guard* off guard. When more than five thousand people attended Hicks's memorial service at the Lane County Fairgrounds, The *Register-Guard* couldn't help but hear about it. And yet, few people on the staff knew who Hicks was or had any inkling of his influence in the community. "We were out of the loop," remembers *Register-Guard* reporter Jeff Wright.

In an end-of-the-century summation, *Register-Guard* columnist Bob Welch listed Hicks as one of the twelve people who most influenced the shaping of Lane County over the past hundred years. "In 1969," he wrote, "Hicks launched a congregation of 75—infused by the 'Jesus Movement'—that turned into one of Lane County's largest churches." Steve Overman, under whose pastorship Faith Center has continued to grow, reminisced that people flocked unshaved and unbathed to the gym that then comprised the worship hall. Self-described as "come-as-you-are," Faith Center—although now a bastion of conservative, albeit charismatic, Christianity—was countercultural in the early 1970s, what First Christian pastor Dan Bryant described as "the happening church."

Collaborations

Eclectic by nature, collaborations in Eugene have been many and vigorous. The following are only a few of the more successful ones from recent decades.

• Steve Overman has been an unusually active bridge builder not only locally, but also internationally. For seven years he partici-

pated in a dialogue on the international level that brought together representatives from Pentecostal and Roman Catholic
churches, even taking Overman to the Vatican for a meeting with
Pope John Paul II. A report published in 1998 speaks of the "scandal of a divided witness." Overman said in a *Register-Guard* interview that "When you're preaching a message of conciliation and
you can't get along with each other, that's a scandal. Brothers and
sisters in Christ need to learn to walk together."

In 1999, Overman noted that the lay of the land in Eugene-
Springfield religious circles since the early '60s had been a kind of
separatism. Catholic churches had their own association of priests
and leaders; the liberal liturgical mainline Protestants had their
organization; and the Evangelical and Pentecostal churches had
theirs—the still-active Lane Association of Evangelicals. The ecu-
menical-interfaith Eugene Ministerial Association had become
depleted.

Overman said that in the mid-1990s, he began to wonder—
do we have any duty toward our civic community as pastors for
different churches to gather once in a while and stand before God
on behalf of the city? John Koekkoek recalled that the idea was
batted around between pastors, but that "it took somebody of
Steve's stature to make it happen."

For nearly four years now, Catholic and Protestant pastors that
range the whole spectrum from fundamentalist to extreme liberal
have met quarterly over lunch to pray for the city. Although the
first several gatherings took place at Faith Center, now they move
from church to church. The half-hour prayer service "takes on the
flavor of the place they are meeting," Overman reported. The au-
tumn 1999 gathering, for example, which met at the First Congregational Church, included images of God as both mother and
father. Such exchange, Overman said, builds tolerance and understanding as well as fellowship. Koekkoek sees it as "truly an attempt to reconcile, to demonstrate that we have more things that
unite us instead of divide us.

Out of the pastors' prayer meetings emerged what Overman

described as a precedent-setting event, a standing-room-only joint worship service held at the Lane County Fairgrounds on Pentecost Sunday in June 2000 that drew more than five thousand people. Virtually every Christian church in the Eugene-Springfield area was represented.

• When Temple Beth Israel was sprayed with gunfire by racist skinheads during the Passover season in March 1994, First Christian's Dan Bryant was among the first to respond. He quickly organized nightly vigils at the temple, which were staffed by a diverse range of churches—including Methodists, Unitarians, Mormons, and Baptists—as well as non-church groups. The vigils served as an expression of outrage against the shooting, as well as an act of solidarity to give Jews a sense of safety as they visited their synagogue during Passover. A *Register-Guard* account of the subsequent honoring of Bryant—he was declared "a righteous gentile," and a tree was planted in his honor on a hillside near Jerusalem—quotes members of the Jewish Federation as saying Bryant "played a key role in stabilizing, and then helping to heal, a wounded Jewish community."

Rabbi Myron Kinberg, known in part for his social activism, was already very much involved with Christian clergy when Bryant arrived in Eugene in 1991. Bryant remembers that the Eugene Ministerial Association held traditional Thanksgiving eve services which alternated between First Christian, First Congregational and Central Presbyterian. About that time Gary Powell came to pastor First Methodist, which then hosted the Anne Frank touring exhibit, what Bryant described as a "pivotal event" that really fostered a relationship between First Methodist and Temple Beth Israel. TBI was invited into that ministerial association, and the group became truly interfaith. It was to die out but be reborn in November 1994 as Two Rivers Interfaith Ministry (TRIM).

Bryant recalls that he and fellow pastors, Greg Flint and Tiare Mathison-Bowie (now the Presbyterian campus minister at the UO), wanted to form a cluster of religious leaders that was broader than Catholic-Protestant. TRIM meets monthly and includes representatives from some of the more liberal Christian churches, Temple Beth Israel, Unity, Unitarian Universalist, Baha'i, Islamic Cultural Center, Buddhist, Religious Science, Christian Science, Hindu, and others.

• Mediator Gayle Landt, who founded the Conflict Resolution Center (an affiliate of both the Oregon Pacific Research Institute and the Appropriate Dispute Resolution Program at the UO law school) began meeting weekly in 1994 with twelve Lane County leaders who represented the traditional Christian community, gay rights activists, and in one case, the Oregon Citizens Alliance (OCA). The OCA's sponsorship of a series of local and state anti-gay initiatives had created a legacy of polarization and bitterness toward conservative Christians. Landt sought to ease polarization between evangelical Christians and gay and lesbian activists through her work.

John Koekkoek, pastor of First Norkenzie Christian Church, was one of those who participated. He remembered it this way: "When Gayle came and talked to me about her idea, I thought it was a good idea but didn't think I'd have forty-plus hours available for participation. But then I thought, 'how long has it been since you've really been in the marketplace' . . . it was probably one of the most meaningfully moving experiences of my life. The awareness of the amount of hostility [the gay and lesbian community] felt from us was hard for me to fathom. I didn't feel it internally, but the more I listened the more I sensed. Nadia [Telsey] looked across at me, said something like, 'I'm aware of the fact you'd probably just as soon see me fry in hell as even be concerned about who I am.' She was about the same age as my oldest daughter. I asked her for her forgiveness. Nadia and I met and embraced. She accepted those were not my feelings. I had a sense of the kind of pain she has felt as a female, Jewish lesbian."

Koekkoek said he felt the people who participated established relationships with one another that were meaningful. "The emphasis was on how to appreciate and value other people without changing our own basic convictions. Gayle told us to remember—when we get through, we're still going to have to live together in this community."

Landt reported that by the end of 1994, "the people in the circle were able to say, 'We love you and this is what we believe the Bible says,' and it worked out because they would demonstrate a kind of Christian love that was credible to people. The conservative Christians' commitment to the Bible was major in their ability to reach common ground, even though that Bible tells them that homosexuality is a sin and it separates people from God."

Conclusion

As the world becomes a global village, so does Eugene. Predominantly of white European descent, Eugeneans are also a weave of Asian, African American, Hispanic, Native American, and many other threads. Our religious and spiritual practices reflect the cultures we brought with us to this place and the multitudinal ways in which the mixture of practices have sparked new ones. We are a microcosm of what is becoming America's increasingly pluralistic society, and we are eclectic not just because we have a university that attracts people from different cultures who have different spiritual beliefs, and not just because of the persistence of '60s counterculture.

Even when Christian faith *was* the norm, when it was mainstream rather than countercultural to attend a mainline Christian church, Eugene housed alternative seekers. Spiritualists, for example, had a strong presence in Lane County in the mid-1800s.

We have every right to hold our heads high in regard to our eclecticism. That's who we are. That's the way we've always been. "The 1906 census shows Oregon to have been a hotbed for new and unusual religions of the time," according to University of Washington professor Rodney Stark. In a *Register-Guard* article by Jeff Wright, Stark asserted, "astrologers and self-described healers have always felt at home here." The same article reported that Oregon ranked third in the nation in terms of the rate of centers and shrines devoted to apparitions of the Virgin Mary.

Pastor Sherry Lady emphasized our intense diversity—Eugene spawned that quintessential hippie celebration, the Oregon Country Fair, but it also drew tens of thousands of searching Christian men to Autzen Stadium for Promise Keepers gatherings in the summers of 1996 and 1998.

Nearly everyone I talked with emphasized the westward movement, which brought with it people who were uneasy with the status quo. Eugeneans are still that way. We're people on a journey, and we always will be.

Bibliography

Moore, Lucia W., Nina W. McCornack & Gladys W. McCready. *The Story of Eugene*. New York: Stratford House, 1949.

The Register-Guard, selected articles, 1996–1999.

Velasco, Dorothy. *Lane County: An Illustrated History of the Emerald Empire*. Windsor Publications, 1985.

Zuckerman, Phil. *Strife in the Sanctuary: Religious Schism in a Jewish Community*. Walnut Creek, Calif.: Altamira Press, 1999.

UNCOMMON SCHOOLS

by Debra Gwartney

WHEN HERMAN LAWSON—a teacher, principal, and administrator for Eugene District schools—neared the end of his thirty-five-year career, he realized layers of local school history were drifting into obscurity. Little effort had been made to interview the district's early teachers, many of whom had passed away by the time Lawson began thinking about preserving the historic record. Each time the school district moved its administrative headquarters—from the first building at 11th and Willamette (which later served for many years as Eugene's City Hall) to the vacated Washington Street School and then to the current site on Monroe Street—mounds of documents were thrown out rather than preserved because of the expense of archiving them.

Eugene's district has a rich past. Full of pioneer spirit in the early days, it demonstrated unabashed creativity as the city's modern era set in at the end of the 1950s, and a bold approach to education sparked in the 1960s that holds to this day. Though many early accounts of public education in Eugene turned to ashes when the administration building burned in 1910, Lawson was determined to reconstruct as much history as he could compile, lest the city be left without the context of its efforts to educate children.

Herman Lawson gave up his post as assistant to the superintendent in 1983 and began to write his book. In 1985, he finished *A System of Uncommon Schools: The History of School District 4J.*

Innovation is at the heart of the educator's account. Indeed,

the ingenuity of staff and administrators is a major theme for 4J
and has been since the district's beginnings in 1855. For instance,
the district, fourth to be established in the county, was one of the
first in the state to establish a high school, in 1897. Classes held in
the superintendent's office and at the district's first real school-
house, Central School, were a rare opportunity for older students.
Most districts in the state and the country believed an eighth-
grade education was enough. This community, however, wanted
more advanced opportunities for young people and rallied to support the construction of a high school. In 1903, Eugene High
opened at 11th Avenue and Willamette.

Many other innovations followed. Eugene was one of the first
districts in the state to have a woman serve on the school board;
her term began in 1904. In 1937, the district was the first nationally to create a single-salary schedule, putting elementary and secondary teachers, and men and women, on an even par. For some
school districts in the nation, that wasn't a priority until late in
the century.

In the 1930s another educational development came to life:
the Eugene Vocational School. In a series of articles written for
Lane Community College in 1976, educator David Butler explained
how the school came to be. The Great Depression "had Eugene on
its knees" by the mid-1930s, causing more than 2,500 young people
to roam the city, unskilled and uneducated, Butler wrote. The
dire situation, stretched over years, caused the state's director of
vocational education, O.D. Adams, to quietly circulate a ques-
tionnaire among business owners in Eugene asking what training
was needed for those so desperately out of work. Adams returned
to Salem to create a vocational program for Eugene.

It was a challenge. Through depression years, a general dis-
taste for "manual training" kept public education concentrated on
traditional reading, writing, and arithmetic lessons. The reality of
the depression and a virtual halt to Eugene's economy made it
clear that young people had to be taught practical skills. But where
would the money come from? In 1934, with bad times hammer-

ing down on the city, the school board was forced to close two schools, Patterson and Geary, and had "pared its operating budget to the bone," according to Butler. Patterson School was soon demolished, but Geary—located at 4th Avenue and Madison—remained standing. It looked to many like a good site for a vocational school. A series of "bull sessions" with civic leaders and the state's vocational education department deepened the community's commitment to vocational education. But no one knew, precisely, how to proceed.

"There were few, if any, models to follow," Butler wrote. "The industry or union-affiliated vocational schools were rich, well-equipped, and thorough. They were also a hundred light years away from anything a struggling school district could afford."

On January 4, 1938, the *Eugene Register-Guard* announced the possibility of a vocational school in the city, a cooperative between School District No. 4 and the state. Improved district budgets and legislative support would allow the school to open and make it the first such school in the nation—in years to come it would be much emulated. On February 1 "at a broken down old grade school on Fourth Ave. and Madison Street in Eugene, the Eugene Vocational School opened for business," Butler wrote. "It was to stay in business for 27 years."

With free tuition, the Eugene Vocational School thrived in the post–World War II years, helping thousands of veterans return to the workforce. But by the 1960s, modernized Eugene had broader requirements. Young people sought a more well-rounded education in combination with practical skills. With support from the legislature and the school district, Eugene Vocational School was transformed into Lane Community College.

As the community college was finding ways to serve older students, the Eugene school district was busy fueling innovation at the elementary, middle school, and high school levels.

By mid-century, Eugene's school district had become a powerhouse in the state. Legislation that encouraged, even pushed, small districts to consolidate into larger ones caused eight smaller districts to join District No. 4, which in 1945 became 4J. Sometimes, Lawson said, "a bitter battle was waged" in the rural communities over the decision to stay autonomous but under-funded or to melt into the big pot. Those that joined included Spencer Butte, Santa Clara, Willagillespie, College Crest, Bailey Hill, River Road, Oak Hill, Willakenzie, Fox Hollow and Coburg.

Of the nearby school districts, only Bethel opted to remain independent. In 1948, residents of the Irving, Danebo, and Bethel districts voted to consolidate themselves, rather than join the Eugene school district. The merger brought the elementary student population to 517. A few months later, Malabon residents voted to join Bethel as well.

By October of that year, Bethel district voters approved a $650,000 bond measure to build additions onto elementary schools and to begin construction on Willamette High School, which opened in 1949.

"I think Bethel has remained separate because it all comes down to the pride people have had in their district," said Gordon Slate, a Bethel teacher for twenty-eight years, in a community statement on the district's history. "Twenty-five or thirty years ago consolidation might have been helpful, because Eugene had many, many more services than we had at that time. But as we have grown, the ability of this district to achieve its goals and the ability of people to sit down and talk and discuss things, have led to a district that has a very strong base."

Scott Lowell, a long-time resident and Willamette High graduate agreed that the decision not to consolidate was best. "I think of Bethel School District as 'big enough to serve, small enough to care,' " he said. "There is a real pride in this community because we are separate and distinct from Eugene. It's almost like a small-town atmosphere where the high school is the center of activity."

In the 1950s, with nearly 14,000 students, "construction [in 4J] became a way of life," Lawson said. Plans for a second high school—

North Eugene High (which caused Eugene High to become South
Eugene High)—were drawn up in 1951. The doors of that school
opened in 1957, much to the relief of overcrowded high schoolers
and their families. Dozens of other schools were built, and teachers were hired by the droves, for newly increased salaries.

These were hectic times, the fast-growth years. "Buildings were
going up right and left and older buildings, like Edison and Dunn,
had additions built," said Lawson. "In a year or two the additions
were full and we'd be out building again."

It had to be done on a shoestring, though—even in those days,
the budget was constrained. "Buildings were put up rapidly and
inexpensively," Lawson said. Architects knew the budgetary limits, so designed boxy buildings with flat roofs. "Cheap to build;
very expensive to maintain," he said.

Lawson recalled that in 1961, when he was principal of the
newly erected Parker Elementary School, a woman came in to complain about all the "palaces" 4-J was building. "It was a rainy day,"
he said, and he calmly escorted the angry woman to the long hall-
way of the school, which was strewn with buckets catching a steady
flow of drips from the poorly constructed, flat roof. In retelling the
story, Lawson shrugged: "Some palace."

Getting enough space for students was only one consideration in
those days. As the population of the district burgeoned, the superintendent pushed for new ways to educate students. In the late
1950s, Superintendent Millard Z. Pond—like his colleagues all
over the country—was looking for ways to respond to President
Eisenhower's encouragement to bring new energy, a spark of imagination, to the way young people were taught. The country was
feeling whipped by the launch of Russia's Sputnik in 1957, and
the president wanted a generation of citizens more far-reaching in
inventiveness, students able to imagine space travel and rocket
building. Pond embraced the challenge, advocating new approaches
to teaching and furiously writing grants to obtain funding for the
innovations.

In 1960, the Eugene Project was born. Introducing such education concepts as the open classroom and team teaching, and abolishing the traditional grading system, the program—funded in part by a $335,000 three-year grant from the Rockefeller Fund for the Advancement of Education—changed the way 4J approached learning. The twelve-step plan that was the backbone of the Eugene Project even suggested that television be used in the classroom as a teaching tool—unheard of in those days. Another step proposed a program for older students and provided funding for that effort, a move that helped the Eugene Vocational School transform into Lane Community College.

As the project got rolling, teaching innovations in Eugene gained national attention. Because of its level of excellence, the district was invited to send several teachers to Stanford University for a two-year training program. They returned in the early 1960s with a framework called the Social Living Program. The idea was to combine themes in classes such as history, geography, and language arts, so students would experience more comprehensive learning.

Roosevelt Middle School, on 24th and Hilyard Street, took on the program fully. The innovations at that school were so lauded that educators and administrators from all over the nation came to Roosevelt to observe and learn. Back in 1915, Eugene's school district boldly took the step of creating one of the nation's first junior high schools, Lawson said. "But it was in the 1960s that the middle school in Eugene truly became innovative."

Change didn't come without some level of public dissent, however. Parents who wanted their children taught "the basics" voiced concern at board meetings. Some parents and community members formed a lay committee to closely scrutinize 4J. "We'd see them parked outside the playgrounds, watching everything teachers did with students," Lawson said.

Instead of allowing the negative response to alarm him, though, Pond encouraged community activity and scrutiny. In fact, he asked that more lay committees be formed to advise on nearly all aspects of the district. The trend of parental involvement in 4J that continues to this day has its roots in Pond's reaction.

Over time, some of the most extreme innovations begun in the 1960s were tempered. Judy Wenger, a lifetime resident of Eugene and twenty-year 4J veteran who teaches at Roosevelt, said that when she joined the faculty in 1979 the movement for no grades was going strong. "I remember my mentor, Ray Scofield, saying that you can't penalize students with grades if you want them to try something new," she said.

For the first years of Wenger's time at Roosevelt, the school still operated on a credit/no credit basis. But parents in the early 1980s asserted pressure on the school, Wenger said, demanding that students who excelled be recognized for that level of work. Under that pressure, Roosevelt adopted a more traditional grading system.

David Piercy, current assistant to the superintendent of 4J, said that when he and his family moved to Eugene in 1977, they found some of the innovations were a bit tough to accept, particularly the "open enrollment" policy that made it possible for children to attend any school in the district. "Our first hit was that we had a choice where to send our own child, but it was almost a negative hit," he said. "We came here valuing the concept of the neighborhood school, and we first resented the district's policy that took children away. It was especially tough because we lived in the Whiteaker neighborhood, and the school was really suffering."

Piercy said he and his wife, former state representative Kitty Piercy, soon came to realize that open enrollment worked for families who had "kids with different needs," although they continue to support the concept of neighborhood schools. "When I arrived, I saw immediately a set of independent schools that were innovative, creative, different. Not all the policies were ones I personally agreed with, but there was synergy and energy in the schools," he said.

Although Pond may have launched that "synergy and energy," most long-time observers of the school district believe it was one man, Superintendent Tom Payzant, who made 4J truly dynamic.

A Harvard graduate, the thirty-two-year-old Payzant was the obvious candidate when he interviewed for the position in 1973, according to Jim Sellers, *Register-Guard* education reporter at that time. "He was knocking baseballs out of the park," Sellers said. "He said the right things. Not necessarily the things the board wanted to hear, but [he provided] the kinds of change and energy the board was seeking."

The board hired the young superintendent to shake the district up, and shake he did. This "star from the East," as former school board member Frank Nearing describes Payzant, "barely had his feet under the desk" before he came to the board with a series of recommendations for change. "He told us to 'vote me up or vote me down,' letting us know how straightforward he was and that he was clearly in charge," Nearing said. "I asked Jim Sellers his first impression of Payzant. Sellers's response was, 'Wow.' "

Changes came swiftly and dramatically. Payzant quickly established the open enrollment policy, for instance, so the community felt as if there was a true choice and a real reason to get involved with the district, according to Piercy. "Parents tend to be more supportive of public school systems if they have a choice and get to help design programs," Piercy said. "That was Payzant's thinking."

The new superintendent was also determined to establish kindergartens in the district. For years voters had rejected bond levy after bond levy that included the formation of kindergartens. It was only after the school board winnowed the budget down and excluded kindergarten that local levies—the primary source of school funding in those days—passed. But Payzant told the board he'd have none of the community "game playing," according to Lawson, who served as his assistant superintendent. "He advised us to hold firm, to tell the community that this is our budget, this is what we need to keep schools open and to keep giving it back to them in whole until it passed."

A *Register-Guard* editorial warned Payzant that the question had been raised seven times since 1968 and that the community had spoken. "The school board must face the fact that the public is not in the mood nor has the funds to pay for added services," the paper stated. But, astonishingly, Payzant's unprecedented forcefulness worked. The levy passed, though narrowly, in 1974. Kindergartens were added to schools, to the delight of many and the consternation of quite a few. With five-year-olds streaming into the district, Payzant's detractors grew in number and launched a recall effort against the board, which quickly failed.

Payzant clearly thrilled a dimension of the community by reorganizing the administration to encourage new, creative thinking. He also deftly managed to put into place the state's new collective bargaining law that allowed, for the first time, legal teacher strikes. The young super also pushed hard for alternative schools. He wanted 4J to be a national leader in creating educational alternatives, and it quickly became so. The Magnet Arts School opened as Eugene's first alternative school in 1974 with 150 students enrolled and used the arts and creative process to teach a traditional curriculum. Soon after, the alternative called Eastside opened in Edison Elementary School. It wasn't long until other alternatives bloomed: A Spanish bilingual program at Meadowlark Elementary that soon became the district's Spanish immersion program; a French immersion program at Fox Hollow Elementary; a Japanese immersion program—Yujin Gakuen—the first of its kind in the nation. In 1984, the International High School (IHS), first at South Eugene High and later at Sheldon and Churchill High Schools, was born. An alternative school in international studies for grades nine through twelve, IHS was a college preparatory program that taught global understanding and communication, cultural differences, and the human condition.

Although Payzant left Eugene in 1978 before many of the alternatives were established, his push was clearly the impetus for the influx of 4J's well-known alternative schools. Yet, a troubled dissent followed the superintendent through many of his sweeping decisions. Nearing recalled, for instance, a program in the district in which sixteen master teachers, headquartered at the administration building, were on-call for teachers who needed special expertise. The master teachers stepped in to teach workshops in math, reading, science, and music that were beyond the regular teachers' abilities. A district-wide survey ordered by Payzant discovered that the master teachers' services were a low priority. Within months, Payzant had dismantled the system and reassigned each of the master teachers to ordinary posts. "It was a real kick in the pants to the ego of these teachers, but Payzant believed it was the best use of personnel," said Nearing. "He wasn't afraid to make decisions like that."

In 1976, one of the largest conflicts ever experienced at 4J took place under Payzant's leadership. Payzant's early marching orders—described to him even in his interview—was to "do something about secondary education." Nearing said that same mandate was repeated strongly after his first-year review with the board. "That was the firecracker," Nearing said. Within weeks, Payzant returned with a recommendation to move three high school principals from their schools.

Although it was commonplace to move elementary and middle school principals to keep their jobs lively, Lawson said, it was unheard of to move well-established high school principals. "No one else would have had the nerve to do it," he said. "It turned out to be the biggest rhubarb the district has ever seen."

Sellers said Payzant's decision created an unprecedented uproar in the city. "Movement in the elementary and middle school engendered no controversy. It never caused news coverage," Sellers said. "But those high school principals had been in their jobs a long time. They had a lot of loyalties built up among their constituents. They had basically built fiefdoms; Payzant knew their loyalties were not to the board and superintendent. It was time for new blood."

Again, Payzant was swift in his decision. One April day he called in the three popular high school principals and three popular junior high school principals and told them, in essence, that they were all switching jobs. Cliff Moffitt, principal of South Eugene High, would move to Madison Junior High, while Roosevelt Middle School's Don Jackson would move to South. Sheldon's principal, Wayne Flynn, was reassigned to Roosevelt, while Madison Middle School's Brad Templeman would move to Sheldon. At Churchill High School, Principal Charles Zollinger was to be replaced by Sue Leabo, the principal at Spencer Butte, while Zollinger would move to Cal Young Middle School.

In other words, nearly the whole city would be affected by the change. The town went wild. Within days, a community movement to oust the board and superintendent formed. That group immediately filed suit, citing an infraction of the Oregon Public Meetings Law. In response, a community group in support of Payzant formed. In early May, 600 citizens turned out at a public meeting on the issue, which many observers described as a "bitter confrontation."

By summer, the three high school principals had filed a suit against the district; in December, a judge ruled that the three had to be reinstated to their high school posts. The school board, however, won on appeal. The principals retaliated by appealing to the State Supreme Court, which ruled in 1979 that Payzant and the board were within their rights to transfer the principals, but that the principals were also within their rights to file a complaint with the Fair Practices Board. In the meantime, a circuit court judge had ruled that by discussing specific policy instructions with the superintendent in a closed-door executive session, the board had violated the Oregon Public Meetings Law. By that time the lawsuits were settled, however, Payzant was in Oklahoma City, where he launched a successful career as a school administrator that would take him next to San Diego and finally to his current position as superintendent of schools in Boston. The principals dropped the matter and abided by the court's decision.

The mess had a lasting impact. Not only were school boards and public bodies all over the state put on notice that they had to abide by the Oregon Public Meetings Law, citizens in Eugene also formed another recall effort in the late 1970s. That recall vote failed, but most of the board was replaced in the next election by anti-Payzant forces.

Within a year, with Superintendent Tom Dorland at the helm, that board would face the Eugene School District's first strike, a walkout that lasted ten days and caused unprecedented scenes of ugly dispute among teachers and administrators. A 1973 Collective Bargaining law passed by the state legislature allowed for public school teachers to leave their posts if contract negotiations failed. It took less than six years for Eugene 4J teachers to take advantage of that provision. The school district, with an enrollment of just over 19,000 students then, saw most of their 1,200 teachers fail to return to school when the year began in fall 1979. Dorland quickly hired more than 700 replacement teachers so that children missed only two days of instruction, but from the beginning the hostilities between the teachers and the substitutes caused a sense of despair within the city. At least two dozen of the replacements quit, so fearful were they of potential violence.

The key issue at stake was salaries, with the two sides $700,000 apart when they first came to the table. By the time the strike settled nine days later, the teachers received a substantial raise, but morale was so damaged at the district that Dorland resigned barely a year later.

With the sense of hostility still fairly fresh in the public's mind, Eugeneans were astonished when a second 4J strike occurred nine years after the first. Then-superintendent Margaret Nichols decided that, in order to avoid the polarization and violence of the earlier strike, she would cancel school. From April 8 until April 28, 1988, 4J schoolchildren had an unexpected holiday. Finally, when the two sides—who were disputing about both pay raises and retirement benefits—showed no sign of settling, Nichols relented and began hiring replacement teachers. As many had anticipated, the sight of replacement teachers rolling in on buses infuriated the weary, beleaguered strikers, and hostilities broke out. Teachers were arrested day after day, a move that seemed only to further ignite the situation. Finally, late Friday afternoon May 8, the teachers union voted to ratify an agreement with the school board, and teachers dashed back to their classrooms, relieved that they could finally return to their jobs.

The past two decades—most of which were guided by Superintendent Margaret Nichols, a beloved leader who died of cancer in 1998—have seen many changes in the district, perhaps more subtle and more driven by societal shifts than what happened under Pond and Payzant. From the perspective of Roosevelt's Judy Wenger, the changes have brought new challenges. Where class sizes were restricted, at the end of the '70s, to twenty-four students, it's now common to see thirty-five or more students crammed in a classroom. "It's impossible to get around to every kid," Wenger said. "There's a lot less personal feedback now."

Technology is another huge shift. "There's a hum in the class we've never heard before," she said. One of the surprise effects of technology is the way gadgets separate students by socio-economic class. "The 'have-nots' are shown up like never before when wealthier kids come in with the fanciest hand-held calculators, the disc-players, and headphones," she said.

Wenger has also found her day crowded with more "other" teaching. The anti-violence lessons, the HIV lessons, the meaning behind pledging allegiance to the flag, for example. And she worries about the diminished "school unity" that used to come from school sports, as well as the new trend of carrying enormous and heavy backpacks to school every day. "Also, there's just more fear now," she said. "Kids fear change and are uneasy when their world changes, as it does so often now. So many kids now act out of fear, fear of getting a bad grade, fear of the future. Where am I going? Will I get into college?"

For 4J specifically, the major shift of the past ten years is the erosion of local control as the state legislature has assumed nearly all responsibility for funding in the wake of Measure 5 and 47. These property tax limitation measures have led to the demise of art, music, and sports programs in many schools. Librarians, counselors, and teachers aides have been laid off in large numbers. In addition, with legislated school standards and school testing, some teachers and administrators feel they have lost the ability to create their own timing, their own curriculum, their own teaching styles. "With everyone focusing on outcomes, it limits the abilities of schools to be unique, innovative, and energetic," Piercy said.

"The state standards are very unfortunate," added Lawson. "What I learned about students years ago was that children learn in different ways. To teach them the same way in the same time is like lining them up on the street and telling them to run the 100-yard dash and get to the finish line at the same time. It's not good."

And, yet, it's what 4J is faced with: the stringency of state testing and the "outcome" model of education. A school district that has been a shining example of innovation is now being forced to find a way to be the same as every other district in the state.

At the same time, Piercy said, many parents, teachers, and community members believe it's necessary to take a hard look at the alternative schools, to measure their successes and to ensure that they truly are quantifiably different, and that they are equitable. "Access to the programs is a huge issue we will look at," Piercy said. "Does everyone have a chance to participate? Are there subtle forms of discrimination? Is there access to transportation?"

Innovations are still popping up at 4J: from the program offered to public school students at the Center for Appropriate Transport, where kids get an education while learning to build and maintain bicycles, to the support homeschooled children are given by the district if they need help with specific subjects parents are unable to teach. Also recently established is a 4J "cyberschool," where students are able to take courses and fulfill credits from their own home computers.

Sadly, though, the year 2000 dawned with the 145-year-old

school district in perhaps its most discouraged state ever. In January, Superintendent George Russell, who took over leadership of 4J upon Margaret Nichols's death, proposed to the school board that an election should be held in the spring asking the public to support a local option levy. "But even if it passed, we'd still be looking at a shortfall of $2 million to $3.5 million the following year, and double that the next year," he said. In May, voters approved the $6 million levy, but Russell still recommended a $1.2 million cut to keep the district afloat.

Russell said that state property tax relief measures, as well as the legislature's control of school funding, have had a tremendously negative impact on the school district. "A significant decrease in counselors, librarians, teachers' aides—all those adults who used to have daily interaction with kids are gone," he said. "And so many of the innovations in the school district developed in the 1960s and 1970s have been eroded away."

For instance, when Russell joined the district in the early 1970s, 4J was acclaimed throughout the nation for being the only school district with elementary school counselors. "Essentially, now there are no counselors in elementary schools," he said. "And when we start talking about innovation and how we want to provide for children, we find it hard to talk about because of our resource situation."

Perhaps, Russell said, as funds dwindle and the strong cadre of teachers loyal to 4J for the past twenty to thirty years retires, the district will have to "give up some of the old and traditional ways of educating kids." Perhaps more of them will have to learn from home, by computer. Perhaps paid, trained staff will have to be replaced by senior citizens and other community members who want to volunteer at the schools.

"We have to face the fact that many of the programs that attracted folks to 4J are pretty much gone, specifically at elementary level. Also, so many electives have been eliminated at the high schools that children have a lot of free time and that's troubling to many parents," he said. " I was hopeful that once we got a local option levy that we'd be able to use the money for restoration of programs that made us outstanding. But, in fact, we'll have to use those funds to simply maintain the bare bones."

Bibliography

Bethel School District. "Why be Independent?" Eugene.

———. "The 'Ol District Office." Eugene.

———. "In the Beginning." Eugene.

Butler, David. Fourth and Madison. Eugene: Lane Community College, 1976.

Lawson, Herman. A System of Uncommon Schools: The History of Eugene School District 4J, 1854-1985. Eugene: School District 4J 1985

Moore, Lucia W., Nina W. McCornack & Gladys W. McCready. *The Story of Eugene*. New York: Stratford House, 1949.

The Register-Guard, 12 Sep. 1972–15 Sep. 1995.

School District 4J. "About 4J." Eugene.

———. "The History of Yujin Gakuen." Eugene.

———. "International High School." Eugene.

———. "Meadowlark History." Eugene.

DOING MORE WITH LESS:

THE HISTORY OF THE

UNIVERSITY OF OREGON

By Keith Richard

IN DECEMBER 1943 Donald M. Erb, president of the University of Oregon, died of pneumonia. Within the next several months the university prepared for the end of World War II and the resulting crush of students anticipated with the enactment of federal legislation creating the G. I. Bill. The leadership of the university was in the hands of an acting president, Orlando J. Hollis, and a search to find a new president was postponed for more than one year. During this critical period the administration made many decisions that would have an impact on the long-term future of the university and its students.

Through Hollis's leadership his advisors correctly anticipated the immediate needs of the university and, ultimately, met most of those needs. One of the greatest obstacles of the increased enrollment was the lack of campus facilities to accommodate the students—in classroom space and housing. A second problem was the need to hire faculty to meet the academic requirements of the students. In many ways it was easier to meet the latter than the former as it took several years to construct the necessary buildings and facilities. Indeed a majority of these were not ready until after the crush of veterans departed from campus.

The one overriding problem that influenced each and every decision—and that continues to influence campus decision-makers today—was a base budget too small to meet demands, both immediate and long-range. The budget for higher education was not even equal with the pre-depression budget when adjusted for inflation. And postwar inflation created a problem as the funds available continually fell short of costs. Throughout its history the UO has learned how to do more with less through innovation and by stretching the available resources.

Harry Newburn (1944–1953)

By the time Harry K. Newburn arrived to assume the presidency, the fundamental changes to meet the challenges were in place. These included moves toward acquiring temporary housing for married students—with and without children—establishing day care for the children of parents who were in school or working, arranging living quarters for bachelor students, and expanding the use of dormitories.

Newburn was new to the scene, but his advisors were not, and they knew from experience how to manage the crisis with amazing foresight and very careful planning. For example, when they realized incoming students with children needed day-care facilities, they established them within the student housing units where they were needed. The advisors didn't hesitate, nor did they set up committees to look into the situation. They took immediate actions to address immediate problems.

Newburn had been kept fully involved in the efforts to meet the needs, so when he took charge, the momentum did not slow. His first challenge was to get deans and department heads to start looking for new faculty to fill the gaps created by the growing influx of students. In fall 1944 2,245 students were enrolled at the university; by fall 1946, enrollment was up to 6,367, and 56 percent of these students were veterans. In addition, few faculty members returned from the service. In a report from the registrar, by 1946, the university increased its number of faculty 32 percent but their credit hours jumped a whopping 67 percent.

In October 1942 the Oregon State Board of Higher Education reversed a decision made a decade earlier that had transferred all upper-division and graduate work in science from the UO to Oregon State College (now Oregon State University). However, the return of the sciences was postponed until the end of World War II in 1946, and Newburn was in a position to hire an almost complete science faculty. This opportunity proved fortuitous as it allowed him the flexibility to hire the best possible faculty. In addition, that faculty was able to have a major influence on the basic development and direction of the new science library collection because almost all science materials had been transferred to OSC in the mid-1930s.

Newburn, speaking to the problems facing the postwar university, set a goal that his various successors have accepted in one way or another. He observed that the university stood at a threshold to its future—it could choose to continue on the path of a second-rate state university or it could choose a higher path, which would lead to a ranking among the first tier of state universities. It was his intention to direct the university toward the latter, a course the UO has successfully pursued since that time, even when the budget for higher education in Oregon was lagging far behind other comparable states.

Through a referendum the voters approved the expenditure of unspent and unbudgeted tax money that had accumulated during World War II for needed state buildings throughout Oregon. This was a godsend for the university as no state money had been spent on buildings or campus development since the 1925 construction of Condon Hall. Although a building boom had occurred during the 1930s, it was mostly federal money, some private donations, and student building fees that paid for all construction and campus development from 1925 through 1946.

As a result of this investment by voters, the university erected several buildings, including Robinson Theatre, Pacific Hall, Gilbert Hall, and an addition to the library, as well as completing major remodeling projects in several of the older buildings.

Temporary buildings constructed for administrative use included the Officers' Club from Camp, a former Army basic training post during World War II that was located between Corvallis and Monmouth. The building was transported to the campus in large pieces and reassembled at the corner of 13th and Emerald to house the registrar, business office, counseling center, and other programs from 1946 to 1988. In addition, other surplus buildings used during the war were moved to campus for temporary use. Trailer houses from Troutdale and surplus housing used to house ship builders in Vancouver, Washington, were disassembled and moved to campus for married students with and without children. These buildings, named Amazon Married Student Housing, were used until 1996. Former military Quonset huts were also brought to campus and used as classrooms and a cafeteria for newly created dormitories, which were also former military buildings. Even houses that were no longer needed at the Hanford Nuclear Reservation were moved to campus and used to house married students and faculty with families. The last of these buildings was torn down in 1998. At the end of the century, prefabricated buildings purchased from a Texas company to serve as married-student housing were still in use by the university.

In 1946 the student body and the alumni became determined to complete the dream of the students on campus in 1923 to build a student union. Since no state funds could be used for this purpose, the Alumni Association in cooperation with the leaders of the student government commenced a drive to raise the necessary funds. Ernest Haycox, a UO alumnus, noted author, and the creator of the modern western novel, led the drive. The campaign lasted four years, and in November 1950, the Erb Memorial Union opened, named in honor of President Donald Erb who had in the midst of World War II suggested that when the war ended the students should resurrect the student union dream and make it a reality. Sadly, Haycox died of cancer before the building was completed.

Carson Hall, the first women's dormitory to be constructed since 1921, opened in 1948. No state funds were used for dormitories because the residents pay for these facilities through their dormitory fees. Virgil Earl Hall joined John Straub Hall as a men's dormitory in 1954. In 1975 Straub Hall was converted to classroom, laboratory, and faculty office use.

In 1946 the State Board changed its rules and allowed the UO and OSC to have separate graduate schools. Since the reorganization of higher education in 1933, the UO, OSC, and the UO's Medical and Dental Schools in Portland were administered jointly as a single graduate program. This change in rules allowed Newburn to appoint a graduate dean and to create a graduate school on the campus. The research activities, and any funding associated with research, were also given over to the graduate school.

In the early 1950s the board again changed the rules on graduate work when it approved a rule that allowed the three teacher colleges (Monmouth, Ashland, and LaGrande) to commence offering master's degrees in education. This was almost immediately followed by approval to allow the UO and OSC to offer degrees in elementary education—previously the exclusive domain of the three teacher colleges. In turn each of the education colleges in Monmouth, Ashland, and LaGrande received the right to offer secondary education as well as general education degrees.

A major change in the administration of athletics took place in 1947 when Newburn became determined to end the fifty-plus year policy of allowing the students to have a major hand in the operation of athletics. He established the position of athletic director and put the major responsibility of running the department in his hands. The students would still help fund athletics through a student fee, which, at that time, allowed free entrance to all home athletic events. However, the students would have little say in the hiring of coaches and the use of funds. This change was in line with the national trend to remove athletics from what had been a regionally based operation for the most part toward a national enterprise.

O. Meredith Wilson (1954–1960)

Harry Newburn left the presidency in 1953 and was, in 1954, replaced by O. Meredith Wilson. Wilson brought with him strong credentials as a nationally known administrator, scholar, and intellectual who had had a great influence on the recent educational changes in higher education.

Wilson, who undertook and expanded the path set by Newburn, made several long-lasting changes to the university that continued moving the institution in a new direction. Like his predecessor, Wilson was saddled with a poorly funded state institution that had a growing reputation for excellence. His major contributions included the full development of the graduate school, the establishment of various institutes in the sciences (where federal and private research funds were available), the continuing quest for and placement of outstanding teachers (who could work on both the undergraduate and graduate level), and a continuing modernization of university administration. He made his goals clear in a 1960 statement, reported by *Old Oregon* magazine: "The assumption is that these institutes will direct some of the central energies of staff toward the graduate programs while not forgetting the fact that all graduate education in Oregon will depend upon how well the students are prepared at the undergraduate level."

Quality development in the sciences reflected Wilson's vision for the university. Terrill Hill was chosen to establish the first institute, Theoretical Chemistry. Then Aaron Novick was hired, and the Institute of Molecular Biology, by far the most noted of the several UO institutes, was created. Novick's practice of hiring additional research faculty and accepting interdisciplinary research made this institute successful and set a standard that other institutions have followed. Although long in coming, this interdisciplinary approach to teaching and research has found acceptance within other departments of the university.

Both Newburn and Wilson urged their deans to find the best-qualified people with the hope they would come at a salary the university could offer. In some instances the chancellor put a cap on any salary offers, making it difficult to negotiate with a candidate. In at least one instance, when Wilson approved a salary much higher than had been previously authorized, he defended this action by pointing out that "... education is not a bottom-line business" when it came to what was best for the students, the state, and society.

Throughout his tenure, Wilson was disappointed by the lack of fiscal commitment by legislators in Salem to education in general and to higher education specifically. He observed that the price difference between mediocrity and excellence was very little, but the rewards were great. And he was continually confounded by the failure of the legislature and governor to grasp this fact—a perennial concern in the years that followed.

Arthur S. Flemming (1961–1968)
The University of Minnesota took Wilson as their president in 1960. Arthur S. Flemming, secretary of Health, Education, and Welfare in the Eisenhower Administration, replaced Wilson. Flemming was not a stranger to most Oregonians. Just before the end of the Eisenhower administration, Flemming had cast doubt on the purity of Oregon cranberries because of a pesticide scare. Thus his appointment was met with some skepticism by Oregonians who remembered the fiasco.

Flemming turned out to be different from his predecessors in a number of ways. He was not a scholar and he did not have a PhD. He was politically oriented and, though a Republican, very liberal. But his method of management created some problems.

Although the administrative structure remained more or less the same as that under Wilson, Flemming worked with his administrators differently. His method of management was the military model: He was the general and all others were staff members. He delegated very little to his deans and immediate assistants. Even long-standing delegations of authority were ignored. Flemming made almost every decision.

Flemming also felt it was necessary to be directly involved in almost all aspects of student and university administration. He became very popular with the students, was trusted by and fully available to them. His door was truly open to one and all.

During the Flemming years the federal government created new programs and expanded older programs that would direct federal aid onto American college and university campuses. With his federal connections, Flemming knew how to turn on the faucets. He appointed Ray Hawk as his liaison with the myriad of granting agencies in Washington, D.C.

Flemming envisioned a "public university" that was not wholly dependent upon any one source of funds to sustain its growth. He commenced putting an emphasis on gifts to the Development Fund, which had been created by President Clark to serve as the private fundraising arm of the university. Private gift giving increased during his tenure, with the drive for funds for the construction of Autzen Stadium and a $1.5 million gift from Lila Acheson Wallace, a UO alumna from the class of 1917.

Although the State of Oregon enjoyed a succession of years of prosperity, the budgets in higher education did not see any dramatic increase. Federal funds coming to campus did increase, however, becoming part of the budget on which the university depended. It was an opportunity that allowed for fuller development during the sixties, but also created a financial setback when the federal money was no longer available.

Many minority programs were created with the federal money. Innovations in the College of Education programs expanded the curriculum and were supported by federal grants. Federal funds available to support graduate and undergraduate students created a dramatic increase in enrollment. A School of Librarianship—the university's first new professional school since 1920—was established in 1966.

With the federal tap flowing, the university was able to add to its building inventory. A humanities building, Prince Lucien Campbell Hall, was constructed with almost all federal dollars;

the Library gained an addition, the science complex was expanded, and the Clinical Services building was constructed—all with federal money.

Flemming was never one to avoid controversy as he involved himself in the fight for fluoridation of Eugene's water supply and defended the decades-old university policy that allowed recognized student or faculty groups to speak on campus. Flemming stood on the side of the students supporting the visit of Gus Hall, the General Secretary of the Communist Party of the U.S.A. Flemming also stood by the right of the UO literary quarterly to publish controversial material that some detractors considered obscene.

To Flemming, a dynamic campus had to bubble with ideas of all sorts, even those he personally rejected. So when the students hurled insults and eggs at a speaker in front of the EMU, Flemming expressed his disgust with these students because they wanted to reject the right to speak if they did not like the speaker or the message. As a result of this incident, the Free Speech Platform was established in front of the EMU. He strongly supported the move to have a Peace Corps training center on campus, to allow students to go to Mississippi and register voters, to work on environmental issues, and to get involved in the everyday life of the community.

Flemming announced his resignation, effective in June 1968. A year later, in large part because of his work, the University of Oregon was invited to become a member of the Association of American Universities. This was the most select and prestigious association of private and public universities in the United States. The UO had initially received a look of interest by the AAU in the late 1920s, but the lack of a quality graduate school and a research-oriented faculty kept the UO from receiving an invitation. Building on the work of Newburn and Wilson, Arthur Flemming was able to get the UO over the hump and into the AAU.

The students were taken aback when they learned that the search committee established to find a successor to Flemming was to be dominated by faculty and administrators. These students had learned well the lessons of the 1960s, and they immediately voiced opposition and petitioned to have an equal voice on the committee. In short order, Johnson Hall was occupied by protesting students, and after several days of occupation, the Chancellor agreed to change the composition of the committee. Those inside the building accepted this compromise, but those outside either hesitated or refused to accept it, creating new pressures and a continuing controversy.

Charles Johnson (1968–1969)

During the academic year 1968–69 the university was headed by an acting president—Charles Johnson, dean of the College of Arts and Sciences. Overall this particular year saw more concentrated disruptions than any other in the late 1960s and was probably the most difficult period for the university during all of the Vietnam War years. During this time, students organized large protest demonstrations against the war, some of which included breaking windows, spray painting slogans on walls, and bombing and torching buildings. The most serious fire destroyed Esslinger Hall in May 1970, and a bomb planted outside of Johnson Hall in 1969 almost killed two university employees in the basement. Students also held demonstrations on other social issues, advocating a ban on non-union lettuce and grapes. They erected poverty shacks on the lawns in front of the EMU and Johnson Hall, hoping to attract attention to the plight of southern blacks and urban poor who didn't have adequate housing.

Johnson worked long hours with student leaders to find a middle ground. State of Oregon politicians got involved through public statements or through letters to Johnson—a few in support of his efforts, but most condemning him and the university. No middle ground existed; compromise was impossible. Johnson's health deteriorated rapidly because of stress, but his determination to find sensible solutions remained strong. Eventually, he was placed under the care of his physician. Shortly after commencement 1969, Charles Johnson died in an automobile accident.

Robert D. Clark (1969–1975)

Robert D. Clark, the eleventh president of the university, was to have little respite. Appointed in June 1969, Clark was returning to the university after a brief sojourn as president at San Jose State. At SJS he had developed a reputation for fairness and understanding. He was not afraid to speak out in opposition to the war and racial intolerance, or to stand up to Governor Ronald Reagan when Clark felt academic freedom was being placed in jeopardy. In his honor SJS named their library after him.

However, at the UO the students did not know Clark. They knew he would not be a Flemming, and so they tested Clark for two years to see if he was indeed what his reputation stated. Those two years were rough—with bombings, vandalism, fires (including the burning down of Esslinger Hall), and repeated large-scale demonstrations against poverty, ROTC, military recruitment, and war, and for the environment and migrant laborer rights. Faculty meetings were disrupted. The faculty was divided about what should be done. But in the end Clark stood firm, as he said he would, in his determination that the protests—no matter how earnest, sincere, or worthy—would not destroy the university. Because he stood firm and did not panic or overreact, he was able to face the governor, the legislature, the citizens, and the intellectual community with an institution that had suffered, but had survived.

During 1971 and 1972, the national and state economy took a nose dive. Federal dollars disappeared, and state dollars evaporated because of a $19 million shortfall in the state's welfare budget. The university suffered severe cuts. A major financial dilemma was unfolding. The demonstrations and protests had put off a number of donors, and the Development Fund saw what had been a growing generosity of gifts fade from view. The university faced an overall 10 percent budget cut.

Clark appointed a small committee consisting of faculty, students, and administrators to seek ways of cutting the budget without doing harm to the entire enterprise. This committee was named "Hearing Panel on University Priorities," a title that indicated its idealized assignment. What could have been a balanced look at the university as a whole instead became a defense of territory exercise, beginning with the choosing of sides and ending with disputes over conclusions. However, in some instances HPUP did delineate some areas that were of fundamental value to the university, and they were not cut. Among these programs were the library book budget, library staffing, and graduate programs. Ironically, the State of Oregon had a budget surplus at the end of the biennial in 1973.

Clark retired from the presidency and the UO in June 1975. He was the first UO president to do so. An active member of the faculty since 1943, he had served in a number of administrative positions at the university and was a key in the creation of the Honors College. It was named in his honor when he retired.

William Boyd (1975–1980)

Over the next five years the university entered a period of relative calm and stability. William Boyd was appointed president in 1975 and served until 1980. It is difficult to separate the years of service of Boyd from his successor, Paul Olum, as the period is almost seamless.

Soon after his arrival on campus Boyd began reorganizing the central administration. This included unloading much of the day-to-day operations of the academic side of the university onto the provost. For this to work he felt he needed a new provost and appointed Paul Olum.

The two worked smoothly as Olum accepted more and more of the delegated responsibility. As provost, Olum raised the standard for tenure and pushed the various deans and departments to raise their standards when seeking new faculty.

During the Boyd years minority programs were reexamined and studied, resulting in some administrative changes and a more centralized and streamlined group of programs. For example, positions of special councilors for minorities in financial aid and admissions were eliminated as the emphasis shifted to making all councilors sensitive to minority needs. The budget of the institution remained stable. Graduate admissions had been capped for a number of years, but with the suspension and subsequent closing of the School of Librarianship, more than 125 graduate student slots for other programs were created. The bulk of these were given over to the science programs.

President Boyd was not a strong supporter of athletics, and when in 1979–80 a scandal involving falsified transcripts and fake transfer credits was revealed in the football program, Boyd was extremely disturbed. He strongly condemned these blatant acts of cheating, dismissing some coaches and freezing or reducing the salaries of others.

Paul Olum (1980–1989)

Boyd resigned in 1980, accepting a position with the Johnson Foundation of Racine, Wisconsin. Paul Olum became the acting president and within the year was appointed president. Almost immediately he faced a budget crisis that was acerbated by cuts of $7 million that had been made in the early 1970s and never restored.

This round of cuts kept 10 percent of the open teaching positions unfilled and resulted in an overall budget cut of 7.1 percent, which translated into a base budget reduction of $1.84 million. $2,283,000 was cut from the university budget by the end of 1985. A tuition freeze accompanied these cuts, and to make matters worse, enrollment increased dramatically, mandating a need to expand. But because of the budget cuts and tuition freeze, it was difficult to sustain quality without sacrifice elsewhere.

During the Olum years the dollar was stretched beyond what others thought possible as the university continued to enhance its reputation through dogged determination and a refusal to surrender its goals or ideals. The university continued to hire quality faculty in targeted disciplines, moving funds to sustain quality. And the faculty in the sciences, education, business administration, and other departments, made concerted efforts to apply for more federal grants and increase funding through that route.

Olum, unlike most presidents of the post–World War II era, thoroughly enjoyed the competitive nature of athletics. He was a competitor by nature and enjoyed the contest whether it was with a physics or math problem, a budget that needed to be stretched to fit, or an athletic competition.

It was during Olum's presidency that the Riverfront Research Park was created. The university originally purchased the land in the mid-1960s to save the riverfront area for its own needs with some areas designated for parking and the majority of it set aside for use as playing fields for physical education and intramural games. The funds used to purchase the land in the 1960s came from auxiliary budgets (i.e. non-state generated funds created through parking fees, dormitories, and physical education).

But Olum became convinced that the university could tap its research arm to work cooperatively with private entrepreneurs as had been done in North Carolina and in and around Stanford. The plans were drawn, and the debate on campus commenced. Opponents to the conversion of this land from its undeveloped status, accepting the playing field plans but not the parking lots as a given, made their case over a long period of time. They did force some compromise in the Olum plan, but the basic idea stood.

The city and the state bought into the plan as a form of economic development, and funding for the preparation of the site came directly from the state and from the city's urban renewal funds. Currently, the area is being slowly developed, but opponents continue to fight for the preservation of wetlands, the riverbank, and the vegetation that borders the river.

A major coup for the university came when it was able to tap the Department of Energy of the federal government for money to construct new science buildings and to remodel the older science buildings on campus. The UO liaison with Washington, D.C., Charlene Curry, made the initial contact to get the funds. Once the contacts were made and both of Oregon's U.S. senators were onboard, Olum and John Moseley, the vice president for research, moved in to complete the package. The UO received $34 million for the projects, and the result made an immediate impact on the science faculty and recruitment for new faculty and graduate students.

Paul Olum was forced to retire from the presidency when he turned sixty-five. The State Board had come under strong political pressure, because Olum had offended a number of important people through the force of his personality and his strong belief in the university and its mission. He had fought a new budget plan, which he felt was based on error and would perpetually punish the university through built-in disadvantage. The university had the largest enrollment in the state, but the enrollment dollars that were seen as surplus by the Chancellor were given to the other state colleges. Olum publicly fought to retain this money for UO programs, faculty, and students. He believed success was being punished, and the students were being robbed of their tuition money. This budget process was recently changed as it was found to be fundamentally unsound and biased.

The announcement of Olum's forced retirement caused demonstrations on campus, civic condemnation, and in the end, a sincere celebration of the presidency of Paul Olum and all he did for the University of Oregon during some bleak years.

Myles Brand (1989–1994)

Myles Brand was chosen as Olum's successor and arrived on campus on July 1, 1989. Brand had been provost at Ohio State University and was seen as a rising administrator in higher education. Many on campus anticipated that he would not remain at the university for long.

Brand was interested in increasing the external private funding of the university to help protect it from the fluctuations experienced in the past. He felt stable funding would allow the flexibility needed to plan for the future growth and development of the university. However, in midstream Oregon voters put a halt to all planning when they passed a measure that capped and rolled back property taxes. This action pushed the support of public education onto the state budget; thus higher education, along with all other state agencies, faced severe budget cuts.

The university faced the single largest reduction in its budget since the start of the Great Depression. The already fiscally abused base budget of the institution was again on the chopping block, and all of the decisions on how to absorb the cuts had to be made within a very short time frame.

Along with his provost, Norman Wessels, Brand was forced to consider options that no past president had confronted. The College of Health, Physical Education, and Recreation, the teacher education program within the College of Education, the speech department, and the Bureau of Governmental Research were all eliminated.

In all, some $10 million, twenty-two degree programs in four colleges, and 200 faculty positions were eliminated. Tuition increased to the point that the UO began the trend of receiving more money from the students through tuition than from the State of Oregon. At a university assembly meeting in 1991, Brand began using the term "state-assisted university" rather than "state-supported university" as had been the case in the past.

For almost his entire tenure, Brand faced the dilemma of living with a budget that was repeatedly too small to support what is the flagship university of the state. He did push hard for the full use of the university foundation to find outside sources of funding, and he worked hard to bring the plight of the university to the attention of the legislature, the governor, and the citizens. His efforts were rewarded through increased private donations—including what was then the single largest gift the university had ever received, $10 million to the College of Business Administration.

In 1994 Brand accepted the presidency of Indiana University. His successor, Dave Frohnmayer, had been the dean of the School of Law. Prior to that, he had been the three-time-elected state attorney general and had been a state representative and law professor.

During his administration the UO has found a more positive budget situation—somewhat more stable, but still underfunded. For example, in a 1951 economic impact statement, the funds received from the State of Oregon to support the university amounted to 68 percent of its general education budget. In 1999, this figure was 22 percent.

Private fundraising has continued apace making additional buildings, facilities, and remodels possible. The private funds have also created some endowed chairs, but on the whole, the struggle continues because of the erosion of the budget throughout the years.

The University of Oregon is the oldest public university in Oregon. In 2001 it will celebrate its 125th year of service to the state. If its past is any indication of the future, the state will continue to cut the university's budget, and the university will continue to stretch its available dollars, continuing on the path spelled out by Presidents Newburn and Wilson—to become a public university of the first rank in this nation.

Bibliography

Oregon Daily Emerald, selected articles, 1944–1999.

The Oregon Journal, selected articles, 1945–1965.

Oregon Quarterly, selected articles 1943–1999.

The Oregonian and *The Sunday Oregonian*, selected articles, 1944–1999.

The Register-Guard, selected articles, 1944–1999.

University of Oregon. *Catalog and Bulletin*. 1943–44 through 1998–99.

———. *Economic Impact of the University of Oregon*, 1951–1990.

———. "Minutes of the University of Oregon Faculty and Assembly," 1943–1999.

———. *Report of the Registrar*, 1944–1995.

———. *University of Oregon Facts*, 1999–2000.

———. *The University of Oregon Reports to All Oregonians*, 1998.

A CITY OF HELPERS:

EUGENE'S SOCIAL SERVICES

By Cynthia Whitfield

IN AN ESSAY featured in the 1949 Oregon Blue Book, former governor Douglas McKay talked about the "tremendous growth in Oregon's population, the greatest percentage in the nation." At that time Oregon had 1.6 million people, a gain of 49.3 percent since World War II. McKay cautioned Oregonians to welcome newcomers while avoiding "the creation of anything that even remotely resembles the slum conditions that too often follow a concentration of population."

Eugene, at least, seemed to heed McKay's warning. In the last fifty years of the twentieth century, the community grew tremendously but took care of those in need without sacrificing the city's livability. Terry McDonald, executive director of the Eugene branch of St. Vincent de Paul (SVdP) said, "Eugene has managed to avoid the kinds of problems that prevent grassroots social-service development. We have no ghettos, no red-light district, no major industrial blight. We're unique because we don't have major ethnic and social-class divisions."

Though Eugene boasted a strong tradition of social-service innovation and creativity, many human-service workers said the scope of social-service delivery remained a qualified success. In a town where wage levels were low, resources sometimes fell short of need, in spite of good programs and intentions.

Still, the per-capita breadth of services in Eugene was one of the nation's highest, according to McDonald, who studied the issue and consulted with social-service agencies around the country. He believed social-service efforts began in earnest after World War II, when Eugene grew tremendously, as Lane County became the "Emerald City," providing large amounts of timber for the country. Along with the influx of people, social-service needs grew, and agencies such as Catholic Charities, SVdP, Goodwill, and others stepped up their programs.

Later, the 1960s counterculture movement spawned "alternative" social-service agencies meant to deliver services in a more egalitarian manner. The goal was to provide what clients wanted, rather than what agencies thought they should get. Finally, the fall of the timber industry in the 1980s created widespread unemployment and homelessness, prompting new systems aimed at increasing affordable housing and food distribution.

Eugene's impressive mix of social services was undoubtedly related to its status as a well-educated college-town community, in a state where grassroots activism is celebrated. The city's diverse base of social-service groups and agencies—including private charities, religious organizations, nonprofit agencies, and government-sponsored programs—all contributed to the vital amalgam of human services at the beginning of the twenty-first century. Despite competition for funding, the organizations coexisted quite comfortably.

Early Social-Service Systems

Originally, Eugene's social-service system paralleled others in cities of its size across the country. Except for small groups of individuals forming their own service systems and religious organizations, most social-service agencies were based in Portland. The 1949–1950 *Blue Book* lists numerous organizations serving indigent men, women, and children through agencies based there. Those who needed these services were sent to institutions in the big city. For instance, the Boys and Girls Aid Society of Oregon was founded in 1885 to serve poor, orphaned, and abused children from all counties in the state. These children were packed off to Portland, and, if possible, returned later to their homes. More recently, keeping children in their own communities was deemed more important.

The Portland institutions were outgrowths of the nation's first social-service systems. The late 1800s and early 1900s saw the development of organized agencies that provided human services, partly in response to the influx of immigrants and displaced farmers who flocked to American cities. The Society for the Prevention of Cruelty to Children, the American Pediatric Society, and the American Association for the Study and Prevention of Infant Mortality emerged around the turn of the century.

Oregonians with mental and physical disabilities often were cared for in institutions. And it was common practice to send poor children to live in more affluent homes, where they became indentured servants. Most people who needed help relied on local relief funds run by religious and nonreligious agencies or custodial institutions such as alms houses or poorhouses.

In early twentieth-century Eugene, religious groups such as SVdP, the Salvation Army, and Catholic Charities provided much help for those in need. The secular Goodwill Industries focused on training people with disabilities to perform jobs at its stores or, when possible, in the community. And like other states, Oregon was home to less-centralized women's "societies" that helped counsel the needy and dispensed goods, such as milk, groceries, and clothing. Many of these societies were backed by philanthropic groups and were free to allocate resources to families and individuals without administrative controls or standards. According to *The Story of Eugene* by Moore, McCornack, and McCready, late-nineteenth- and early-twentieth-century efforts to provide help to those in need were often "taken care of by donation parties." These consisted mainly of churches collecting and distributing clothing and supplies.

A popular method of gathering food for the hungry still exists—the school-based canned-food drive. As early as the late 1880s, Eugene children brought canned goods to school for later distribution by clubs and societies to help combat poverty. There was one big difference though: Children carted home-canned, rather than store-bought, food to school. Federal and state governments did not take major responsibility for helping those in need until the Great Depression resulted in massive unemployment and poverty.

The First Wave

Since the 1950s, Eugene developed a remarkably diverse base of social-service agencies. Terry McDonald of SVdP said social-service efforts in Eugene occurred in waves. "The first wave was in the 1950s, when this organization, Catholic Charities, Goodwill, and others really got going here," he said.

McDonald is a second-generation head of the country's largest and most diverse SVdP organization. His father, H.C. "Mac" McDonald, was hired in 1953 as a "temporary, acting unpaid director" of the Eugene branch of the nonprofit agency. In 1955 Mac was hired permanently and, according to meeting minutes, received $250 per month "or the profits from the agency's thrift store sales, whichever is greater." Terry joined his father at SVdP in 1971 when he was twenty-one. He described himself as a "good Catholic boy interested in social justice."

Terry became executive director of the organization in 1984, and under his leadership SVdP developed from a simple thrift store and emergency-aid agency into a dynamic and diverse agency that provides a wide variety of services. "When I started work here," McDonald said, "my father showed me the budget and said, 'This is all we'll be able to do. There's not much of a chance we'll ever have more to work with.' " But in 1999, what the organization spent in just ten days equaled the amount of its entire 1971 operating budget.

By the close of the century, SVdP was serving as a model for recycling and managing renewable resources. The organization diverted dumpsters full of scrap wood that was combined with pine to create new wood products, which were then sold to help finance the organization's social-service programs. SVdP's glass factory made and sold beautiful glass products from recycled glass. It rebuilt and recycled two hundred mattress sets each month. Some of these items were sold in SVdP's local stores, some were given to needy families, and some were shipped to locations around the nation and the world. These large-scale recycling efforts received national attention.

Catholic Charities, which changed its name to Catholic Community Services in 1984, also served the Eugene community throughout most of the twentieth century. In 1957 social worker Frank Nearing began working for Catholic Charities of Eugene in an office above the attic of SVdP's salvage store. The two organizations cooperated with each other and held joint monthly meetings. Nearing's primary duties were running a foster children's program.

After the state-run Children's Services Division took over those duties in the mid-1960s, Catholic Charities purchased an old house at 522 East 13th Avenue and, under Nearing's direction, made it a home for unwed mothers. Nearing also offered marriage and family counseling. The need for the home faded when the prejudice toward unwed mothers lessened, and abortion became legal. In the late 1970s Nearing proposed that the house become a "home away from home" for out-of-town Sacred Heart patients undergoing treatment. Families of patients were also welcome at the home. Nearing remained director of what he dubbed the "Murnane Guest House" (after Monsignor Murnane, who oversaw both SVdP and Catholic Charities) until his retirement in 1984.

However, religious organizations weren't the only game in town. A variety of nonreligious social-service organizations sprang up in the 1940s and 1950s, most notably the Lane County Community Chest. The Community Chest, precursor of United Way, evolved out of a need to coordinate local agency fund-raising efforts. A fact-finding committee met on January 6, 1942, to discuss "the need for coordinated action in the matter of raising funds for continued operation of charitable, character building agencies of Eugene." Present at this first meeting was Alton F. Baker, publisher of the *Eugene Register-Guard* and the first campaign chair of the organization. Throughout that year other meetings followed, which included representatives of the various agencies, such as the Salvation Army, Boy Scouts, and YMCA.

Father Leipzig, pastor of St. Mary's Catholic Church during the '30s and '40s, made a special plea to be included in the Community Chest on behalf of SVdP. He pointed out that SVdP cared for "people in charity homes, old people's homes, city jails, hospitals, etc., regardless of whether they were of the Catholic faith or not." He noted that the Salvation Army, YMCA, and other groups slated for inclusion were strictly Protestant, and that it might be beneficial to include an agency from the Catholic community. The board was rather lukewarm about his proposal and told him they'd think about it. Monsignor Murnane reportedly strode into a later meeting and said, "If you don't admit us, I'll go to our people and tell them to contribute only to Catholic Charities." St. Vincent's was subsequently invited into the fund.

The first funds were dispensed in 1943 through the Eugene Community Chest, after an unexpectedly fruitful fundraising campaign. The goal was to raise $39,043, but contributions amounted to a whopping $67,200, which went to benefit the Boy Scouts, Girl Scouts, Salvation Army, St. Vincent de Paul, and two branches of the YMCA. The Chest also allocated money to a variety of war-relief organizations.

In 1947 the organization changed its name to Lane County Chest, Inc., and extended its giving beyond Eugene's city limits. Agencies were told to submit two budgets—one for Eugene and one for outlying areas. By the 1960s the organization was raising funds for forty-two agencies, and in 1975 it became the United Way of Lane County. Funds raised and programs helped through United Way continued to grow. In 1999 it served sixty-four programs through forty-two agencies and had a budget of more than $3 million.

The Second Wave

The philosophy of helping others, according to Nearing, developed slowly from providing a somewhat narrow range of aid—food, foster care, or institutional care—to providing a larger menu of services aimed at empowering people to make their own decisions. Although this attitude shift is evident as early as the late '40s, it exploded in the late 1960s when concerns with issues of equality, individuality, and self-determination began to grow. In addition, the country's material prosperity after World War II convinced people that the richest country on earth should increase its level of services to the needy, that it was both possible and desirable to share the wealth.

The '60s also introduced another concept into the mix. Young activists embraced the idea of seeing clients as peers who had problems like everyone else and made a conscious effort not to develop the condescending attitudes that sometimes permeated social-service organizations. All these conditions made Eugene ripe for the second wave of social-service activity that began in the early 1970s, when agencies such as White Bird, Food for Lane County, Looking Glass, Womenspace, and others made their appearance.

One of the first post-1960s grassroots agencies was Looking Glass, born in 1970. The shelter rose out of a need to help teenage runaways and "incorrigible" children. From those humble beginnings it grew into an organization that "takes into account the educational, mental-health, substance abuse status, and counseling needs of youth," according to agency literature. During Jim Forbes's twenty-seven-year tenure at Looking Glass he "learned how to blend a big-hearted mission with a get-the-job-done approach."

The organization decided to view its glass as half full rather than half empty, Forbes said. "We decided to become optimistic rather than take on a victim role." He believed social-service personnel need to be wary of a tendency to spend too much time feeling sorry for themselves and assuming others aren't interested in helping. "Once we went out in the community and worked to build positive relationships, the help came. But that only happened after our own attitude changed," he explained.

By 2000, Looking Glass was serving more than 7,500 young people and families in Lane County through nine separate programs—a far cry from its beginnings with a budget of $3,000, twenty volunteers, and a runaway shelter. "We've had a lot of impact," Forbes said. "We've been visited by international groups throughout the state and nation."

One of the most visible grassroots social-service agencies in Eugene is White Bird Clinic. The agency has provided low-cost medical care, outpatient drug-and-alcohol treatment, twenty-four-hour crisis intervention, counseling, a mobile crisis-care unit, state-licensed human services training, and more. White Bird began after graduate students from the University of Oregon, members of the counterculture, and professional health-care workers met in 1969 and decided to "do things differently," said clinical coordinator Bob Dritz, a twenty-four-year veteran of the program. "We organized as a collective rather than a hierarchy. We also looked at an alternative way of delivering health care and alternative-health-care practices, including prevention, which was not an established concept at the time."

The primary focus of the original group was dealing with "problems starting to crop up around the extensive recreational use of drugs, often working with people who were alienated from the system and didn't trust the standard lines of care," Dritz said. "We started putting our fingers in the holes in the dike, and our toes in others, and basically dealt with the chores no one else wanted because they didn't pay." These chores included caring for people with little money and running programs, such as crisis intervention, which don't generate money.

White Bird first opened with a free medical clinic and twenty-four-hour drug hot line. Within a few years the clinic's range widened, and the agency continued to add new programs as the "people we were addressing changed," said Dritz. Over the years, the clinic developed from a organization created to serve the counterculture to a system designed to help "everyone who was having trouble getting access to care," he explained.

Though the range of services available in Eugene is "outstanding for its size," Dritz noted, "in other senses there is a very shallow depth of services." He said he'd seen cities that made him jealous in terms of what they could provide to clients. "Lane County and the City of Eugene are average in terms of the resources they put behind human services," he said. "There are areas where they've contributed a lot, and areas where they've been stingy, leading to more needs." White Bird struggled amid the rising costs of medical care while receiving only "small pots" of money from federal, state, county, and Eugene-Springfield sources. Sliding fee scales helped some, and the agency billed Medicare and Medicaid when possible.

But because the need was constant, resources fell short there as they do with all social-service agencies. Many grassroots agencies make do without sufficient support, depending instead on fundraising, grant writing, and volunteers. Because the level of support generated through these resources varied, it was sometimes difficult to provide consistent services. According to some observers in the field, the funding issue is not surprising, considering the lack of available city and county capital, especially as the area scrambled to find ways to replace the revenue generated during the timber industry's heyday.

Social services aimed at providing help for people struggling to escape abusive relationships or recover from physical and/or sexual abuse developed during the late '70s and early '80s. Awareness of these issues spread largely through the efforts of the women's movement and subsequent media attention. One of the first battered-women's shelters in Oregon opened in Eugene after a group of women returned from the 1975 Oregon Political Women's Caucus. Although they didn't know each other before the trip, on the way home they decided to tackle the problems of battered women in their own community.

"Shelters were just starting to spring up across the country," explained Kate Barkley, Womenspace's community outreach director. "These women were determined to open one in Eugene. They started posting flyers and met regularly with each other. A core group of about seven people opened the first shelter house in 1977. Before that, they were providing support for women by talking to them on their private phones and letting them sleep on their couches." Womenspace was operated completely by women, which Barkley said was important at that time in the women's movement. The organization got its nonprofit status, renovated the first shelter house, and opened in early January. By the following July, it had to move to bigger quarters because the need was so great. It moved again in the mid-1980s.

In 2000, the shelter housed 150 women and 300 children per year. Barkley said a primary focus of Womenspace has been community education and social change. Employees and volunteers worked with police and health and mental-health professionals to help them better understand the problems of battered women. They also worked to provide services to women leaving the shelter and re-entering the community.

Around the same time the plight of battered women came into the national consciousness, an awareness of the devastation wrought by child abuse also began to emerge. The Relief Nursery, an organization designed to provide a safe place for kids, was created to give parents "a little time away from their children," according to executive director Jean Phelps. Many of the agency's clients were involved with the state-run Children's Services Division (CSD), because of poor or abusive parenting. Relief Nursery creators hoped to help relieve the stress of parenting and lessen the potential for child abuse. The agency came onto the scene in 1976, thanks to the efforts of CSD caseworkers Mary Ellen Eiler and Lynn Frohnmayer, along with volunteers from the Junior League. The Central Presbyterian Church donated space for the program.

Besides providing respite care for parents who abuse or are at risk of abusing their children, the Relief Nursery offered counseling for both children and parents. By the end of the century, this

Eugene agency served as a model for similar programs across the country, which it helped foster in Cottage Grove, Salem, and Portland, with more sites planned.

Unfortunately, some children are so badly damaged by abuse, they need intense, specialized care away from their families. Jasper Mountain and the Child Center were started after community members brainstormed about ways to help abused children who were not adequately treated by existing social-service agencies. Jasper Mountain provided a residential treatment center for Lane County children suffering severe trauma from sexual abuse. The Child Center offered day-treatment counseling and schooling for children aged three to twelve with hard-to-manage emotional and behavioral problems. "Traditional once-a-week therapy isn't enough for these children," explained the Child Center school psychologist Laramie Palmer. The center also ran an outreach program providing weekly individual and family therapy for people needing less intensive services.

Nicole Bennett came to VOICES as a frightened woman determined to deal with problems resulting from years of sexual and physical abuse. "We're the only organization in our community whose sole purpose is to work with survivors of sex abuse," she noted. As executive director of VOICES, Bennett has been the only paid staff member at the small Eugene agency. But their size belies the importance of their services, according to Bennett, who noted, "Victims of child abuse who haven't worked through their issues have a greater incidence of mental illness, earn lower wages, and are often unable to work at all."

The mainstay of VOICES has been a peer support group facilitated by two volunteers, who also survived sexual abuse. The organization offered a parenting group to help formerly abused adults recognize how that abuse affects parenting. Clients who had difficulty being touched, sedated, or rendered helpless in any way were accompanied to potentially frightening settings, such as dentists' and doctors' offices.

With such a variety of services available, some social-service

innovators saw a need for an organization capable of steering clients to the agencies most likely to assist them. Direction Service
formed to help individuals who have family members with disabilities find appropriate resources. Marshall Peter's years at Direction Service led him to believe Eugene's status as a mecca of
social services is complex. "We're often described as a resource-rich
community because of the diversity of human- and social-service
agencies here," Peter said. "We're fortunate to have a lot of organizations doing outstanding and even nationally noteworthy work. I
think we're especially distinguished in terms of programs for children and youth."

Direction Service came a long way from its beginnings, in 1977,
as a federally funded project at the University of Oregon. By 1982
it had demonstrated to the community the importance of case
management and received support from the Educational Service
District. Though it landed a large grant in 1999, the organization
continued to struggle.

Peter credited the University of Oregon with providing exceptional social-service personnel, who like Eugene and elect to stay
once their training is over. These workers have tended to be the
ones who wrote grants and brought funding and program innovation to Eugene. "At the university we have one of the finest special
education training programs in the country," he said. "In particular we've made gains in the areas of helping children with developmental disabilities and behavior problems." He added that Eugene always attracted "large numbers of starry-eye idealists who
have very active concerns about social issues and public policy.
These people are often willing to work for next to nothing if they
think they can make a difference."

On the other hand, many baby boomers became self-absorbed
and preoccupied with financial security and material accumulation. The ranks of nonprofit workers could thin dangerously. Government agencies are able to pay employees more than most nonprofit agencies even though such employees work just as hard.
Many nonprofit employees work without retirement plans or medi-

cal and dental insurance. Peter noted, "Some will need social services themselves when they retire. We need to better compensate
nonprofit employees. That objective would probably be best met
through public policy channels."

Jim Forbes of Looking Glass said local trends have been moving toward providing comprehensive services, rather than forcing
already stressed clients to run around seeking various kinds of help
from different agencies. The wisdom of this system is evident. "In
the past, most agencies specialized in the kind of help they offered—dealing only with alcoholism or juvenile crime, for instance,"
Forbes explained. "But many people seeking services don't fall solely
within such narrow boxes. We've developed a continuum of care
for young people and their families. If they show up to our service
system, we're able to broker their entire social-services needs and
make referrals to those services we can't provide."

Other agencies, such as Womenspace, have developed similar
"wrap-around" services. However, consolidating agencies into fewer,
larger organizations can have drawbacks. It might make the system more efficient, explained Peter, but clients lose consumer choice.
Agency innovation and creativity might also be hampered by a
larger, more bureaucratic system. A better solution, he argued, is
convincing government agencies to contract-out appropriate jobs
to nonprofit agencies. "There are some things better dealt with by
government agencies, but other things are best handled by smaller
community agencies," Peter said.

The Third Wave

The final wave of new social-service activity came during the 1980s
on the heels of Lane County's recession. McDonald recalled, "In
1982 the volume of need for social services increased when many
jobs in the timber industry disappeared and we began to deal with
the homeless." St. Vincent de Paul started up affordable housing
programs, something that remains a major goal of the organization. Each year SVdP completed 65 to 150 low-income housing
units. McDonald was instrumental in creating the Interfaith Emer-

gency Shelter, which opened in 1989 and provided the homeless with nighttime sleeping space at various faith centers in town. The First Place Family Shelter opened in 1990, offering daytime services such as day care and job-search help. SVdP also developed programs aimed at helping tenants become better renters in order to break the cycle of homelessness. Numerous other organizations took on important work—among them, Food for Lane County, the Alvord-Taylor homes for the mentally retarded, ARC of Lane County, and the Pearl Buck Center.

Back in 1952 the Community Chest's annual report lamented that costs were exceeding resources, especially in light of "inflation," which hadn't led to a comparable "inflation of giving." It ended with an appeal to businesses and individual donors to set "new standards of giving" annually increasing their contributions. Although such appeals continue, Eugene was able to establish and maintain a rich variety of social services, even though resources always fell short of human needs.

The disparity between need and resources slowed efforts to attain the human-service utopia many Eugeneans envisioned. Good ideas and good intentions come and go with fluctuating cultural trends. However, many Eugene residents remain committed to working toward the goal of perfecting social-service delivery by endeavoring to help as many people as possible.

Bibliography

The Catholic Sentinel, June 11, 1982.

"Minutes from Community Chest meetings," 1942–1957.

Oregon Blue Book: 1949–1950, compiled by Earl. T. Newbry. Salem: State Printing Department.

The Register-Guard, selected articles, 1940–1989.

THE BUSINESS OF HEALING

By Alice Tallmadge

TO GET A handle on the quantum transformation that has occurred in health care in Eugene over the past half century, take a
moment to time-travel back to the medical world of the 1950s. Be
sure to tune your mind to black and white, for that pretty much
was what Eugene's health-care community looked like—straight-
line, reputable, conservative, independent, mostly male, and fairly
intolerant of anything that veered from tradition. Back then,
Eugene's physicians served a population of about 35,000, including Springfield and Cottage Grove, which had no hospitals of their
own. Your physician, like almost all the other doctors in the area,
would have had an independent practice, probably located in the
medical center building on Broadway between Oak and Pearl or
the Tiffany Building at 8th and Willamette. For the most part,
these Eugene physicians were a genial bunch, coming together
regularly at medical society meetings, comparing notes, exchang-
ing new information and experiences. Very independent, they nevertheless were yoked together by a common commitment to medicine.

Your doctor was a general practitioner and a trusted friend
and confidant. He knew your sleep patterns, the names of your
kids, all about your bum knee. He charged between $3.50 and
$5.00 for an hour-long office visit, during about half of which
he'd just talk and listen. If you had symptoms that needed treatment, he didn't have many drugs to choose from. The major pharmaceuticals at his disposal were penicillin and sulfa. He hadn't
heard of cortisone, and if you came down with a bad case of poison

oak, you ended up in the hospital getting treated with wet compresses. If you had high blood pressure, he offered only sedation. He couldn't give you antidepressants, birth control pills, or anything to help lower your cholesterol. Roughage? He'd never heard of it. An ulcer? Drink milk. Bad back? Traction.

If you were pregnant, your predelivery prep included having your pubic area fully shaved. Your feet were secured in stirrups throughout your labor. You also may have had your hands tied down to insure that your surroundings remained sterile. And your husband was barred from the delivery room. In those days, too, abortions were illegal, although your doctor may have been one of the few Eugene physicians willing to take measures that created a "spontaneous" miscarriage.

If you needed hospitalization, you were sent to one of the city's three facilities: the Eugene Hospital and Clinic (EHC), Sacred Heart Hospital, or the fifteen-bed osteopathic Valley Lane Hospital on West Broadway. Your doctor assisted in your surgery and certainly showed up for follow-up care during your recovery, which likely meant several days in the hospital. And although you got good care in those facilities, there were a host of surgeries you didn't find in any of them, including open-heart surgery, kidney dialysis, organ transplants, and laparoscopic surgery. You didn't have the diagnostic benefits of ultrasound, MRIs, or CT scans. There were no neonatal intensive care units, sketchy rehabilitation services, and few psychiatric in-patients.

To access those advances, you must zoom forward to the 1960s and beyond, when changes in diagnoses, technology, and treatment came to Eugene, slowly at first and then at warp speed. Quality specialists who settled in the area found substantial support at EHC and particularly at Eugene's primary health-care facility, Sacred Heart Hospital. Sacred Heart's first nuclear medicine appeared in 1959, its in-patient mental health unit in 1969; cardiac intensive care became available in 1966, and in 1971, open-heart surgery. Hemodialysis became available in 1975, a neonatal intensive unit in 1977, magnetic resonance imaging in 1987, and cardiac catheterization in 1991. New equipment allowed better detection of prostate cancer, more accurate diagnoses of osteoporosis, more sophisticated treatment of arrhythmias, and safer cranial tumor and spinal surgeries. The new diagnostic and treatment techniques, says Don Hill, a Eugene doctor who began his practice in 1954 and retired in 1995, "allow many types of surgery we never even thought of." Philosophies guiding obstetrics practices have changed enormously, he says. And the cornucopia of available pharmaceuticals allows people to live with conditions that formerly would have killed them or made their quality of life dismal.

But all of these advances came at a cost. Post–World War II laws exempted health-care packages from taxes. Employers used health benefits as an incentive to attract workers, who then made good use of benefits. The establishment of the federally funded Medicare program in 1966 boosted the use of health-care services even more, filling hospital beds and patient rosters. This heavy use of services, rapid development in medical technology, and the lack of caps on service charges led to astronomical increases in health-care costs. The government introduced more limits on Medicare reimbursements. Then, in the mid-1980s, the insurance industry introduced a cost-saving model known as the managed-care model of service delivery. The model introduced such practices as formulaic reimbursement, tighter physician oversight regarding treatment procedures, and, in some cases, rewarded physicians who limited their patients' treatment options. Like physicians elsewhere, Eugene doctors have had powerful reactions to the new system.

Although admitting it has slowed rising health-care costs, older physicians especially believe managed care has torn the heart out of what they consider the practice of medicine to be. Hill says he routinely spent appointment time with his patients getting to know details about their lives. He developed close relationships with scores of area families—some that spanned generations. "I had a sense of satisfaction," he says about his practice. "But now doctors don't have the time, they don't get to know the patient. I talk to

younger fellows in practice now; they're not happy. They're looking for ways out."

Donald England, who has practiced in Eugene since 1953,
agrees that "many doctors don't like it. Patients don't like it." But,
he adds, "if you're going to survive, that's what you have to do."
Locally, some of the fallout from trying to keep costs down led to
the formation of physicians' groups who found themselves in competition with each other. Effects of the new system hit the Eugene
area with particular punch in the early and mid-1990s, when an
insurance company owned by PeaceHealth (Sacred Heart's parent
company) set up provider plans that excluded some local physicians from seeing patients who were on certain insurance panels.
For some, the sting of that exclusion persists, says Mark Herring, a
Springfield neurologist. "There's been an erosion of any kind of
camaraderie and friendship that used to be enjoyed by physicians
in Eugene and between Eugene and Springfield," he says. "People
have had to circle the wagons, join different camps, focus on the
business of medicine rather than on the issue of providing health
care."

Walls, Floors, and Windows

It's a tasty piece of historical irony that Eugene was a testing ground
for a very early experiment in prepaid health-care delivery. The
area's first hospital, the Eugene Hospital and Clinic, opened in
1922 as a partnership among six Eugene physicians who auctioned
their homes to pay for the construction. Early on, the Booth-Kelly
lumber firm agreed to pay the clinic a set monthly amount per
worker to cover the medical bills of employees and their families.
According to a self-published history of the EHC written by Larry
W. Hirons, the prepaid contract was particularly fitting for rural
timber workers. "While lumbermen frequently came to town and
frequently had money, the money and the men just as frequently
parted company before they got to the doctor," Hirons writes. In
the late 1920s the hospital struck a similar deal with Southern
Pacific Railroad. In 1931 the State Industrial Accident Commis-

sion also signed a contract to have EHC provide care for all injured workers in Lane County, at the insurance rate of three cents per worker per workday.

The plans proved to be a lifeline for the EHC during the depression, providing a dependable source of monthly revenue. Overall, the contracts worked, says Donald England. "They were good for the patients, good for the doctors." But the practice also made EHC somewhat suspicious in the eyes of other local physicians. In the 1930s anything even vaguely suggestive of socialized medicine was considered suspect, points out John Bascom, a Eugene doctor. "Physicians thought they would end up being controlled and losing." But by the mid-1950s almost half of EHC's patients were on prepaid plans. We got a reputation," England says. "We were at odds with the rest of the community."

The plucky Eugene Clinic was well loved by the physicians who worked there, and it continually stretched the walls of the clinic, leading to an extension in 1955 and an entirely new, 84,000-foot facility in 1965. It purportedly also had "one of the largest oblong luncheon tables in the city," where staff routinely sat down to eat, debate, consult, and relax. EHC physicians had operating privileges at Sacred Heart but maintained their own distinct identity. Sacred Heart was owned and operated by Catholic nuns, and Eugene still harbored some anti-Catholic sentiment. "A lot of patients came to the clinic just because we weren't part of Sacred Heart," says England, who hung his whites at EHC for most of his forty-seven years in practice.

Just slightly more than a stone's throw away from EHC, Sacred Heart was going through its own evolution during those same years. The hospital's first incarnation was the sixty-bed Pacific Christian Hospital. Built in 1924, it went through a number of hands and in the depression almost fell into bankruptcy. A handful of local physicians arranged for the Bellevue-based Sisters of St. Joseph of Newark to acquire the building. Four sisters arrived in 1936 to take on the task of revitalizing the hospital, which had been renamed Sacred Heart General Hospital. Revitalize they did, and Sacred Heart began to expand. In 1951 construction brought bed capacity to 275; in 1965 it increased to 366. A six-story main building, replacing older beds and expanding the emergency room, was completed in 1981, and renovations and expansions continue to this day.

Sacred Heart never intended to be a small-town facility. Between 1960 and 1990, the hospital established itself as the most comprehensive medical center between Portland and San Francisco. Its willingness to provide a great breadth and depth of services attracted quality specialists. It grew to offer sophisticated diagnoses and treatments for a host of medical conditions, including trauma care, cardiac surgery, hip replacements, cardiac intensive care, oncology, rehabilitation services, hemodialysis, stroke treatment, neonatal intensive care, and prenatal care for low-income women.

The hospital's open-heart surgery unit, established by Robert P. Hodam in 1971, illustrates how the hospital worked in partnership with specialists. According to a 1996 interview with Hodam, the hospital agreed to spend thousands of dollars on needed equipment. In turn, Hodam trained nurses and recruited another specialist from Portland to assist him. In 1971 a Junction City resident became the hospital's first open-heart patient. Before the unit was established, the hospital was sending fifty to sixty cardiac cases a year to Portland or Stanford University. That first year, Hodam and his team performed sixty-five open-heart surgeries. They doubled that number the following year. Today, four cardiac surgeons and eleven cardiologists staff the Oregon Heart Center, which serves about one thousand patients annually. In 1999 the center received national recognition as one of the top one hundred cardiac centers in the country.

Throughout the '70s and '80s, Sacred Heart saw increasing revenues. The funds were channeled back into the nonprofit facility. Still, says Sister Monica Heeran, the hospital's administrator from 1973 to 1988, "we always had a goal to make a good bottom line." The hospital became one of the area's largest charitable donors, absorbing millions in charity care and giving away thousands of dollars annually for health-related projects.

But in the late 1980s Sacred Heart, like hospitals across the country, found itself responding to the pressures of increased healthcare costs and diminishing government Medicare reimbursements. Subsequent years saw positions being eliminated, first through attrition, then through elimination. In fiscal year 1994 the hospital reported a net income that was less than half of the previous year's, its lowest revenue margin in twenty-four years.

The hospital spun through many changes during the next decade. Its Bellevue-based parent organization, Health and Hospital Services, changed its name to PeaceHealth. In 1995 Sacred Heart Health System also changed its name to PeaceHealth, and Sacred Heart became Sacred Heart Medical Center. In 1995 fifty-five physicians at the Eugene Clinic voted to integrate with PeaceHealth, putting an end to seventy-two years of independence. The forty-one-physician Oregon Medical Group, as a whole, declined to integrate with the system, although eleven doctors did so independently.

Sacred Heart's assumption of local physician groups concerned some who felt the Catholic-associated hospital's position prohibiting abortion on its premises could reduce women's access to the procedure. Community concern became evident when the obstetric group Women's Care Associates was considering becoming part of PeaceHealth. Although the group and Sacred Heart were able to come to an agreement that allowed physicians to perform abortions at an independent location, Women's Care never integrated into the PeaceHealth system.

Sacred Heart remains a massive ship in Eugene's health-care harbor. The city's largest private employer, it provides full- and part-time jobs for about 3,400 area residents. Its reach extends west to Florence, south to Cottage Grove, east to Springfield and, for some services, includes Douglas, Coos, Linn, and Benton counties. (PeaceHealth also operates hospitals in Ketchikan, Alaska, and in Bellingham and Longview, Washington.) Some have maintained the hospital wears two community hats. A July 1996 story in *The Register-Guard* described one "image" of Sacred Heart as that of a supremely efficient hospital that provides advanced life-saving techniques for a wide community and "gives away millions of dollars in medical and social services." But "Sacred Heart is also part of a profit-motivated corporation, PeaceHealth, and a king-size real estate developer," the article continued. "The corporation's sprawling property acquisitions—and vigorous efforts to collect debts from uninsured but solvent patients—have earned it the nickname, 'Sacred Wallet.' "

The facility has had its own internal struggles. Scars remain from a bitter ten-week nurses' strike in 1980. And the integration period of the mid-1990s, when some physicians found themselves more competitive than collaborative, was a time of particular "internal and external angst," says PeaceHealth spokesperson Beverly Mayhew. Buffeted by two decades of unceasing change and challenge, the hospital community has struggled to find its footing, Mayhew says. "This industry ended the twentieth century under tremendous pressure, tremendous change. We are trying to find the balance that will sustain us."

Parallel Healing

The 1970s and 1980s saw a parallel — and unparalleled — expansion in alternative healing modalities. Naturopathic medicine, chiropractic care, acupuncture, massage, midwifery, and a host of other practices sprung up throughout Eugene in the post–Vietnam era. It's unclear why Eugene became such a mecca for alternative practitioners. Certainly, the late 1960s gave birth to a nationwide disaffection with many mainstream institutions. The rise of both the "hippie" movement and the women's movement fueled interest in diet, herbs, organic foods, and alternative forms of healing. Many people who embraced such independent practices found their way to Eugene, which by the mid-1970s was home to dozens of experimental, cooperative businesses. The presence of two natural-healing schools in Portland also assured a steady source of practitioners.

Stephen Messer came to Eugene in 1979 after graduating from the National College of Naturopathic Medicine in Portland. At first, his practice went well. But after an economic recession slammed the Northwest in the early 1980s, many of his clients had to leave town to find work. "I went to work in a funky office on Willamette Street," he remembers. "The roof leaked, there was no receptionist. It was really bare bones." Still, the public continued to be drawn to alternative healing approaches, and, as Eugene and the rest of Oregon climbed out of the financial doldrums, people became more willing to try them.

In 2000, Eugene's local yellow pages listed eighteen acupuncturists, sixteen naturopathic physicians, and scores of chiropractors and massage therapists. Messer says in the last twenty years he has seen a "sea change" in the Eugene community's acceptance of "complementary modalities." Acupuncture, for instance, now is routinely used at White Bird Clinic and other drug and alcohol treatment centers. It's also effectively used in treating migraines, chemotherapy-induced nausea, and upper-respiratory complaints. Chiropractic treatments are used for sinus problems, headaches, and allergies. Increasingly, insurance policies offer coverage for some alternative treatments because customers demand them. "First we were outsiders," Messer says. "Now we're part of the whole milieu of medicine."

The public has been far more willing to embrace alternative options than the local physician community, say many alternative practitioners. Physicians have showed their skepticism, alternative practitioners say, by refusing to send records on patients or refusing to refer patients or simply not considering the possibility that healing may come in different forms. Chiropractic physician Vip Short says that, although chiropractics is about the most established and least "fringe" of local alternative options, he doesn't recall getting any referrals from local physicians in his first six years of practice. It's only been since 1989, he says, after making contact with a local physician who is open to different types of treat-ments, that he began getting referrals. "It only takes one angel in that 'other' professional community," says Short. "And he had those magic letters: M.D."

Managed care also set back local physicians' acceptance of al-ternative health practices. Because of increased oversight, even the more receptive physicians "started folding up, started towing the line," says Eugene acupuncturist Larry Weinstein. He says, "The few doctors we got referrals from are gone, or they've had the fear of God put into them by the insurance companies." In other ways, however, Weinstein says managed care has turned out to be a boon for his practice. Increasingly, clients dissatisfied with their physi-cians' abbreviated checkups are willing to pay out-of-pocket to see a practitioner who not only can treat their symptoms, but who also has time for them. "Managed Care has created an emotional vacuum," says Weinstein. "Patients need human contact. They're crying for someone to sit down and listen to them. And they come to us because we listen."

Messer is confident that the evolution that has made his shelves bulge with patient records isn't going to reverse itself. He acknowl-edges that he is not yet allowed to treat patients at Sacred Heart Medical Center, even though naturopathic physicians are allowed to treat patients in Portland and Seattle-area hospitals. But he says that acceptance from the mainstream is simply a matter of time. "It will happen," says Messer. "There's no doubt about it."

On the Front Lines

Throughout the past few decades, individuals in the local medical community have emerged who defy categorization. These indi-viduals have bucked the status quo in their own corner of the com-munity and, in doing so, have helped to usher in changes that benefited others.

Emily Fergus Merritt left a teaching job at the University of Washington to follow her husband to Eugene in 1965. At the time, there were fewer than five female physicians in Eugene.

"When I got here, I was a total *persona non grata*," she says. "I had to prove myself. It took a while." Fergus began her practice as an internist, attracting teenage girls and post-menopausal women who were "tired of male doctors." She later became a kidney specialist, establishing Eugene's first dialysis unit with her partner. "I used to take new women doctors to lunch when they first came to town," she says. "There were so few of us."

Donald Woomer, an obstetrician-gynecologist, did his share of shaking up the status quo in 1973 when he became one of the first physicians in the country to use certified nurse midwives in a private obstetrics practice. Woomer says he encountered "vigorous resistance" when he first approached his peers at Sacred Heart about using nurse midwives. "But I had enough rapport that no one outright wanted to refuse me," he says. Within just a few years his practice grew from fifteen deliveries a month to eighty, a client-load that kept a crew of four doctors and four nurse midwives working full time. Although it hasn't been a smooth road, nurse midwives continue to be an option for local mothers-to-be.

Donna Howell, a coordinator for home health and hospice at Sacred Heart, put herself on the front lines of fighting for adequate pain management thirty years ago. Back then, Howell says, pain at the end of life was accepted as a given. As a rule local physicians "wouldn't order [enough] morphine," she says. "They feared making people drug addicts." But it was nurses, not physicians, who witnessed the horrible pain people were forced to endure before dying. "I would come home from work shattered by the pain my patients had to go through," she says. Howell decided to learn as much as she could about pain management. She attended workshops all over the country, learning how physicians in other communities managed dying patients' pain. She became even more convinced that it was attitudes, not medical facts, that kept Eugene physicians from prescribing adequate pain-killing drugs. For years she badgered physicians, forcing them to tell her face to face why they would not increase morphine dosages. Over time her persistence worked. By 1999, she says, most physicians were readily prescribing adequate pain medication. "People are very courageous and wonderful," says Howell, who has witnessed hundreds of deaths. "If they have support, if their pain is under control, they can die with tremendous courage and dignity."

Vision, volunteers, and dedication on the part of scores of individuals also made possible White Bird Clinic, the community's low-income health clinic. Since 1970 White Bird has provided health services to low-income patients, along with the indigent, those struggling with substance abuse, the mentally ill, and non-English-speaking immigrants. Bob Dritz, clinic director, says clients include people who work but can't afford insurance, people who qualify for the Oregon Health Plan but don't have the skills to use it, and undocumented residents who don't qualify for the Oregon Health Plan. According to Mike Weinstein, who came to the clinic in 1983, more than sixty local physicians volunteer at White Bird. For many of these doctors, the clinic is the only environment where they can practice medicine the "old-fashioned" way—with a minimum of paperwork, a lot of collegial sharing, and an emphasis on patient-physician interaction.

Those involved in the health-care community fifty years ago could not have predicted today's advances, and it's very difficult to predict what the next fifty years will bring. Certainly, we can expect more research and procedure breakthroughs in areas such as trauma care, cancer, auto-immune disorders, and genetic diseases. Hopefully, the same will hold true for conditions, such as diabetes and spinal cord degeneration, that have stymied physicians for decades. Technology and computer-assisted procedures will continue to make possible a broader array of diagnoses and treatments. On the heels of the last tumultuous decades of the twentieth century, many hope the future will improve communication among physicians and specialists, physicians and patients, physicians and those who administer health plans, and mainstream and alternative providers. Perhaps the pendulum will swing back toward prioritizing patients the system was meant to serve.

Acupuncturist Marvin Finklestein is one practitioner working toward such goals. Part of a group of caregivers from across the health-care spectrum exploring ways to better manage pain, he says, "We've realized that working together works better for the patient." Bev Mayhew says Sacred Heart Medical Center is strengthening its priority on patient care. "We are realizing with greater clarity than we have in recent years that we need to focus all of our efforts on the patient and the patient's family," she says. "We let ourselves get off track by all of the changes hitting this industry so hard."

Messer says the pendulum has swung as far away from health-care consumers as it can. Over the past several decades, he says, "medicine has gone from doctor-centered to insurance-centered, and is now going to be more client-centered," he predicts. "People aren't willing to stand for a paternal or hierarchical structure anymore. They want to be cocreators of their health care. The patient has to be part of the equation."

Bibliography

Hirons, Larry W. "A History of the Eugene Hospital and Clinic, 1923–1973."

PeaceHealth Public Affairs, "A History of Sacred Heart Medical Center."

The Register-Guard, selected articles, 1988–1996.

MAKING THE ARTS MATTER

By Lois Wadsworth

IN THE FALL of 1974 when I moved to Eugene, downtown felt like the center of a vibrant, exciting city—a great place to live. For five years I spent every weekday lunch hour downtown and soon realized that the exciting sense that something was happening was primarily the result of an active visual arts, theater, and music scene. Art happenings added to the excitement of being on the downtown mall, and performance was frequently integrated with art show openings.

Unfortunately, the city's liveliness failed to survive the economic recession of the early 1980s. Downtown anchor businesses moved to Valley River Center or closed their doors. Art galleries and theaters shut down. Empty buildings and dwindling pedestrians contrasted with the beehive of activity that had previously swarmed through downtown.

Most people who live in Eugene would probably agree that we collectively feel better about our city when people are drawn to downtown, as happens during the annual Eugene Celebration, for example. All who are interested in preserving the spirit of revitalization that manifested itself in the core downtown area at the end of the century after many years of decline should take a good look at what makes such areas attractive. The architecture of public buildings and art in public places are two visual arts elements that beautify downtown. An active visual arts scene that includes both commercial and nonprofit galleries is also part of that picture.

In the years since 1950, public funding from government has played an important role in directly and indirectly fostering the visual arts. Leaders and stewards of the arts have arisen from the city's many institutions. Local artists have been influenced by teachers and curricula at the University of Oregon, Lane Community College, and Maude Kerns Art Center. Civic-minded public artists from Jan Zach to David Joyce to John Rose have left their marks on the city, while seminal art galleries such as the White Lotus Gallery, Open Gallery, the Museum of Art at the university, and the Jacobs Gallery have created the necessary interfaces between artists and the public.

Overview of Public Funding for the Arts

The federal government has been a major player in funding the visual arts scene nationally as well as in Eugene, with programs such as the Works Project Administration–funded works of fine and decorative arts of the 1930s, the post–World War II GI Bill that sent American servicemen and women to the nation's colleges, and the Comprehensive Employment and Training Act (CETA) funds of the 1970s that helped launch individual artists and arts organizations. CETA funds were administered through state, municipal, and nonprofit local agencies such as the Lane Regional Arts Council (LRAC), now the Lane Arts Council (LAC). Other federal funds for the visual arts came from agencies such as the National Endowment for the Arts (NEA), for example, which also disbursed grants through state and local art agencies, such as the Oregon Arts Commission (OAC).

Another source of public funding that had a direct impact on local arts were the state and local "percent for the arts" ordinances. Oregon's 1975 percent-for-art ordinance (ORS 276.075) applies to state-owned buildings and reflects the recognition that "the visual arts contribute to and provide experiences which are conducive to the enrichment and betterment of the social and physical environment." If the state builds new buildings or remodels old buildings to the tune of $100,000 or more, one percent of the direct costs must be set aside for the acquisition of art.

In August 1981, the Eugene City Council passed Eugene Ordinance 18849, which mandated that the city spend one percent of the cost of new construction or remodeling that totaled more than $50,000 on art works. "The commissioning of art works in public places, in addition to furthering the policy of fostering and developing artists, enriches public perception of government buildings, parks, malls, and the like," the ordinance read in part. Even before the passage of Ordinance 18849, the Eugene City Council voluntarily dedicated $200,000 for artwork for the Hult Center and the adjoining conference center. Kirsten Jones, a Eugene public art consultant and former city employee, described this action as "a catalyst for the passage of the ordinance."

Commercial art galleries receive no public funding, but Eugene's not-for-profit art galleries—the University of Oregon's Museum of Art (UOMA), Maude Kerns Art Center gallery, the Gallery at the Airport, and the Hult Center's Jacobs Gallery— receive a mix of public and private funding. The UO provides for the Adell McMillan Gallery and the Laverne Krause Gallery on campus. Likewise, LCC's main campus art gallery is funded through the college.

But other institutions learned to survive without public funding. The Jacobs Gallery went from being a fully staffed, City of Eugene–subsidized space to a volunteer-run, nonprofit gallery. When the Hult Center opened its doors in 1981, Suzanne Pepin, who worked as a consultant for the city's Parks and Recreation Department's Cultural Services, recalls that visual arts advocates and artists, such as Madeleine Liepe and Mark Clarke, urged the city to turn the Jacobs Community Room into an art gallery. (Pepin ran the Jacobs Gallery for twelve years, from 1986 until taking early retirement in 1998.) And the Open Gallery, which was the source of much of the arts revitalization of the 1970s, began as a commercial gallery on the corner of Hilyard and 25th but became a nonprofit with 501(c)3 tax-exempt status, eventually locating in the old Midgley Glass Building near downtown.

In 2000, though the U.S. Congress and the Oregon legislature continued to chip away at public sources of arts funding, the

collective impact of such focused funding on the health of the arts
and the grace of the city proved substantial.

Major Influences

In the 1950s and '60s, there were only a few art galleries in the
city, including High Street Gallery and 12th Street Gallery. Other
than those small spaces, the University of Oregon's Museum of
Art, built by the founder and first dean of the School of Architecture and Allied Arts, Ellis R. Lawrence (1879–1946), was the
only show in town. Lawrence was an influential leader who integrated the fine arts and crafts into the designs of his most famous
buildings—the Knight Library and the Museum of Art—as well
as making them part of the school's curriculum.

According to Associate Director of the Museum of Art Lawrence
Fong, when you consider the arts in Eugene historically, "You recognize traditions founded in architecture and coming from the
integration of craft into the design of our institutions—ranging
from the historic UO buildings to the [downtown] '60s architecture of Poticha-Unthank. What's not as obvious is the support for
the fine arts: painting, printmaking, sculpture, photography."

Leadership in the fine and integrated arts at the university
came from many teachers over many years. One of the most influential postwar teachers was Jack Wilkinson (1913–1974), an energetic oil painter, lithographer, and muralist who taught from
1941 to 1968. Wilkinson's public art work includes Orientation,
a 1957–60 mural at the entrance to Lawrence Hall on campus,
and a 1959 mural for the Lane County Courthouse. But his more
enduring legacy is his influence on the artists who studied with
him.

One important artist and teacher who studied with Wilkinson
was LaVerne Krause (1924–1987), who painted from home while
her children were young and then went to teach at the university
in 1966. There she founded the school's printmaking program.
Printmaker Elizabeth Brinton said a conversation in the 1970s,
when Krause basically told her "to quit whining and get on with

the work," was key to her development as an artist. "She was curt," Brinton said, "but it was so useful to me."

"Energy looking for an outlet" is how Krause was described in a 1979 interview. Krause said about the artistic climate of Eugene, "People here are still in the pleasure-boat stage. Our mentality here for art still isn't very strong." She noted that lacking were "the audience and the galleries."

Krause channeled some of her famous energy into helping to found Oregon Artists Equity and the Northwest Print Council. Krause was awarded the Governor's Art Award in 1980, "the highest honor an Oregon artist can receive," according to *Oregon Painters: The First Hundred Years (1859–1959)*, an index and biographical dictionary by Ginny Allen and Jody Klevit published by Oregon Historical Society Press in 2000. An oil painting by Krause hangs in the Hult Center, and a print is in the council chambers at City Hall.

Likewise, abstract painter Frank Okada influenced many students. "People came here to the university because Frank was here," Lawrence Fong said. Okada taught from 1969 until his retirement in 1998. His public art includes an oil painting at the Hult Center and another in the EMU. Several large oils are on display on the mezzanine level of the Museum of Art.

One of the university's first fine arts photographers, Bernard Freemesser (1927–1977), also reached beyond teaching to the larger culture of the city. Photographer Paul Neevel, who studied with Freemesser, described him as "a very dynamic teacher but abrasive at times." Freemesser helped start the Society for Photographic Education and brought nationally recognized photographers to Oregon, including photojournalist Eugene Smith and California fine-arts photographer Brett Weston. "Freemesser loved the image of the pioneer photographer with his large-format camera out in the wilderness," Neevel said, "but in truth Bernie never got very far from his car."

In 1967, Freemesser also helped start the entirely volunteer-run Photography at Oregon Gallery. Despite losing its gallery in the 1990s, the Photography at Oregon Committee continued to sponsor exhibits and bring in lecturers through its primary fundraiser at the UO Museum of Art, an annual auction of works donated by prominent national and regional photographers, which in 1999 raised $10,000.

David John McCosh (1903–1981) taught at the university from 1934 until he retired in 1972; his 1965 oil painting, *Thicket*, is part of the Hult Center's art collection. McCosh, who inspired a generation of painters, was honored with a series of UOMA exhibitions, October 1993 through June 1994. In the summer of 2000, UOMA held an exhibition of twenty-nine paintings selected by members of the arts community from the museum's David J. McCosh Memorial Collection, established by his widow, painter Anne Kutka McCosh in 1990.

Filling in where the university did not was a community art resource now known as the Maude Kerns Art Center. A group of artists founded the Eugene Art Center in 1951, organized by Maude Kerns (1876–1965), a prolific and important Oregon painter who retired from thirty years of teaching at the university in 1947. The center's mission was to provide classes and exhibition space for area artists. Decades before the concept of "lifelong learning" penetrated academia, people made and studied art in a small building at the Lane County fairgrounds.

For the next twelve years, according to Kerns scholar Mary Helen Burnham, Kerns stepped in to provide or expand housing for the center, which continued to outgrow each improvement. In May 1962, in formal recognition of Kerns's generosity, the center was renamed the Maude Kerns Art Center (MKAC). With the Junior League of Eugene, Kerns, then eighty-six years old, made the down payment on George Miller's Fairmount Presbyterian Church just east of the UO campus, and MKAC moved to its current site.

Two retrospectives of Kerns's work—a 1988 MKAC exhibit and a 1994 Jacobs Gallery exhibit—have helped determine Kerns's place in Oregon's art history. Kerns's greatniece, Leslie Brocklebank, said paintings were borrowed from the Guggenheim and the Seattle and Portland Art Museums for the MKAC show. And for the Jacobs show they discovered some "seventy-five years of paintings, including some very early pieces and paintings done the last year of her life," she said.

Oregon Painters puts Kerns's work in this perspective: "She was an Oregon pioneer in the non-objective style, which placed her at odds with most of the Oregon art community. . . . Maude Kerns enjoyed a strong reputation in the East but was not as well known in her home state of Oregon."

Burnham said that Kerns's work of the 1960–1965 period is "some of her most mature work." And Brocklebank noted, "We don't think of Maude's world-oriented side, but many of her works from all periods of her life were about her interest in international affairs."

In 1968, when Lane Community College moved to its new facility on East 30th Avenue, the art faculty moved from its temporary home at MKAC. Painter and sculptor Harold Hoy has taught at LCC since 1970 and directed the LCC Gallery since 1971. The gallery hosts student and faculty art shows each year, but Hoy has broadened the gallery's scope to include the larger community. His goal has been to show the "best contemporary artists in the Northwest and beyond," he said.

When Hoy retired in June 2000, LCC did not replace the gallery director position because of decreased state funding. Hoy said the position will be run by a committee of volunteers, including textile artist Marilyn Robert. Both the curriculum and the teachers in the visual arts fields at LCC have offered affordable, practical resources for area residents, artists, and craftspeople. Many of the area's fine artists have taught at LCC over the years. For example, photographic sculptor and faculty member David Joyce has taught one of the most popular classes offered—a survival class for artists.

Arts Explosion

A tremendous arts explosion swept the country in the late 1960s and reverberated throughout the 1970s. The long-held, popular but economically unfounded notion that Eugene supports its artists comes from this era. The growth of alternative arts had its origin in the Oregon Country Fair and Saturday Market, both of which began at the end of the 1960s and undoubtedly encouraged many local fine artists to learn crafts to support themselves.

But the fine arts explosion that was part of the '70s national trend toward alternative art spaces really got a kick in the pants when Flora Rudolph opened an experimental art gallery, the Open Gallery, in the mid-1970s. Rudolph, a UO graduate with a fine arts degree in painting, opened the gallery with Richard Heller, and like Krause, they quickly discovered that "people in Eugene went elsewhere to buy art." The gallery evolved into a not-for-profit organization surviving on national and state arts grants and CETA funding into the early 1980s.

"Open Gallery was a magnet," Rudolph said. "So many artists started coming by [that] we set up an Artists' Forum once a month where artists showed slides of their work, and everybody talked about the arts. People were hungry for it." The gallery's focus came to be "creating a community of artists who would generate enough excitement about art that it would spread to the larger community," Rudolph said.

Painter Steven Oshatz recalled that when Open Gallery first opened, the *Eugene Register-Guard* had no arts section and "refused to review art shows." But, he said, "We approached them, and they said they would not publish art reviews unless they were written by accredited journalists—no freelance articles accepted." So he got a grant to hire a recognized art critic—he found Roger Hull, who taught at Willamette University—to review his show at the Open Gallery. But the newspaper "refused to run the review," Oshatz said. "They said they didn't have a section to run it in."

"A new thing is happening in Eugene," began a new arts column by Ellie Spech, a writer from Chicago, in a story on Oshatz in the April 15, 1977 issue of the *Willamette Valley Observer*. Spech called his art style "a little Charles Adams, a pinch of Disney and a pinch of Dada thrown in for good measure." The *Observer* also published a weekly community arts calendar. Fred Crafts, arts reporter for the *Eugene Register-Guard*, wrote an article on Oshatz as part of the paper's weekly arts and entertainment section. In 1982, the *Observer* went under, and a few months later *What's Happening* (later the *Eugene Weekly*) began publication, and by the 1990s covered local news in addition to its comprehensive arts and entertainment calendar, stories, and reviews.

The early 1970s is also the era that gave birth to the Lane Regional Arts Council (LRAC) and the Oregon Arts Commission (OAC). And it was the era of the expanded federal CETA funds for art-related projects, which Lane County first administered. CETA grants had "dramatic effects on the arts in Lane County," according to the 1979 Cultural Guide to Lane County published by the Open Gallery. "Most CETA projects continue to be restricted to public agencies or nonprofit corporations with federal tax-exempt status," the Guide noted. The City of Eugene also had CETA funds, and LRAC handled the Artist in Community grants.

"Selena Roberts at LRAC was dedicated to the personal vision that arts could add vibrancy to the city," said Oshatz, who received a CETA grant "to put the geese-flying mural up at the 5the Street Market" (*Birds in Flight*, which was painted over in 1984). Without the advocacy of such arts professionals as Roberts, Rudolph, and others, the '70s arts explosion would have fizzled sooner.

Rudolph and Heller applied for a large CETA grant for artists and administration for the Open Gallery, which came through in 1976. They immediately created art projects that reached out to and involved the community, such as art displays in storefront windows all over downtown. "Shop owners donated a window of their store, and we set up small art exhibits in them," Rudolph said. The gallery also put "monumental works" in public places, such as in parks, downtown, and on Skinner Butte, and had LTD buses take people to see them. "We brought in national artists to meet Eugene artists and do some kind of public art. Donald Lipski of New York did tiny sculptures for an installation at the Lane County building, and Deborah Butterfield did another installation of life-sized metal horses there," Rudolph said.

And the gallery scene took off. Open Gallery moved into the EWEB-owned Midgley Building. James Aday set up Kairos Gallery, which later became Artists Union Gallery, on Willamette Street. "After Artists Union became an establishment gallery," Oshatz said, "Harold Hoy and Bobby DeVine opened Project Space, an alternative gallery." Not all galleries were downtown, he noted. Mama's Homefried Truckstop, a restaurant near campus, also held curated art shows. "That's where the real artists were shown," Oshatz said.

By the early 1980s, Eugene's economic recession was worsening, and paradoxically that's also when CETA grants became unavailable. Rudolph and Heller closed the Open Gallery. "We showed 320 artists a year, had five artists-in-the-school exhibits every month, and did three major public arts projects a year plus our exhibits," Rudolph said. "I was an available instrument for the alternative arts movement when that energy came through."

Public Art in Public Places

Although downtown activities made the visual arts visible during the 1970s, Eugene's enduring public art owes a great deal to sculptor Jan Zach (1914–1986), who worked before and after that era. He came to the university in 1958 to direct its sculpture department. His public art spans decades and includes several works in various media for the courtyard of the new City Hall in 1964; *Prometheus* (1958), a large cast-iron sculpture outside the UOMA; the stainless steel *Can-Can* (1969) in Meier and Frank's rotunda at Valley River Center; and *Oregon*, a 1973 stainless steel sculpture at the 8th Avenue entrance to the Lane County Public Service Building.

"Zach meant his work to be outdoor pieces," public art consultant Kirsten Jones said. "They were meant to age." But the long-term maintenance of public art has many problems, and Zach's concrete panel bas reliefs at City Hall illustrate one: At some point, someone painted a blue background on the panels, perhaps hoping to "improve" them.

Another problem, since addressed, was the lack of record keeping of public art. One year Jones and fellow city employee Suzanne Pepin were putting together a survey of the city's art for the OAC, and Pepin discovered a standing figure by Zach completely hidden by a big rhododendron at City Hall. It had been forgotten by everyone. Jones noted that the city will have to decide what to do with Zach's sculptures if City Hall ever relocates.

Another public artist, glass artist John Rose, remembered that soon after arriving in Eugene in 1974, he attended a sculpture symposium inspired by Zach at Alton Baker Park. An NEA grant brought six international sculptors to Eugene for the summer-long Oregon International Sculpture Symposium. Rose recalled feeling fortunate to live in a city where such events took place, only to discover that the symposium was a one-time-only event. Several notable pieces of public art were created at the symposium and are on various sites in the city, including two at Alton Baker Park (Bernard Rosenthal's welded Korten steel sculpture and Hugh Townley's group of concrete figures), one at the plaza of the Lane County Public Services Building (Dimitri Hadzi's eight basalt columns), one at the UO (Jack Chamberlain's painted aluminum foil sculpture), and one at the Washington-Jefferson Park (Bruce Beasley's *Big Red*, an abstract painted metal sculpture).

Rose began bringing large sculptural pieces downtown in 1990, and from 1990 to 1998 a temporary show called "Outside Art" brightened the area. Rose, a LAC board member, and Greg Wilbur found artists who agreed to create art and install it on the mall for $100 each. Then they went to Carol Brewster at the City of Eugene who "said yes to the project and expressed a willingness to figure out how to get it through all the committees," Rose said. "You've got to have someone like that to make a project work."

Then they approached downtown-based publisher and building owner Ed Aster, who was embroiled in the controversy over
opening Willamette Street to traffic, which he opposed. He gave
them $900 for the project. They went back to the city and got
another $900. In subsequent years, LAC's Douglas Beauchamp
got the project funded through the city's urban renewal funds so
the artists got paid. "Now the new library project is sucking up all
the urban renewal funds," Rose said, "and there's no funding for
the outdoor sculpture program."

"Outside Art" provided artists "a way to do civic art that had
to last four to six months, rather than forever," Rose said. "They
learned about scale, about what it is to work big." Memorable
sculptural work included Carey Wade's *Big Red Chair* and Aimee
Matilla's tire pieces.

One of the city's most popular, widely recognized public art-
works isn't downtown at all. David Joyce attached individual photographic cutouts of a variety of Eugene citizens to a the wall,
creating a black-and-white photosculptural installation of the "flying" air travelers at the renovated Eugene Airport in August 1989.
The plywood-mounted figures are a continuing source of delight
for travelers.

The Visual Arts Today and Tomorrow

In 2000, there were more than forty commercial galleries or businesses where art was shown in Eugene. The downtown galleries
attract large numbers of people every First Friday of the month,
when new art shows traditionally open. The galleries stay open
later, hold receptions for the artists, and offer snacks and beverages
to encourage the public to meet the artists.

One of the important anchors for the commercial galleries
downtown is the Jacobs Gallery, which received a long-overdue
facelift in spring 2000 thanks to Otto Poticha and lots of volunteer labor. "The gallery is alive now only because of the efforts of
dedicated arts volunteers such as Laurel Fisher and David Joyce,"
Pepin said. Whether an all-volunteer organization with tenuous

financial underpinnings can continue to support noncommercial but quality work by local and regional artists is a question no one can answer. And whether the venue itself, even with improved internal space, is suitable for a municipal art gallery is another sticky point.

The Jacobs has not only served as a gallery for talented artists to interact with the public and learn what worked in their shows and what didn't, but it is also the home of the annual Mayor's Art Show, which is now so large that it challenges the limitations of the gallery's space. This successful exhibit attracts people during the Eugene Celebration who may not attend another art show all year.

On the university campus, planned remodeling and building of the Museum of Art promises that its resources will continue to serve the larger public as well as its first concern: UO students and faculty. Lawrence Fong described the UOMA's mission for the future as being "more representative of the arts of our time and place." It will balance its traditional historic Asian art, he said, "with contemporary arts and issues, and with shows from regional artists, American artists, and from our own collections."

Eugene should plan to develop a privately and publicly funded nonprofit metropolitan gallery to support the visual arts. The Jacobs Gallery attempts to fill this niche, but its location is both too small and too dependent on the Hult Center's hours. Ideally, a metro gallery would be staffed by art professionals neither dependent on the taste of wealthy patrons nor dominated by the concerns of arts organizations. Including a rental-sales gallery would provide additional support to local artists.

But to invigorate the arts scene to approximate the kind of energy that was on the streets in the 1970s, well, that must come both from policies and from artists themselves. I saw the very beginning of such a movement at the March 2000 First Friday. Outside Due Fine Art on Willamette and 8th Avenue, two local artists had set up their paintings. A local performer came by with his accordion, and small groups of people gathered around, looking at art, talking. The ambience was European cosmopolitan. It felt good.

Integration of the visual arts into the cityscape will need to accelerate in the new century, not diminish. People may disagree about the need for public funding of the arts, but public support is essential to create a good-looking, safe, active city center, which in turn helps create a vital civic life.

A LITERARY LIFE

By Michael Kroetch

When John B. Hall launched the master of fine arts program in creative writing at the University of Oregon in 1957, there were only a handful of such programs to be found anywhere. With the program, Hall put Eugene on the map and probably was responsible for the influx of exceptional writers who have, however briefly, called this place home. As with Eugene's visual arts community, the writers who have studied and taught at the UO have been major influences in the literary community.

"It's important that not everyone who graduates from the university leaves the area," noted Erik Muller, coeditor of *Fireweed*, a poetry journal dedicated to Oregon-only authors, from 1989 to 1998. "Those who stay make up the mulch for local activities. They're often the ones who lead workshops and organize readings."

These writers have often captured statewide attention. Literary Arts, Inc., a statewide funding agency based in Portland, has awarded fellowships to many local authors. And for the thirteen years that the organization has sponsored the annual Oregon Book Awards, Eugene-area writers have taken top honors fourteen times in three categories. For poetry: Pimone Triplett '99, Maxine Scates '90, Ingrid Wendt '88, John Haislip '87. For fiction: Ehud Havazelet '99, Peter Ho Davies '98, Tracy Daugherty '96, Chang-rae Lee '95, Diana Abu-Jaber '94. For nonfiction: John Daniel '97, Garrett Hongo '96, Lauren Kessler '94, John Daniel '93, Barry Lopez '87. Several of these writers either taught in or attended the UO's creative writing program.

The UO has also served as a venue for literary activities, exposing the community to writers of national acclaim. Readings by resident and visiting talent have long been popular in town, since the 1960s when the Willamette Writer's Guild hosted them on the UO campus. According to Bill Sweet, editor of Lane Community College's *Denali* as well as owner of The Literary Lion Bookstore from 1980–90 and first president of Lane Literary Guild, "Practically everybody who was anybody came to speak at that time, including W.H. Auden, Robert Penn Warren, and many, many others. The important thing about having such big names was that they created energy and excitement and an audience for other readings by locals. In that way the two fed each other."

But Eugene's literary community isn't entirely a university affair. Muller noted, "One thing that characterizes the community is how heterogeneous it is," he said. "There's a wide variety of achievement here, not just in level, but also in goals. You have everything from performance poets, street poets, conventional to modern ones. And there's a diverse range of ambition from those just happy to write anything at all, to those seeking a Pulitzer."

He listed the Lane Literary Guild's "Windfall Series" as the most regular reading series in the area, but also pointed out the importance of readings at local bookstores such as the UO Bookstore, Mother Kali's, and Tsunami Books.

Roger Moody, sole proprietor of Eugene-based *Silverfish Review*, which recently celebrated its twenty-second year in print, moved here from Indiana in 1974. He did so "because it was an exciting place alive with writing and poetry. There's really something to that, about this place being on the edge of the continent. There's a vortex here that vibrates with creative electricity. People come to Eugene from all over and constantly bring in new ideas. On the downside, despite the flow of energy, there is little, if any, way to financially support them. And that's a problem."

Ingrid Wendt, author of five books and cofounder of the Lane Literary Guild (LLG), is one of many in the literary community who agrees that funding for literary arts is minimal. Although she praised the city's Room Tax Funds for helping the LLG become established and pursue its many missions, she said, "The amount given is never large, in fact disproportionately small, but we're still very grateful. However, overall, I think the literary arts have received, per artist, less than those in other arts. Mostly it's an issue of visibility. There's a perception that the general audience for literary work is smaller than that for performing arts, because you can count the number of seats that are filled in a concert hall, but not the number of readers at home with a book. And because literature is not considered outright entertainment, it often doesn't get promoted and backed nearly as heavily as some of the other more attention-grabbing disciplines."

In contrast, John Witte, editor of the UO-based triquarterly, *Northwest Review*, said the arts always exist outside governmental authority, and used as an example certain Communist-occupied countries and their artistic efflorescence. "Often where the arts are least supported, they thrive the best," he said. "Precious little has been done for the local literary scene, but that may not be a bad thing." He cited the region's great wealth of writing as proof and said most writers he knows ply another trade for money so they can live in the area.

Bill Sweet recently visited Ireland and said he was surprised at the amount of respect given to contemporary authors in that country. "Irish writers are not taxed," he said. "They're supported, celebrated, and you find their images are everywhere, even in beer halls. I think the state can support artists in a much more serious way than they do. Literary arts are essential for us as a people. Why don't we have, as we did in the late '80s and early '90s, a major literary event scheduled into the Hult Center's annual calendar?"

Echoing this opinion, Lauren Kessler, author of nine books and a professor of nineteen years in the University of Oregon's journalism school (the last five spent in the department's literary nonfiction program), noted that all the other major cities on the West Coast—Seattle, Portland, San Francisco—have huge literary festivals, but not Eugene. "Why is that?" she asked. "And it's amazing that *The Register-Guard* pays so little attention to the local literary scene. It's embarrassing for a community that thinks of itself as a cultural mecca."

VENUES AND VISIONARIES

By Brett Campbell

IN 1950, EUGENE hosted—for the last time—the Oregon Trail Pageant. Begun in 1926 to commemorate the anniversary of the first train to cross the new Cascade Mountain route, the triennial production at the Lane County fairgrounds featured great herds of livestock, covered wagons, stunt-flying airplanes, skits and songs, and everything else a proper small-town country shindig should have. A good portion of the citizenry attended or participated in some way: downtown merchants redecorated their shops to get that log-cabin look; farmers brought their animals to town. Each installment of the "trail to rail" show grew bigger; one year, three thousand people gathered onstage at once, and the pageant was said to be the largest in the world. A genuine community celebration of Oregon's pioneer heritage, it was the highlight of the summer, and the city's major performing arts event.

But by 1950, Eugene had outgrown the pageant. The city had become too large for it to operate as a communal event, the way farm families came together to raise a barn. Ranching and the rural traditions the pageant celebrated were already declining as influences on the city's economy and character. The economic and cultural changes that reverberated through the United States after World War II had begun to change the city, so much so that a celebration of livestock and log cabins could no longer encompass the city's performing arts culture. The end of the pageant was a turning point; the rest of the century would see Eugene performing artists and their supporters working hard to overcome the town's small size and cultural isolation to bring first-class theater, dance, and music to the burgeoning audiences.

Venues and visionaries shaped the arts scene over the past fifty years. Performing arts need dedicated people with vision—artists and arts supporters alike—to create performing opportunities. And they need a place to play—affordable venues that give the visionaries a platform for their creativity and audiences a place to be transported beyond mundane concerns. The story of Eugene's performing arts over the last half of the twentieth century is the story of visionaries striving to create art and to find places to perform it.

College Town Boon

The University of Oregon's experience, although beyond the scope of this chapter, is instructive here. A key factor in the UO's superior performing arts programming has been the availability of publicly financed, affordable venues. In 1950, just as the trail-to-rail show was ending, the UO had built a new, four-hundred-seat theater adjacent to Villard Hall. Over the next quarter-century, that space and others at the UO provided the opportunity for one of this region's great visionaries, Horace Robinson, to stage ambitious, innovative productions that won national renown. The theater, later named in his honor, has continued to provide a venue for some of the city's most exciting productions. And one of his students, Ed Ragozzino, who arrived at the UO in 1950, became another of the city's arts visionaries; he would go on to help create other publicly funded performing arts venues at South Eugene High School, Lane Community College, and the Hult Center.

Also in 1950, the UO School of Music undertook a dramatic physical expansion, adding studios and instruction rooms to make it one of the finest facilities on the West Coast and kindling an expansion of its programs. Until the Hult Center was built in the 1980s, the music school's acoustically phenomenal recital hall (named Beall Hall in 1973) was the only true music venue in the area, the setting for dozens of student, faculty, and community ensembles as well as internationally acclaimed guest artists. The school has had an incalculable effect on the city's culture, producing performers and building audiences for ambitious music performances. In fact, the city's premier performing arts institution, the Eugene Symphony, was born at the UO and weaned at Beall.

Until the late 1950s, the school hosted a civic symphony, many of whose players came from the UO. But by the time another visionary, Orval Etter, an amateur cellist who practiced law by day, arrived in Eugene in 1960, no real community orchestra existed. He recalled, "I became the convener of a group of amateur chamber music players who'd gather at [Caroline] Boekelheide's home to play together." The group soon developed into the Emerald Chamber Orchestra.

Beginning in the spring of 1965, the ensemble drew excellent audiences to a series of free concerts at local high schools, incorporating as the Eugene Symphony, founded by Etter, Boekelheide (who would become a major supporter of the symphony), Amy Jo Butler, and Karen Seidel in 1966. With UO violin professor Lawrence Maves on the podium, the music school supplying the scores, and Etter chairing the board, the orchestra gradually improved the quantity and quality of its players and concerts, attracting star international soloists. In the 1970s, the ensemble's concerts moved to Beall Hall, and they soon had to schedule multiple performances of each show to satisfy ticket demand.

But the UO's venues owed first allegiance to its students. By the 1960s, thanks to its music, theater, and dance departments, the UO was producing so many artists and cultivating so many arts lovers that the city needed more and larger performing arts space for those visionaries to play.

All the World's a Stage

Of course, the city did have quite a few performing arts spaces already. In 1950, after two decades of putting on productions in various spaces, the city's leading private theater company, the Very Little Theatre, bought its own building from the city of Eugene— for $3,000. The theater enthusiasts who made up VLT's membership converted the building into a two-hundred-seat playhouse that would, for the rest of the century, present the sort of mainstream, drawing-room comedies and melodramas that many Eugeneans wanted to see. Because it chose its productions based on the wishes of its membership (which eventually grew to well over one hundred members), VLT took few programming risks. But over the decades, it would enjoy a stability rare for theaters of its kind and remain the solid center of Eugene's community theater.

For many years, the main venues for such long-time groups such as the Eugene Gleemen, Cascade Chorus, Symphonic Band, Community Orchestra, Women's Chorus, and Sweet Adelines were the area's churches, and many of them continue to provide an important place to hear music by local performers and groups.

The city's clubs and restaurants and the Eugene Hotel provided the main venues for popular music. In the 1950s and '60s, the main attractions were dinner and dance clubs featuring top local swing bandleaders. Later, a variety of clubs hosted rock, folk, blues, and jazz performers, both local and national. The 1970s saw the emergence of a strong modern jazz scene, centered on the Eugene Hotel and mentored by expatriate New York saxophonist Sonny King, who taught an informal class at South Eugene High and influenced quite a few young musicians who later became stalwarts of the jazz scene. Many clubs and restaurants booked local or national jazz acts, while others featured the music of Eugene's growing counterculture and then witnessed the birth of a thriving blues scene led by Robert Cray and Curtis Salgado, who'd go on to national and regional acclaim, respectively. Larger shows used the fairgrounds and area ballrooms.

But the major venue for big shows was, of all places, the UO's McArthur Court—the only place in town that could hold a big audience of up to eight thousand. In 1943, a group of local music lovers formed what later became the Civic Music Association (CMA), selling memberships, and using the proceeds to bring nationally and internationally recognized performers to its annual

Mac Court concerts. At its peak, the CMA (later known as the Eugene and University Music Association) boasted more than four thousand members, who put up the money to bring increasingly famous performers and some of the world's greatest orchestras.

But Mac Court was, after all, a gym. At one of the CMA shows, the Philadelphia Orchestra's famed conductor, Eugene Ormandy, didn't hesitate to criticize its abysmal acoustics. At another show, as the audience clapped for the great soprano Eileen Farrell to return from intermission, the applause was drowned out by the clattering of a sudden hailstorm on the roof. Water began trickling down as Farrell and the ushers scrambled to save the piano. Clearly, Mac Court wouldn't satisfy the need for a serious performing arts venue.

As early as 1954, a group of Eugene architects had presented a report to city leaders calling for, among other things, a downtown auditorium for cultural events. By the mid-1960s, more and more residents of the growing city were hungry for a more sophisticated performing arts experience.

Ed Ragozzino recognized this, too. In 1963, he participated in forming the Lane County Auditorium Association to help create and finance a real performing arts center for Eugene. To raise funds for the effort, Ragozzino decided to put on summer productions at South Eugene High, with all proceeds going to the LCAA. Despite the sweltering heat in the unairconditioned auditorium, the shows were enormously popular. Ragozzino remembers people passing out during a performance of *The King and I*, being carried outside, revived, and then going back in to see the rest of the show. Those LCAA summer productions, featuring colossal casts and a pit orchestra, earned the arts center effort more than $200,000 over ten years and kept the project in the public eye.

The LCAA, led by businessman-broadcaster Lee Bishop and composed of a dozen or so arts lovers and local movers and shakers who wanted to save a downtown that was already starting to decline, proposed a new center to be funded by a hotel-room tax. Opponents included those opposed to taxes as well as some arts

lovers who worried that investing only in a single, massive performing arts center would ultimately diminish the art scene's diversity. The group got the proposal to the ballot twice, and it lost
each time. Finally, Mayor Gus Keller agreed to make the effort an
official city project, formed the Civic Center Commission, enlisted
former Mayor Les Anderson and Maurie Jacobs, and on the third
try, in 1978, the voters approved an $18.5 million bond levy to
fund the new center. The Eugene Arts Foundation helped raise
funds for many of the amenities.

This vote was probably the critical decision regarding Eugene
performing arts. It demonstrated that the citizens wanted to upgrade the city's performing arts opportunities and were willing to
foot the bill. The new center would bring enormous benefits as
well as difficulties, but there's no question that this decision largely
shaped Eugene performing arts for the rest of the century.

If the Hult Center represented the triumph of mainstream
culture mavens, the apotheosis of Eugene hippie–alternative culture began in 1969, when a number of Eugene activists (led by
Bill and Cynthia Wooten) and artists put together the Renaissance Fair, a benefit for an alternative school. The next year, it
moved out to Veneta and became the Oregon Country Fair, growing from five thousand in attendance to ten times that number in
a three-day continuous happening every summer. Country Fair
performing arts amounted to new-age Vaudeville, featuring not
only folk, rock, and reggae musicians but also performers such as
the Flying Karamazov Brothers, Avner the Eccentric Tightrope
Walker, Artis the Spoonman, and many other characters. With
help from a benefit concert by the Grateful Dead, the Fair owned
its land by the end of the century.

But the counterculture needed a regular venue, and an opportunity soon arose to create one. In 1975, rumors spread that the
historic Woodmen of the World union hall, a major site for dances
since the Depression and the home of some of Eugene's first rock-
'n'-roll bashes, would be sold. In response, a group of performers,
neighbors, and historical preservationists organized in favor of a

community-owned, democratically operated center for the performing arts. The leaseholder agreed to sell the building to the community for $75,000—but only if the group could raise a $10,000 down payment in two weeks. A week later, on December 10, 1975, the committee sponsored the WOWathon—five days of continuing entertainment. With help from the Oregon Country Fair, radio stations KZEL and KLCC, and other counterculture institutions, the group raised the money—then had to fight off city attempts to demolish the building in favor of a parking lot and freeway offramp. Hundreds of WOW Hall supporters packed hearings to turn back the bulldozers.

Despite receiving a few major grants over the years, the hall remained in a precarious financial state, depending on stalwart efforts of volunteers and low-paid staffers to do needed work and raise funds. By 1983—just after the Hult Center became reality—the group paid off the mortgage and the community actually owned the hall, which attracts medium-size rock, reggae, and other music shows, and provides space for plenty of dance classes, occasional theatrical events, and many other local and national performers.

A Seedbed for Start-ups

As the Hult Center and WOW Hall proved (in very different ways), grassroots start-ups can thrive in Eugene, but their financial problems also demonstrate the precariousness of performing arts institutions here.

"We don't have a cultural establishment here that says, 'This is how we've done it for thirty years,' " said Philip Bayles, who helped found the Eugene Opera and Community Choir. "This is a place where, if someone wants to try and do something, there's not a lot of barriers. It's a good place to start things up. In those first few years, you'll get a chance. There's not a lot of money around—fundraising is difficult here—but here is the tolerance and willingness to give it a shot. There is a fertile seedbed here, and once in awhile, a plant gets high enough to survive."

In the 1970s, what many regard as the Golden Age of performing arts in Eugene, grassroots visionaries had a heyday, coax-
ing the city toward a new, more sophisticated arts scene. Alternative arts flourished amid a rich confluence of factors: cheap living
and performance spaces, federal arts money, cafes and restaurants
that catered to the counterculture. The city experienced an influx
of high-energy artists and audiences in their twenties and thirties—many drawn by Eugene's freak-friendly image, courtesy of
Saturday Market and its associated crafts artists, Country Fair, and
the UO.

"The alchemy of all those conditions made Eugene a perfect
spot for an alternative community," said visual artist Steven Oshatz,
who worked on theater productions with many alternative performing artists. The "urban removal" of the 1960s devastated downtown—but the resulting empty storefronts and low property values proved a haven for an emerging alternative arts community.
Several galleries sprang up and hosted groundbreaking visual and
installation art as well as performances by innovative theater groups
such as the New Mime Circus, founded by Sparky Roberts and
James Aday.

Music blossomed, too. The 1970s saw the birth of what would
become the city's single-most internationally recognized institution, the Oregon Bach Festival. Beginning as a small UO class in
choral conducting, the festival steadily grew into a three-week summer extravaganza of classical music, focusing on the great choral
orchestral repertoire. Music director Helmuth Rilling, an up-and-
coming Stuttgart conductor, and executive director Royce Saltzman
(a UO professor) carefully nurtured the festival into one of the
world's great classical music institutions, with national radio broad-
casts, CDs, and dozens of concerts each summer. It's probably the
most significant performing arts institution in Eugene history.
Moreover, Rilling's pioneering lecture-demonstration method
helped develop the city's audience for classical music by showing
listeners some of the beauty and intelligence behind the notes
they hear.

The Bach Festival wasn't the only musical triumph of the '70s. In 1974, Bayles, a music teacher, was conducting the Eugene Community Orchestra, and the members wanted to perform the Hallelujah chorus from Handel's "Messiah" for an Easter concert. This meant they'd need singers. They distributed handbills, held auditions, and decided to become an independent entity, the Eugene Community Chorus (later Concert Choir), which Bayles directed through the early 1980s.

A few years later, in 1977, Bayles and Ginevra Ralph spearheaded the creation of the Eugene Opera. Bayles served as music director for the first decade, and his contacts helped it develop a base of singers and its own orchestra, composed of musicians from throughout the region. Performing first in high school gyms, the opera steadily grew in quality and resources (props, lighting, costumes); by the end of the century, it was able to stage credible performances of such mega-masterworks as Verdi's *Aida* at the Hult Center.

The theater scene gained a new light when Ed Ragozzino left South Eugene High and the LCAA, in 1975, to start the new performing arts program at Lane Community College. During his tenure, LCC staged dozens of impressive productions, using not just LCC students but other members of the community, and became one of the finest community college theater programs in the state.

Toward the end of the 1970s, the Oregon Repertory Theater became a new player in the theater scene. ORT staged shows in the Atrium Building on the downtown mall for several years, but that space lacked the technical capabilities needed for serious theater productions. Still, the company mounted some excellent productions and became famous for its "Midnight Mafia," experimental plays performed at the witching hour for an emerging alternative audience. The company later moved to the Eugene Hotel.

But ORT and many other performing arts groups looked forward to the new performing arts center, which would give them the technical capabilities (theater seating, lighting, large offstage and storage areas) to mount the kind of ambitious productions that their founders envisioned and that the rapidly growing audiences were demanding. The Hult Center opened in September 1982 with a spectacular concert by Marilyn Horne and the Eugene Symphony. With a 2,500-seat concert hall and a 500-seat recital hall, an advanced electronic acoustic enhancements system, and a striking design, the Hult became the focus for the performing arts, hosting big-name performers from all over the world. The Eugene Symphony became its first resident company (followed quickly by the Bach Festival, Eugene Opera, and Eugene Ballet) and commenced ambitious plans: tripling its budget, doubling the number of performances, boosting musicians' wages, and hiring its first professional directors, including the fine new conductor Bill McLaughlin. The Hult's smaller Soreng Theater hosted ORT and then the new Oregon Mozart Players, founded by UO professor Robert Hurwitz, which gave the city a much-needed, first-class chamber orchestra. The Hult also challenged other local companies to upgrade their ambitions to match the expanded facilities and audience capacity. The future looked bright.

All Good Things Must Come To an End

But just after the Hult opened, the economy crashed. Many Eugene performing organizations, run by arts lovers who lacked professional management, financial, marketing, and fundraising skills, proved unable to weather the rougher economic gales and, in some cases, amateurish planning and administration. The federal government's termination of its CETA (Comprehensive Employment Training Act) program at the end of the '70s deprived local arts groups of an important source of funds to hire staff. This had a severe impact on several Eugene arts groups that had become dependent on subsidies. Smaller groups competed with each other for audiences and support, fraying some of the art scene's community spirit.

Larger companies weren't immune. The Civic Music

Association's series ended after almost forty years, and by 1985, the symphony was deep in debt and embroiled in disputes over pay cuts and an acrimonious music director search. Other Hult resident companies groups also sputtered in red ink, while the Hult itself plunged into debt and by 1985 turned to direct city operational support.

Financial straits also doomed many clubs that hosted jazz and folk performers, and those that remained cut back their jazz offerings, which in turn spurred many musicians who formed the backbone of the jazz, blues, and rock scenes to depart for greener pastures.

Theater suffered, too. The ambitious Oregon Repertory Theater soon folded, unable to pay the Soreng Theater's relatively high rent. That loss was partially compensated when Ed Ragozzino left LCC in 1986 to found the Eugene Festival of Musical Theater at the Hult Center. Over its eight-year history, the EFMT pulled off a number of impressive summer productions of big, splashy musicals, drawing some professional actors from Eugene and Portland. But it, too, found the cost of presenting in the Hult too high, and folded in 1994, a victim of escalating musical theater production costs and the scarcity of good new musicals. A couple of progressive dance troupes, Wallflower Collective and Curry-Oslund Company, also left town.

Many blamed the Hult Center for some of the arts community's difficulties. Even before the center was built, a number of local arts supporters had warned that a large, expensive venue might suck up all available arts funding for a few privileged resident companies and encourage the kind of concentration of attention and funding that's an anathema to artistic vitality. They worried that high rental fees would make it impossible for many groups to recoup their rental costs (not just for performances, but also for rehearsals) and that high ticket prices might drive away audiences or consume so much of the family entertainment budget that many Eugeneans wouldn't have time or money to explore smaller community arts events.

All of these predictions came to pass, to some extent, but the Hult did allow larger productions, made Eugene a viable stop for big touring shows going up and down the West Coast, and provided space for the bigger audiences that organizations like the Oregon Bach Festival and Eugene Symphony drew. It surely increased the number, quality, and size of productions available to Eugene audiences. It also boosted the downtown economy by drawing regional arts patrons to Eugene in general and downtown in particular.

On the other hand, having a larger space meant that shows that drew smaller audiences looked like failures, and even shows that sold well usually staged fewer performances than when they were in smaller, cheaper venues; that meant artists didn't have as much of a chance to hone their performances over several shows. Although Silva Hall's large size and high costs often forced even resident companies into relatively conservative programming, the Hult can work well for large-scale, mature works. But it's not so friendly for smaller, more innovative or risky performances; even though the Soreng Theater was supposedly intended for such smaller groups, its poor design and acoustics, lack of flexibility, and expensive rates made it unworkable for many community artists. On balance, the Hult was a valuable addition to a burgeoning performing arts culture, but, as constituted, it proved a mixed blessing for local performing artists and has been too expensive for many of the citizens and artists it was designed to serve.

Signs of Resurgence
Even during the financial drought, some promising artistic seeds began to sprout. One came from the dance world, when Riley Grannan and his wife and fellow choreographer, Toni Pimble, moved back from Germany to his hometown. They cashed in their pensions, bought the Eugene School of Ballet, and soon found a pool of current and former dancers in the region. Initially sharing management with Eugene Opera and moving into the Hult Center, the new Eugene Ballet began with a half dozen performers

dancing mostly classics. Eugene Ballet's careful management and proceeds from its extensive touring schedule enabled it to not only maintain high production values but also to grow. Over the years, EB carefully expanded its staff, budget, and reach, entering into a partnership with the Idaho Ballet that enabled it to stage one hundred performances per year throughout the region and occasionally beyond. EB's eagerness to collaborate with local visual, literary, and musical artists gave its productions a distinctive richness. Other performing arts groups that worked with EB credited Grannan and Pimble for supporting them through advice and collaboration. These and other collaborations helped spawn several companies such as Dance Theater of Oregon, Musical Feet, DanceAbility, Van Ummerson, and TapRoOT, that gave the city a surprisingly varied dance scene in the 1990s.

The theater scene found a new source for more contemporary drama when Actors Cabaret/Mainstage Theater was founded in 1984 by Jim Roberts and South Eugene High School drama coach Joe Zingo. Beginning by staging popular musicals, ACE steadily built its audience until it was able to stage more innovative and contemporary shows along with enough surefire draws to stay in the black. After performing in various spaces, ACE settled into its own downtown theater in 1991, later opening a second, smaller stage next door.

That same year, Lord Leebrick Theater Company arrived and began presenting an increasingly strong schedule of shows, from Shakespeare to contemporary drama—another welcome sign of the performing arts resurgence that accelerated throughout the '90s, despite constant struggles with expensive and inadequate rented space in a former auto repair shop.

In 1999, a new company, Willamette Repertory Theater, directed by Oregon Shakespeare Festival veteran Kirk Boyd, attempted to bring true professional theater to Eugene, using Actor's Equity actors and the Soreng Theater. Boyd's well-planned fundraising campaign made WRT the best shot in years for raising the level of theater performance in Eugene.

Meanwhile, smaller groups such as Encore Theater (in which senior citizens told stories from their lives), Eugene Chamber Theater, Little Apple Productions, and Young Women's Theater Collective all mounted successful, innovative productions at various locations around town.

At decade's end, several smaller arts groups joined in an informal consortium to find a new performance space for alternative and community groups, as existing spaces proved either too expensive, too large, or otherwise unsuitable for such grassroots groups. The recovering economy meant that businesses snapped up the cheap downtown properties that had hosted alternative galleries and performance spaces, few of which could afford higher rents. As a result, the marvelously vital alternative culture scene that existed in the 1970s and early '80s mostly withered away, although some of its stalwarts, such as Sparky Roberts, rose to positions in other institutions and infused them with their exploratory spirit.

By century's end, most of the major arts institutions had taken the painful steps necessary to pull out of debt. The Concert Choir worked its way out of debt and created a smaller sister organization, the Eugene Vocal Arts Ensemble. The Eugene Symphony began to fight its way back from the brink of collapse in 1989, when the board and musicians put aside their differences and agreed to hire a young music director, Marin Alsop, a Leonard Bernstein protégé who loved American music. This proved to be one of the city's most significant performing arts decisions, as Alsop pushed the orchestra to new heights of accomplishment and more exciting, contemporary programming. That helped ESO win major arts grants, which, along with professionalization of fundraising and budgeting, combined to eliminate the debt by 1995. When Alsop left for larger orchestras, the ESO hired a young Peruvian conductor Miguel Harth-Bedoya, who carried on Alsop's high musical standards.

Perhaps the best thing to happen to Eugene performing arts in the 1990s was the Oregon Festival of American Music, founded by James and Ginevra Ralph and Roger Saydack, which initially engaged Marin Alsop to produce orchestral concerts devoted exclusively to American "classical" music—a rather radical proposition even at the end of the twentieth century. OFAM gradually broadened its scope to include folk and roots-based American music, signing up as advisor-performers highly regarded and knowledgeable musicians such as New York pianist-arranger Dick Hyman, Louisiana Cajun revivalist Michael Doucet, and conductor James Paul. By decade's end, OFAM had become one of the most innovative and community-oriented music organizations in the area, pulling off terrific concerts of superior but too-seldom heard American music performed by local players and national guest stars. OFAM also sponsored a strong children's music program and a jazz revival band, the Emerald City Jazz Kings, led by Steve Stone and composed of veteran swing players, whose concerts at Soreng Theater and South Eugene High School regularly sold out.

Other performing arts groups struggled for funds, and to some extent competed for audience dollars and time. But they also collaborated fairly often, bringing voices, instruments, and dancers together for some fine productions. As they grew, many of these groups were able to pay some or all of their performers, but the city still benefited from amateur groups (like Eugene Chamber Singers, Peace Choir, Inspirational Sounds gospel choir, Sacred Harp singers, Soromundi Lesbian Chorus, Emerald Chamber Players, and many others), which played conferences, malls, retirement centers, and other such venues and gatherings.

The Seventh Species composers collective, founded by Gary Noland in 1992, explored the territory between contemporary classical and avant-garde music. Their mentor was Art Maddox, a composer-pianist who arrived in the 1970s who also worked with Mason Williams, the "Classical Gas" composer who'd retired in the area and put on a very popular Christmas show each year at the Hult. And as Oregon found itself increasingly linked to the rest of the multicultural Pacific Rim, world music groups appeared, featuring African drumming, marimba, Latin American music, and Indonesian gamelan percussion orchestras.

But just as the performing arts were making a comeback, the city suffered a double whammy. The passage of two property tax limitation measures in the 1990s had a devastating effect on the arts and schools. Summer parks and recreation performance programs were canceled; the Hult lost a huge portion of its public subsidy (as did many groups), resulting in drastic staff cuts and high rental fees. The center responded by booking more slick, blockbuster road shows, eschewing riskier, forward-looking art, either from outside of town or from the community itself. Its policies and costly operating structure came under sharp criticism from many directions.

"For [the Hult] to become a roadhouse for big touring acts—that's a disservice to the original voters who thought what they were voting for was a place for community performers," says Ed Ragozzino. At century's end, the Hult was reconsidering its role in light of new budget realities and community pressure.

Summary

Considering that only a few decades ago, the highlight of the city's arts culture involved livestock, Eugene's artistic growth has been remarkable. Thanks to many of the visionaries mentioned here (and many others), the city has seen more than its share of exciting, thought-provoking, and entertaining stories, sounds, and spectacles upon its stages. Venues such as the Hult Center, the WOW Hall, the UO, and others gave those visionaries places to stage their dreams. And thanks to thousands of supporters who've worked tirelessly, donating time and money to these visionaries and the campaigns for the venues, Eugene boasts a performing arts scene that's the envy of many towns several times its size.

Yet while the city has grown rapidly in population and sophistication, as the new century opened, its performing arts scene was still coasting on investments (such as the Hult Center and WOW Hall) made a quarter century earlier. Today, the shortage of spaces for certain kinds of productions not suitable for existing venues often deprives Eugene audiences of innovative, affordable, smaller-scale, community-oriented arts. And too many of our finest young artists leave Eugene for cities that do provide such facilities.

Although the Hult Center's size and costs have often forced even resident companies into relatively conservative programming, it can work well for productions by large resident companies and road shows. But it's not so friendly for smaller, more innovative or risky performers. Similarly, though it provides a vital place for rock, reggae, some dance and theater, and smaller road shows, the WOW Hall's age, lack of flexibility, and constant need for cash make it unsuitable for many local performers. The hall pays for its maintenance and operating costs through rental fees, which even with a nonprofit discount, can range from $300 to $600 per night.

Other performance spaces in town have their own limitations. The result is that some kinds of performing arts (the most popular, the biggest) can flourish here, but others (smaller, innovative, experimental, community-oriented) struggle.

"The richness of the arts scene here isn't being viewed by the public that wants to see it because there isn't enough space," complains Lane Arts Council executive director Douglas Beauchamp. "Given the growth in the community and its diversity in population, there's a terrible lack of facilities for rehearsals, planning, experimental presentations, and accommodating a variety of audiences."

Insufficient arts funding poses another major obstacle to artistic progress. History shows that what really makes a cultural capital is significant investment in its own artists—the ones who are most in touch with the community's needs and feelings. And as the twentieth century ended, in the midst of unprecedented state and national prosperity, Eugene was failing to make those investments. Despite some impressive instances of support from private donors and the federal government, at the outset of the twenty-first century, Eugene seems unwilling to place as high a priority on public goods such as performing arts as it did during the flush times of the 1970s.

Again, the groups hit hardest by insufficient investment have been alternative and other community groups. They rely on sweat equity, enormous energy, and volunteered time—stolen from day jobs, family, and sleep—to create innovative art. Even when they can afford to rent spaces, often they're limited to inadequate rehearsal and few performances. Even many of the larger organizations just barely stay afloat.

As the new century opens, and Eugene grows, its population base makes it more able to support the arts, and audiences seem to be getting younger—a good sign for progressive performing arts. A number of visionary artists have settled here recently, meaning that the most important element—people who care about the arts— is in place. If our performing arts are to rise to the level of sophistication to which this city aspires, arts visionaries will again have to show grassroots supporters, potential public and private funders, and political leaders the value of new venues and support for performing arts. If the city has the vision, the venues will follow.

GO DUCKS:

HOW SPORTS AT THE UO HAVE

CHANGED AND CHANGED US—

FOR BETTER AND WORSE.

By Guy Maynard

FOR MY WIFE'S last birthday, I decided to try to buy her an old toy made by a company called Schoenhut in the early part of the twentieth century, even though antiques and collectibles are both her vocation and avocation. My trying to buy her a Schoenhut is like her trying to stump me on the starting lineup of the '74 Kamikaze Kids. Daring, maybe even foolish. What's more, I went shopping for this toy on the Internet auction, e-Bay, a world I'd never ventured into before. So, I was trying to buy something I knew almost nothing about for an expert through a medium I had no experience with. The amazing thing is, it all worked. I got a great toy—a hippopotamus with glass eyes and a leather tail—that she loved for a decent price from an antique seller in Florida, who sent the hippo priority mail all wrapped in shipping peanuts, on top of which sat his bright yellow business card, with a handwritten note on the back: "Thanks for bidding. Go Ducks!!"

I don't know if that man was a football fan or a major college basketball aficionado or even a track fan. I knew from a telephone conversation that Eugene, Oregon, was to him a distant and mysterious place. But when he thought of Eugene, he thought Ducks, which is the nickname of the University of Oregon sports teams.

That's not all that surprising. For many people, the UO is the most recognizable thing about Eugene, and sports are the most visible aspect of the university. Like it or not, then, on some level all of Eugene is connected to the Ducks. And with the track and field championships and NCAA basketball tournament appearances and Rose Bowls of the last half-century, that's more true now than ever. These young men and women playing games are an integral part of what we are, not only to outsiders, but also to ourselves.

Long Green

Of course, there's the money. As the twentieth century ends, UO officials have just announced an $80-million expansion plan for Autzen Stadium that will increase its capacity to 53,800. Eighty million dollars that will reverberate through this city: construction workers, subcontractors, materials, room for 12,000 more people for six Saturdays a year, who just might buy gas and beer and a hotel room and dinner and a Duck tee-shirt or two. And that's just one part—though a huge and historical one—of the big business UO athletics has become.

At the end of World War II, when the returning veterans swelled the enrollment at the UO and brought what had been a dormant athletic program back to life, the university's intercollegiate sports program was run by an athletic board, made up of five faculty members, three alumni, and three students. The board's policies had to be approved by the university president and were carried out by the athletic manager. The university hired Leo Harris as its first athletic director in 1947 in an effort to make the program more professional. The athletic department's budget in that period was around $300,000.

Until the construction of Autzen Stadium, the football team played its Eugene games in Hayward Field, which could hold only 22,000 for football. Most big home games weren't even played in Eugene. The capacity was too small to entice football powers to Eugene, and UO athletic officials didn't want those big draws wasted at Hayward. Only two or three UO football games were played in Eugene each year, and they were likely to be games against Idaho or Washington State, while the Ducks played teams like Washington and USC in Portland's 35,000-seat Multnomah Stadium.

In the late 1940s, the Ducks basketball team played in the same place it does in 2000, McArthur Court, but it was then called the Igloo and held only 7,600. In 1955, capacity was expanded to 9,100, which was upped again to slightly over 10,000 in the early 1970s, when a team whose feistiness earned it the nickname of the Kamikaze Kids attracted full houses of raucous fans and "the Igloo" became "the Pit."

Former athletic director Norv Ritchey, who's had almost continuous ties to UO athletics since he was a freshman baseball player in 1948, says he used to do a circuit speech about what it meant to Eugene to have a 10,000-seat facility like McArthur Court. More than the big basketball crowds it could accommodate, Mac Court meant performers like Louis Armstrong, Harry Belafonte, and Bob Hope had a place to stop between Portland and San Francisco, which not only brought dollars into the community, but also brought prestige to a city that was changing from a lumber and mill town with a liberal arts college into a liberal arts kind of city with a woods-products-based economy.

The building of Autzen in 1967 was a giant step for UO athletics and Eugene. Autzen meant five or six games a year for the home fans, and its capacity of 41,000 meant more seats for members of the general community. And the big games were here. Portland alumni and fans had to come here, and the football powers and their fans had to stay in our hotels and eat at our restaurants. Crowds averaged only 28,500 that first year in Autzen (the team was 2-8), but that still meant that 142,500 fans watched college football in Eugene that year. The year before, the maximum that could have watched was 66,000.

Oregon had known sporadic success throughout its football history. The 1948 team (said by a 1973 UO sports history book to "mark the arrival of big-time, money-making football in Eugene") had gone to the Cotton Bowl only because the University of Washington cast a tie-breaking vote to send California to the Rose Bowl instead of the UO (that's one of the reasons we hate the Huskies). Legendary coach Len Casanova put together a nine-year run in the late 1950s and early 1960s when the Ducks had only two losing seasons and stars like Bob Berry and Mel Renfro led them to three bowl games, including the 1958 Rose Bowl against number-one-rated Ohio State. The relatively new medium of television allowed the entire country to see the Ducks nearly upset the Buckeyes before losing 10–7, bringing national attention to both the UO and the city of Eugene. The 1964 team reached the highest national ranking ever for an Oregon football team, seventh, after winning its first six games of the season.

But that era was followed by a long string of disappointing seasons. Finally, during the 1980s, Coach Rich Brooks gradually turned Oregon into a team that usually won more than it lost. The Ducks finally got back to post-season play, after a twenty-six-year absence, with a trip to the 1989 Independence Bowl where they scored the final seventeen points to win 27–24. But it wasn't until after the Rose Bowl year of 1994–1995, that the Ducks started filling Autzen regularly. In the five years leading up to the Rose Bowl (33-28 record, three bowl games) average home attendance was 36,685. In the five years after the Rose Bowl (40-20 record and four bowl appearances), the Ducks averaged home crowds of just over 43,000—more than Autzen's capacity.

One simple formula to figure out the economic impact of a sporting event, according to UO sports marketing professor Lynn Kahle, is that for every dollar in tickets sales $4 goes into the local economy. Figuring an average ticket price of around $20 over the ten-year span centered on the Rose Bowl (high for the earlier years, low for the more recent), each pre-Rose Bowl game brought about $3 million into the greater Eugene community. In the years since the Rose Bowl, that figure has grown to about $3.5 million per game, which means a highly successful UO football team contributes $3 million per year more to our economy than a moderately successful one. Go Ducks, indeed.

Football is the big contributor, but there are other ways UO athletics puts dollars into the Eugene economy. Autzen has provided a venue for attractions from the Grateful Dead to the Promise Keepers. The athletic department's budget is now more than $25 million, of which only $1.6 million leaves the state, according to the Convention and Visitors Association of Lane County. UO athletics also was on a building binge in the 1990s that has produced the $12-million Casanova Center (offices, locker rooms, and training facilities), $6 million worth of Autzen improvements, more than $2 million in renovations to Mac Court, and the $15-million Moshofsky Center (indoor practice facility).

Eugene's reputation as Track Town USA, nurtured at the UO's Hayward Field, attracts national and world-class meets. The USA Outdoor Track and Field Championships in 1999, for example, brought something like $5 million into the Eugene community. It is ironic that track has become a money maker for the Eugene community because it never has been for the UO. Of course, the UO track program also had a little bit to do with that athletic shoe company in Beaverton, which has contributed mightily to Oregon's economy and whose founder's last name is on a few buildings and programs at the UO. Nike founder Phil Knight had also been a strong financial contributor to UO athletics, until 2000 when his anger over the UO joining a labor rights watchdog organization led him to end all support of the university, which could at least delay the Autzen expansion project.

Money Can't Buy Me Love

But I don't think that guy in Florida was thinking about the Eugene economy when he wrote, "Go Ducks!!" I'd guess it had more to do with how he perceived Eugene's identity. And he's right: UO sports have helped define the kind of community we are. Unlike many slogans attached to sports teams, Track Town USA is not marketing hype or wishful thinking. It is a reflection of a reality that took root in this community beginning in the 1950s and reached full bloom in the 1960s.

When Bill Bowerman came to coach the UO track and field team in 1949, the program had a long history of regional success under long-time coach Bill Hayward. But Oregon had not made much of a mark on a national level, and track meets were long, dull affairs that didn't have much appeal for spectators. But Bowerman changed the pace of track meets, tightening the schedule of events so meets offered an exciting afternoon of athletic entertainment. He also made Eugene a city of participants. Shortly after becoming track coach, Bowerman started an all-comers meet for grade-school athletes and later expanded it to include high-school and college-age athletes. In 1957, he and North Eugene High School track coach Bob Newland formed the Emerald Empire Athletic Association (which later became the Oregon Track Club) to promote track, provide training and facilities, and bring big meets to Eugene. By the early 1970s, 400 to 500 participants showed up for each of five summertime all-comers meets, and Oregon fans were used to seeing national championships and Olympic trials at Hayward Field. Bowerman also convinced Americans, and especially Eugeneans, that jogging was one of the best fitness activities.

While kids in other parts of the country pretended to be star football or baseball players, Mark Kirchmeier—who was nine years old when Oregon won its first national championship at Hayward Field in 1962—remembers that kids in Eugene would pretend to be mile runner Dyrol Burleson or other Oregon track stars. Runners—from Bill Dellinger to Burleson to Steve Prefontaine to kids at all-comers meets to men and women chugging slowly through our parks in the rain—became an integral part of Eugene's identity, something sure to make any thirty-second summary of what kind of city we are.

As track took hold in Eugene, the city was changing, too. A mill town with a small liberal arts college before the war, Eugene was slowly shifting to becoming more of a liberal arts college town with a timber-based economy. And "track is a liberal arts kind of sport," as Kirchmeier puts it. As post-war prosperity increased the mobility of Americans, more liberal-arts types were attracted to Eugene's natural beauty and maverick spirit. And the nationally televised image of Pre—his hair, flowing in the breeze his stride created—circling a roaring Hayward Field, and the camera occasionally straying to the majestic firs outside the field only added to Eugene's mystique. It's hard to measure how important that image was to the kind of people who were attracted to Eugene in the great migration of the late 1960s and early 1970s, and how important those people are to the character of the city at the end of the twentieth century, but I believe that its influence was enormous.

UO track won four national championships under Bowerman, and the men's team won one under his successor, Bill Dellinger. The women's team, which wasn't even allowed to have meets at Hayward Field until 1972, won a national championship in 1985. Though Eugene maintains an undeniable claim to the title of Track Town, most fans point to the mid-1970s as the end of the golden age of UO track.

The Eugene community strongly identified with other UO sports as well. In the early 1970s, the intense style of basketball coach Dick Harter's Kamikaze Kids had fans rocking the scoreboard at Mac Court, goading one opposing coach into calling them "deranged idiots." It was a label embraced by many who found particular glory in rooting for the David Ducks who in one stretch slew the Goliaths of UCLA in three consecutive games.

Then there was the 1995 Rose Bowl team. In 1994, at midseason, the UO football team was 4-3 and clinging to a narrow lead in the closing minutes of a game against the University of Washington at Autzen Stadium. But the Huskies had driven to Oregon's ten-yard-line with just enough time left to score the winning touchdown—and most Oregon fans, me among them, were resigned to the fact that they would—when a freshman cornerback intercepted a Washington pass and returned it ninety-seven yards for a win-clinching Oregon touchdown. A photo by *Register-Guard* photographer Andy Nelson of Kenny Wheaton's interception captures a singularly euphoric moment in the history of UO sports and Eugene: Wheaton seemingly alone on the field stepping surely toward the distant goal line, fans in the near background, jaws dropped, arms raised in celebration or pointing toward Wheaton's glorious destination, eyes wide, leaping, shouting, astonished, smiling—except for the few purple-clad fans in the slightly blurred background who grimaced, hands to mouth in shock. Of course that interception and win sent Oregon on its way to the Rose Bowl in 1995, an event that truly was a Eugene community celebration.

Lynn Kahle remembers being in a Safeway in early December that year when a friend challenged him to find a single person in the store not wearing a piece of clothing related to UO sports. He couldn't do it. At events in the Los Angeles area leading up to the game, for Eugeneans it was like being at Valley River Center or the Fifth Street Market because it was impossible to go for more than a few minutes without seeing someone you knew from Eugene. In a book about that Rose Bowl season, former UO sports information director George Beres tells a story of a woman who wanted to teach blind people to cross streets on January 2, the day of the game, but couldn't because there was no traffic. The streets of Eugene were deserted. Those who hadn't made the trip to Los Angeles were at home in front of the television. "It's weird, man," said the Ducks star tight end Josh Wilcox, using a particularly Eugenean analogy, "we're bigger than the Grateful Dead."

Changes

UO athletics has also helped change us. Eugene is a city whose black population has been largely invisible to the white majority population through much of its history, but African Americans have long had a presence on the UO athletic fields. Even in the pre–World War II years, black players could be found on various UO sports teams, as well as on campus. In the first ten or fifteen

years after the war, black players were still a small part of UO
athletics. But as the 1950s ended and the 1960s began, African
Americans began taking more prominent roles: Otis Davis and
Harry Jerome in track; Willie West, Cleveland Jones, Mel Renfro
in football. Also during that time, when teams traveled into areas
that were still segregated, the UO athletic department began in-
sisting that black players be allowed to stay with the team and
would only go to the hotels and restaurants where they could.
Norv Ritchey, then associate athletic director, says that the UO's
insistence that Mel Renfro and three other black football players
be allowed to stay with the team in the Shamrock Hilton Hotel in
Houston, Texas, in 1962 was a major step toward the desegrega-
tion of that hotel.

Black participation in UO sports increased steadily throughout the 1960s and early 1970s. But perhaps the first African American athletes to connect to the heart of the Eugene community—in
a way that had kids imitating them at recess—were the members
of the Kamikaze Kids of 1972–77, first Ronnie Lee, then Greg
Ballard, Stu Jackson, and Ernie Kent. That team packed the Pit
because of its exciting and hard-nosed style of play, and the players made an extra effort to become involved in both the larger
Eugene community and the small black community within it.
"Those guys made a tremendous difference in the city because
they gave of themselves to the community," says Edwin Coleman,
a UO emeritus professor of English. Too often, before and since
that time, the only connection between each community and black
athletes has been that of fans and entertainers.

It's still not easy being a black athlete in Eugene. There are far
more black men (particularly because of football and basketball)
than black women athletes on campus. Black athletes are put in
the difficult position of being celebrities on the field and are still
under a microscope in predominantly white Eugene, so any problems they have are magnified. Star quarterback Akili Smith, who
played for the Ducks in 1997 and 1998, had some run-ins with
local police—none of which led to convictions—that many be-

lieve would never have happened if he'd been white. Perhaps for that reason, according to Coleman, most black athletes tend to stay in a closed group and come and go from Eugene without making any lasting connections with either the university community or the city.

UO athletics has had a lasting effect on racial relations in Eugene, Coleman believes, through the African Americans who came to Eugene to play sports and chose to stay—like Lane County Commissioner Bobby Green—or have come back—like Kent, who became the first black head coach in UO history when he was hired as the men's basketball coach in 1997. Green, who moved from New Orleans to play football for the Ducks from 1972 to 1975, says he never would have come to Eugene except to play football and never expected to stay. Twenty-five years later, Green and his wife have raised five children here, and he has become a community leader, serving as a Eugene city councilor and Lane County commissioner. Although he says that Eugene still has lots of ways to grow to become a community of true racial tolerance, "At least now, we're able to have the conversation. Twenty years ago, we couldn't have even gotten it started." Both Coleman and Green say that though athletics has played some role in the slowly changing racial climate in Eugene, it is the university as a whole that is the strongest force for change.

UO sports have also played a part in the changing roles of women. Up until the early '70s, women's athletics was an extracurricular activity within the physical education department. The basketball team met one night during its season and played a four-game schedule. The softball team met twice a week and played five games. The teams shared one set of uniforms. In 1970, when the volleyball team put on an exhibition at half-time of a basketball game to raise money to go to the national tournament (where they took fourth place), a couple of volleyball players had to take their uniform shirts from the basketball players, who were using them that day.

Title IX of the 1972 Education Amendments Act changed all

that by mandating equal educational opportunities for women in many areas, including athletics. A Title IX review conducted at the UO in the mid-1970s concluded, in essence, that the inequalities were so great that developing a separate-but-equal women's program was impossible. Emblematic of the situation were the travel plans for one of the first coed track meets, which was to be held at Washington State University in Pullman in 1977. The men were scheduled to fly and the women were going to take a bus to the same meet, according to Becky Sisley, who was women's athletic director at the time. Everybody ended up taking the bus, a fitting metaphor for the UO's approach to Title IX compliance. The UO decided the best path to compliance was for men's and women's athletics to merge, or, more precisely, for the women's program to be annexed to the men's. Especially in those early years, that meant more that the men had to ride the bus than that women got to fly. Men's track scholarships were cut—the beginning of the demise of Oregon's track glory, many believe. Eventually baseball and men's and women's swimming and gymnastics were cut. Some are quick to blame the Title IX mandate for gender equality for those losses, but Sisley points out that it is the weight of the high costs associated with scholarship-hungry football that forced the cuts on the men's side of the scale.

The event usually cited as signifying that women's athletics had connected with the Eugene community in a profoundly different way was an exhibition basketball game with the South Korean national team in February 1979. That 1978–79 team, coached by Elwin Heiny with stars Julie Cushing and freshman Bev Smith, was on its way to a 23-2 record. So insiders like Sisley knew something exciting was happening, but they weren't fully ready for the 5,766 people who showed up for an exhibition women's basketball game. Average home attendance that year was 946. There weren't enough ticket takers to handle the crowd, and the turnout was headline news throughout the state. The *Eugene Register-Guard* compared the event to Patty Hearst being set free, the U.S. establishing relations with communist China, and snow falling on the

Mohave Desert. The fans showed, said the newspaper, "that there was room in their hearts—and their pocketbooks—for the women." The Ducks won, beating a team that had been ranked fifth in the world. "That one single event," recalls Sisley, "showed that we are here, this is something special, and it's only going to get better."

Sisley believes that the rise of women's sports at the UO was both a cause and a result of "very progressive" attitudes towards girls' sports in Oregon high schools. The steadily increasing exposure and prestige of women's athletics at the university contributed greatly to more youth sports programs for girls and more girls turning out for them. Between 1985 and 1995, the number of girls teams in soccer, volleyball, basketball, and softball in the Eugene-area Kidsports youth leagues increased from 263 to 857.

Women's basketball remains the most visible of the women's sports. Attendance at Mac Court grew rapidly in the Bev Smith years to average almost 3,000 per game in 1981–82, a peak unmatched until the 1996–97 team coached by Jody Runge attracted an average crowd of 3,500. Runge, who took over in 1993, built a new winning tradition for Oregon basketball that had developed a loyal following of more than 5,000 per game in 1998–99. In some ways, it's a different sort of crowd than shows up for other UO sports. In a book about the 1994–95 UO women's basketball team, author Lauren Kessler describes one segment of the crowd: "The reason they come here is the intimacy.... They can't get this feeling of connectedness at a men's game with its big, boisterous crowds, the TV cameras, the two-hundred-thousand-dollar a year coach. Here they feel part of an extended family." And, of course, there are the young girls in the stands: "They are of that protected, preadolescent age when girls can have big dreams, that time before they learn the hard lessons about what girls should and shouldn't hope for, what real women can and can't do." On the playgrounds, they can dream of being Oregon stars like Shaquala Williams or Brianne Meharry.

Go Ducks?

University of Oregon athletics offers many things to the Eugene community: money, entertainment, heroes, identification, reflected glory, shared sorrows, connections between the university and community members who don't have a clue (or care to) about molecular biology or the latest trends in literary criticism. Sports is our most-shared spectacle, a place where conversations can begin and passing acquaintances can find a common ground: "How 'bout them Ducks?"

In the latter half of the twentieth century, UO sports and the Eugene community have grown together: We are more sophisticated, more diverse, more open, more prosperous, a bigger dot on most people's maps. And yet, we are also bigger, more elite, less personal, more expensive, more demanding and expectant, more market-driven—and drifting from our roots and our traditions.

In the early 1970s, the resignation of well-respected football coach Jerry Frei, forced by media, alumni, and donors dissatisfied by his win-loss record, led many to question the direction of college athletics. UO president Robert Clark responded, "I don't think we need to be the biggest of the big. I think we can play well, win our share of games and be satisfied." Sounds like the quaint sentiments of a bygone era, doesn't it?

The UO football team now talks regularly of competing for a national championship, and its facilities, if not its ranking yet, put it in a class with the Nebraskas and Michigans of the football world. Head coach Mike Bellotti makes in the neighborhood of $700,000 a year, $550,000 more than university president Dave Frohnmayer, at an institution where low faculty salaries are commonly recognized as a serious problem. The $80-million plan to expand Autzen was announced at a time when lower-than-expected enrollments were forcing administrators to consider reductions in funding for UO academic programs. Although most of the Autzen money is coming from private donations, there is something unbalanced and unsettling about the comparative financial situations of the central purpose of the university and an extracurricular activity. Athletic teams wear a corporate logo on their uniforms, and the Oregon Duck no longer appears anywhere on football uniforms—in part, at least, because it would impede marketing them. The Oregon–Oregon State athletic competitions in 1999 had a corporate sponsor, and in the television advertisement by that sponsor for the football game between those rivals, the announcer spoke of the Or-EE-gone versus Or-EE-gone State game. Geez.

I am a sports fan. I am a Ducks fan. I went to the 1995 Rose Bowl and the 1996 Cotton Bowl. I stamped my feet in the third balcony of Mac Court when Greg Ballard hit the shot to beat UCLA in 1976. I am a football season-ticket holder and a donor to the Duck Athletic Fund. I am convinced that the men and women who direct the UO athletic programs are both remarkably decent and tremendously talented people. But I feel a growing distance from the UO teams and from the athletic fortress growing around Autzen Stadium. I just recently learned that the expansion of Autzen Stadium means I must significantly (significantly!) increase my donation or I can no longer keep the seats I have had for the past five years, just like long-time ticket holders were displaced when Mac Court courtside seats were made more comfortable for the big donors. Kids, families, students, the non-rich are moved further from the action, to the fringes or out of the picture altogether.

At the start of the twenty-first century, two events have dramatically shown the nature of the crossroads where the UO sports program finds itself. One was Phil Knight's dramatic withdrawal of his support from the UO (reports say he had pledged $30 million toward the Autzen project) because he didn't approve of the university joining the Worker Rights Consortium—a group with plans to monitor working conditions at factories where university-licensed apparel is produced. Knight's action apparently put the stadium project in jeopardy, and some even went so far as to say that it threatened the long-term success of all aspects of UO athletics. If that's true then it seems that UO athletics has become too dependent on the kindness of rich people—and, in this case, one very rich person with very clear business interests in athletics. That's a dangerous road.

The other event was something that didn't happen. Basketball coach Ernie Kent didn't leave the UO and take a Notre Dame job that offered more money, more prestige, and a better chance of winning a national championship sooner. Without having access to the inner working of Kent's mind, I have to believe that he stayed because of the things that make the UO different from places like Notre Dame: the fervor of Mac Court, the love the community shows for teams that play hard and win their "share of games"—the kind of teams that Kent played on and coaches—and the qualities that make Eugene, Eugene, and the UO, the UO. Qualities, apparently, that all of Notre Dame's money couldn't buy. A road that fosters those connections and those qualities is a road the Ducks ought to take.

Success can be the cruelest master. Winning is, of course, the bottom line in sports, but no matter what Vince Lombardi said, winning is not the only thing. Remember how we mocked the complacent fans at Pauley Pavilion who got spoiled by the winning UCLA basketball teams or the no-shows at USC football games? Part of what makes rooting for the Ducks so much fun is that we aren't UCLA or USC (or even the damned Huskies); we are the University of Oregon from a small city where the loggers and the hippies and the professors and the computer geeks and the feminists and the construction workers can fight like hell over most anything but cheer together when we beat the rich and the powerful teams from the big cities. Do we really want to become one of them?

Even the women's basketball program, which still has some of the intimacy and innocence of the earlier days of UO athletics, will lose the very things that now differentiate it from the men's games if the program succeeds the way everyone wants it to. The UO volleyball coach quit this year because, according to *Register-Guard* columnist Ron Bellamy, even minor sports can't afford to lose in the new climate in UO athletics.

How do we slow this spiral of success feeding growth, which feeds more success and more growth, until we no longer recognize or particularly like what we have become? If we can dream of regular trips to the Rose Bowls and national championships, why can't we dream of an athletic program that aspires to a success that keeps it connected to the academic pursuits of the university and to all parts of the community of Eugene?

How about if Oregon athletics spreads its wealth, so more success does not separate it further from the community but rather connects it more? How about ten cents of every dollar donated to the UO athletics going to a fund that supports university-wide academic programs? At the very least, the university should stop the subsidy of the athletic program, which amounted to about $1.7 million in 1999. Part of the justification of the Autzen expansion is that it will generate additional revenue that can reduce that subsidy and help finance more women's sports. Let's make that a promise instead of a hope. If funds can be raised for all these buildings, why not for the ongoing operation of the athletic department, so it's not draining funds that could support academic programs?

How about the UO leading efforts to further reduce football scholarships? Most people believe that the reduction of football scholarships from 105 to 85 reduced the dominance of the football powers, making college football more competitive and exciting and making it possible for schools like Oregon to compete for championships. Still, eighty-five scholarships for a sport that eleven men play at a time is excessive, the equivalent of thirty-eight scholarships for a five-person basketball team. How about moving toward sixty-five scholarships for football, still more than the rosters of professional football teams, and the savings could go to increasing support for women's programs or track?

How about students becoming involved again in athletic governance, especially in matters having to do with traditions and image—like uniforms and logos? It is, after all, their university.

How about if lines are clearly drawn for all to see what corporate and donor money can buy and what it can't?

How about ensuring that there will always be end-zone seats at Autzen and third-balcony seats at Mac Court set aside at reasonable prices for kids and families, for all games? Right now, it costs a family of two adults and two children at least $54 to go to a single Duck football game, and general admission buyers get squeezed out for the biggest games. Let's make sure the expanded Autzen always has room for families and kids and that prices are made more affordable. Luxury boxes and sky suites may bring in the big bucks, but filling them can't make a town jump for joy like we did when it really sunk in that Kenny Wheaton was going to score.

Let's go Ducks—someplace a little bit different from all those big-time programs we've taken such pleasure in beating, a place where the UO and all parts of the community can meet and truly celebrate.

Bibliography

Beres, George. *Year of the Duck, 1995.* Eugene: Northwest Sportscene, 1995.

The History of Oregon Athletics. Eugene: Oregon Daily Emerald, 1973.

Kessler, Laura. *Full Court Press.* New York: Dutton, 1997.

Old Oregon, selected articles.

The Register-Guard, selected articles.

Roses For Oregon, Eugene: Guard Publishing, 1995.

University of Oregon Athletic Department. "Media Guides" (Track & Field, 1999; Football, 1999; Men's Basketball, 1999-2000; Women's Basketball, 1999-2000).

EVERYBODY PLAYS:

PARKS AND RECREATION IN EUGENE

by Gary Turley

A YOUNG BOY learns how to handle a bow and arrow. A middle-aged man with a history of heart problems jogs on Pre's Trail, preparing to run his first marathon. A group of white-collar workers escapes from the daily office grind by snowshoeing into the backcountry on a weekend wilderness adventure. A flyfisher stands knee-deep in the Willamette River, making gentle casts in search of a fat, juicy trout. A swarm of second-grade girls surrounds a bouncing soccer ball, oblivious to the shouts of their coaches and parents along the sideline. Mature men and women flock to neighborhood fields and gyms to keep fit and perhaps to relive the memories of youthful athletic glory. Senior citizens gather at a community center for folk dancing. A great-grandmother puts the finishing touches on a pot she has just thrown, her hair still damp from her daily swim in the nearby pool.

These are the faces of recreation in the Emerald Empire, nestled at the southern end of the Willamette Valley and within sixty miles of the mountains to the east and the ocean to the west. These are the faces of citizens who over the last half-century have reveled in the area's unparalleled natural resources and been both the impetus behind and the beneficiaries of its unrivaled recreational opportunities. They have lobbied zealously and crafted public-private partnerships to establish and preserve open spaces for public use. They have organized to ward off private development along the banks of the Willamette River, a waterway described in a 1960 report as the "one great natural recreational feature" of the area and that is the setting for one of the nation's most extensive systems of bike trails. They have supported, through taxes and bond measures, the development of a parks and recreation department that over the years has used creative staffing techniques and flexible program management to offer everything from archery to Ultimate Frisbee.

But this, too, is the face of recreation in Eugene at the dawn of the twenty-first century: more people making more demands on a finite supply of public spaces, facilities, and services. If the city has been more vigilant than most in managing growth and if its citizens can point to a long tradition of widespread public support for recreation, it, too, has been vulnerable to the same forces of increased population and tightened budgets common to communities across the country. In the 1960s and 1970s, considered Eugene's high-water mark for area recreation, the city became nationally known for its commitment to parks and physical fitness as well as its innovative recreation department. By the 1990s, although Eugeneans continued to rate the community's parks and recreation system highly, they seemed increasingly reluctant to set aside spaces for public use or to fund an expanded range of affordable recreation programs. When voters approved a bond measure in 1998 to fund new parks and the renovation of existing facilities, it was the first yes vote in almost a quarter of a century.

The Old Swimming Hole

Shortly after he built his cabin along the banks of the Willamette River in the mid-1800s, Eugene Skinner teamed with Charnel Mulligan to donate land south of the river as the site for Lane County's first courthouse. The space, which now includes the Park Blocks, remained vacant but over the years served as the young community's first public meeting place. In 1906, a year after the adoption of a home rule charter allowed the city to "purchase, hold, and receive property for use as City parks," Thomas Hendricks donated forty-seven acres of his hilltop holding east of the University of Oregon, which the city added to thirty-one acres of adjoining property to create Hendricks Park.

Eugene's efforts in the years prior to World War II to build a recreation program were occasionally significant but generally modest and intermittent. In 1920 the city passed its first park improvement bond issue, which authorized $10,000 to renovate existing park facilities and to build free campgrounds, including automobile campgrounds near a popular swimming area on the Willamette River. The successful levy that created the Public Recreation and Playground Fund in 1927 was the first measure devoted expressly to recreational programs. It established a five-member playground commission, a forerunner of the modern parks and recreation department, to administer a small youth summer recreation program. Frank Chambers, a local banker, donated 4.3 acres to establish Kiwanis Park in 1932, and six years later Eugeneans voted to spend $500,000 to purchase 280 acres on Spencer Butte.

On the eve of the war, Eugene had six city parks and a sturdy tradition of public and private efforts to expand the community's store of public spaces. However, the existing parks were largely unimproved, there were no public swimming pools, and the city had only $6,000 set aside in its playground budget.

The establishment of a recreation commission in 1944 marked a turning point. In surveying the state of Eugene recreation and recommending changes, the citizen advisory group provided a link to the past, but also put area recreation on modern footing. It endorsed the long-standing commitment to preserving open spaces as parks and recommended that the city move even more aggressively in acquiring and improving such public spaces. At the same time, it urged a greater emphasis on creating neighborhood parks and developing them as centers for expanded recreational activities and programs. It also recommended the construction of a public swimming pool.

The commission's recommendations were put into effect almost immediately. In 1946 the city consolidated recreation services in the Eugene Parks and Recreation Department and named

Don January as its first superintendent, establishing a year-round parks and recreation program. That same year voters approved a $700,000 park levy and the city broke ground for Jefferson Pool, located at the fairgrounds on land donated by Lane County. The Century Progress Fund, another volunteer citizen group, began a fundraising drive that culminated in the acquisition of ninety acres, including most of what is now Amazon Park.

By the end of the decade voters approved an additional $1 million levy for long-range park acquisition and development. Forty-six acres on the southern and western edges of the city became Westmoreland Park. In 1951 George Owen, a local lumberman, donated a two-acre site along the Willamette River to the city. The Eugene Rose Society adopted the land and, after planting some 400 rose bushes, created the Owens Rose Garden. In similar fashion, the Eugene Rhododendron Society planted rhododendrons and azaleas on ten acres of land in Hendricks Park that formerly had been used for deer pens.

Other public-private partnerships active at the time added to the area's supply of public space. In the midst of its drive to acquire Amazon Park, the Century Progress Fund organized another campaign, this time to purchase a former garbage dump just south of Amazon Park, now Tugman Park. A number of other park sites, including Gateway Park, were developed as the result of donations by private citizens or fundraising efforts by civic organizations. Perhaps the most ambitious partnership effort came after Eva Johnson informed the city in 1960 that the late Celeste Campbell had left $50,000 to purchase land along the Willamette River for parks. The city coveted one six-acre parcel in particular, but the owners were asking $120,000, substantially more than the city could afford. At that point three Eugene businessmen—Maurie Jacobs, Alton Baker Jr., and Ehrman Guistina—stepped in and recruited seven other residents to contribute $5,000 each toward the purchase price. After extended negotiations with the owners of the property and donations from a number of other citizens, the site was purchased and eventually turned over to the city.

What had been a relatively small community before the war quickly became a city energized by the arrival of thousands of new-comers attracted by the area's natural amenities and eager to set down roots. With population growth came demands for additional programs and facilities, particularly in the city's new neighbor-hoods. In 1948 the city opened Jefferson Pool, its first public swim-ming facility, at the fairgrounds on land donated by Lane County, and Amazon Pool, in South Eugene, opened in 1957.

When the parks and recreation department staff gathered late in 1965 to plan for the future, they realized how ill-prepared they were for growth. The following spring Eugeneans would go to the polls to vote on a $1.7 million levy that would authorize the con-struction of two new swimming pools and four new community centers. There was little doubt the measure would pass. "The sup-port for recreation was overwhelming," recalled Dave Pompel, a native who returned to Eugene that year to work for the depart-ment under director Ed Smith and stayed on until his retirement in 1996. "Good recreation programs were a real priority. Some people took it as a right of living in Eugene, almost like public education." The proposed recreation measure reflected widespread support not only for building new facilities, but also for putting them square in the heart of the neighborhoods they would serve. Each new community center would offer a broad-based program, with something for everyone.

On the eve of the 1966 levy, however, Smith oversaw a small staff—only five full-time employees—that operated a short list of programs and classes on a relatively modest budget. "The offerings were very limited," Pompel admitted. Other than its school-based youth summer recreation program and the two swimming pools, the department supervised only a few activities at Monroe Park, Washington Park, and a small senior center in Skinner Butte Park, usually available for free or for what amounted to a token registra-tion fee. The department grappled with the prospect of suddenly going from a small and narrowly focused operation to a large and comprehensive one. It was difficult to imagine how the department, in its current form, could get the most out of the proposed new facilities.

The problem was tradition. The prevailing philosophy was to organize a recreation department around a staff of professionals trained in recreation management and to rely on that staff not only to supervise facilities, but also serve as instructors for all or most of the classes and programs. As a result, the offerings were limited to what the staff could physically handle and was skilled in. More than that, the traditional approach was vulnerable to a cycle that almost guaranteed modest growth: limited programs, thus low participation rates, thus little support for a larger staff, thus limited programs.

The department could go to city officials and ask for the money to significantly enlarge its staff. But Smith and his colleagues came up with a different, and deceptively simple, idea: Why not charge a small participation fee for individual classes and recruit instructors from outside the department, experts in their field or craft, to lead them? "The idea was that if we put on quality programs, people would come," Pompel said. "We didn't think people would be upset about paying if they had instructors who knew what they were doing." But the staff knew there were no guarantees the new approach would work. "As far as we knew," Pompel said, "no one else in the country was doing it."

Once put in place, the program produced immediate and dramatic results, embraced by both instructors, whose time and expertise were modestly rewarded, and participants, who didn't mind paying two or three or even ten dollars each for the opportunity to learn a craft or skill from one of the area's finest. Within a few years the program offerings expanded from a few classes here and there to a wide range of activities, according to Pompel, and participation rates jumped from about 25 percent capacity to nearly full capacity. By putting individual classes on a self-supporting basis, according to Pompel, the department was no longer completely at the mercy of its budget allocations. It was able to try new things and could respond quickly and directly to suggestions and ideas.

"We told the instructors, 'It's your baby,' " Pompel said. " 'You tell us what you want to teach.' "

A graduate student who had recently arrived from the East Coast asked why the department didn't offer a Frisbee class. Not only was one started, but the graduate student taught it. "We had some instructors who taught for twenty to thirty years," Pompel said. Moreover, a significant number ended up as permanent staff members, freeing up staffers trained in recreation management to assume their primary roles as supervisors at the community centers. And, most important, the public overwhelmingly endorsed the enhanced program offerings. "We never had single person say a class wasn't worth it," Pompel said. "Not only were we able to offer more programs, we also upgraded all the programs."

Pompel described the next fifteen years as a "golden age" for the parks and recreation department. The Sheldon Meadows and Westmoreland Centers opened the following year, marking the first real commitment to a year-round slate of activities. Echo Hollow Pool was dedicated in 1969. In 1973 the Amazon Community Center held its grand opening to show off its new youth building and arts and crafts center. It was the final community park facility financed by the 1966 levy. In 1968 Smith announced the appointment of a new cultural arts coordinator to oversee programs in drama, music, art, dance, and arts and crafts. As Dan George, coordinator for community centers and schools, said in a 1975 interview, the department felt an obligation to offer its constituency the widest possible range of recreational options. It particularly targeted youths and senior citizens. It entered a partnership with the school district to make use of school gyms on the weekends for youth activities. It also took over control of the Celeste Campbell Senior Community Center, opened in 1958 by the Emerald Empire Council for the Aging with donated equipment in a borrowed building, and developed it into one of the top senior programs in the state.

The one consistent note that sounded throughout this period of dynamic growth was the need to satisfy the recreational inter-

ests of the area's youth. The parks and recreation department filled
the summer with youth programs, and school athletics for junior
high youths and older were well organized and well financed. Early
in the 1950s two volunteer parent groups, one in the Ferry Street
Bridge area and one in South Eugene, decided to pool their resources to create a baseball program for younger children. And
they were determined that it wouldn't be just another Little League.

A Way to Play

When Ralph Myers, then a college student and recently married,
became the Eugene Boys Athletic Association's first and only full-
time staffer in 1956, he thought it was going to be a temporary
position. "But as time went by," he recalled of the private, nonprofit organization started by his father and a number of other
parents, "I saw the thing start to snowball." More like an avalanche. Little did Myers know that he would remain at the helm
of one of the country's most successful and innovative youth sports
organizations for almost four decades.

It started in the winter of 1953, with ten basketball teams
comprising some ninety boys. At its core from day one, said Myers,
was its vision of competitive athletics within the framework of good
sportsmanship and equal participation for all, supported by volunteers and donations from the business community. The idea
was to get as many kids as possible involved, in a setting that
didn't follow the competitive ethos of Little League and wouldn't
be simply a training ground for future high school athletes.

The philosophy, according to Myers, was geared to the masses.
"I don't think we could have the type of program we have with a
high level of competition," he said. "It would run off the borderline kid." And that commitment never wavered, even as the program grew from those original ninety boys playing one sport to a
year-round schedule that now involves more than 25,000 area boys
and girls. "If a kid wants to play, he or she gets to play," said
Kidsports chief executive officer Bob Josephson in 1994. "We will
find a way."

The numbers certainly back up that claim. In the spring of 1954, following that first winter of basketball, the program expanded to include baseball. The budget was $1,500. In 1960, after a city-wide ballot measure to fund football in the junior high schools was soundly defeated, the organization added football to make the program year-round. It continued to serve only boys until 1974, when sports for girls were added and the group became the Eugene Sports Program. By 1979, 8,431 youths in six boys' and four girls' sports were participating. A staff of eleven managed an annual budget of $350,000, backed up by a thirteen-member board of directors and 1,500 volunteers. The budget hit the $500,000 mark in 1985 and continued to grow, until by the mid-1990s more than 25,000 kids were involved and the budget passed the $1.5 million mark. According to Kidsports estimates, the organization reached about 60 percent of the households in the Eugene-Springfield metropolitan area.

That Kidsports and the thousands of volunteers who make it run have been able to sustain such growth is a testament to its bedrock philosophy, put in place at the beginning and little changed since. "Kidsports was designed as a community, with the schools to help with the facilities, the community to supply the volunteers, and the business community to supply the funds to operate the program," said Myers. The program uses public facilities and receives modest subsidies from public agencies, but it does not rely on direct tax support; participation fees are supplemented by donations and sponsorships. In 1968 Mayor Gus Keller said that such a program couldn't be managed by the city for less than twice the cost.

Ron Howard participated in the program and later coached his four boys as they went through it—by his estimate, more than thirty baseball, soccer, basketball, and football teams. He got involved the same way many Kidsports coaches get involved: The kids needed a coach. He was standing on the sidelines with other parents when a Kidsports official informed him that his five-year-old son's team was without a soccer coach. Howard told the official that he knew nothing about the game. "Hey!" the official replied. "They're five years old. All you gotta do is teach them how to kick a ball and run up and down the field."

Howard later joined one of Kidsports's many volunteer boards, served nine years on the main board of directors, and at the end of the century served on the organization's endowment board. He remembered when one of his son's teams went undefeated for several years running, but he also treasured the fact that Kidsports had stuck to its original goals of maximizing opportunity while minimizing the stress associated with ultracompetitiveness. "It's still a great organization," he said. Yes, he admitted, there will always be a faction of parents who get very frustrated by anything less than perfection, be it the coaches, the referees, or the facilities. Yes, he experienced firsthand the effects of a baseball coach whose teaching and people skills left a lot to be desired—so lacking were they, in fact, that one of his boys quit that team and never played baseball again. And yes, the "everybody plays" ethos has been more or less a formal policy for the last ten or fifteen years. It's better for everybody involved to have it written down, he said.

Early in his coaching career, Howard had assembled a group of boys to tell them who had made the top team and who would be playing in the lower divisions. "I never liked to use the word 'cut'," he said of his coaching philosophy, and he didn't use the word that day. Afterward, the father of one of the boys who did not make the top team approached him. The family had just moved into the area. He thanked Howard for the way he handled the situation. Howard appreciated the compliment but took it as an endorsement not of his personal approach, but of the program's guiding philosophy.

Early in the 1990s, Kidsports officials started asking around: Was Kidsports unique? They asked in Salem, Portland, Medford, even out of state. The answer, said Howard, was always the same: No other community had a youth athletic program even remotely close to Kidsports.

Make Me Room to Play

During the 1960s and the 1970s the parks system both reflected and encouraged the city's growing recreational needs. It had established four community centers, expanded its offerings of organized recreation, formed a popular outdoor education program under the leadership of Mel Jackson, and stepped up its efforts to acquire additional land for public use. Eugeneans could choose from a long list of activities, centered on swimming programs for all ages as well as flourishing adult basketball and softball leagues, but also including everything from art classes to instruction in Zen meditation. The running craze, traceable to Bill Bowerman and his hugely successful track and field program at the University of Oregon, exploded on the local scene and put Eugene at the forefront of an international fitness movement.

Throughout this period Eugeneans consistently rated the area's open spaces as one of its prime attractions and vigorously supported measures to protect them. In 1972, as part of its review of several housing projects proposed for the South Hills, the city council commissioned a study of the area, which was completed two years later. Among its recommendations was the goal of integrating future housing developments into natural areas in a way that provided for recreational space and preserved wildlife and vegetation. The report also identified several potential park sites, and in 1976, funded by a $5 million levy, the city created Hawkins Heights Park, Skyline Park, and Crest Drive Park. In 1972 voters approved a bond measure that authorized continued purchases of land along the Willamette River. Those purchases, part of the West Bank Acquisition Plan, eventually led to the creation of a superb system of bike trails and dedicated bike bridges, as well as protecting the riverbank from private development.

By 1980 the city had a network of parks comprising approximately 1,500 acres. Over the next several years, however, the economy faltered, and for the first time the historically high ratio of open space to population began to decline significantly; by 1995 Eugene had set aside less than two-thirds of the acreage recommended by a national survey for its neighborhood parks. Pompel said that the recession made city officials increasingly reluctant to go to voters for more money and created what he called an "either-or mentality," in which some local leaders pitted a dollar for recreation against a dollar for the police or the fire department. Rather than cutting costs across the board, the city began cutting whole programs, particularly those that served the entire community rather than a specific constituency. The situation was "real political," Pompel said, and "really started limiting our opportunities." He remembers the 1980s and early 1990s as a period of almost continual downsizing and increasingly crowded facilities. A number of potential bond measures "never got off the ground." The department was asked to cover more of its overhead costs by boosting participation fees, especially for its popular adult athletic programs. "Registration didn't go down," said Pompel, "but we definitely started serving a different base of participants. Now we weren't programming for everyone, but only those who could afford."

So dire did the department's budgetary travails become that in the mid-1980s it even temporarily suspended what Pompel said was the foundation of the entire department, the youth summer recreation program. In 1987 the police department pledged to fund youth recreation programs out of its own budget—"they understood the value of getting youth involved in athletics," Pompel said—but the proposal withered for lack of support from the city.

Perhaps the legacy of those difficult years was one reason Eugeneans were so hopeful that a 1998 bond measure—$25 million earmarked for parks and open space—would prove to be the first step in a new era of growth and vitality. The measure would fund the renovation of Amazon Pool, the improvement of almost thirty existing parks, and the development of new open spaces and facilities. In an August 2000 guest editorial in *The Register-Guard*, city councilor Nancy Nathanson gave an optimistic progress report, writing of projects "humming along," "unique" public-private partnerships, and the "many hours of labor and thousands of dollars" citizens had donated to create new parks.

Of course, the five-year-old child leaning intently over the mobile she is making from plastic CD molds doesn't know from shrinking budgets or administrative realignments or shifting political priorities or public-private partnerships, unique or otherwise. She's excited because her arts class, a one-week session at the Amazon Community Center taught by professional artists, gets to go swimming at Amazon Pool later in the afternoon. Better yet, it's the same day as her swimming lessons at the same pool. She's in the Flipper class. On summer weekends she often rides bikes with her parents along the river or flies a kite in Alton Baker Park or hikes to the top of Mount Pisgah or Spencer Butte. This is her vision of recreation in Eugene, and she has no reason to believe it won't be even bigger and better next summer, when she starts playing Kidsports soccer.

ODD DUCKS

By Steve McQuiddy

I HAVE CALLED Eugene home for most of the past twenty years, and during that time I have traveled, not only in this country but to other parts of the world. When people ask where I'm from, I tell them Eugene, Oregon, and their response nearly always goes something like this: "Eugene . . . isn't that where the hippies and weirdoes are?"

Well yes, I say, and start to say something more, but then I just smile. Because what can you say? Eugene *is* where the hippies and weirdoes are. The hippies and weirdoes and a whole lot more. Back in the early 1990s when a couple of sixties fugitives surfaced here, a national newspaper article said Oregon "harbors an abundance of activists, free spirits, odd ducks and loose cannons." They said Oregon but they meant Eugene. Because Eugene is where you'll find lawyers wearing ponytails and clown pants, where a south hills estate might have an old school bus with wooden shingle siding parked out back, where people on bicycles sing to trees, and where babbling, drooling, and public nudity are called grounding, focusing, and personal space; where it rains nine months of the year but cars don't rust, and where the local public health organization is run by a group of so-called hippies but is one of the most successful in all the land.

Now, any sizable city has its oddballs and eccentrics, most every small town has its village idiot, and even out in the desert you'll find your cranky old hermit living in a sod hut and talking to the rattlesnakes and prairie dogs. But Eugene seems to have a concentration of the fringe element, and because of that, a reputation.

You wonder how it got this way. Was there some cataclysmic event or chain of circumstances that attracted the carnival crowd? Is there a supernatural power at work? Is it the climate or the soil? Is there stuff in the water?

Perhaps it had something to do with the Oregon Trail. With all due respect to our pioneer legends, anyone who would strike out on foot, hauling along their family and a wagon, for six months or more across two thousand miles of unknown territory with no real certainty of what lay at the end would have to be, at least to some degree, "touched." Sure, they came to sink their plow into the fertile earth and build a life in this pristine land—no one's kidding when they call Oregon God's country. But they also came here to get away—to escape being drafted into the Civil War, to leave behind unpaid debts, social disgrace, family obligations, and narrow-minded neighbors. Noble and ignoble, they tended to value the individual over society, and when you put enough true individuals together it's bound to be a colorful mix.

From the very beginning Eugene seemed to straddle the line—sometimes literally. When the first Lane County Courthouse went up in 1855, two founding settlers, Eugene Skinner and Charnel Mulligan, had donated land for the building. Rather than cause bad feelings, county commissioners chose to put the courthouse smack on the boundary line between the two properties. As the town grew, however, it turned out the building was in the middle of what is now 8th Avenue, and so had to be moved—a fair illustration of another peculiar Eugene quality: the compromise that must later be fixed.

Maybe our *feng shui* is askew. The first town plat included a Water Street, along the river about where Skinner Butte Park is now, but the area flooded so frequently back then that the town was replatted onto higher ground, and Water Street removed from the map. Confusion still reigns on the streets of Eugene. Try telling someone the difference between Franklin Boulevard and Broadway. Direct them through the one-way grid downtown. Answer why the Ferry Street Bridge comes off Coburg Road on one side of the river, crosses where Mill Street should be and connects to Broadway—or is it Franklin?—on the other. Tell them why River Road isn't on the river. Then explain how we have a north and south bank of the Willamette when the river itself runs north.

Maybe it's inherited from the jail. In the 1870s a local contractor outfitted the city jail with walls "double lined with lumber an inch and a half thick, with three ten-penny nails in every square inch inside." The building was declared escape-proof, and citizens were shocked when a few months later a prisoner cut his way out with an old case knife. Or perhaps the observatory tainted the municipal gene pool. In 1888 the University of Oregon built a modest observatory on Skinner Butte. But the perpetually overcast skies made stargazing impractical, and the project was abandoned. The building sat like a skeleton above the town and became "a mecca for vagrants, for small boys, for lovers, and other trespassers." [3]

We could almost have blamed it on the Dukhobors. In 1924 nearly eight thousand members of the Russian religious sect that eschewed government authority planned to move to Eugene from Canada. The local chapters of the American Legion and the Ku Klux Klan actively opposed the move, but it wasn't called off until the Dukhobor leader was killed by a bomb (presumably planted by his own people) that obliterated his train car in British Columbia.

Eccentricity hardly means incompetence, and there have been successful local people whose individuality was very much a mark of their character. Lord Nelson ("Nels") Roney of Eugene, Oregon's master builder of nearly one hundred covered bridges, painted his structures red. He signed them, too, as would an artist sign a painting. And after he finished a job in the far reaches of the county, he would head off into the woods, hunting and fishing his way home. George Melvin Miller, brother of the flamboyant poet Joaquin

Miller, outlined plans for a human-powered flying machine, which he patented in 1892, but never got off the drawing board. Miller later promoted a transcontinental highway running from New York City to the Lane County port of Florence. Nothing had come of it by his death in 1933, but if you look at a map today you can see Highway 20 running from the Atlantic seaboard at Boston to Newport on the Pacific Coast.

The forests and rivers and the mountains and sea coast such a short distance away no doubt have influenced the mindset here. They breed a kind of wildness, an independence not found just anywhere, says author Ken Kesey, who grew up in Lane County and now lives in Pleasant Hill. "What's really special and different is that we weren't afraid to experiment, to go with confidence and excitement, knowing that you stand a good chance of survival." Kesey, whose *One Flew Over the Cuckoo's Nest* and *Sometimes a Great Notion* remark quite a bit on the effect one individual can have on society, told a story in 1963 about an old accordion he and his brother found in a covered drainage ditch when they were kids in Springfield. They tried to play the instrument, he said, but couldn't get it to work. So they opened it up, and down inside the valves and bellows, stuck in a corner, was a tiny piece of paper with a message that said, "What the hell are you looking in here for, Daisy Mae?"

"Well, I achieved some kind of *sartori* right there," Kesey said, "knowing that *somebody* had *sometime* a very *long* while ago gone in there and put that sign in that accordion, and he's betting all the time that *someday* somebody's going to come along and *find* it. A mystery for people to wonder about." [6]

Strong individuals in highly visible positions were certainly a factor. Wayne Morse, the combative University of Oregon law school dean, labor arbitrator, and politician, called Eugene home from 1929 until his death in 1974. As the "Tiger of the Senate" from 1944 to 1968, he served as a Republican, Independent, and Democrat—leaving a mark that resonates to this day. "Don't send me back to Washington," he said in 1950, "unless you want me to sit in the Senate a free man—free to vote in the public interest as the facts and my conscience dictate."

Stories abound also of William "Bill" Tugman, outspoken editor of the *Eugene Register-Guard* from 1927 to 1954. Tugman, who ran the newspaper not only as a chronicler but as a watchdog of the city, would sometimes wonder aloud why Eugene was such a "particularly contentious community," recalled long-time *Register-Guard* writer Dan Wyant in 1993. "Some of us on his news staff wondered if Tugman realized that his hard-hitting editorials were one of the prime reasons the community seemed stirred up much of the time." [9]

Another tale tells of Tugman's early days when he was approached by members of Eugene's Rotary, Kiwanis, and Lions clubs. Each wanted him to join, and the young editor obliged all three, signing a personal check each time. When the club representatives realized what he had done, they returned to Tugman and explained that he must choose only one. Tugman then asked for the checks back, tore them up, and said, "I appreciate your interest, gentlemen, but if I cannot join all service clubs, as an editor I cannot favor one. You are very courteous, and I thank you." Throughout his time in Eugene, he never joined any business group.

Iconoclastic businessman Archie Weinstein left his brand on the town. Born in New York at the turn of the last century, he came to the University of Oregon about 1918, but was blackballed by fraternities due to his Jewish faith. He left to work in family stores throughout eastern Oregon but eventually returned to Eugene and became a champion of small business owners, or "the little guy." He worked 100-hour weeks at his surplus store, located where the Hult Center is now. He put an anti-tank gun for sale in his front window. He beat Remington and Sunbeam in court when they tried to bar him from selling their products below market value. At age sixty-seven, he bought the tallest apartment building in Eugene and topped it with a circular penthouse, where he lived with his twenty-nine-year-old wife. At seventy-five, he was elected county commissioner, and his battles with fellow commissioner Jerry Rust (whom he dubbed the "hippie tree planter") became legend. He fought with *The Register-Guard*, the business establishment, and especially politicians. "They're all liars, full of bull," he said at age ninety-one, after a series of strokes confined him to a wheelchair. "If I could walk, I'd give 'em all hell."

Records are somewhat skimpier on the women, but we know they were—and are — here. Maude Kerns, the artist who forsook a New York career to remain in Eugene and care for her mother, and who willed funding for an art center to the town; Laverne Krause, another artist who balanced her work, family, and promoting the work of others; Joan Gratz, who lived in a tiny house on Patterson Street and did Claymation for the California Raisins commercials and later for Coca-Cola ads; Sidney Herbert, who has dedicated her life to the League of Women Voters, the Oregon Bach Festival, and is lately studying to become an Episcopal priest . . . are all individuals whom Cynthia Wooten, the well-known community advocate and former legislator, calls "extraordinary, larger than life."

There was no shortage of unique characters who simply came and went their own way. A fellow named "Rosie" Cluer was a sign painter who lived with his mother on Olive Street. "He was the town drunk," recalls Bill Gardner, who lived nearby in the 1930s. But Cluer was so harmless that parents let their children visit him at his shop, Gardner says. "He was as gentle as the day is long." Gardner also says he had heard that when the city needed a sign painted, they'd arrest Cluer, sober him up in jail, and have him paint the sign. "When he painted he had a steady hand."

Willie Knickerbocker was another favorite with children, if not the entire town. The "father of bicycling in Eugene" pedaled everywhere he went, from the time he got his first bike in the 1890s until just a few years before his death in 1960, at age ninety-two. He was a short, wiry man—not very bright, people said—and had legs like steel bands. He lived at the family homestead out by Deadmond Ferry and would pedal the ten-mile round trip to

Eugene. He wore a baseball cap and rubber boots, he rode an old "direct drive" model with no coaster brakes, and he'd stop by using sheer leg power on the pedals. He rode to Portland, the coast, over the mountains to Sisters, and up to The Dalles. One story had him riding to Mexico and back in the days before the roads were paved. He didn't talk much, but he loved attention when he got on that bike. He'd ride out to the grade schools and do tricks for the kids, including his famous "high kick"—putting one foot on the seat and kicking the other high in the air. At the annual Pet Parade during the 1950s and 1960s, he decorated his bike with crepe paper and raccoon tails and performed for the crowd. "Willie would ride his bike around the block just to do more tricks for the people," recalled Ethan Newman, long-time Eugene postmaster and historical authority, in 1978.

Willie was an entertainer, but he also had a message—quite a few, in fact. He would hand-deliver letters to the editor at the *Eugene Register-Guard*, signed simply "W.K." Many were one-liners: "I saw a rooster in the rain, eating gravel to grind his grain," and "I saw Oregon go from geese to gas." In 1978 Dan Sellard, a *Register-Guard* reporter, spearheaded a motion to name the new bicycle-path bridge at Judkins Point for Willie. Officials agreed, and today a plaque there bears his name.

The University of Oregon is a natural haven for eccentric behavior and, probably more than anything else, has helped give Eugene its reputation in the last forty years. It's easy now to forget that for most of the past century Eugene called itself the lumber capital of the world and, aside from the UO, was much like its neighbors. "Without the university," said radio personality Wendy Ray in 1990, "we're Roseburg."

A walk down 13th Avenue just west of the university, particularly on a sunny day, proves this ain't Roseburg. In the one-block microcosm between Alder and Kincaid, you can find coffee shops and sushi bars, donuts and tabouli, signs written in half a dozen languages and a barber shop with a world map sprouting a hundred colored pins. The sidewalks run like a river with students and teachers, secretaries and street people, musicians and malcontents, Bible-thumpers, petition-hawkers, panhandlers and puppy dogs. "They're all here," wrote *The Register-Guard*'s Bob Welch in 1990. "Joe College, Betty Coed, Professor Plum, The Thinker, Frog, Zeus, Franklin, Rabbit, Eagle Park Slim, and Cookie Szakacs, founder and CEO of Cookie's Corner, a hot dog stand."

Cookie is gone today, but a bronze plaque in the bricks on her old corner at the gates of the university remind us that she was there. Eagle Park Slim shows up from time to time, playing his timeless blues guitar with bells on his hands and blowing his old kazoo. Zeus, who wore women's dresses and lived on the streets, was taken down by tuberculosis—although the legend lives on of the time he supposedly swallowed some Barbie doll heads and had to have his stomach pumped. Frog is still around, hawking his joke books, as the 2000 version of Joe College and Betty Coed head for Starbucks down on the corner that used to be Guido's, that used to be Duffy's, that used to be the Lemon O burger bar.

The main student hangout for decades was the College Side Inn, built in the 1920s, where the UO bookstore is now. In the early 1960s the intellectuals and radicals gathered there, and the spirit spread when the New World Coffee House opened down the street and around the corner on Alder. "There was a kind of beatnik elite," says Cynthia Wooten. "And the Odyssey brought the so-called hippie presence downtown."

The Odyssey Coffee House was opened by Wooten and her husband Bill in the late 1960s, at 713 Willamette. This was before urban renewal, the Hult Center, the Hilton, and the downtown mall. At the corner of 7th Avenue was Pope's Donut Shop, with the donuts traveling on a conveyor belt in the storefront window and old Mrs. Pope in her glasses and hair net and pink starched apron, coming to work at four o'clock in the morning. "She looked as stoic as ever, through the sixties and early seventies, as all kinds of people descended on her," Wooten says, adding that during the Second World War there was a brothel upstairs. "She told me."

The Odyssey became such a hotspot for bohemians, intellectuals, and radicals that the Wootens were accused of being funded by the Communist Party. There was actually a hearing held in city hall. "It was July 1969, the night of the moon landing, and it was *hot*," Wooten recalls. "On one side sat our accusers, on the other sat the respondents. It felt like a trial." But there was no real evidence against the Wootens, so nothing came of it. The problem, Wooten says, was that the conservative community couldn't believe that these young people with strange clothes and ideas were possibly up to any good. The Establishment felt threatened, and the scenes acted out in Eugene were like so many others across the land at the time. "We were investigated, our phones were tapped," Wooten says. "It was like we were space aliens come here to destroy their lives . . . Except we weren't space aliens, and we weren't trying to destroy anything. We came here to demonstrate an alternative way of being alive."

At least one Odyssey regular was a communist. Or a former communist—the word was that he'd been kicked out of the party in the 1920s for being too radical. He was Russell Dell, born in Michigan in 1899, and—according to stories that may or may not have been true—he knew Emma Goldman, fought in the Spanish Civil War, walked across Russia during the Bolshevik Revolution, and rode a unicycle in a circus. He came to Eugene in the early 1970s, and called himself a "revolutionist, Marxian scholar, and dialectician." He also said his name was Stupid.

Stupid adopted the town and became a kind of surrogate father to alternative groups like the Hoedads tree-planting cooperative. His needs were few, and he slept wherever he happened to be that night, claiming that he was welcome at a hundred different homes in town. He was a fixture at the 5th Street Public Market after it opened in 1976, doing odd jobs, repairing the wooden chairs, and bringing boxes of fruit and nuts for children. With his orator's voice, shock of white hair, and long, sweeping eyebrows, he held court at various tables in the cafe seating area and wrote pamphlets called "Stupid's Comments on Current Events." Offering a kind of wit and wisdom with an edge, the booklets featured sayings like "Keep America green...Hose down a politician!" and "Stupid's idea for maintaining world peace...Universal, unconditional, compulsory cannibalism. If ya kill it, ya gotta eat it."

He was described as "the market philosopher" and "an anarchist, but a friendly one." When he died in 1982, from mistakenly eating poison wild mushrooms, it was front-page news, and the Hoedads held an Irish wake. [1]

Uncle Ray was a bit like Stupid in that he considered all of Eugene his home. He spent twenty years here on the streets, pushing his trademark shopping cart filled with bottles and cans and junk. He looked like Father Time's tough cousin, with his long gray beard, baseball cap, Salem cigarettes, and bottle of Night Train. He was a scrounger, not a beggar, and was well-known around the West University neighborhood. He sometimes played harmonica at Mama's Homefried Truck Stop on 14th Avenue just off Kincaid, and later frequented Poppi's restaurant on 13th, where the Sacred Heart Hospital parking garage is now. He'd water the flowers and trees in the bower-like courtyard, and sometimes sleep in an alcove out back. "I knew him from the first day we got the restaurant in 1978," remarked owner Poppi Cottam. "He came with the restaurant, more or less."

Ray didn't talk much about his past. He'd seen heavy combat in World War II, then came home and got married, but it didn't work out. Some say there was a "Dear John" letter involved. He drifted around the west, arriving in Eugene in the late 1960s. He made no apologies for his drinking; he ranted and raved and sometimes got arrested. "What a man wants to do in his life, he does it," he'd say, "and that isn't easy." Then he'd turn and growl, "I don't give a damn! That isn't easy, either!" But he was also a kind man—even wise—and students might find themselves sitting outside on a dark night, facing some crisis of spirit, and talking to Uncle Ray. He listened and believed that considering an outside perspective was essential to understanding. "Try consideration," he often said, and sometimes people did.

When they found Uncle Ray's body in 1988, under a piece of carpet in an old garage where he'd lay down to sleep or to die, he was wearing two shirts, a sweater, a jacket, and two pairs of pants. He had a watch on each wrist, three pens, a tire gauge, and a corncob pipe. He also had nearly $7,000 in a bank account, accrued from veterans and social security benefits. "By our standards, it was a sad thing. By his standards, he was perfectly normal," explained Poppi Cottam. "He was free of our standards."

Individuals . . . that's what this place is about. Individuals living together in a sometimes astounding mix. Once you pull the lid off the Pandora's box of Eugene's contradictory collective character, all you can do is hang on for the ride. How else to explain the White Bird Medical Clinic, Saturday Market, the Oregon Country Fair, and Toby's tofu pâté? Pro-growth advocates, no-growth advocates, the cross on Skinner Butte, the flag on Skinner Butte, a harmonic convergence on Skinner Butte, a coffee house across from the jail, and eagles soaring above bumper-to-bumper traffic on the Ferry Street Bridge? A communist on the city council, a communist running for mayor, another candidate campaigning in a jester's cap? Six pages of churches in the telephone book, a Christian college, a Bible college, a Christian publishing house, an anarchist collective, the Eugene Celebration's slug queen, a Disney character for the state university's mascot, and the guy who built houses in trees? Host of the annual Oregon Logging Conference, the birthplace of jogging in America, and more VW buses per capita than an old hippie's Woodstock flashback? Percon, Hyundai, tree-sitting, patchouli oil, a million miles of bicycle trails, the Riverfront Research Park, B.R.I.N.G. Recycling, pallet recycling, Alice Soderwall's Glass Station, the Growers Market, Project Safe Run, the Hemlock Society, Birth to Three, the Gizmo electric car, and Peddler's Express? Not to mention countless ads for rolfing, Reiki, rapid eye therapy, shamanic healing, soul retrieval, warm pool therapy, herbal body wraps, chakra cleansing, acupuncture, acupressure, structural integration, Breena, Qi Gong, triple spiral

healing, and the Orgone accumulation box. Tack on the thirty-
year downtown mall debacle, the probability that your restaurant
waiter has a Ph.D., and that in a county called the "covered bridge
capital of the west" residents voted to build a bicycle bridge that
looks like San Francisco's Golden Gate, and you begin to wonder
just exactly what "weird" means.

It's because of the rain, says Don Bishoff, the long-time columnist (now retired) at *The Register-Guard*. "Faced with the annual inevitability of nine months of perpetual pouring, our municipal psyche has unconsciously created a defense mechanism:
Screwball Syndrome. It keeps us distracted from the woeful weather
we love to hate." Bishoff, who has seen his share of dreamers, ge-
niuses and nut cases come and go, reminds us that Eugene has
long been a town divided. "Since I moved here in 1960, Eugene
has had its own John Birch Society chapter and outposts of every
screaming left-wing protest group of the sixties and seventies."
Most of the groups are less extreme these days, but no less zealous,
he says. "The perpetual push-pull tension probably makes this
the most maddening town to govern outside of Italy. But damn,
it's a fun place to live."

Maybe that's what it is, and all that it is—Eugene is this way
because we want it to be. People come here by choice, and they
stay for the same reason. Bridge builders or street people, the ones
who leave a mark have an investment here—and it's personal. "The
magic of Eugene really is in its people," says Cynthia Wooten.
"There's a collective growth and consciousness." Then, at the end
of a ninety-minute phone interview, during which she also prepared dinner, she adds almost as an afterthought, "In some ways
it's better to not unveil the mysteries, or try to quantify why Eugene is unique."

And this is where Hershel comes in. Hershel Bloom, who works
at White Bird, the co-op organization that offers help to everyone—homeless or depressed, abused or addicted, people who need
clothes, medical care, schooling, shelter, or just someone to talk
to. Hershel has worked there for many years. He listens, and he

communicates in many ways. He draws pictures. With both his
hands. He plays guitar and is continually writing a long song that
is continually changing—a song about the history of Eugene, naming all the people and all the changes that have come and gone. He
calls it "Loose Change," and sometimes he'll play it for an hour or
more, switching lines, making some up, and if you want to know
where he's coming from, take a deep breath and read this line out
loud, straight through, without a rest: *I see myself in a process to
gently light upon an unseen ledge within the darkest moment after I
must have prepared something out of nothing in the lost and churning
of the unknown at a point where some go crazy while others never come
back.*

Eugene might be, as some say, lost in time. We might be, as the
national media prefers to believe, stuck in the sixties. But we might
be so far ahead of the pack that as we circle around to pass the
crowd again they see us coming from behind and think that's where
we started. A recent PBS documentary about New York City had
various authorities singing praises to that town. Among other things,
they said that New York sets the tone for the rest of the country.
Well, they're wrong. New York sets the tone for the middle of the
country, which happens to be a really big chunk. What New York
doesn't understand is that west of the Rockies and beyond the
thousand or so miles of high desert and over that string of volca-
noes called the Cascades is where the real pioneers are, including
the pioneers of the imagination. Because it's not just the visionaries who made the West, but also the ones with visions, any kind of
visions: hallucinations, illuminations, illusions and delusions, night-
mares and dreams. Dreams of grandeur, dreams of gold, dreams of
water and quiet, and dreams of finding God. Or if not finding the
God, then the freedom to follow their own. Freedom, that's the
other thing you find out here. Freedom to run your own life, freedom to choose. Freedom to choose where to work, freedom to
choose not to work at all. Freedom to walk in the woods, to pray to
the moon, to stand outside your front door at dawn wearing noth-

ing but a set of bagpipes and the desire to play them. Freedom to dream of a world where freedom is real and nobody's crazy no matter what they do.

I don't know if such a world exists, but I know there's a place where you can think it possible: here, in Eugene. Whatever hope we have is waiting and it's right here. There's an odd logic at work in this town, and it has become the standard. You can't put your finger on it because you can't describe it in terms of anything else. Now and again a fashion or fad will come along and give it a name—karma, coincidence, synchronicity—but though the names may come and go, that inexplicable quality has been here all along. And whether idealized or ignored, whether a magnet for crowds or the place they desert like the tide going out, still it remains: this notion of order in seeming chaos, increasing evidence that the unrelated is anything but, the idea that we might not have to blow it after all.

It comes to you in pieces out here, like riddles and clues, fragments that are actually self-contained parts of the whole. And maybe it sounds quirky and surreal, this talk of time and intuition, maybe it smacks of metaphysical breakfast cereal—and God knows there are enough ding-dongs filling in the cracks around here, and God knows the national psychosis has arrived like the first new strains of an epidemic, and God knows the outlet malls and distribution warehouses are turning the open farmlands from green to brown and gray—but this place is also weird. Weird in that nothing seems to happen, and yet somehow everything does. And whether or not it's the work of some higher power, whether or not it's magnetic fields, polar instability, UFOs or the CIA, whether or not it's the collective remains of the psychedelic consciousness, or whether or not it's just plain luck, there's no denying that something is happening here. And proof enough is in the line of cars rolling up I-5 like wagons in a train.

Bibliography

1. Bellamy, Ron. "Stupid leaves colorful legacy," *Eugene Register-Guard*, 29 October 1982.
2. Haswell, Ken. "Citizens want to honor King of Cyclists," *Oregon Daily Emerald* (Eugene), 30 March 1978.
3. Lish, Gordon. "Ken Kesey: A Celebration of Excellence." *Genesis West 5* (Fall 1963).
4. Mantia, Patty. "A familiar face is gone: Uncle Ray," Eugene *Register-Guard*, 12 February 1988.
5. Nelson, Lee H. "A Century of Oregon Covered Bridges." *Oregon Historical Quarterly*, 61:2 (1960).
6. Nelson, Lee, and Martin Schmitt. "Sic Transit Observatorium." *The Call Number*, April 1955.
7. Price, Warren G. *The Eugene Register-Guard: A Citizen of Its Community, Volume I*. Portland: Binford & Mort, 1976.
8. Walling, A.G. *Illustrated History of Lane County, Oregon*. Portland, Ore.: Walling, 1884.
9. Wyant, Dan. "William Tugman: Last of the Crusading Editors." *Lane County Historian*, 38:1 (1993).

AUTHORS AND EDITORS

Ed Alverson is the Willamette Valley stewardship ecologist for The Nature Conservancy, a position he has held since 1991. He received a master's in botany from Oregon State University in 1989. He has written for a variety of publications about natural history and ecology and recently completed a biographical essay on the botanist David Douglas for a forthcoming book about the botanical history of the Pacific Northwest.

Rosemary Howe Camozzi is editor of *The Business News* and a former reporter for the *Corvallis Gazette-Times*.

Brett Campbell is a writer and former magazine editor who teaches magazine writing at the University of Oregon. He writes for a variety of publications and often covers contemporary and classical music.

Alice Evans has lived in Eugene since 1983. She has a master's in journalism from Indiana University and is editor of *Midwifery Today*, an international journal for midwives and other birth practitioners. She also works as a freelance editor and writer and has written about religion for *Christianity Today*, *Oregon Quarterly*, and *Eugene Weekly*.

Debra Gwartney is a freelance writer and assistant director of the University of Oregon creative writing program. She was previously editor of the *Eugene Weekly* and Lane County correspondent for *The Oregonian*.

Michael Kroetch has worked in a wide variety of artistic media. Two of his plays have won national contests. Five of his videos have received top honors by American Film Institute. He is currently working on several screenplays and a history/trivia book on the University of Oregon. He has two short story collections awaiting publication and a novel in development. He is the literary arts columnist for the *Eugene Weekly* and a citizen of Eugene for twenty years.

Guy Maynard is a Eugene writer and the editor of *Oregon Quarterly* magazine, the award-winning magazine of the University of Oregon. He is a lifelong fan of the Boston Red Sox, good training for the often bittersweet adventure of following Oregon Ducks sports, which he has done since moving to the state more than twenty-five years ago.

Steve McQuiddy is a former editor of the *Lane County Historian* and an honorary director of the Oregon Cultural Heritage Commission. He has published many stories on colorful characters in Pacific Northwest history and is currently recasting them into a book.

Ken Metzler is a retired professor of journalism and author of five books and editor of another. The latter, *Yesterday's Adventure*, is a photo book of Lane County History, published by the Lane County Historical Society. Metzler has a bachelor's from the University of Oregon and a master's from Northwestern University and has lived in Eugene since 1956.

Gretchen Miller is an administrative law judge for the state of Oregon and an adjunct professor at the University of Oregon Department of Planning, Public Policy and Management. She is presently working for the Oregon Central Hearings Officer Panel.

Peggy Nagae is an attorney and corporate consultant, specializing in organizational change, leadership development, and diversity issues.

Keith Richard served as archivist at the University of Oregon from 1972 until retirement in 1996. He holds a master's of science and a master's of library science from the UO. He has published articles on Oregon's history in *Oregon Historical Quarterly* and *Old Oregon* and is coeditor of the book *A Down-Easter in the Far West: The Reminiscence of James Neall in Oregon and California 1845–50*.

Karen Seidel served as a senior research associate at the University of Oregon's Bureau of Governmental Research and Service from 1963 to 1994. She has been a member of the Board of Directors of the City Club of Eugene and also a member of its Research Committee. She serves on the Eugene Masonic Cemetery Association's Board of Directors and is a member of the Lane County Boundary Commission. She has authored two articles for *Lane County Historian*, among other writings.

Alan Siporin has been with KLCC radio for nearly twenty years, serving as talk show host, commentator, editor, producer, and trainer. From 1984 to 1994, he was National Public Radio's primary reporter for Oregon stories. He has also written for *The New York Times* and other publications. Prior to his career as a journalist, Siporin was an activist for social change, participating in civil rights and antiwar efforts in Nebraska in the 1960s, and numerous community-building efforts in Eugene beginning with his arrival here in 1970.

Jonathan Stafford pursued graduate studies at the University of Oregon in the department of mathematics. After a master's degree and further study toward a Ph.D., it became apparent that there was no work in that field, so he apprenticed to be an archi-

tect with his father, becoming registered in 1982. Stafford has
served on several neighborhood projects, advisory boards, and planning committees. He is a member of the City Club of Eugene.
Jonathan and his wife, Molly Stafford, have two grown sons, Jason
and Shad, who currently live in Portland.

Alice Tallmadge moved to Eugene from Boston in 1977. She
received a master's degree from the University of Oregon School of
Journalism in 1987 and has worked for a variety of media outlets.
Currently, she is the Lane and Douglas Counties correspondent
for *The (Portland) Oregonian.*

David Thompson is editor of *Getting Ready*, a life-skills magazine for at-risk youth, and a former reporter for *The Herald-Times*,
in Bloomington, Indiana.

Gary Turley is a life-long sports participant and fan who was
born and raised in Eugene. He is the former editor of *Travelin'* and
the current editor of *Mercator's World*. He looks forward to coaching one of the teams his five-year-old daughter, Katherine, is sure
to play on, through Kidsports.

John Van Landingham has served as a staff attorney with Lane
County Law and Advocacy Center since 1977. He was a member
of the Eugene Planning Commission from 1987 to 1999 and has
served on dozens of public committees and nonprofit boards. He
was appointed to the Land Conservation and Development Commission in 2000. He received the Oregon Chapter of the American
Planning Association's 1992 annual award for Distinguished Planning by a Community Planner. He has worshipped Betty Niven
since 1979 and frequently describes his own planning effective-
ness goal as "striving to be half the planner Niven was."

Lois Wadsworth has lived in Eugene for more than twenty-five
years. She has a bachelor's and a master's in journalism from the

University of Oregon. A cofounder of *Eugene Weekly*, she has worked for the paper since 1991 and is now the executive arts editor and literary editor. She reviews films, books, performances, the visual arts, and music, and edits a twice-yearly books issue. Previously she worked as a technical writer for the City of Eugene and was involved inn community access television.

Nancy Webber is a writer and filmmaker. Before pursuing a master's in journalism from the University of Oregon, she spent about twenty years working on public policy issues at the local, state, and national levels. She has also produced a documentary that aired on Oregon Public Broadcasting about commercial navigation on the Columbia River and a video about retraining mill workers and loggers through the "Jobs in the Woods" program.

Ross West earned a bachelor's in literature from the College of Creative Studies at the University of California at Santa Barbara (1980) before moving to Eugene to pursue an MFA in creative writing from the University of Oregon (1984). He was a freelance writer for ten years before taking a position as the science writer in the UO Office of Communications, where he also serves as assistant director and the writer-editor of the UO's research magazine *Inquiry*. His writing has appeared in *Orion Nature Quarterly*, *New Realities*, *Oregon Business*, *Oregon Heritage*, *Public Power*, *Ruralite*, *ICON Thoughtstyle*, *Persimmon Hill*, etc., and, regularly, *Oregon Quarterly*. Having never possessed a driver's license, he is a lifelong pedestrian, car-pooler, and rider of bicycles, buses, ferries, trains, subways, and airplanes.

Cynthia Whitfield is a Eugene freelance writer. She has written numerous articles for *The Register-Guard*, *The Oregon Clarion*, *Career Views* Magazine, *Mom's Action*, and other publications. She lives with her husband, Don Hein, and her four children, two of whom she homeschools. She became particularly acquainted with social services after her youngest son, Jalen, was diagnosed with autism.

Kimber Williams is a feature writer at *The Register-Guard* newspaper, where she has worked since 1990. She received her master's of science degree in journalism from the University of Oregon. Williams has reported for newspapers and freelanced for magazines and other publishing projects for seventeen years.

Cheri Brooks has worked in Eugene as an editor and writer for more than a decade. Her work has appeared in a number of publications, including *Oregon Quarterly* and the *Register-Guard*, and she has she has worked with community groups, businesses, and nonprofit organizations on their publications. She currently lives with her daughter, Jade, in West Eugene.

Kathleen Holt recently moved to Portland after living in Eugene for ten years. She is assistant editor of *Oregon Quarterly* magazine, the magazine of the University of Oregon, and has worked on freelance editing projects for various local organizations. She has also won awards for her fiction and essay writing, including a Literary Arts Women Writers Fellowship and a Hedgebrook residency.

ACKNOWLEDGEMENTS

The editors and authors would like to acknowledge the following people for their assistance with this project. This book would never have been possible without them.

First and foremost, Kathy Madison, who was our primary contact in the City Club and served on the editorial advisory board and the City Club board of directors. She had the vision for this project and provided us the tools and support to pull the whole thing together.

Karen Seidel who first conceived the idea for the book. Susan Ban, for her quiet but steady support. Alice Parman for her invaluable guidance and advice. Frank Gibson for his help in seeing the project through.

The editorial advisory board for the City Club of Eugene History Project: Steve Gordon, Charles Henry, Kathy Madison, Adell McMillan, Jan Oliver, Keith Richard, and Henny Willis. They formulated the structure and scope of the book and ensured that it would be written by a diverse group of authors with varied viewpoints.

The City Club board of directors: Susan Ban, David Pompel, Kathy Madison, Karen Seidel, Jackie Mikalonis, Chuck Reul, Dave Kleger, Rebecca Force, Charles Dalton, Sam Frear, Alan Zelenka, Frank Gibson, Nancy Gines Mason, Don Kahle, Sally Weston, Sue Aufort, Carolyn Kranzler, George Kloeppel, and Dan Bryant.

Katherine Getta, for her graphic design assistance and for her

426 THE CITY CLUB OF EUGENE

photo of Hendrick's Park that graces the cover, and Carter McKenzie, for her fine proofreading skills.

For their help with the photography in this book: Lane County Historical Museum, the University of Oregon Division of Special Collections and University Archives, Dot Dotson's, Cress Bates at Lane Council of Governments, Eugene School District 4J, Lane Transit District, the City of Eugene Parks and Recreation Division, Hope Pressman, Deborah Weese and John Jordan-Cascade at PeaceHealth Medical Center, St. Vincent de Paul, Spencer Gross, U.S. Army Corps of Engineers, and the Pearl Buck Center.

Last but not least, the following individuals used their keen eyes and vivid memories to review one or more of the essays for accuracy and clarity:

Evelyn Anderton
Lois Barton
Ed Bergeron
Ann Bettman
Don Bishoff
Jim Carlson
Jan Childs
John Crane
Paul Ehinger
Dave Fidanque
Lawrence Fong
Jim Forbes
Sam Frear
Terry Glaspey
Dan Goldrich
Steve Gordon
Ken Guzowski
Margaret Hallock
Beth Hege Piatote

Charles Henry
Don Hill
Tim Ingalsbee
Kirsten Jones
Dennis Lueck
Beverly Mayhew
Terry McDonald
Hugh McKinley
Adell McMillan
Stephen Messer
Ken Metzler
Ralph Myers
Jan Oliver
Marshall Peter
Dave Pompel
Hope Pressman
Jim Ralph
Dave Reinhard
Norv Ritchey
Brian Rooney
Karen Seidel
Sally Sheklow
Becky Sisley
Mike Thoele
Jenny Ulum
Dom Vetri
Louise Wade
Ray Wiley
Diane Wiley
Cynthia Wooten
Jeff Wright

Sources

All of the authors used the archives of *The Register-Guard* in the course of researching their essays. We are grateful to the newspaper for being the main source of Eugene's written history over the years.

For most authors, the primary method of research was conducted in the form of interviews. The following individuals have been very helpful to the writers and editors of this book. Many were interviewed for several essays. Others provided key information, guidance, and advice. We sincerely thank them all and apologize to any we may have neglected to mention.

Don Allen
Silvia Alloway
John Alltucker
Cordy Anderson
Dorothy Anderson
Les Anderson
Bahati Ansari
Bjo Ashwill
Ken Babbs
Denny Baker
Vilma Baker
Scott Barkhurst
Kate Barkley
Lois Barton
John Bascom
Ruth Bascom
Philip Bayles
Terry Bean
Douglas Beauchamp
Nicole Bennett
George Beres

Ed Bergeron
Ed Bingham
Don Bishoff
Diane Bishop
Lee Bishop
Silas Trim Bissell
Alfred Bloom
Bob Bojorcas
Elizabeth Brinton
Leslie Brocklebank
Abe Brooks
W.A. Brooksby
Alan Brown
Dena Brown
Pastor Dan Bryant
Jan Burg
Mary Helen Burnham
Alfonso Cabrera
Beth Campbell
Neila Campbell
Roscoe Caron
Lawrence Carter
Carolyn Chambers
Jan Childs
Cristina Cipres-Jacome
Robert D. Clark
Edwin Coleman
Angie Collas-Dean
Jennifer Craig
Richard Crawford
Jim Croteau
Wilma Crowe
Pat Cusick
Jane DeGidio
John Dellenback

Bob Dritz
Jain Elliott
Vicki Elmer
Donald England
Orval Etter
Dave Fidanque
Melvin Finkelstein
Laurel Fisher
Pastor Gregory Flint
Lawrence Fong
Jim Forbes
Tommy Fox
Lynn Frohnmayer
Jim Garcia
Bill Gardner
Harvey Ginsberg
Mike Gleason
Dan Goldrich
Steve Gordon
Riley Grannan
Charles Gray
Bobby Green
Norma Grier
Ken Guzowski
Debra Gwartney
Tom Hager
John Haislip
Margaret Hallock
Mark Harris
Ray Hawk
Alicia Hayes
Diane Nechak Hazen
Paul Headley
Bonnie Henderson
Sarah Hendrickson

Charles Henry
Sister Monica Herran
Mark Herring
Bob Hibschman
Kathryn "Catalina" Hidalgo
Don Hill
Robert P. Hodam
Kimball Hodge
Garrett Hongo
Kevin Hornbuckle
Ron Howard
Tom Howard
Donna Howell
Harold Hoy
Julieta Hughet
Don and Helen Hunter
Lorraine Hunter
Rabbi Yitzhak Husbands-Hankin
Lorraine Ironplow
Jerry Jacobson
Art Johnson
Benton Johnson
Bern Johnson
Jim Johnson
Angel Jones
Eric Jones
Guadalupe Jones
Kirsten Jones
Misa Joo
Lynn Kahle
Ed Kenyon
Ken Kesey
Lauren Kessler
Patricia O'Connell Killen
Mark Kirchmeier

Jamie Klundt
Pastor John Koekkoek
Associate Pastor Sherry Lady
Gayle Landt
Tom Larsen
George Lauris
Herman Lawson
Lisa Lawton
Ada Lee
Bobby Lee
Jeff Lewis
Pollyanna Lind
Diamond Livingston
Glen Love
Ray Lowe
Allen Lowe
Scott Lowell
Tony Lum
Laurie MacLain
Marion Malcolm
Beverly Mayhew
Marilyn Mays
Terry McDonald
Hugh McKinley
Marion Toepke McLean
Anet Mconel
Mary Meier
Harriet Merrick
Emily Fergus Merritt
Stephen Messer
Kim Metzler
Jeff Miller
Willie Mims
Fred Mohr
Roger Moody

Armando Morales
Ken Morrow
Eric Muller
Ralph Myers
Ken Nagao
Frank Nearing
Paul Neevel
Bill Nelson
Reverend Carl Nelson
Paul Nicholson
Betty Niven
Mary O'Brien
Frank Okada
Steven Oshatz
Pastor Steve Overman
Laramie Palmer
Lyllye Parker
Dave Pedersen
Suzanne Pepin
Marshall Peter
Bob Peters
Jean Phelps
Linda Phelps
David Piercy
Toni Pimble
Earl Pomeroy
Dave Pompel
Charles Porter
John Porter
Bill Powell
Don Powell
Jan Powers
Glen Purdy
Guadalupe Quinn
Ed Ragozzino

Jim Ralph
Fred Rankin
Wendy Ray
Diane Retallack
John Reynolds
Keith Richard
Greg Rikhoff
Norv Ritchey
Jim Roberts
Sparky Roberts
Don Robinson
Horace Robinson
John Rose
Lawrence Ross
Lela Ross
Sarah and Randy Ross
Flora Rudolph
George Russell
Ralph Salisbury
Maura Scanlon
Tom Schwetz
Karen Seidel
Jim Sellers
Tim Shea
Sally Sheklow
Jim Shoemaker
Vip Short
Marc Siegel
Charlene Simpson
Becky Sisley
Nick Sixkiller
Gordon Slate
Dwight Souers
Twila Souers
Caleb Standefer

Rodney Stark
Steve Stone
Lotte Streisinger
Wallace Swanson
Bill Sweet
Susan Sygall
Paula Taylor
Dirk Ten Brinke
Ken Tollenaar
Bob Tompson
Kate Tompson
Jim Torrey
David Toyama
Bob Tricket
Cheri Turpin
Dee Unthank
Rebecca Urhausen
Clair van Bloem
Dorothy Velasco
Dom Vetri
Ansellmo Villanueva
Rose Marie Villanueva
Louise Wade
Erica Waechter
Mary Wagner
George Watson
Sally Weaver
Barbara Weinstein
Larry Weinstein
Mike Weinstein
Ingrid Wendt
Judy Wenger
William Wheatley
Reverend David White
George Wickes

Ray Wiley
Tom Williams
John Witte
Jim Witzig
Carl Woideck
Donald Woomer
Cynthia Wooten
Jeff Wright
Susan Zadoff
Ron Zahn
St. Mary's Catholic Church
Staff of All Women's Health Services

Contributors

This book was made possible by the generous contributions of the following organizations and individuals.

City of Eugene
Wayne & Jean Tate
Total Communications
Eugene Downtown Rotary
Qwest
Hyundai Semiconductor America
Karen Seidel
PeaceHealth
Robert D. Clark
Theodore Palmer
Lane Transit District
Tim Brinton
Carolyn Chambers
Kathy Madison & Armen Kevrekian
Adell McMillan
Lane County
Obie Media Corp.

CAWOOD
Carolyn Kranzler Architect AIA
Ruth Miller
Hugh & Sue Prichard
Michael Warshafsky & Sinde Fitz
Hope Hughes Pressman
Cascade Manor
Michael & Nancy Rose
Frank Gibson
Dorothy Anderson
John & Ruth Bascom
Lew Bowers
Cathy Briner
Jan Childs
Liz DeShelter
Don & Laurel Fisher
Kloos Consulting
Bruce McKinlay
Public Relations Services
Bob Rutledge & Susan Ban
Oregon Country Fair
Robertson/Sherwood/Architects PC
Tykeson Foundation
The Ulum Group
Sally Weston
Ann Cahill Fidanque